Discourse and Dominion in the Fourteenth Century

Also by Jesse M. Gellrich

The Idea of the Book in the Middle Ages:
Language Theory, Mythology, and Fiction

Discourse and Dominion in the Fourteenth Century

ORAL CONTEXTS OF WRITING IN PHILOSOPHY, POLITICS, AND POETRY

Jesse M. Gellrich

PRINCETON UNIVERSITY PRESS
PRINCETON, NEW JERSEY

Copyright © 1995 by Princeton University Press
Published by Princeton University Press, 41 William Street,
Princeton, New Jersey 08540
In the United Kingdom: Princeton University Press, Chichester, West Sussex

Library of Congress Cataloging-in-Publication Data

Gellrich, Jesse M., 1942–
Discourse and dominion in the fourteenth century: oral contexts of
writing in philosophy, politics, and poetry / Jesse M. Gellrich.
p.   cm.
Includes bibliographical references and index.
ISBN 0-691-03749-3 (CL)
1. English literature—Middle English, 1100–1500—History and
criticism.   2. Oral tradition—England.   3. Great Britain—
History—14th century—Historiography.   4. Politics and
literature—Great Britain—History.   5. Great Britain—
Civilization—1066–1485.   6. Written communication—England.
7. Discourse analysis, Literary.   8. Oral-formulaic analysis.
9. Philosophy, Medieval.   10. England—Languages.   I. Title.
PR275.072G45   1995
302.2'242'042209023—dc20   94-3761
                                                                  CIP

This book has been composed in Postscript Type 1 Palatino

Princeton University Press books are printed on acid-free paper and meet the
guidelines for permanence and durability of the Committee on Production Guidelines
for Book Longevity of the Council on Library Resources

Printed in the United States of America

1 3 5 7 9 10 8 6 4 2

This book is for Michelle

———————————————

CONTENTS

Preface   ix

Acknowledgments   xiii

Introduction

CHAPTER ONE
Vox Literata: On the Uses of Oral and Written Language in
the Later Middle Ages   3

PART ONE: *Philosophy*

CHAPTER TWO
The Voice of the Sign and the Semiology of Dominion in the
Work of Ockham   39

CHAPTER THREE
"Real Language" and the Rule of the Book in the Work of
Wyclif   79

PART TWO: *Politics*

CHAPTER FOUR
Orality and Rhetoric in the Chronicle History of Edward III   123

CHAPTER FIVE
The Politics of Literacy in the Reign of Richard II   151

PART THREE: *Poetry*

CHAPTER SIX
The Spell of the Ax: Diglossia and History in *Sir Gawain and
the Green Knight*   195

CHAPTER SEVEN
"Withouten Any Repplicacioun": Discourse and Dominion
in the *Knight's Tale*   227

Bibliography   273

Index   297

PREFACE

THIS BOOK is occasioned by an increasing body of scholarship which has qualified the assumption that the rise of literacy in the middle ages put an end to oral tradition. Fourteenth-century England is often regarded as confirmation of this shift in Western history. And for that reason I have explored examples from three areas—philosophy, historiography, and poetry—which suggest to me that oral characteristics of communicating and thinking still survive, albeit in embedded or implied formations.

Attempting to account for oral influence on the basis of written records has been a subject of much discussion in several scholarly disciplines. I follow the lead of others who have maintained that writing itself is vital evidence for understanding how the oral channel of language may persist. In particular, fourteenth-century studies have already demonstrated that oral influence is apparent in poetry, manuscript illumination, and the arts of memory. It is now possible, therefore, to attempt a more synthetic view of how and why orality continued at all in this century when manuscripts and books were used more than ever before.

A principle emerging from each of the parts of this book is that one mode of language is an imitation of the other. Most commonly we observe the idea, stemming from the early middle ages and antiquity, that writing imitates spoken language. But how this principle is understood and exercised differs widely in the examples I have studied. The self-consciousness with which the two modes, spoken and written, reflect on each other is sometimes acute, as in certain passages of poetry. "Self-reflexivity" or "metalanguage" is familiar in poems containing images or figures of their own mode as narrative or representation; but it is also true that poetic language in general can be called metalinguistic, and one of the most notable implications of this factor is the extent to which oral and written modes comment on each other in certain contexts.

Such acknowledgment about the status of different media raises the question of whether or not other disciplines of writing are similarly involved in exploring their own use of oral and written forms. Both philosophers and historians took a definite interest in this problem; but they also resolve it quite differently, some leaning toward the writtenness of their own projects, others toward its imitation of spoken language. As a result of such contrasting attitudes, it is no wonder that

modern scholarly assessments have not been able to mark in any
decisive way where oral custom ends and the influence of literacy
commences.

I take this dilemma to be a reflection of medieval arguments themselves about the nature of language. So long as imitation remains the
model of language, we are forced into the situation of locating change
in either the source or the copy, orality or literacy. A look at scholarship
on the problem confirms again and again that literacy is reckoned to
be an unprecedented power of historical change. But how, then, do we
explain the persistence of orality in a world making an extraordinary
use of books? And how also do we account for the paradox that a
social group with only minimal or no literate competence illustrates
the influence of skills learned from writing? These are not new questions in the history of literacy. But I suggest an alternative approach to
them.

Instead of looking for an answer in oral tradition or in the technology of writing, I argue that the power of language consists in *displacement*, the capacity of one mode of language to take the place of the
other, to make the source disappear into the copy. Writing is commonly
masked as oral, and just as often spoken language is veiled as inscription—one channel of language is the guise or disguise of the other. But
how the difference between them is mediated and accommodated
spells out the differences among the disciplines in fourteenth-century
England. This claim about the power of displacement is well appreciated from the work of Sigmund Freud, Karl Marx, and Jacques Derrida. But it has no application, as far as I know, to scholarship on
literacy, or to the integration of philosophy, historiography, and poetry
in England during the later middle ages.

The following chapters are concerned with two general matters, first,
identifying the margin between spoken and written modes, and second, assessing how that margin was understood. In the Introduction I
use these two issues in order to show that orality and literacy are not
only identifiable properties in books and manuscripts; they also indicate different theoretical ideas, social values, and ways of experiencing
the world. In Part One I take up two representative philosophers of
the century, since both were intensely concerned with the status of
language. Unquestionably, they represent the high watermark of literate achievement, and thus to probe for the "oral context" of their
assumptions would appear irrelevant. But their differences on the
question of the linguistic sign provide a way of showing that "orality,"
understood as an instrument of displacing language as mere inscription, exerted subtle and unexpected influence on a number of their
philosophical arguments, such as the nature of evidence, validation,

authority, and history. For instance, the prominence of "voice" in the logic of William of Ockham qualifies the reduction of his so-called "nominalism" and thus confirms other recent assessments of him. John Wyclif swings back in the other direction, as he would fortify what he takes to be the artificiality of writing and history with the presence of the spoken word.

Part Two considers how historians of the time actually tried to represent past and present events. Chroniclers working during the reigns of Edward III (1327–77) and Richard II (1377–99) acknowledged their indebtedness to rhetorical commonplaces and generic forms for writing history. But the use of such "literary" forms appears in a new light when the chronicles are studied for evidence of oral displacement. The rhetoric of the historian as eyewitness appears as a strategy for vitalizing and validating the record as oral testimony from the past; and the observer then takes on the interests of the political and social causes represented. This kind of elision between record and event is well known in the early efforts of medieval historiography, but it also betokens the oral-literate split of the times and the limited attempt to engage it in this discipline. As a result an "oral chronicle" is embedded in the texts of record, creating a picture of chivalry and a story of heroism that the fourteenth century wanted to believe about itself.

Part Three analyzes two poetic romances that address very different attention to these matters of language and history. Romance, the genre associated with historical problems, is also the occasion for unsettling typically medieval attitudes toward the past, as other scholars have noted. Although several medieval poems are relevant, I choose two that employ both oral and written modes in an assessment of the value of chivalry as a political ideal. Without direct reference to fourteenth-century events or people, both poems are all the more pertinent to my inquiry. As explorations of voice, writing, and literary figuration in general, these works comment on the displacement of language as an instrument of dominion in their time, leaving us with a sense of nostalgia that will not mitigate the idealizations of power and history set forth in other disciplines.

The fourteenth century in England presents an exemplary test case for the reformulation of literacy under way in many areas of scholarship today. Not only was this century a cultural watershed in the development of written language; it also illustrates how inadequately a rigid model fits the facts of linguistic experience. Those facts, such as they are, indicate that "literacy," however we define it, must include a much more *pragmatic competence*—one inclined to accommodate, and thus be changed by, the difference between voice and writing, oral priority and textual criticism. Although inquiry into the control of discourse and the exercise of dominion had been confronted prior to the fourteenth century, never before were these problems developed with such scrutiny and consequence. It is unique to this time. And it is uniquely English.

Finally, a word is in order about translation and documentation. Unless otherwise noted, translations from foreign languages are my own and are always included in the text. Constraints of space have made it necessary to limit the amount of original quotation that could be cited. And thus I have provided original words or phrases only where absolutely essential to an argument. Similarly, the notes abbreviate all documentation and include very little commentary; they are designed to be read with the Bibliography, which provides a full reference for each source cited or consulted. Middle English, however, is quoted in the original, with obscure passages paraphrased in the text.

Baton Rouge
1993

ACKNOWLEDGMENTS

THE FIRST DEBT I wish to acknowledge in this book is to the scholars who have preceded me. My reliance on them appears throughout the footnotes, which unfortunately do not reflect adequately my appreciation for the silent conversations I have had with their work since I began. Without the extraordinary contributions of people in many fields, I simply could not have proceeded. Among others who have assisted me, I wish to acknowledge the American Council of Learned Societies, which awarded me a fellowship for 1986–87 to undertake research and writing in the early stages of the project. The College of Arts and Sciences at Louisiana State University subvented the fellowship during that year and released me from all teaching duties. I am grateful to both institutions for their generous support. Librarians at many locations have provided invaluable assistance, in particular at the Middleton and Hill Libraries (Louisiana State University), Firestone Library (Princeton University), Pierpont Morgan Library (New York City), and Houghton Library (Harvard University). Elaine Smyth and Dennison Beach have been especially helpful with research problems.

Various professional organizations and institutions have graciously invited me to represent my work during the last few years. I am grateful for opportunities to speak at: the American Philological Association Convention (New York City, 1987), the Midwest Modern Language Association Convention (Columbus, 1987), the International Society for Comparative Literature Convention (Munich, 1988), the Pennsylvania Symposium on Medieval and Renaissance Studies (University of Pennsylvania, 1989), the Program on Technology and Sexual Difference (Oregon State University, 1990), the French and Francophone Foundation Colloquium (Louisiana State University, 1990), the Symposium on Oral and Written Traditions in the Middle Ages (New York University, 1990), the Symposium on Language and Society in the Middle Ages (Tulane University, 1991), and the International Symposium on the Theory and Practice of Translation in the Middle Ages (University of Wales, 1991). I am indebted to the organizers and audiences of these events for responses that helped me with the arguments of this book.

In my department at LSU I have received much needed assistance from colleagues: Gale Carrithers for responding to sections of chapters one and two, John Fischer for countless directions about computer software, and James Olney for general support of my work. A few pages in chapter one were originally drafted in an essay that appeared in *Philological Quarterly* 67 (1988): 461–73, 480. At Princeton University Press I am grateful for the editorial resourcefulness of Robert E. Brown, whose scholarly dedication and rare vision have marked academic publishing for many years. The two anonymous readers for the Press provided engaging responses to my claims and several important suggestions about bibliography: the book has profited from both of their reports. So too has it benefited from the production editing of Beth Gianfagna and the assiduous proofreading of my copy editor, Roy Thomas.

The personal encouragement of family and friends has been a continuous resource to me during the course of this project. I am thankful specifically to Anna Gellrich for her fine undergraduate essay on Shakespeare's *Richard II* and to Mary and Martin Carver for their unceasing appreciation of my daily efforts.

But the help *non plus ultra* has come from my wife, Michelle, who read every chapter of the manuscript with painstaking care and uncompromising criticism. Her shrewd and lucid insight into my arguments has influenced this study from the outset, and I am more grateful to her than the dedication of this book can ever express.

Introduction

Chapter One

VOX LITERATA: ON THE USES OF ORAL AND WRITTEN LANGUAGE IN THE LATER MIDDLE AGES

Grammar is the knowledge of how to speak
without error.
—Hugh of St. Victor, *Didascalicon*

INTRODUCTION

Scholarship on oral and written language has generally assumed that since medieval societies developed after the advent of inscription, they do not illustrate what has been called "primary orality, the pristine orality of cultures with no knowledge of writing."[1] But neither can they be called "illiterate," if we mean by that term that they were untouched by the influence of writing, including the skills it encouraged. Rather, we are dealing with a historical situation in which orality persists in "residual" form, and its principal channel of expression is the written word itself. From this point of view, medieval writing has sometimes been described as a form of "secondary orality" or of "mixed orality."[2]

For instance, it has recently been argued that among the Carolingians in the early middle ages Latin may have been spoken and written by a much wider sector of society than hitherto supposed; and thus literacy in Latin circulated freely in a culture with other languages that were exclusively oral.[3] In England between the Norman Conquest (1066) and the death of Edward I (1307), the transition from oral "memory to written record," as it has been described, was well under way. And yet we cannot say of this period that England was now literate in Latin, or in the vernacular languages, for that matter. Even during the time of Edward, written documents were not used by literates in a way that assured their efficacy as proof.[4]

Writing was regarded with attitudes formed over many centuries in

---

[1] Ong, *Orality and Literacy*, p. 1. Cf. pp. 6, 11, 31–75.

[2] Ong, "Oral Residue in Tudor Prose Style"; Zumthor, *Introduction à la poésie orale*. Though Ong uses "secondary" to describe electronic orality, his category has been extended broadly to include the "orality within literate culture," e.g., by Bäuml, "Medieval Texts and Oral-Formulaic Composition," pp. 34 and 47n.15.

[3] McKitterick, *The Carolinginans and the Written Word*, ch. 1, and p. 273. Cf. Auerbach, *Literary Language and Its Public*, p. 254.

[4] Clanchy, *From Memory to Written Record*.

which it was absent or nascent. It was thus received within a culture still used to oral ways of communicating and conducting the affairs of domestic and governmental life. Academic and religious communities, for instance, in the eleventh and twelfth centuries, present a special case since they evolved around written documents and books. But it would be oversimplified to assume that the academic wall kept out influences from a world going on busily in the old oral ways of doing things. Rather, the community of the text, or "textual community" as it has been conveniently called, was the result of social and oral habits interacting strongly with the special skills of reading and interpreting manuscripts.[5]

Such considerations clearly indicate that literacy no longer signifies a complete and final separation from the "oral tradition" of the past or present. But where to draw the line of departure in theoretical and historical terms remains a problem. Some time ago, Erich Auerbach remarked with reference to the Carolingians that there was no "Bildung-ssprache," no language of general culture which expressed the actual living conditions of society, in spite of the fact that documents and books were influencing cultural life.[6] Even if we assume the proposal that Latin was more widespread at this time, Auerbach's insight into the contested situation of a literacy influenced by oral circumstances remains to be explained.

In England poetry and prose composed in Anglo-Saxon have often been documented for the evidence of "oral performance" and "oral transmission." But a recent study has shown that "literature" in the sense of written, crafted composition is also a figure or motif in the writing itself. Bede's story of Caedmon or the Old English riddles replace spontaneous "improvisation" with the "craft" of the text, so that the poem is acknowledged as a "self-consciously crafted expression of a literate aesthetic."[7] A similar acknowledgment of the oral-literate divide has been studied in French manuscripts and books of the thirteenth and fourteenth centuries. In this case, however, the evidence suggests a leaning decidedly in the opposite direction: "writing retained a certain dimension of orality"; poets and rubricators "appropriated the language of oral declamation"; now we have "the performative quality of the medieval book" preserved in both the themes and layout of the documents.[8]

[5] Stock, *The Implications of Literacy.*

[6] Auerbach, *Literary Language and Its Public*, p. 255. Bäuml, "Varieties and Consequences of Medieval Literacy and Illiteracy," uses Auerbach in arguing for "the social function of literacy" (p. 239). Cf. D. H. Green, "Orality and Reading."

[7] Lerer, *Literacy and Power in Anglo-Saxon Literature*, pp. 42–48, 112–13.

[8] Huot, *From Song to Book*, pp. 2, 3. See Camille, "The Book of Signs" and "Visual Signs of the Sacred Page," for orality in romanesque and gothic illuminated manuscripts.

Outside the poetic traditions of the later middle ages, deciding upon where to mark the end of oral influence and the beginning of literate experience is more difficult. John of Salisbury, for instance, insists in the *Metalogicon* that Latin "grammar alone has the unique privilege of making one 'lettered.'"[9] Two centuries later, Margery Kempe, a woman without any formal education and no training in Latin, demonstrates unequivocally that contact with literates could produce a shared competence in being able to "write," since she produced by dictation a book about her own life and thought. To accommodate the gap between a literacy exclusively in Latin and its apparent influence on social experience, the familiar terms "vernacular literacy" and the "literacy of the laity" have been of some use.[10]

But the interaction between these two orders of language and social reality is more complicated than these terms allow, especially in the trilingual environment of England during the 1300s. In this chapter I reconsider the problem by following the lead of scholars in other disciplines, chiefly the social sciences, who have asked whether written language is "autonomous" in relation to oral contexts or "dependent" on them in some vital way.[11] This question, although not as yet asked forthrightly about medieval literacy in general, is relevant if only because anthropologists, ethnographers, and critical theorists have used medieval evidence to support one side of the debate or the other—that writing is an "autonomous competence" as opposed to a context-dependent "ideology."

On the one hand, the development of writing in the middle ages illustrates pointedly how literacy may be understood as a "technology of the mind," a special set of "skills" fostered by learning to write and read. Reference, classification, validation, documentation, logic, rationality, scientific methodology, and many other "advances" have been documented in medieval writing in the interest of arguing that literacy is an autonomous activity, since it can be transported from one community to another. On the other hand, medieval evidence clearly leans in the opposite direction as well, toward the oral contexts of society. Individuals skilled in writing are members of a unique class, an educated elite, which marks a sharp division from social groups with little or no training in the written word. Literacy, therefore, is a cultural form

---

[9] *Metalogicon*, p. 71.

[10] See the review by Parkes, "The Literacy of the Laity," which includes a critique of Thompson's original equation of literacy with Latinity (*The Literacy of the Laity in the Middle Ages*).

[11] See Goody and Watt, "The Consequences of Literacy," and Goody, ed., *Literacy in Traditional Societies* and *The Domestication of the Savage Mind*, in contrast with critiques by Street, *Literacy in Theory and Practice*, and Graff, *The Literacy Myth* (see also Graff, *The Labyrinths of Literacy* and *The Legacies of Literacy*).

tied specifically to social experience: it is "context-dependent," since it is responsible for the development of social patterns. When understood as the formation of such patterns, writing then becomes the "ideology" of culture. And it has been understood precisely in that way at various moments of the medieval past, such as in the Carolingian period, when Latin was instituted as both the written and spoken language of the land.[12]

Accordingly, to turn to the middle ages for evidence of whether "literacy" is autonomous or ideological presents theoretical and historical difficulties of no little moment. For the evidence seems to fall on both sides of the fence. The learned language of literates would appear to be a citadel of specialized competence, locked away with precious books in clerical scriptoria. Literacy thus effects a powerful division or "diglossia" of social class: Latin was the *high* language of the literate, those in superior places and devoted to lofty purposes, such as law, government, theology, philosophy, and poetry. In contrast, vernacular languages were *low* and oral; they circulated throughout the schools of hard knocks in street and countryside. Although such a division of "tongues" is not exclusive to the Western middle ages, no other instance of it, so it has been argued, "seems to have had an effect on the entirety of the human race comparable to that of medieval cultural diglossia."[13]

But appreciating this situation presents no little difficulty, since we can trace the history of literacy (on the basis of documents) much more easily than we can explain the persistence of oral customs. Indeed, this dilemma has been called the "central problem of the Middle Ages . . . the relation of orality to a world making ever-increasing use of texts."[14] Since we are not dealing with orality per se, but with oral properties embedded in books, manuscripts, and other artifacts, I suggest that we direct this inquiry toward how the technology of writing was *used* by various social groups. An otherwise autonomous skill became the expression of individual or group interests as it was transported from

[12] McKitterick, ed., *The Uses of Literacy in Early Mediaeval Europe*, p. 320: literacy was not only a "technology," but also "a mentality, a form of ideology through which power could be constructed and influence exerted, a frame of mind and a framer of minds." Following Street's criticism, Goody, *The Logic of Writing and the Organization of Society*, p. 172, argues for the "relative autonomy of the written tradition," which promotes the "structural autonomy" of certain institutions; "any divergence between the domain of priest and king . . . implicit in oral societies now becomes explicit and can take on an 'ideological' dimension."

[13] Ong, *Orality and Literacy*, pp. 4–5, 8.

[14] Stock, *The Implications of Literacy*, pp. 14 ff., and "Medieval Literacy, Linguistic Theory, and Social Organization," p. 16. McLuhan, in *The Gutenberg Galaxy*, responded presciently to this problem after reading Lord, Parry, and Chaytor.

one community to another. It is not a matter of whether medieval literacy conforms to an autonomous model identified with the technology of writing, or to a context-dependent ideology from the oral world. The problem is: how did the autonomous character of writing become subordinated to ideological factors in society?

The answer will not tell us why *orality* persisted, for it is not a question of "primary orality" or of the "audible word." Rather, medieval materials present us with a *structure* in which writing exists in specific relation to spoken language. It is this structure which prevails, not one valence or the other, speech or script, voice or letter; and it prevails not only in language but in society as well. Medieval scholarship has tried, with some success, to avoid dividing these issues too simply by proposing such formulations as "secondary orality," "vernacular literacy," and "textuality." But it has not questioned sufficiently why medieval evidence lends itself so readily to resolution in one model or the other, the autonomy of language or its ideology. I suggest that this question has been bypassed thus far because of the particular ways in which writing was related to oral custom in the later middle ages. We need to look more carefully at the structure of this relation, and to ask why it does not prompt such inquiry on its own.

St. Augustine

In order to pursue this question, I turn first to St. Augustine, because he illustrates a clear effort to account for language in its own right, as an autonomous human ability.

> When they called anything by name, and moved the body towards it while they spoke, I saw and gathered that the thing they wished to point out was called by the name they then uttered; and that they did mean this was made plain by the motion of the body, even by the natural language of all nations expressed by the countenance, glance of the eye, movement of other members, and by the sound of the voice indicating the affections of the mind, as it seeks, possesses, rejects, or avoids. So it was that by frequently hearing words, in duly placed sentences, I gradually gathered what things they were the signs of; and having formed my mouth to the utterance of these signs, I thereby expressed my wishes.

Although in this passage from the *Confessiones*, Augustine recounts his earliest memories of how he learned to speak as a child, he writes "under the perspective of eternity" (*sub specie aeternitatis*), and his assumptions reflect his mature thoughts on the subject of language. In drawing an alignment between the utterance of words and a speaker's effort to act out or mime their signification through facial expressions and bodily movements, Augustine implicitly conceives of a word as the name or label of a person, event, or thing; and language in general becomes a simulacrum of the physical gestures of the body, an imitation of "the natural language of all people" (*uerbis naturalibus omnium gentium*).[15] In *De magistro* Augustine instructs his young son, Adeodatus, in many of these same ideas about words, but this time applied to the act of reading: "when a word is written, a sign is made in the eyes by which that sign which pertains to the ears comes into the mind."[16] Like learning to speak, reading is a process of learning to identify the letters seen by the eyes on parchment, wax, or stone with the physical act of shaping the mouth into audible sounds, which are in turn synonymous with what the ears receive and the mind comprehends.

Among Augustine's many reflections on language, these passages from the *Confessiones* and *De magistro* highlight a point that is not always obvious, notably the relation between voice or the oral word and the written language of texts. One of the few to confront this factor, Ludwig Wittgenstein has observed: "Augustine does not speak of there being any difference between kinds of word"; the formulation in the *Confessiones* is accurate for only a small circumscribed area of linguistic functions; it reduces all of language to "phonological script" in which each letter designates a specific sound.[17] For Augustine's model of equivalence—between utterance and letter, word and object, name and person—does not take into account adequately the use or functionality of language, which may be demonstrated, in Wittgenstein's illustration, by thinking of words not as gestures and names but as "tools in a box" or "handles" in the cabin of a locomotive.[18] Many handles or tools may look alike, but they perform vastly different functions. So it is with words, and Wittgenstein's simple metaphor demonstrates how far away from *use* Augustine's model for language remains.

Wittgenstein's critique of the "phonological" aspect of Augustine's view of language will be recognized for its similarity, if not identity, with Jacques Derrida's sense of the "phonocentric" determination of written language in the Western tradition.[19] Presuming an identity between voice and the act of pointing, Augustine establishes the phone as the prior, self-evident equivalent of gesture, the "presence" of its signification; he thus gives birth to a phonocentric hierarchy of gradually decreasing terms—including speaking, gesturing, listening, writ-

[15] *Confessiones* 1.8.7.

[16] *De magistro* 4.8.165.

[17] Wittgenstein, *Philosophical Investigations* 1.2, 4.

[18] Ibid., 1.6–7.

[19] Derrida, *Of Grammatology*, part 1.

ing, and reading. In Augustine's formulation, if we comprehend the letter when it is identified as the copy of prior speech, then the oral word inevitably enjoys a privileged status denied to writing. Thus writing must appeal to speaking for authentication.

The extent to which these logocentric preferences inform other areas of Augustine's thought may be suggested by considering how conceptions such as God's "writing" and his "book" become metaphors of voice in his theology; or, in contrast, we may note how human writing is relegated to the shadows—what Augustine calls the *regio dissimilitudinis*—where it proceeds best when it is conceived of as an imitation of speech, when it patronizes the more perfect order in the lost paradise of the oral word.[20] Thus Augustine's reflection on language in these examples involves a binary structure in which voice is the prior term and writing is secondary, a diminished likeness, even an "unlikeness," reminiscent of the fallen domain over which the *Vox Dei* presides. Because of the binarism exemplified by this structure, writtenness and fallenness are coupled together, and Augustine repeated the connection in various ways. Language became a matrix for the study of divine significations; its role in the analysis of particular historical situations does not emerge in his work. As one recent commentator remarks, Augustine does not give us a distinct historical Christ or a sense of the past as past; he makes all Christians "memoryless," since verbal signs "mirror" an eternal truth.[21] The autonomy of language is fully achieved in such a metaphorical sense of writing; its functional interests have been bypassed, along with the details of history.

Secondary Orality

It is a long way from the rarefied atmosphere of Augustinian theory to the argument for the "ideological" context of language, but there is a symmetry between the two that is relevant at this point. Although Augustine describes the idea of voice in its divine and human exemplars, his speculation is not entirely "academic" or safely removed from the hands of outside interests. For he *subordinates* writing to voice when the letter is represented as a fall away from the origin of its "authorship" and dominion. In principle, the hierarchy organizing speech over script is to be found as well in the social history of writing when it is received, as it commonly was, to be a species of oral language. The understanding of writing as speech written down, which medieval

[20] *Confessiones* 7.10.103. Cf. Ferguson, "Saint Augustine's Region of Unlikeness," and Gellrich, *The Idea of the Book in the Middle Ages*, pp. 112–22.

[21] See Coleman, *Ancient and Medieval Memories*, p. 100; cf. pp. 105–106, on *De trinitate*: "the sign is wholly adequately identical to the signified."

evidence illustrates again and again, assumes plainly that writing is
second to speech. And thus the so-called "secondary orality" of medieval culture is more medieval than it knows: first comes voice, writing
follows. Augustine would agree, and so would many later commentators. In and of itself, the written word is an empty thing, lost from its
origin, and wandering near death, as Paul enjoined when he warned
that the "letter killeth" (2 Cor. 3.6).[22] Gregory of Tours is not far behind
when he complained about the tyranny of grammar and syntax. And
Gregory the Great would part ways with literacy once and for all,
though not without a drop of hyperbole: "I do not shun at all the
confusion of barbarians. I despise the proper constructions and cases,
because I think it very unfitting that the words of the celestial oracle
should be restricted by the rules of Donatus."[23] Under the weight of
such a hierarchy of opinion, it is small wonder that the autonomous
skill of this new technology took its place quietly within an idea of
voice as first and foremost.

In this way, theoretical considerations of language are not at all
unrelated to the social history of "oral tradition." To the contrary, it is
fair to suggest that the binary structure which subordinates the letter
is also a cultural form in which the oral word, in principle or in
practice, prevails over the production and dissemination of written
language. As a category for explaining the "residue" of oral properties
in written language, "secondary orality" presumes that speech gradually loses the high ground to the advent of writing, whereas in medieval sources we have abundant evidence that the struggle is far from
over. The practice of oral reading illustrates dramatically the controlling structure of the oral and aural word. Although reading marks the
passing into history of a "primary" oralism, it still preserves the vestige
of a social context in which communication by word of mouth took
precedence. In this sense, a new and relatively autonomous "technology" existed from the beginning within the subordinating context of
oral practice. Writing arrives already dependent upon context.

Even in the academic world of fifth-century Athens, Plato's students
experienced philosophy and poetry as "listeners" rather than silent
"readers."[24] In the late Roman period, Augustine probably read texts
as most of his contemporaries did, by vocalizing script. Word separa-

[22] See Kelber, *The Oral and the Written Gospel*, p. 168, for "Paul as an oral traditionalist
who objects to the Law not on legal, but ultimately on linguistic grounds." See Bäuml,
"Medieval Texts and Oral-Formulaic Composition," pp. 41–45, for qualifications of "secondary orality" and poetic genesis.

[23] Both cited in Vising, *Anglo-Norman Language and Literature*, p. 27.

[24] Havelock, *A Preface to Plato*, p. 38: "Over and over again, the relationship of the
student or the public to poetry is assumed to be that of listeners, not readers, and the

tion, which is all we know in an age of print, was unknown to Augustine. A written Latin text of his time, says one commentator, was "like modern musical notation": it was comprehensible only when "performed orally to others or to oneself."[25] Spelling was entirely phonetic, and therefore letter and syllable, rather than individual words spaced out and duly punctuated across a line, were the determinants of pronunciation, which was the preeminent vehicle of understanding.[26]

Nor was composition a silent activity. We know that Cicero's scribe was Tiros and that Caesar, Pliny the Elder, and Augustine also used scribes to whom they dictated orally. Although Augustine and Hilary added marginal rubrics to some of their commentaries, following the rubrication introduced into the Bible by Jerome, they composed without word separation. The practice remained in place at least through the seventh century, as we may see in the *Etymologiarum* of Isidore of Seville, whose scribes used word division in the headings but not in the text. After Isidore, texts using word separation may be found, for instance, on the Continent in the eighth century, though they are unusual. In England and Ireland, however, they are more ordinary by this time. The significance of the change should not be underestimated: with spaces of separation, Latin words became segments comprehensible without syllabic pronunciation. Certainly Augustine or Ambrose would understand a Latin substantive as a single entity if he saw it inscribed; but the habit of reading and writing aloud was so common that exceptions to it are reported with astonishment, as we may note in Augustine's account of watching Ambrose read without moving his lips: "His eyes were drawn through the pages, and his heart probed the meaning, but his voice and tongue were quiet."[27] Yet lest we think that Augustine is here underwriting an objective and autonomous role for reading the written word, we must recall that the entire episode illustrates the allegory of reading for the secret, spiritual sense concealed beneath the dead letter. And that is a *use* of literacy which is much more than "academic."

The reading skills of Ambrose, surely exceptional in the world of fourth-century Milan, became somewhat familiar in subsequent centuries with the gradual introduction of word division. But, although monasteries in Europe and Britain during the ninth and tenth centuries

---

relationship of the poet to his public or his constituency is always that of a reciter and/or an actor, never of a writer." Cf. pp. 21, 22, 26–27, 36–45.

[25] Saenger, "Silent Reading," p. 371. Cf. Chaytor, *From Script to Print*, ch. 2.

[26] Cf. Saenger's notion of script as musical notation with Kittay, "Utterance Unmoored," p. 215: "Words as units do not exist on the page . . . writing did not bring with it the ideographic status of the word."

[27] *Confessiones* 6.3.75.

were entirely hospitable to the silent reading and copying of texts, the
brethren did not proceed in complete silence, despite the exercise of
rules enforcing it. Unlike Ambrose, they read alone in *sotto voce*, moving their lips and mumbling; or they read aloud to each other in
groups, a commonplace scene frequently depicted in the art of the
illuminated page. Composition was also oral, since a scribe copied
what he read by vocalizing a text in front of him, or what another read
quietly to him in a cell or scriptorium. Copyists were the ventrilo-
quists, so to speak, of "the voices of the pages."[28] And many of them,
according to the samples studied by one recent analyst, may have been
unable to comprehend what they copied—they had an "oral" response
to the text.[29]

When Peter the Venerable in the twelfth century praises monks for
copying in silence, he implies that reading and copying are still carried
on aloud. Such activities were apparently not construed as violations
of rules of silence, since Bernard of Chartres, for example, issued
orders prohibiting dictation and composition during Lent, except for
only a special few. The orality of reading is assumed by Hugh of St.
Victor throughout the *Didascalicon*: defining *grammatica* for his pupils,
Hugh does not even think to remark on its basis in inscription: "Grammar is the knowledge of how to speak [*loquendi*] without error."[30] And
if we turn to the physical layout of Old French manuscripts, we may
note how the scribe, as one commentator puts it, "'speaks' in red ink."[31]

The "audible" quality of such script is perhaps most lucidly preserved in medieval arts of memory. Scholarship continues to demonstrate that the rise of literacy did not replace reliance on memory, since
books often illustrate mnemonic techniques of earlier times, when oral
memorization was essential for the preservation of knowledge.[32] Writing and monastic *ruminatio*, the silent "talk" of meditation, are commonly figured in metaphors of "digestion," which suggests the continued appeal to the oral sense of language. From this point of view,
writing follows the steps of memorial invention, dictation, and copying. The act of inscribing is last, and it may not even have been
performed by the author. Accordingly, it is not surprising to find that

[28] Leclercq, *The Love of Learning and the Desire for God*, p. 19. Cf. Chaytor, *From Script to Print*, pp. 19, 116; McLuhan, *The Gutenberg Galaxy*, pp. 92–93.

[29] See Troll, "The Illiterate Mode of Written Communication," p. 116.

[30] *Eruditionis didascalicae* 2.31 (*Patrologia Latina*, henceforth *PL*, 176, 765). Cf. 4.16 (*PL* 176, 789): "The word 'gloss' is Greek, and it means tongue, because, in a way, it bespeaks the meaning of the word under it."

[31] Huot, *From Song to Book*, p. 38.

[32] E.g., Carruthers, *The Book of Memory*, pp. 10, 111, 194. Cf. Yates, *The Art of Memory*.

memory in this context was not an instrument for appreciating the pastness of the past.[33] For the mastication of words was spiritual nutrition
necessary to "blanch the memory of men's personal pasts within the
monastic Jerusalem." Herewith the voice of memory completely over-
powers its inscription, for the end of memory is "oblivion."[34]

PARADOX

Although life in the medieval monastery felt the influence of Augustine
in many ways, it would be wrong to suggest that the practice of
reading and writing took shape specifically around his theory of the
genesis of language. But it is not so far wrong to see a structural
parallel between his formulation of voice as an origin that writing
imitates and the medieval practice of imitating in writing the speech
recited or memorized from the manuscript page. Writing proceeded
under the dictation of voice in every sense of the term, just as both
speech and writing were themselves efforts to imitate the more mysterious reaches of the *Vox Dei*. The word "paradox" belongs somewhere
in this discussion, since it is obvious that no medieval cleric would
imagine that his language was actually synonymous with its source,
especially if that source were the speech of God. "Oral literacy" or
"literate orality" would appear to be a harmless enough paradox for
characterizing a letter that is not speech and a speech that is not
writing—not in their own *esse*, at any rate.

But, *paradox* here is part of the problem, for it masks the controlling
structure of the opposition between these two aspects of expression by
suggesting that it is more apparent than real. There is no contradiction
between voice and letter. Writing is speech written down. What could
be more medieval? Priscian, whose name is synonymous with language study throughout the centuries, said as much when he insisted
that the kind of expression worthy of consideration is *vox literata*, the
"lettered voice," or utterance of the mouth filtered through the discipline of "letters."[35] Imitation is the model here organizing the relation
of voice to writing by encouraging the notion that the copy is little
different from the source. The margin between the two thus elides, and
any distinction between the autonomy of writing and its use fades as
well when writing is subsumed within the fullness and presence of the

[33] Coleman, *Ancient and Medieval Memories*, p. 138.

[34] Ibid., pp. 145, 154–55. NB Coleman's striking difference from Carruthers (*The Book
of Memory*) on memory as a "book."

[35] *Institutiones Grammaticae* 2:5. Cf. Aristotle, *Poetics* 20.2: the written "letter is an
indivisible sound."

oral word. Function does not play a significant role in such a model, since language is an ideal of which speaking and writing are simply the imitations. As Wittgenstein observes of the *Confessiones*, Augustine assumes that a child learning a language is like someone traveling in a foreign country without a knowledge of the language of that country, "that is, as if it already had a language, only not this one."[36] Language, in other words, preexists the speaking subject, who remains merely a vehicle through which it passes. In the name of "autonomy," language has rarely served such specific theological and social uses.

Thus, if "paradox" will not do as a description of the relation between oral and written, then what *is* a serviceable alternative? As Augustine represented in theory what medieval reading tended to illustrate in practice, the structure of the relation between voice and letter did not grant each mode equal standing. Reading the written word in Latin, for instance, in the study of the sacred page or its commentary, was synonymous with listening to the voice of its author: spoken and written were recto and verso of the same communicative act. The relation of the two modes is thus not a "paradox," for it is governed by a *discourse* within each which restricts or denies the import of difference between them. The implicit or explicit exercise of this denial is made in the name of an origin that assumes *dominion* over the copy: writing is the "domain" of what voice would set out to occupy. In this way, writing is inhabited by the discourse of voice. It is this ideal of language that Gregory the Great speaks for when he denies grammar by throwing out his Donatus.

DISCOURSE AND DOMINION

"Literacy" in Latin, therefore, is only partially understood when it is thought to be competence in the grammar of case and number on the page of the manuscript or the memory. To the contrary, it is a symbiosis of oral and written. Locating its authority in the identity of *vox* with *littera*, it is small wonder that Latin was installed as *the* model for literacy in the middle ages, keeping the vernacular languages on the other side of the diglossic border. Dante, Boccaccio, Guillaume de Lorris, Jean de Meung, and Chaucer all bear ample testimony to this hierarchy in their apologies for the difference of vernacular writing. But they acknowledge not only the difference of another tongue; they also mark a historical shift in which the vernacular is no longer simply a spoken language; each of them assumes for his own work the import and authority traditionally associated only with the written form of

[36] Wittgenstein, *Philosophical Investigations* 1.15–16.

Latin. Such arguments for the vernaculars surely ought to qualify the customary identification of literacy with Latinity.

However, redrawing the map to allow room for languages other than Latin does not really redress the question of literacy in the later middle ages. As every reader of medieval writing is aware, the challenge of the vernacular is that the spoken tongue rivals the dignity of Latin productions by virtue of its *writtenness*. It is customary to see this rivalry as a "battle of the books," the vested interests of the *antiqui* in contest with the departures of the *moderni*. But the conflict between different tongues also calls attention to a conflict within each of them between spoken and written, oral and textual. The rise of the vernacular is the historical moment of this difference, but it is to be found long before and well-entrenched in the tradition of Latin literacy, where the subordination of letter to voice was so familiar that it was hardly ever questioned as a model for language.[37] Thus illustrations from both Latin and the vernaculars are relevant to the ways in which spoken and written language are related. Neither linguistic family is presumed to have a more natural inclination toward the discovery of difference between voice and letter than the other. The inclination is conferred entirely by convention. And that is why I am arguing for an alignment between theoretical reflection on language and the social practice of orality.

But by the same token, it is in the Latin traditions that we see refined confirmation of the notion that writing is a mirror of speech. And in this commitment, the dominion of voice, as I have characterized it, asserts itself as the discourse of writing. It is not that the difference of writing was unknown or misperceived, although vernacular developments enunciated it in a new key. Rather, this difference is *occluded* within a discourse of voice as prior and originary. For writing to justify itself as something more than artificial, a mere adjunct to spoken language, it had to present itself at the origin of speech, as the voice of the author. The discourse of language creates an occlusion by tending to hide the source of utterance in the effect, by trying to say that the voice at the source is synonymous with the resulting expression. Why bother about difference in such a circumstance, when writing is bending over backwards to imitate the *vivam vocem* itself?

The persistence of that occlusion should not be underestimated: it established the dominion of Latin as *the* model for literacy throughout the middle ages; it held at arm's length productions in the vernacular

---

[37] NB that Huot, *From Song to Book*, p. 39, argues for the "creative tension between oral and written format" in OF manuscripts; Lerer, *Literacy and Power*, p. 195, charts "the making of a literate imagination" in the oral context of OE verse.

well beyond the advent of printed books in the fifteenth century; and it is the distant progenitor of a historiography that would insist even today on defining "culture" by appeal to a model in "literacy."[38] In order to appreciate the difference of writing (both the division between linguistic groups and also their intrinsic differential structures), we need to see much more critically than we have that a notion of orality as "secondary" has an unavoidably problematical history in the middle ages and specifically in the concept of literacy modeled upon the subordination of letter to voice. It remains a stunning irony of medieval history that the dominion of this model over the centuries was assured by doubt and suspicion about the very instrument of its perpetuation—inscription itself. For it is not "orality" that persisted as a "secondary" form in the middle ages, but rather the occlusion that prevented the difference within language and between different languages from having a standing of any real consequence. And finally, we cannot say that the qualification of literacy as an autonomous technology was a cultural "program" self-consciously pursued from century to century. Rather, it was simply the way things were, which is another way of saying that literacy was context-dependent or "ideological." Whether or not writing would find a way out of this situation remains to be seen.

LINGUISTIC CRISIS

We have already noticed the manifestation of oral control in the pronunciation and dictation of script in monastic circumstances of reading and copying. Another version of this control is apparent in the possibility that oral reading in the twelfth century encouraged a situation of orthodoxy and social stasis: if intellectual endeavors were too bold or latitudinarian, "they were subject to peer correction and control in the very act of their formulation and publication."[39] For example, the success of the Cathar heresy was not the result of circulating a body of forbidden books for silent meditation, but of communicating information by word of mouth. On the other hand, silent reading allowed private responses to arise without the sanction of an audience of present listeners. In the thirteenth century, Joachim de Fiore's *Liber figurarum*, a heretical text of intricate designs and figures, was intended

---

[38] E.g., see the responses to Bloom's *The Closing of the American Mind* and Hirsch's *Cultural Literacy* in Gless and Smith, eds., "The Politics of Liberal Education" (esp. Rorty on "pragmatic" literacy, pp. 227–34).

[39] Saenger, "Silent Reading," p. 399.

for private study, which—it seems fair to surmise—encouraged "individual critical thinking and contributed ultimately to the development of scepticism and intellectual heresy."[40] One need only look to England and the Lollard heresy of the later fourteenth century for further evidence of containing crisis by curtailing the written word: the movement was quashed on various occasions by the suppression of manuscript-books, the possession of which was grounds for formal charges of heresy.[41]

Such historical events illustrate my earlier point that the power of change does not issue from one channel of language or the other, voice or writing. Neither term of this duality is presumed to have an internal force more potent than the other. Such an opposition might be proposed for an oral society, such as the South American Nambikwara, who—as Claude Lévi-Strauss argues—receive writing as an instrument of violence and imperialist power.[42] But just as readily that opposition will be falsified, as Derrida demonstrates in his critique of Levi-Strauss' account, since the scene of violence is already taking place among the Nambikwara, who have no writing yet nonetheless manifest the exertion of power and difference by *imitating* Lévi-Strauss' writing and notetaking. Contrary to what the anthropologist takes for granted about writing as violence and imperialist power, the writing lesson, says Derrida, "was not the scene of an *origin* but only that of the imitation of writing."[43] One might conclude that this critique obliterates all difference between speech and writing and points to the self-disclosing violence in the orality of a people without writing. Such a view, furthermore, might lead to the assumption that Derrida holds out for a "paradise" beyond difference, such as the medieval myth of a pristine orality prior to the fall into linguistic confusion.[44]

But Derrida makes a different point, and the medieval example of phonocentrism enunciates it. Among the tribesmen, it is the act of imitating speech by writing that carries out the exertion of social dominion and hierarchization. The power of imitation is not a mysterious force ready to unleash itself from either voice or text; the imitated copy is not a resource in which power is contained. Rather, the power of imitation consists within its action, in the *displacement* it urges by seeming to make the source disappear into the copy. One mode of language is staged as the other, so that critical differences between

[40] Ibid.
[41] See Aston, "Lollardy and Literacy," p. 352.
[42] Lévi-Strauss, *Tristes Tropiques*, pp. 294 ff.
[43] Derrida, *Of Grammatology*, p. 127.
[44] See Bloch, *Etymologies and Genealogies*, pp. 9–10.

them no longer seem to have import. Within that suppression, the potential for opposition is deferred, but collision waits for its moment. Thus to speak of the "power of literacy" versus the dominance of "oral tradition" bypasses the action of displacement which put out of play the opposition between these major cultural investments. Dominion "originated" in neither talk nor text, but in the displacement that made writing look like the voice of authority.

TEXTUALITY

Anyone who has explored the reception of writing in the middle ages has confronted the fact that it was often the occasion of contest, if not outright collision, between different segments of society. For instance, a recent study of the eleventh and twelfth centuries has shown that the impact of written texts (of philosophy and theology) on groups who sought to understand them did not initiate sudden change but rather the "transformation" and mutual "interdependence" of orality and literacy. Oral customs continued to function "within a universe of communications governed by texts."[45] It was less important whether texts were actually present, since a community might very well think, analyze, and behave as if they were. Thus, texts began to inform not only how experience was understood but also how people actually experienced events of their world: they began, so to speak, to "live texts." For a person could be "literate" (that is, have a minimal knowledge of Latin grammar and syntax), but not be able to use texts. And similarly, one could be "textual" and have assimilated the habits of analysis and reference learned from listening to texts read, yet still not show the genuine literacy of a *magister* (teacher).[46]

We may regard such situations, according to this study, not as the assertion of orality or literacy per se but rather as the development of a third category combining the two of them, "textuality."[47] This application of the term allows for the possibility of resolving the potential conflict between oral practices and the new skills of literacy; the "text" becomes the occasion for reconciling disagreement and eventually influencing group behavior. Those involved in the process constitute a "textual community" that is a new amalgam of differing intellectual and social practices. The Cistercian order, for example, may be considered such a textual community, since its source of authority existed ultimately in a written document and it experienced on a daily basis

[45] Stock, *The Implications of Literacy*, p. 3. Cf. McLuhan, *The Gutenberg Galaxy*, on the "interiorization" of script in oral language, pp. 18, 24, 40, 54, 58, 76.

[46] Stock, *The Implications of Literacy*, pp. 4, 6, 42–59.

[47] Ibid., pp. 44, 90–92, and passim.

inevitable conflicts with the community outside of the text and the monastery walls. But while differences between customs of literacy and orality were bound to be changed by acculturation, this process was not a dramatic standoff between a hostile society and a community committed to pondering documents and living according to them. For oral habits prevailed within the community itself through the disciplines of conducting ritual or discussion without the physical presence of texts, as well as through the vocalized reading of texts in manuscript production. Although such practices are indebted to writing, the cultural conditions of orality are still present, especially when the discipline of reciting aloud the interpretations agreed upon by a community subdues, if it does not silence, the occasion of opposition that might otherwise arise in the private encounter with the written page.

It will be apparent that this concept of "textuality" encourages the notion of resolving ("transforming") cultural and intellectual difference, and it does so by identifying the text with "rationality."[48] Analysis, reference, logic, and the other skills of reading are now modeled by the text, so that the "logic of writing" appears to be the appropriate "organization of society."[49] But let us note that this alignment of text with logic or rationality changes significantly the role of social context in the assessment of literacy. An appreciation of the development of writing within definite social circumstances is now qualified by appeal to a completely translinguistic category. Literacy in this configuration can be called "context-dependent," but only in the sense that it has successfully displaced the autonomy of the technology in which it is founded to begin with. Now it is no longer "secondary orality" which persists, but a new principle beyond history itself, the "rationality of the text." This development realizes exactly the concept of *displacement* I have been describing. The difference between linguistic and social activities is apparently reconciled by virtue of an order or hierarchy in which the logic of the text is ultimately taken as the prior term.

I have argued that the subject literacy in the middle ages appears to present us with choosing between oral and written influences whenever imitation is the model of language. To study this point in finer detail, let me follow the arguments of Anselm of Canterbury, who has been offered in illustration of the idea that medieval theorists themselves identified textuality with rationality. My sense is that his subtle formulations of "word" and "text" in the *Monologion* and *Proslogion* also illustrate the powerful success of displacement in language.

---

[48] Ibid., pp. 10, 111–12, 252, and passim.
[49] See, e.g., Goody, *The Logic of Writing*, who refers to Stock for this idea, pp. 176–77.

IMITATION AS DISPLACEMENT

As Anselm sets out to address his brethren and a wider, imagined audience, he figures both of them as present in his mind and engaged in conversation with him. His aim is to comprehend and represent what they believed, and understanding, in this circumstance, is tantamount to discussing, explaining, and creating a new text.[50] Through an interior "dramatic dialogue," an unwritten "text"—like a transcendent form—is constructed before it is represented in writing. The oral word in the mind is projected eventually as the written word on the page, and the text is, accordingly, an intermediary for a discussion ongoing internally as well as in the world. Because it organizes everyday colloquy into a rationalized coherent object, the text in this conception mediates between conflicting forces: it defers confrontation. Herein, let us observe, is the reassertion of oral priority, which is made quite explicit by Anselm himself in his preference for interior dialogue over writing and in his striving for a literacy that is best illustrated by the art of public speaking.

Anselm did not arrive at these reflections on the orality of the textual by accident, but in the context of extended reflections on the nature of the linguistic sign. In the *Monologion*, he argues that *verba* ("words") "are the likenesses and images" of the objects to which they correspond. Mimesis is the model of linguistic competence in this formulation, since the truth of a verbal likeness is determined by how precisely it represents its object. "For all words of the kind by which we say things in the mind, that is, by which we think, are similitudes and images of the things of which they are the words."[51] Linguistic similitude, moreover, not only explains the correspondence between thought and reality; it is also vital to the process by which thought reflects on itself. If, according to Anselm, we think in words (*dicimus, id est cogitamus*), then "the mind conceiving of itself gives birth to an image of itself in its own thinking; or rather, thinking is its own image."[52] He goes on to observe that the mind "cannot be separated from its own image except by thought itself."[53] But his metaphor of self-reflection as "birth" is all to the point of his emphasis on the mental concept as the

[50] Stock, *The Implications of Literacy*, p. 333. The "speaking" of memory in Anselm is also covered by Coleman, *Ancient and Medieval Memories*, pp. 155–68.

[51] Anselm of Canterbury. *Monologion* 48.18–20. On the relevance of this principle to later scholasticism, esp. Aquinas, see Lonergan, *Verbum*, pp. 1, 7, 23, 46–47.

[52] *Monologion* 52.12–15. On this Anselmian principle, see Coleman, *Ancient and Medieval Memories*, p. 164: "To think of a thing which we remember is 'to speak' this thing mentally."

[53] *Monologion* 52.27–28

word spoken in the mind: since thought gives birth to itself, so is "the image of the mind its own word."[54]

In subsequent chapters of the *Monologion*, Anselm draws out the Trinitarian suggestions that any medieval student would see in his discussion of thought fathering its own *imago* as *verbum*. The connection follows effortlessly from a theory of the concept so committed to imitation. Yet the notion of conceptual similitude also helps to clarify Anselm's assumptions about the text: as the word is an imitation of *cogitans* or of *res*, so too is the text the site of a mediation between the silent, interior dialogues spoken in the mind and the confusing world of everyday communication. It is conceived in the recognition of real differences between the conceptual, transcendent order and the physical universe, but it remains the ground on which those differing forces come to terms; such a meeting would be impossible without a theory of what they have in common, which is the priority of voice in their formulation. Anselm extends and refines these analyses of word and text in the *Proslogion* and *De grammatico*; but, as these treatises have been studied, he does not abandon the model of oral exchange for written discourse.[55] Even when he turns to comparing and contrasting the speech of common people (*populi*) with the more refined language of those who engage in logical disputation (*dialectici*), he does not oppose speech to writing. The *populi* employ grammar based on oral usage; the *dialectici* speak according to the norms set by texts. However, popular speech too has rules informed by written models; because of individual variation, it may show greater flexibility than the technical language of logic, which must be confined by rules of subordination. But the two modes do not differ in kind.

In this respect, Anselm is fairly representative of other writers, such as Bernard of Clairvaux and Peter Abelard, who also had much to say on the topic of mental language and its expression in speaking and writing. Like Anselm, neither of them entertains the possibility of an opposition or conflict between spoken and written. Rather, they illustrate with Anselm the "transformation" of these two modes within the society that took shape around their teaching: the group adopts "a rationality inseparable from the text."[56] And yet it remains rooted in the bedrock of oral habits of thought and discourse rather than in the silent, private response of an individual mind proceeding without the

[54] *Monologion* 52.28. For comparable formulations of *verbum* in Aquinas, see Lonergan, *Verbum*, pp. 45, 191, 206. Cf. Coleman, *Ancient and Medieval Memories*, p. 164.

[55] Stock, *The Implications of Literacy*, p. 361: "Reflection is rational not because of its rationalism . . . but because, within Anselm's mind and afterwards, it involves playing out a set of 'speech-acts' as texts."

[56] Ibid., p. 523; for Abelard, see pp. 362–403; for Bernard, pp. 403–54.

sanction of public performance and response. It has been concluded
that the textual communities of the middle ages effect, by means of
texts, a separation of "experience . . . from ratiocination about it" and
that written documents constitute "forms of mediation" between the
raw data of experience and the concepts of a transcendent order.[57]
What is true of Anselm seems equally accurate for Bernard and Abelard: the text is a symbolic extension of the mind, of its ongoing,
internal dialogues. The model of imitation informing these typical
medieval theories of language and textuality is very firmly situated. It
leads inevitably to the identification of the text with rationality, and
literacy in Latin with the organization of society.

However, are we really thinking here about "rationality" as the
model of social order? The text, to be sure, is associated with all the
familiar "skills" of literacy, such as logic, validation, reference, and so
forth. And yet as the imitation of speech, silent or spoken, writing is
no longer an autonomous skill but a definite context-dependent expression of the needs of a specific time and place. Although textuality
appeals to an autonomous model—indeed *the* model of autonomy
itself, rationality—it nonetheless conceives of that model as a function
or use. The text is an ideological instrument by virtue of its success in
displacing the potential difference between voice and letter, mental
and textual, literacy and society. It is, need I say, brilliantly successful
in this capacity, since the order of the community is made to seem
synonymous with the order of writing itself. But "order" in this case
is not something "natural" to text or speech. It is, rather, the unequivocal logic that subordinates one to the other in the interests of social
norms. Thus to trace the power of social change back to a principle
like "textuality" does not take account of the displacement at the heart
of transforming one property of language into another. And that is
why such a theory can bypass almost without realizing it the contribution of vernacular languages within the larger cultural context of
literacy in the later middle ages.[58]

ORAL MYTHOLOGY

One way to appreciate further what is at stake in this compromise is
to compare the orality of medieval forms with evidence from an archaic past in which language does not maintain a very scrupulous
separation between signifier and signified reference. The medieval

[57] Ibid., p. 531. Similarly, see Lerer, *Literacy and Power*, p. 195: "oral culture is mediated
by writing" in *Beowulf*; on rationality and writing, p. 122.

[58] See the reviews of Stock by Nichols in *Speculum* (1986) and Vance in *Diacritics*
(1985). Cf. Carruthers, *The Book of Memory*, p. 32.

scene, to be sure, is a long way off, but the archaic example will be useful for considering the possible connection between the persistence of oral forms and the interests of dominion in the middle ages. It is, of course, well recognized that orality is illustrated in the cultures we call "mythological," the archaic societies in which writing as we know it is not practiced, such as the world of the Nambikwara today or the cultures of Europe and Britain during the Neolithic period, which Christianity eventually encountered. But only in the last few years has it been asserted that "orality" might profitably be studied interchange-ably with "mythologizing" modes of thinking and communicating. One scholar has taken significant steps in this direction by revising the theory of myth in the work of Lévi-Strauss and exploring how "the characterisation of the 'savage mind' as 'pre-historical' or atemporal relates to the distinction between literate and pre-literate societies."[59] Among the various areas that would benefit from this suggestion, the theoretical insights that have been reached about both myth and orality deserve attention for the light they may shed on each other. To begin with, a connection between these two categories is facilitated by the specific nature of the medieval traditions under discussion here. For one of the most typifying features of mythologizing thought, as pointed out in a variety of anthropological and theoretical studies, is its determination to resist or resolve contradiction. Lévi-Strauss has discussed myth in terms of "mediation," the site of "transformations" between contrary aspects of legends separated by time and geographi-cal location. He maintains that myth "totalizes" because it refuses to leave anything "alien" to itself.[60] Roland Barthes has argued a similar point: myth "organizes a world that is without contradictions."[61] In reference to many aspects of ancient Roman religion, Georges Dumézil has demonstrated the preoccupation of myth with justifying and af-firming the "structure, the elements, the connections, the balances" which prevent a society from disintegrating.[62] Considering Dumézil's theory of the "three functions"—of those who provide, those who pray, and those who fight—Georges Duby has offered a new appreciation of the internal structure of hierarchy as it contributed to the enduring stability of feudal society in the middle ages.[63]

Although no one would insist on a univocal theory for a category

[59] Goody, *Domestication of the Savage Mind*, p. 15 and passim. Discussion of Lévi Strauss occurs throughout the book. See also Finnegan, *Literacy and Orality*.

[60] Lévi-Strauss, *The Savage Mind*, pp. 10, 245; Lévi-Strauss, *Structural Anthropology*, pp. 216–17, 226, 229.

[61] Barthes, *Mythologies*, p. 143.

[62] Dumézil, *The Destiny of the Warrior*, p. 3.

[63] Duby, *The Early Growth of the European Economy* and *The Three Orders*.

such as myth, the evidence of its stabilizing function in social organization is continually pointed out, specifically in medieval cultural
forms. Duby's approach is only one of several ways of explaining the
many variations on the medieval myth of hierarchy. The mediation of
contradiction and crisis is the other side of this mythology, and that
factor aligns it with many kinds of oral practices in the middle ages.
For oralism, like myth, is distinguishable preeminently by its resistance
to alien modes in the determination of preserving its own integrity and
unity: the oral group, in a vestige of tribal solidarity, asserts itself
against others, not necessarily as a gesture of aggression but of continuing self-definition. If oral cultures may be called "agonistically
programmed," they are so paradoxically because of a more abiding
need to protect the "familiarity" and "equilibrium or homeostasis" of
the social unit.[64]

Nowhere is this thrust more suggestive than in medieval metaphors
of script used for divine voice, as in the Book of God's Work and the
Book of His Word. As divine utterance, these Texts embody the unity
of a transcendent intention, and the disciplines devoted to studying
them—the exegesis of the Bible and of the physical universe—extrapo-
late a variety of possible readings within the context of a controlling
foreknowledge of that intention. To recall only one striking example
of this hermeneutic, we may note Hugh of St. Victor's comment, from
the *Didascalicon*, that in Holy Writ there may be "many things which
seem to be opposed to each other" and others that seem "absurd"; but
finally the Divine Page "admits no opposition."[65] Other cultural forms
also appear to hold on to a mythologic from the past by virtue of their
totalizing commitments—for instance, the gothic facade, window, and
column; or the elaborate continuity of ideas about number, harmony,
and music stemming from the *Timaeus*; or the edifice-like style of
illuminated manuscript pages and book covers. Like these illustrations, the oral transformation of writing which marks written language
from Augustine through the end of manuscript culture in the fifteenth
century is similarly invested in preserving the status quo as it sup-
presses or defers an alien and "killing" letter.[66] In attitudes of this sort,

---

[64] Ong, *Orality and Literacy*, pp. 43–46.

[65] *Eruditionis didascalicae* 6.4 (*PL* 176, 802). Cf. my discussion in *The Idea of the Book*,
ch. 3.

[66] Goody, *Domestication of the Savage Mind*, p. 14: "What happens here is part and
parcel of the tendency of oral cultures towards cultural homeostasis; those innumerable
mutations of culture that emerge in the ordinary course of verbal interaction are either
adopted by the interacting group or they get eliminated in the process of transmission
from one generation to the next." Cf. Ong, *Orality and Literacy*, p. 46.

the two tongues of oral and written speak with one voice, and that is why they do not debate the possibility of a split within.

Or we may turn to *rhetorica*, the third discipline of the trivium, since it preserved demonstrably the art of public eloquence which from its origins in antiquity was always an oral mode.[67] Because it is so agonistic, as Aristotle maintained, so postured against the opposition, we might be correct to say of rhetoric what Hugh said of Scripture: it too admits no internal contradiction, and that is its myth. The longevity of these oral properties, which extend well into the seventeenth century, must have been reinforced by influences of medieval mythology which were much more pervasive than acquired skills such as oratory or exegesis; for they are, after all, latecomers on the scene of writing. The alphabet had a history of little over three thousand years by 1400, whereas oral communication went back over five hundred millennia. In a manuscript culture that was itself still on the margin of illiteracy for so many centuries, orality is hardly the product of educational disciplines like *rhetorica*; rather, it is a far-reaching social infrastructure. Only such a wide foundation can explain how a cultural tradition so bent on validating knowledge in old books did not give way to flourishing excursions into the gap between voice and letter long before the revolutions of the sixteenth century. The answer, as McLuhan once pointed out, is that "the 'text' was felt to be the immediate voice of an *auctor*, and was authoritative in an oral way."[68]

THE MAGIC OF WRITING

To explore the possibilities of the mythology of the "lettered voice," we may turn from theoretical speculation about the linguistic sign and the text to further examples of writing in the social history of the later middle ages. For instance, the meaning of "literacy" in England from the Norman Conquest to the death of Edward I in 1307 was nothing like having scholarly competence with Latin books of philosophy, law, or literature.[69] For the term *litteratus* in England at this time could simply distinguish someone who possessed a rudimentary reading knowledge of Latin from a person who did not, a *laycus* (layperson). *Litteratus* thus designated the minimal ability to read an elementary

[67] Ong, *Rhetoric, Romance, and Technology*, p. 28: "Rhetoric, despite its deep involvement in the written medium, retained its earlier expressly oral contours intact."

[68] *The Gutenberg Galaxy*, p. 104. Cf. Ong, *Rhetoric, Romance, and Technology*, p. 46: oral elements "survived centuries of manuscript culture because in the teaching and practice of expression this manuscript culture retained very live connections with the preliterate oral-aural world."

[69] See Clanchy, *From Memory to Written Record*, pp. 175–201.

document in order to conduct business as a landlord, operate a shop, or serve on a jury. As *layci* (laypersons) could not read, neither did they have the same advantages of those *litterati* who were trained in ecclesiastical schools and could claim "benefit of clergy." A *clericus*—a university student—had such privileges and was *litteratus*, though not necessarily erudite. But that benefit, in the later middle ages, could save someone's life: a felon accused of murder could claim "benefit of clergy" by demonstrating only the barest ability to read a verse or two from the Vulgate Bible and thereby escape the death penalty.[70] Accordingly, if knowledge of Latin became more widespread in England between 1100 and 1300, the laity were "literate" in only a minimal sense, since a little competence in the language could keep one out of jail or assist a business transaction. And it was even more minimal for women, who would have had the benefit of Latin only by word of mouth, inside a nunnery or out, since they were ineligible for formal education.

These factors bear witness to a culture in which reading and writing were simply ancillary to familiar oral custom; literate skills in thirteenth-century Britain did not sweep away traditional ways of conducting life. As the manifestation of educated thought processes, literacy was a possibility for only a privileged few. The kings of England were among them, since they were educated in Latin from Henry I forward. Henry II was known as *litteratus* in the privileged sense, according to Peter of Blois, who says that the king took recreation in private reading and puzzling over difficult *quaestiones* with court *clerici*.[71] But these examples are exceptions. For others in society, Latin was learned at home or church by ear, and only remotely from texts. Among the peasant class, learning Latin proceeded obviously at a snail's pace. An educated *litteratus* from the peasants is nearly a medieval miracle, and the biography of Robert Grosseteste is a case in point—if in fact he was of peasant origins. Among the knightly class, Latin was also acquired from oral exchange, which means that real competence in it was a rarity. By and large, the practical "literacy of the laity" through the reign of Edward I designates a society still grounded in orality. And the oral world of the *litterati*—as paradoxical as it may sound to us—is evidenced by many striking facts of legal and economic history in these years of medieval England.

For instance, it has been shown that charters in the twelfth century were oral documents. They might be addressed to "all those seeing

---

[70] See Gabel, *Benefit of Clergy*, pp. 68–88.

[71] *PL* 207.198; Robertson and Sheppard, eds., *Materials for the History of Thomas Becket*, 7.573. See Clanchy, *From Memory to Written Record*, p. 186.

and hearing these letters, in the future and in the present," or to "all who shall hear and see this charter." Some charters conclude with a "goodbye" formula, *valete*, as if the maker of the document had just conversed with his audience.[72] Personal wills of the twelfth century are also oral acts, despite their written form. They include the audience of persons present as witnesses to a testator announcing a bequest, "with his own mouth." The witnesses "saw, were present, and heard" the actual words spoken by the maker of the will.[73] The document itself does not validate the transaction, which is completed at the moment of verbal exchange rather than in writing. The written as witness to the spoken is especially well illustrated in documents recording the transfer of land or the making of gifts. To such documents it was common to attach some object personal to the donor such as a ring or a knife or an actual piece of the land being transferred (a clump of sod). Tied by strips of parchment or skin extending from the document itself, such objects are not strictly speaking "symbolic," since they were physical parts of what the writing described. Thus attached, the object and the written word are of the same order, and the document itself is not considered for what it "signifies" but for what it actually embod-ies—a donor's gratuity or a seller's property.

That the maker of a document was somehow immanent in writing takes on supernatural proportions during the practice of *levatio cartae*, when parchment, stylus, and ink were physically deposited on the plot of ground changing hands. The instruments of the transfer became "impregnated with earthly forces"; the "signed" act was, in essence, an imitation of the holy rite of transaction and the written document became "a quasi-magical object," since even a *carta sine litteris* (a "docu-ment without letters") had binding legal strength.[74] These examples bespeak not the kind of writing recognized as a reference system but rather the continuum typical of mythological unions between natural and supernatural, chthonic powers and human beings. A mind-set bred on such a "mytho-logic" would hardly be predisposed to ponder a diglossia between the written word and the voice of the person who dictated it. It is no surprise, therefore, to find writing venerated as an object with magical properties—as we do, for instance, on the Conti-nent in the eleventh and twelfth centuries. During ceremonies of in-vestiture or marriage, the exchange of vows was done orally, but documents and other physical objects were included eventually in the rituals at this time as written records became more common. Oral

---

[72] See Clanchy, *From Memory to Written Record*, pp. 202 ff.
[73] Ibid., p. 203.
[74] Cited in Stock, *The Implications of Literacy*, p. 48.

features of such exchanges were then accompanied by taking up the *festuca*, an object such as a wand, rod, or bit of thatch, in order to confirm the bond. Thus, "ratifying" (*festucare*) the union was synonymous with exchanging the words between vassal and lord or husband and wife; and the *festuca* was a *signum et symbolum traditionis*—a "sign and symbol of the tradition" of investiture or marriage. Accordingly, to break the bond, *exfestucare*, the objects of ritual were cast away.[75] In historical materials of this sort, it is superfluous to think of writing as an artificial representation of an absent intention or meaning, since the words of the document recording the ritual are immanent in the vows spoken and the objects exchanged.

The magic of the written word is perhaps predictable in rituals of this sort; but that it persists as well in legal procedure witnesses the strength of deep social habits holding on to emerging forms of communication. In England, law was "published" by proclamation commonly from the twelfth century through the fourteenth. Although the *Magna Carta* (of 1215) is the precedent for writing legislation, it too was read publicly, and apparently so widely that it was not even recorded officially in the royal archives. Public reading of law, which was frequently done both in Latin and English, obviously met the needs of a society by and large unable to read, but the practice appealed also to the more indefinable expectation of a preliterate world where the *viva vox* simply had more power than script. Notwithstanding the increasing use of written documents, legal practice through the thirteenth century continued to privilege the oral word. In the twelfth century, a court summons was made not in writing but through oral proclamation delivered by summoners or criers (*curatores*) to the accused. In London an individual charged with a crime could be summoned by a bell to the court of Husting—a notification rather impossible to ignore, since the great bell of St. Paul's might be invoked in witness to the crier's summons. The arbitrariness of such communications was probably curtailed in Henry II's reign, when writs were used along with summonses.[76]

The power of the oral word is particularly notable in the procedures of court trials. A litigant made use of an "advocate," called a *forespeca* in Anglo-Saxon and a *perorator* or *narrator* in Latin. Such a person was not a lawyer but someone who spoke in the right style before the court, with proper emphasis and clarity. An attorney also had a role in the proceedings but was not as important as the *narrator*, whose pleading (called a *narratio*) constituted the primary defense of the litigant. The

[75] Ibid., pp. 49–50.
[76] Clanchy, *From Memory to Written Record*, pp. 220–26.

narrator could not be the true representative of the litigant, who had to be present in person, nor could the lawyer. But the prominence of the oral is unmistakable in this context, since the *narrator* was "an extension of the litigant's faculty of speech," the sine qua non of defense.[77] The force of the spoken word in pleadings was as equally mysterious as the means for deciding innocence or guilt. After the pleadings were heard and the written evidence was read aloud, truth or blame was determined by looking for "signs" in the plaintiff and defendant, some physical evidence in their behavior that might betoken the "accuracy" of a decision. Instead of an indicator of right or wrong, the verdict was an instance of "divination," a suspension of the rules of analysis and validation taught by texts in favor of a reliance on the mythological power of "signs" to "tell the truth." Legal practice in England was to change in the twelfth century with the new emphasis on "recognitions" and the critical analysis of evidence.[78] But the prerogative assumed for the spoken word prevailed over written testimony in procedures of law through the end of the thirteenth century.

The link between oral and mythological may also be studied in the signing of legal and other documents by means of special *seals*, which appear to illustrate the strength of mystical and magical influence more than the advance of literacy. Before the use of seals, a simple cross was commonly executed on a document to signify the authority of the maker, whose own name, in such an instance, was far less important for validating the writing than calling on the witness of Christ's sign. This displacement of the written by the power of a sign was effected even more vividly when the seal was a precious and rare object. The maker of the document did not have to write, since he had both his name and the *signum* of his family or house together in one object that could be reproduced endlessly. As it has been noted, "seals perpetuated pre-literate customs in an automated and literate form and thus prevented documentary proof from being followed through to the ultimate point of dispensing with symbolic objects altogether." Because a seal gave a document a certain authoritative status, it might endure longer: it turned the document into a "relic" since, once seen and touched, the seal gave the authenticity of the maker's actual intentions "which no writing could adequately convey."[79] And when a seal was carved from a gemstone, it was regarded as a talisman identifying the

[77] Ibid., p. 221.

[78] *Recognitiones* were specific answers to questions about the facts of a case. Introduced into England after the Norman Conquest, they were originally oral in form but eventually developed as a combination of spoken and written evidence. See Stock, *The Implications of Literacy*, pp. 58–59.

[79] Clanchy, *From Memory to Written Record*, p. 245.

bearer with great personages of the past and with mysterious power. Because it impressed upon a document the evidence of antiquity and the world of the dead, the seal fulfilled not simply the preference of speech over writing; rather, it superseded both by turning language into magic. If we regard the magic in these examples of writing in manuscript culture simply as an illustration of a so-called medieval fascination with the exotic, we ignore its connection with the monastic custom of reading by listening to the "voices of the pages": both of these forms of signing and reading must have flourished as a result of oral traditions holding on in many areas of culture in the later middle ages—and all the more firmly because the validation of writing as the image of speaking stemmed from *auctores* like Augustine.

Resistance to Writing

I have been suggesting that representation of the sort illustrated in medieval oral customs paradoxically obscured writing as something other than voice, and that this occlusion sharply guided the ideological interests of literacy. But the persistence of the oral was assured no certain fate; for it is tantamount to the *parole* (the material quality in speaking or writing) which may be dictated by a governing *langue* determined to avoid difference, but which inevitably challenges and changes the parental myth of discourse. The evidence of suppression and resistance, accordingly, is of particular relevance to this interchange, for it illustrates where linguistic crisis is making contact with social crisis. It is relevant to turn now to a few more instances of the medieval resistance to writing and thus probe further my underlying assumption that theoretical questions about language are part and parcel of its social uses.

We have already seen expressions of this resistance in the old practice of *levatio cartae*, in which writing was ritualized as a viaticum with the spirits of earth. The social conditions behind such practices were very slow to change. In medieval England, for example, "people had to be persuaded—and it was difficult to do—that documentary proof was a sufficient improvement on existing methods."[80] The "advantage" of writing was hardly self-evident, since even literates proceeded in familiar oral customs without recognizing how documents might assure new methods of proof. Few instances of the intrusion of the conflict veiled behind the oral representation of writing are as graphic as the investiture controversy between Anselm of Canterbury and

[80] Ibid., p. 231.

King Henry I in 1101. The letters from Pope Paschal II to Henry and Anselm enjoining governmental investiture of ecclesiastical offices were sealed by the Papal See and composed so elegantly that they remain among the most extraordinary *cartae* created in the middle ages. And yet they were vituperatively defied by Henry's bishops, who argued that the pope himself had told them in person that the king was to be allowed investiture. Oral priorities make their appearance even in Eadmer's account of the matter, which is represented in dialogue form as a dramatic standoff between Anselm's monks and Henry's bishops—an illustration of the old oral penchant for flyting common in heroic narrative.

Anselm's monks:	"But what about the evidence of the letters?"
Henry's bishops:	"As we don't accept the evidence of monks against bishops, why should we accept that of a sheepskin?"
Anselm's monks:	"Shame on you! Are not the Gospels written down on sheepskins?"

The conflict is not simply between what was said in Rome versus what was read in England; it concerns the breakdown of voice imitated in the *cartae*, which are traduced further by Henry's partisans as "the skins of wethers blackened with ink and weighted with a little lump of lead."[81] If writing does not possess the magical property of speaking for its author, it is nothing.

The forgery tradition in England is yet another instance of imitation tearing under the pressure of difference between speech and writing. It developed because written documents outpaced oral tradition among the customs of laying claim to land and property by ecclesiastical and aristocratic houses. And the result was that *scriptores* were set to work inventing documents "verifying" land holdings by church and state which had been previously claimed simply by word of mouth. In 1238 Archbishop Simon Langton wrote to Pope Gregory IX: "Holy Father, there is not a single sort of forgery that is not perpetrated in the Church of Canterbury. For they have forged in gold, in lead, in wax, and in every kind of metal."[82] The practice long outlasted the lament, but the tension suppressed under the old orality of the written was out in the open: the aversion to writing was plain in the act. For if anyone could steal it, manipulate it, change it, and misrepresent it, who could trust it?

These are not extraordinary examples of attitudes toward writing in

[81] Cited by Clanchy, *From Memory to Written Record*, p. 209. On flyting, see Parks, *Verbal Duelling in Heroic Narrative*.

[82] Clanchy, *From Memory to Written Record*, p. 234.

thirteenth-century England; but neither are they exclusive, since we
may note in Anglo-Saxon poetic traditions the imagery of craft and
skill identified with writing and represented in objects of enormous
value, such as bejeweled book covers.[83] It may even be the case that
such fictions of the text in the poem respond to specific social attitudes
which were not entirely hospitable to the new technology of the written document. In the fourteenth century, the situation of literacy shifts
dramatically, as writing in English and French, not just Latin, is widely
practiced at court, in parliament, and in business affairs. And yet the
evidence of this advancement in communication and learning should
not create the impression, as it sometimes does especially in the study
of law or poetry, that we have arrived in an age when writing has
parted ways once and for all with the oral customs of society. For we
still have to reckon with the persistence of memorial techniques from
the past, as well as the continuing appeal to spoken models of language for validating the authority, credibility, and confidence of the
written word.[84]

Fourteenth-century studies have taken some note of these issues in
the production and illumination of manuscripts. For example, it has
been recently observed of nonliturgical manuscripts that if a single
picture was to be painted in a manuscript, it was not a depiction of
events described in the text but of the author or narrator. This evidence
in a wide range of late medieval pictures indicates a familiar appeal to
the author as the source of truth, but it also suggests strongly that the
document is a record of something spoken. Such illuminations are the
result of "a state of mind which perceived the speaker as more significant than the marvels of which he spoke."[85] We may note similar
evidence in manuscripts from the 1380s and 1390s, when production
moved from provincial districts to the city of London. Though we
know little about professional scribes at this time, it is apparent that
inscription was still made from oral dictation, and that the copyist may
have had little or no knowledge of the material he was producing. John
Lydgate makes ironic use of this apparently common assumption when
he compares himself as lover to a "skryvener" who knows of love only
what "his maister beside doth endyte."[86] Scribes were "artisans" of the

[83] As Lerer, *Literacy and Power*, has argued for the riddles, *Beowulf*, and *Durham*.

[84] On fourteenth-century evidence of memory, see Carruthers, *The Book of Memory*,
pp. 160 ff.

[85] Scott, "Design, Decoration and Illustration," p. 47.

[86] Lydgate, "Complaint of the Black Knight," l. 196, in *Minor Poems*. See Christianson,
"Evidence for the Study of London's Late Medieval Manuscript-Book Trade," pp. 87–89;
and Edwards and Pearsall, "The Manuscripts of the Major English Poetic Texts," pp.
257–62.

page, not scholars of it, and they worked in all likelihood independently, rather than in large scriptoria.[87]

These considerations about how texts were produced and illuminated suggest that literacy was certainly on the rise in fourteenth-century London; but they also indicate what I have been calling the "oral context" of writing. In the following chapters, I will pursue this claim in the evidence of writing from several disciplines of this century. For now let me conclude by noting that the appeal to the author for meaning arises in response to the specific limitations of manuscript culture. Because writing illustrates, by virtue of its evidence as a document, that reference to the author can no longer be taken for granted, it realizes the margin of its difference from spoken language; but it also leads inevitably to the discovery of another margin, the potential division within both speech and writing between what is uttered and what is meant. This discovery is a self-consciousness as fundamental as learning to read and write in any age, and yet it is no less useful for studying the impact of writing on oral contexts in the middle ages.[88] It suggests that a hesitation about writing or a resistance to it may be a way of concealing the illusion that there is no split, or none of any real consequence, between spoken and written, utterance and meaning.

However, it would be incomplete to remark of the examples thus far that writing illustrates a self-awareness speaking does not possess. It would be more useful to suggest that the historical conditions of diglossia betoken an insight into both modes: speaking no less than writing is inhabited by the potential for realizing the difference between its own medium and its capacity to convey a message; how this potential split was negotiated spells out the difference between the oral and written orientations of a particular social context.[89] Oral circumstances of communicating tend to resist diglossic difference, since a speaker has the advantage of reading audience response, prefiguring questions, clarifying the direction of argument, and so forth. Communication in this channel is manifestly more context-dependent.

On the other hand, a written document has no such privileges, as the oral characteristics of charters and wills illustrate. We have a direct,

[87] See Christianson, "Evidence for the Study of London's Late Medieval Manuscript-Book Trade," p. 96. The arrival of paper in England during this time did not affect book production, since it was rarely used in writing; see Lyall, "Materials: The Paper Revolution," pp. 7, 12.

[88] See Goody, *Interface Between the Written and the Oral*, p. 269, on the diglossia between spoken and written channels of language, and within speech itself: as "a visual component to language, writing alters not only the external models . . . but also the internal ones. . . . It alters them in ways that feed back to the structure of speech and of perception."

[89] On this split in manuscript illumination, see Camille, "The Book of Signs."

and sometimes amusing, insight into the problem when we observe a poet personifying his written composition as a "messenger" (the commonplace "envoy") who is urged to "explain" the meaning of the words when the author is no longer present to do so.[90] Similarly, it seems possible that precious images of the text in Old English poetry witness not only an emerging "literary aesthetic";[91] they may also constitute a metatextual defense against an oral skepticism broadly based in society at large. If that is the case, then poems like *Durham* offer unexpected evidence of cultural diglossia in their time. Cut loose from the context of the author's voice, writing must get by on its own. Such examples set in high relief a point that has been made about writing in general, that it is "decontextualizing."[92] It is not autotelically closed off into a system untouched by outside influence; it exists by virtue of such influence, and thus its autonomy is always open to compromise.

ORALITY REDEFINED

In this regard, the "orality" of the customs that existed side-by-side with the rise of literacy in the later middle ages needs to be reformulated: the appearance of oral habits does not constitute a resurgence of "primary" oralism, the tribal consciousness of preliterate societies from the archaic ages that Christianity transformed in Europe and Britain. Rather, in view of the tendency to comprehend writing as a version of speaking or else, in extreme cases, to distrust it, the evidence of oral properties embedded within a document or text may be redefined as the orientation of a discourse to foreclose or deny systematically the recognition of its own differentiation. What defines orality as a "tradition" is precisely this denial.

The implications of denial in language deserve extended study. For in a society of many languages and dialects, such as the trilingual environment of fourteenth-century England, literacy can no longer be grounded in the precepts of an Anselm, *dicimus, it est cogitamus*, let alone in Latinity. The influence of literacy on historical change was never felt with greater force than in this century, and yet it did not come about because of the power of the written word itself, as so often assumed. Understanding cultural change in terms of "secondary oral-

[90] E.g., Middle English lyrics beginning, "Go, litel bille." Cf. Chaucer's "Go, litel boke" at the end of *Troilus and Criseyde*.

[91] Lerer, *Literacy and Power*, pp. 113, 195. In contrast, see Near, "Anticipating Alienation," pp. 323 ff.

[92] See Goody, *The Logic of Writing*, p. 175.

ity" and the "textuality" of certain communities has been more helpful; but neither of these formulations has taken adequate notice of the compromises wrought by the imitative model of language which they presuppose. My argument is that the power of change arises from the *displacement* inherent in the medieval assimilation of written and oral language. Either channel of communication can be the "voice" of dominion, but it proceeds from neither per se. The power of language consists in its capacity to deny opposition to its own utterance in either channel. Language "has" dominion when it becomes a kind of "domain" or "property" in its own right, held by a special few and protected by the class divisions of society. It has no context other than its own self-assertion. And in this sense its "property" is its "propriety." Thus the decontextualizing possibility of language in the written channel is a potential threat or antibody in the system of controlling meaning and asserting power. At all costs writing *must* be construed as voice, if the status quo is to continue.

The ideology of writing, therefore, is a definite consequence of medieval attitudes toward language. But such an ideology is by no means monolithic. We cannot speak of the "ideology of medieval literacy," not without serious oversight of the resistance suppressed within it, beginning with the Latin suppression of the vernaculars. For another attitude toward writing, an appreciation of its autonomy, was also at large—indeed had always been. The problem is that it was so often compromised as the unrecognized and unheard "voice" of the letter itself. Writing is "uncompromising" when its expression pays specific attention to the difference between statement and implication, and features that difference as an event of language in its own right. The language of poetry, of course, specializes in that kind of attention, since it plays out the properties of discourse to comment on an object or event and also on itself as a medium of communication. Medieval poetic figures of the text as "artifact," which occur in Old English and in other literatures as well, betoken the oral contexts from which they emerge, not only the accomplishments of literacy. But they also illustrate the metalinguistic commitment of poetic language in general. In this respect, the poetic traditions of a particular context may be of enormous value in understanding the place of orality and writing in the language of other disciplines. That assumption is the organizing principle of the remaining parts of this book. I argue that metalanguage creates an environment that is not hospitable to displacement, for the denial of difference cannot finally succeed the capacity of one mode of language to echo its alternative. Metalanguage is, accordingly, the theoretical and historical dislocation of the dominion in discourse which defines orality as a mode of writing in the first place. Poetry, however, is one of the more accessible forms of this dislocation.[93] It is much more difficult to trace in other disciplines, such as the language of philosophy and historigraphy.

It will be apparent by now that the question of the autonomy or ideology of medieval literacy inevitably applies as well to the vantage from which that subject is approached in these pages. To assume the autonomous nature of inquiry immediately recalls the medieval model, in which writing was regarded as the reiteration of timeless lessons from the past, and history was bypassed along with the functionality of language, as Wittgenstein observed of Augustine. On the other hand, to assume that all language is ideologically motivated may acknowledge the relativity of any historicism, but it also bypasses a critical factor of its own, the displacement of writing which constituted the discourse of dominion in the middle ages. Taking account of such binarism has become a familiar strategy in modern theoretical discussions of language. My problem will be to engage a stance "between" the two oppositions without compromising an historical appreciation of the fourteenth century. Accordingly, I study the *writing* of philosophy, historiography, and poetry for what it says about specific objects or events, but more importantly for the ways in which it may or may not acknowledge its own capacity as an instrument of communication. Modulations of this acknowledgment can be measured in each of these medieval disciplines, and the degree to which they compare in self-disclosure provides insight into the role of language in society at the time. I think that is an historical claim to make about the culture, even if it is derived from remote theoretical reflection. I begin with the philosophers, since they develop language theory in rarefied academic quarters at both ends of the century. What they may reveal about oral context remains to be seen.

[93] See Mueller, *The Native Tongue and the Word*, on the "orality" of ME prose. In contrast, Coleman, *Medieval Readers and Writers*, pp. 27–28, sees ME prose as a model of "literacy" and poetry as the channel for the survival of "orality."

PART ONE

Philosophy

Chapter Two

THE VOICE OF THE SIGN AND THE SEMIOLOGY OF DOMINION IN THE WORK OF OCKHAM

Section I
ON THE SIGN

Sight is often deceived; hearing serves as guarantee.
—Ambrose, *Commentary on Luke*

INTRODUCTION

"Manuscript culture in the west remained always marginally oral."[1] As a description of the influence of literacy on the European middle ages, this proposition attempts to characterize the seemingly paradoxical situation in which cultural traditions handed down by word of mouth persisted in spite of changes introduced by writing and reading. Although thought processes and behavior were gradually altered by such developments, particularly after the printing press, this claim suggests that the borderline established by the advent of script was much more fluid than it may appear; and written versions of epic poetry or chronicle history which rely on oral conventions offer convenient illustration. But if the idea of "marginal orality" is a phenomenon of manuscript culture in general, then we are obliged to inquire about its relevance to enterprises with little apparent orientation toward the oral past, such as the philosophical projects undertaken during the fourteenth century. Is there any point of thinking about major philosophical problems, such as the discussion of "mental language," in relation to the wider cultural context of an orality persisting against the advance of written tradition?

Among fourteenth-century philosophers in England, William of Ockham presents a particularly challenging test of this question, since he is more rigorously concerned with language as the basis of knowledge than any other thinker of his time. Seeking to purge scholastic epistemology of Platonic and Neoplatonic colorations, he began by reducing

---

[1] Ong, *Orality and Literacy*, p. 119. NB "manuscript cultures remained largely oral-aural even in retrieval of material preserved in texts" (ibid.).

the categories of "substance" and "universality" to nominal topics in the mind, not as having real being in themselves. For this radical move he has been commonly identified as a "nominalist," a title he has worn especially outside the discipline of philosophy. But he would probably have repudiated that label as more appropriate to his forebears, Abelard in particular, because he was also interested fundamentally in what he called *cognitio rei particularis* ("cognition of the particular thing"). This determination has earned him another identity, that of philosophical "realist," and he has even been compared in one recent appraisal to Locke as a precursor of British empiricism.[2]

Between nominalism and realism, we may be hard put to situate Ockham. But I begin with this difference of opinion because it is in part explainable by inadequate scholarly attention to an apparently innocent term in his epistemology, namely the role of *vox* ("word," "voice"). It will be obvious from the outset that this term does not assume a frame of reference specifically in spoken language; nor is it discretely written or mental, the other categories considered by Ockham. Accepting one or the other of these neat divisions is familiar in a readerly appreciation of texts. Yet the fate of *vox* in Ockham's epistemology is not so easily fixed, and it is precisely the fluidity or marginality of the term which invites further exploration. While he addressed the ambiguity of *vox* as a way of exposing uncertainty in scholastic realism, Ockham did not use it to acknowledge what would be called today the "metalanguage" of his own philosophical procedure. His arguments move in a different direction, away from imputing to logic the fluidity he would otherwise recognize in one of its fundamental terms. The reasons for this leaning are rooted in the philosophy of language which he inherited, and I will pay some attention to it; but they are also related to the leaning of Ockham's time, toward the familiarity of oral customs in society at large as well as in the ongoing work of producing script in clerical scriptoria. I do not suggest, of course, that we can turn to his texts as we can to poetry or chronicle history for "evidence" of a reliance on oral tradition. Rather, we must look elsewhere—specifically to his detailed arguments about the relation of *vox* to individual things. For although he settled this problem in new ways, he also sees it with the eyes and ears of someone long used to hearing the spoken word control its written representations. And in this subordination, Ockham's epistemology is not as far as we might presume it to be from the premise of Ambrose

---

[2] Adams, *William Ockham* 1:549–50. Cf. Boehner, "The Realistic Conceptualism of William of Ockham," and Courtenay, *Schools and Scholars in Fourteenth-Century England*, p. 19.

cited at the outset, that hearing is prior to seeing, or from the social context of oral tradition in his time.[3]

THE INDIVIDUAL

That Ockham stressed the priority of evident knowledge is not a particularly unusual move in the history of medieval philosophy. But he was an innovator with this topic insofar as he varied considerably the means by which knowledge might be validated. He has sometimes been thought of as a medieval Aristotle, loosely because he accepted—without specific defense—the categories of substance and quality.[4] For Ockham they were the only concrete realities (res permanentes), unlike other Aristotelian categories (quantity, relation, etc.) which he regarded as merely convenient ways of describing permanent things. And yet Ockham's arguments are often directly opposed to Aristotle, particularly to the scholastic interpretations of his works. A suitable example is Aristotle's epistemological premise, taken over fully by Aquinas, that "the soul never thinks without an image." For Aquinas this principle means that the proper objects of knowledge are intelligible ideas (or species); the mind can know directly only universals. Particular knowledge, the cognition of individuals, is first known by the senses and then received via abstraction in the intellect exclusively as a likeness, or similitudo, of the particular. The mind does not know individual things immediately or directly, but only as mediated by images. For as Aristotle also said, "There is nothing in the intellect which was not first in the senses."[5]

In the context of this commitment to the origin of knowledge in universal being, Ockham's departure did not come from renewed interest in Aristotelian empiricism, but more immediately from Duns Scotus' refined considerations of "intuitive knowledge."[6] Although intuition had been a concern for both Aristotle and the scholastics, it was regarded by them primarily as a function of the senses. Scotus took a different view of the matter, because he sought to account for the

---

[3] Cf. Tachau, Vision and Certitude in the Age of Ockham, on vision, p. 147. For the "lost opportunity" of philosophical scholarship to look into the relevance of orality, see Stock, Listening for the Text, p. 147.

[4] Adams, William Ockham 1:277. See also Courtenay, Schools and Scholars, p. 200, and Leff, William of Ockham, p. 139.

[5] Aquinas, Summa Theologiae 1.12, q. 86.a.1, pp. 90, 92 (Aristotle, De anima 3.7.431b2). See Day, Intuitive Cognition, pp. 26, 129–30, 143–46; Tachau, Vision and Certitude, p. 135.

[6] Wolter, The Philosophical Theology of John Duns Scotus, pp. 99–102. See also Adams, "Intuitive Cognition, Certainty and Skepticism in William of Ockham," pp. 389–98, and William Ockham 1:495 ff; Tachau, Vision and Certitude, pp. 118–25; Coleman, Ancient and Medieval Memories, 475–78.

impasse reached by previous epistemological theories which had shut off the intellect from direct knowledge of existing things. Scotus argued that the mind does indeed have such immediate knowledge, as it is capable of intuitive awareness of what exists and does not exist. Since this capability was not possible within the order of the intellect alone (which can know only what is abstracted from the senses), Scotus introduced a breakthrough from mind to world that Ockham would eventually develop. The immediate cognition postulated by Scotus included not just the existence of a particular thing but also an awareness of its intelligible species. However, intuition does not have the same power as reason (*ratio*) to judge and analyze a species because it is of a different order. Through reason the intellect has a second means of direct apprehension, not of the particular but rather of the species or universals contained by it. Therefore, such cognition is still mediated since it is of a representation stripped of its limitations in materiality. Rationality for Scotus remains the superior order of knowledge insofar as its object is the domain of concepts; but without the power of intuition, the intellect has no way to account for the existence or nonexistence of its objects of knowledge.

Haecceitas

This is not to say, however, that intuitive knowledge is of that property of an individual which differentiates it from all others in a class—what the Scotists described as *haecceitas* ("thisness").[7] In general, *haecceity* was designed to solve the problem posed by Scotus that the descent of substantial form into its material accidents does not explain how a particular thing is individual; matter alone cannot be a principle of individuation. He reasoned that if a "common principle" of matter could be abstracted from material accidents, then matter per se could no longer be described as strictly individuating. Thus individuality must be explained by a third entity, which he called *haecceitas*. Beyond the accidental *differentiae* in a class of particulars, the individuation of an essential form is an act limiting it to "this" singular instance as opposed to "that" one. We are able to know such instances, according to this principle, insofar as we can perceive intuitively and rationally their accidental differences, but not because we can know their essential *haecceitas*. Of this individuating difference, we can have no direct, immediate knowledge in this life.

Ockham did not incorporate *haecceitas* into his vocabulary of terms

[7] See Wolter, *Philosophical Theology of Duns Scotus*, pp. 88–97; Coleman, *Ancient and Medieval Memories*, pp. 471–75, 485, 492.

for discussions of ontology, and the reasons are readily available.[8] He would have had no use for this principle since it attempts to account for the individuality of a particular thing within the realist split of substantial form and material accident. Ockham denied this split at the outset because he believed, as one commentator puts it, that "nothing can individuate or be individuated by anything extrinsic to itself."[9] But *haecceitas* poses another problem that would have bothered Ockham: it involves a tautology that prevents the immediate apprehension of the individual.

Though Scotus assumes the ambiguities of his term, he does not probe the extent to which they may precede his metaphysical applications of it. *Haecceitas* essentially functions for him as a way of accounting for an individuating identity without generalizing matter into a common principle on a par with the universality of substance. In order to account for what is left unexplained about the identity of "this" singular thing beyond the separation of its essence from its accidents, Scotus appeals to a linguistic model: "thisness" must be included to account for what essence and accident leave out. But even though Scotus acknowledged the limitations of providing such an account, the pronoun *haec* points to an invented nominative category (*haecceitas*) which "names" what cannot be named in reality and thus is not "nominative" in any strict sense. The noun simply points back to or repeats—it does not "denominate"—the referent of the pronoun.[10] Such a situation of unknowability may have articulated Scotus' epistemological conviction, but it cannot conceal that language, too, has reached a referential impasse. As the noun form repeats its anterior pronoun, the linguistic representation does little more than point back to itself, not "denominatively" to something else: the object of representation in *haecceitas* can only be known as a linguistic repetition. Scotus fully recognized the inability of language to identify an individual in this way, since the mind itself cannot do it. But he would have objected surely to the inevitable conclusion about language implied by his principle of *haecceitas*: in reflecting only itself, representation cannot avoid being repetition, and language more broadly is self-referential and metalinguistic at the very moment when it is seeking reference. Before it can account for the indeterminacy of knowing individuals, *haecceitas* begs the question. It conceals the repetition inhabiting representation from the outset.

[8] The critique attributed to him is cited by Boehner, *Collected Articles on Ockham*, p. 81; see also pp. 376 and 398.

[9] Adams, *William Ockham* 1:68; cf. p. 41.

[10] Cf. Adams, *William Ockham* 1:55: Ockham departs from *haecceitas* because it fails to be "denominative" of the individual.

Beyond Mediation?

If Ockham sought to avoid such a circularity, it remains to be seen how successful he was in arriving at a more adequate epistemology of the thing. He begins, as noted, by contesting accounts of knowledge that proceed hierarchically, in the Thomistic sense, from essence to thing. He moves instead from the bottom up, so to speak, starting with "evident knowledge" (*notitia evidens*), which he says is always of the unmediated present. Unlike Scotus, who stressed the difference between intuitive and abstract knowledge (*notitia intuitiva* and *notitia abstractiva*), Ockham remained confident that we have evident knowledge about the world of contingent facts, and therefore he never called it into question.[11] Abstract knowledge, on the other hand, apprehends specific objects but *cannot* determine whether they exist or do not exist. That knowledge is *intuitiva*, Ockham writes, "in virtue of which any contingent truth can be known evidently, especially of the present. But abstract knowledge is that in virtue of which a contingent thing cannot be known evidently to exist or not to exist."[12] For instance, I can have intuitive knowledge that an object in my hand is white, and that knowledge is evident; but once it disappears from my possession and I no longer have the evidence of it, my cognition of the object is abstract. Consequently, abstract and intuitive knowledge both concern the same objects but differ *per modum* ("in the mode") of their knowing.

The basis of knowledge in evidence rather than in natures and essences challenges fundamentally the Thomistic and Scotist a priori of the universal because it revises the status of the concept in the mind. For the scholastics it had unquestionable ontological status, insofar as it was the result of what reason abstracted from individual things—the *esse* giving them form. But Ockham was not satisfied with the indifference of abstraction to existence and nonexistence; for him the ontology of the concept is shifted into the realm of the hypothetical until intuition confirms the evidence of it. And at that point, the ontology of the concept is located in the specific individual of which it is the abstraction, not in the *esse* separable from it or in a transcendent Aristotelian category. In short, the concept is a sign (*signum*), rather than a real entity in the scholastic sense.

So far it has been assumed that evident knowledge for Ockham means something like empirical evidence, stripped of any impediments of mediation. However, as soon as the concept (*conceptus*) enters

---

[11] See Wood, "Intuitive Cognition and Divine Omnipotence," p. 61; Day, *Intuitive Cognition*, pp. 148 ff.

[12] *Ordinatio* 1: Prologue, 31–32.

the discussion, Ockham quite deliberately begins to describe mental acts by appeal to linguistic models, such as "term," "word," "sentence," and "proposition" (*terminus, incomplexum, verum complexum,* and *propositio contingens*). Even though the use of linguistic categories appears to interpose a mediation in front of cognition of the particular thing, Ockham maintained that "evident knowledge is the cognition of any true proposition caused sufficiently by an immediate or mediate [*immediata vel mediata*] knowledge of terms."[13] With this statement Ockham sets aside Scotist principles of epistemology insofar as he does not acknowledge the categorical separation of essential form, accidental differences, and the *haecceitas* distinguishing individuals. But we ought to ask whether or not Ockham has been able to penetrate as well the *haecceitas* of language. In what sense exactly is the cognition of a proposition "evident"? Is it evident in the same way as the intuition of the particular thing? There is no facile resolution to this problem in the logical treatises, and the author himself is the first to bear witness to it when he vacillates on how to define the concept: was it a *fictum* or an *intellectio*?

Fictum or Intellectio

As a *fictum*, the concept is a representation in the mind like an image, similitude, or phantasm; as an *intellectio*, it is the act of understanding, the process of cognition itself. The term *fictum*, the past participle of *fingo*, means "to form" or "shape," especially by art, as in the making of statues, but also "to form" by instruction and "shape" through language, "to form mentally or in speech."[14] Hence it is the root of *fictio*—'making," "fashioning," "feigning," "supposition," and "fiction." Ockham's eventual hesitation with the term derives from this sense of it as an end product or result of understanding, the "object" rather than the "act," as recently noted.[15] For instance, as product rather than process, *fictum* blurs the distinction between *ens rationis* ("thought objects") and *ens reale* ("real things"). On the one hand, objects which do not exist in reality—'figments" (*figmenta*) of the mind such as the chimera or goat-lion—would be, epistemologically speaking, no different from real things; and on the other, Aristotle's categories, which signify being existing only outside of the mind, would perforce comprehend mental objects as physical qualities. Whiteness or heat, the qualities of corporal things, would then be indistinguishable from

---

[13] *Ordinatio* 1: Prologue, 5–6. See Tachau, *Vision and Certitude,* p. 122.

[14] Lewis and Short, *A Latin Dictionary,* s.v. *fingo;* Du Cange, *Glossarium,* s.v. *fictus.*

[15] Adams, *William Ockham* 1:74 ff.

thought objects, which would in turn be actually hot or white according to the thing perceived.[16] The gap, therefore, between *ens rationis* and *ens reale* could not be closed by a sense of the concept as a *fictum*, and Ockham eventually qualified his entire thinking on the matter, with apparent assistance from Richard Campsall, by developing a theory of the *intellectio*.[17]

His revision is quite plain: "the *fictum* impedes cognition of the thing"; it is not the thing known nor the cognition itself, but a "third medium separating the other two."[18] He sought to penetrate this *tertium medium* in various ways. "What," he asks, "is that thing in the soul which is such a sign?"

> It ought to be said that diverse opinions are articulated about it. Some say that it is nothing but what is shaped [*fictum*] by the soul. Others, that it is a certain quality existing in the soul as in a subject, distinct from the act of understanding. Others say that it is the act of understanding [*actus intelligendi*]. And the reason for this last opinion is that "it is vain to do with many what can be done with fewer." For everything that can be saved by positing [the concept as] something distinct from the act of understanding can be saved without such a distinction, so that to supposit for something else and signify something else can belong to the act of understanding just as it can belong to any other sign. Therefore beyond the act of understanding it is not necessary to posit anything else.[19]

This vivid instance of Ockham's so-called "razor" operates in various other reductions of the concept.[20] And yet the move toward the immediacy of knowledge attempted here still leaves a critical point unexplored. Although Ockham gradually objected to the *fictum* because of its representationality, he proceeds to define the act of understanding in terms of the signs and language "spoken" in the mind. "The act of understanding," he argues, "by which I understand people is a natural sign of people, in the same way as groaning is natural sign of sickness or weeping of sadness; it is such a sign because it can stand for people in mental propositions, just as voice [*vox*] can stand for things in spoken propositions."[21]

The act of understanding is like the spoken word. But the correspon-

---

[16] See Ockham on the *Perihermenias* (ed. Boehner) in Boehner, "Realistic Conceptualism," pp. 328–29. Reliance on the *De trinitate* (e.g., *Ordinatio* 1:2.8.276–89) also limits Ockham's discussion of the concept; see Coleman, *Ancient and Medieval Memories*, p. 526.

[17] See Tachau, *Vision and Certitude*, pp. 148–64. Cf. Leff, *William of Ockham*, pp. 96–104.

[18] *Quodlibet* 4.q.35.

[19] *Logica* 1.12.42–43. ('Suppositing" to be covered shortly.)

[20] E.g., *Quodlibet* 4.q.10, where the distinction is also on understanding as an act.

[21] *Logica* 1.15.53.

dence here is not a crude likeness between mind and language—a semantic thesis Ockham ridiculed.[22] Representation is more subtle in his analysis, since it reflects the processes of conception and causality. Yet when he turns to describe exactly how universal concepts of the mind proceed, he nonetheless reverts to familiar forms of representation: the concept is an imitation of audible (or inaudible) speaking— of a person's *vox*. "Universal concepts," he says, "declare, express, explain, convey, and signify the substances of things" (and his verbs are "declarant, exprimunt, explicant, important, et significant").[23] This formulation is recognizably different from the concept as a representative *fictum*; it is also a long way from Duns Scotus' notion of the knowledge of essential being and the *haecceitas* of the individual. But it postulates the concept by repeating a "medium" of its own—the linguistic model of *vox* taken as the prior term of the immediacy and evidence of knowledge. The self-referentiality of the Scotist *haecceitas* has found its way into Ockham's attempt to establish the *intellectio* as an act superseding all intermediaries. A concept of "voice" has yet to be separated finally from the "voice" of the concept in Ockham's epistemology.

This point poses the question of the degree to which *vox* may qualify Ockham's broader epistemological project of defining the unmediated signification of evidence. When he takes up the distinction between mental, spoken, and written signs in the *Logica*, he attempts to put such qualifications to rest, and his modern commentators, by and large, have followed suit.[24] For he assumes that evidence unimpeded by any intermediary, such as the linguistic sign, prevails a priori in the acquisition of knowledge. What remains to be seen, however, is whether or not this assumption is carried forward in texts that debate the difference between evidence and its signs. Before the *Logica*, Ockham had already argued a distinction between knowledge that is accessible from signs and other kinds of understanding. In the *Ordinatio* he says that a sign in general is anything that causes one to remember something previously known. In the most fundamental sense a sign "re-presents." As representation, it is already the repetition of what a person knew in the past. "And such cognition," says Ockham, "can be called the

---

[22] Adams, *William Ockham* 1:306. On "representare," see Boehner, "Realistic Conceptualism," pp. 312–14.

[23] *Logica* 1.17.60. Boehner, "Realistic Conceptualism," p. 311: "It is . . . Ockham's genuine teaching that universal concepts are in the relation of similarity with reality, that there is a correspondence between them and a representation of the one by the other."

[24] E.g., Boehner, "Ockham's Theory of Signification," pp. 201–32; Loux, "The Ontology of William of Ockham," pp. 1–21. Adams, *William Ockham* 1:84: Ockham was "a staunch defender of direct realism in epistemology"; cf. Tachau, *Vision and Certitude*, pp. 152–53.

representation of the other [*repraesentativum alterius*]."[25] In this formulation, a knower understands a "vestige" (*vestigium*) or an "image"
(*imago*); he or she has a "remembrance of something known habitually
[*habitualiter*]."[26] That the signification of a sign depends on some anterior knowledge is plain, Ockham observes, in the example of the
viewer looking at a statue of Hercules: without previous knowledge
of who Hercules was, how could he possibly be distinguished from
Socrates? But, in opposition to knowledge through signs, Ockham
argues for what he calls "primary" cognition, which is "immediate"
(*immediate*) and not dependent on prior linguistic or other *signa*.[27] He
maintains that such cognition occurs when "knowledge of a singular
is the cause of knowledge of a universal, and [when] knowledge of
premises [in a syllogism] is the cause of knowledge of the conclusion."[28] In these acts, Ockham maintains, the mind is not recalling or
representing something previously known. The mediation of *signum*
or *imago* and the temporal lag of presenting again what was anteriorly
known is foreclosed. The act of cognition (*intellectio*) is present to itself.
Voice does not—so it appears—figure in the process.

One might question how clean Ockham's cut is between "mediate"
and "immediate" cognition in view of the fact that the act of knowledge which he says does not proceed from sign to sign is illustrated
by the movement from singular to universal and from premise to
conclusion, entities that remain for him fundamentally linguistic.[29]
And the opposition is even more questionable in the first chapter of
the *Logica*, where Ockham says that the sign "is anything which when
apprehended makes something else come to mind; however, it does
not cause the mind to arrive at cognition for the first time . . . but at
actual cognition [only] after habitual knowledge of a thing."[30] In this
sense, "the voice signifies naturally, just as any effect signifies at least
its cause."[31] But Ockham contrasts this general definition of the *signum*
to the more restricted sense in which he has been using the term.
"Signs," he says, are words in a proposition that "supposit" for their
signifieds or are "added" to other signs in a sentence, as are verbs and

[25] *Ordinatio* 2:9.545.
[26] *Ordinatio* 2:9.544.
[27] *Ordinatio* 2:3.544–45.
[28] *Ordinatio* 2:9.544.
[29] Cf. Adams, *William Ockham* 1:350–51, on the ambiguity of how the mental concept
"presents itself." Coleman, *Ancient and Medieval Memories*, pp. 519–26, sees no ambiguity,
stressing instead habitual knowledge as the basis for memory and history.
[30] *Logica* 1.1.8–9.
[31] *Logica* 1.1.9.

other parts of speech.[32] Because such signs are decided on by an act of will to be joined with certain signified meanings, they are not "natural" but "imposed" (*imponuntur*) by common agreement—*ad placitum* or *secundum voluntarium institutionem*.[33] Ockham concludes that "when this [sense of the] term 'sign' has been accepted, voice is not the natural sign of anything."[34] That is to say, spoken—and written—words are "conventional" or "artificial." But they are no less capable, he assumes, of overcoming the gap created by signs in general, the habitual knowledge that is the mediated "representation of the other." Although spoken and written signs are artificial, Ockham continues to argue that they are able to signify *immediante*. This position would appear to be more relevant to the inaudible language of the mind, since it is associated with the act of understanding. But Ockham insists on the direct signification of both spoken *and* unspoken modes despite the integrity of their opposition. The claim invites us to ask how distinct it really is: does *vox* determine or become determined by the immediacy of the act of knowing?

SPEECH AND WRITING

Opening the *Logica* by separating "spoken" and "written terms" (*termini prolati, scripti*) from "conceptual terms" and "mental words" (*termini concepti, verba mentalia*), Ockham appeals to Augustine's *De trinitate*, book 14.[35] He accepts the customary tripartite structure of word, concept, and signified thing, but he objects to the traditional explanation (such as Boethius' commentary on Aristotle) that words signify concepts which in turn signify things. Mediating between word and thing, the concept, according to Ockham, gets in the way of direct signification and, a fortiori, the evident knowledge of individuals. He addresses this dilemma by acknowledging, with Augustine, that "spoken words" (*voces*) signify concepts; but, departing from him, Ockham insists that "spoken words are subordinated to concepts."[36] That is, spoken words do not always "signify concepts of the soul primarily and properly," but rather—and here is his departure—"spoken words are imposed for signifying those same things which are signified by mental concepts."[37] What had formerly been understood as the exclu-

[32] Ibid.
[33] *Logica* 1.1.8.
[34] *Logica* 1.1.9.
[35] *Logica* 1.1.7.
[36] Ibid.
[37] *Logica* 1.1.8.

sive provenance of the concept, its power to signify a thing, is now granted by subordination to the power of the spoken word itself: direct signification is thus preserved in this epistemology of the individual. And, furthermore, it is carried out by the written word as well, since Ockham maintains that the same correspondence existing between spoken words and concepts "holds between spoken words and those which are in writing."[38]

To specify further the relation of mental and spoken or written terms, Ockham goes on to explain the "parts of speech" in the mind. He says that it is necessary to postulate such things as "mental nouns, verbs, adverbs, conjunctions, and prepositions" because "every element of spoken discourse corresponds to those mental words in the mind; and therefore, just as those parts of the vocal proposition are distinct because of the necessity of imposed signification, so also are the corresponding parts of the mental propositions distinct."[39] As terms in spoken or written discourse obey the rules of grammar, so also are the words on the page of the mind controlled by the same demands for distinct *partes orationis*.[40]

Ockham clearly insists on the difference between spoken and mental orders of language, but the one has elided into his conception of the other.[41] It would seem that the immediacy of understanding has not been compromised by this elision, since voice, be it mental or material, is an act and not an image of knowing. And yet when Ockham goes on to say that speech and writing are related by "subordination" to mental language, the broader meaning of the sign as the *habitus* or recollection of something previously known is inevitably involved. For the word signifies an object, but the act of understanding that word depends on the recollection and repetition of knowledge, which is itself a previous sign or concept. Thus the "immediacy" of the spoken word is more putative than real: as the "expression" or "declaration" of the concept, *vox* must be qualified by the temporal status of a past act of understanding. The spoken is, as a result, both prior and present, notwithstanding Ockham's emphasis on it as *primam cognitionem*. What announces itself *hic et nunc* in the mind is also spoken and mediated by habitual knowledge.

The implication of this point is that even though Ockham separates mental from material language, present concepts from past acts of understanding, he does not focus on the overlap of these oppositions

[38] Ibid.

[39] *Logica* 1.3.14.

[40] See *Quodlibet* 5.q.8 and *Logica* 1.3.12 for even more refined correspondences between the grammar of spoken and mental languages.

[41] Adams, *William Ockham* 1:341, 350, 359, 377, has also noted this "overlap."

in order to allow their reflexivity or metalanguage to play itself out. Rather he describes the relation between these different orders of language as a hierarchy, in which *termini concepti* or *verba mentalia* have priority over their "artificial" representations.[42] This is not to say, of course, that Ockham has returned to the universal concept embraced by scholastic realists. Nor has he followed the early nominalists who reduced every category of being to *flatus vocis*, the mere emptiness of breath. In stressing knowledge of concepts as a knowledge of language, it may seem that he introduces an appreciation for the pastness of past acts of understanding.[43] But I have been suggesting that the *vox* of knowing does not fortify exclusively a theory of mediated understanding in Ockham's epistemology. He argues for temporality at the same time as he would have *vox* be the immediate act of knowing. We might speculate about the source of this dilemma and point (with at least one other critic) to Aristotle, who gave Ockham no little difficulty with the principle that whatever is in the intellect was first in the senses.[44] However, my purpose is to study the role of *vox*, in order to see whether it continues to blur the distinction between mental and material language, present and past knowledge. Supposition theory is the next place to look, since it is central to this problem.

Suppositio

A commonplace among the speculative grammarians of the twelfth and thirteenth centuries, *suppositio* describes that "property" (*proprietas*) of language in which one term "takes the place of another" for the purpose of signifying meaning. In the sentence, "this person is Plato," "person" can supposit for or take the place of "Plato," just as "this" can be a pronoun of "person."[45] Since such a pronominal substituting of *nomina* is characteristic of the function of signs in general, *suppositio* is absolutely basic to Ockham's sign theory. But the term is complicated by a figurative dislocation of reference which is also a part of the elusiveness of mental and spoken signs that I have been describing. As the *signum* in language can be something that "takes the place of" something else or is "added" to something else, so does *supponere*

---

[42] Cf. Loux, "Ontology of William of Ockham," p. 4: "Ockham insists on the ontological priority of mental language." Similarly, cf. Adams, *William Ockham* 1:351, despite the "overlap" she notes between mental and conventional.

[43] See Coleman, *Ancient and Medieval Memories*, pp. 526, 537.

[44] Tachau, *Vision and Certitude*, p. 135.

[45] *Logica* 1.63.193. See Kretzmann, Kenny, and Pinborg, eds., *The Cambridge History of Later Medieval Philosophy*, pp. 188–96; Boehner, "Ockham's Theory of Supposition and the Notion of Truth," pp. 232–67; Adams, *William Ockham* 1:317–82.

mean: (1) to "substitute" or fill up an absence left by the removal of
something, to "hypothecate"; and (2) to "supplement" in the sense of
to "complete" or "subjoin" to something already present.[46] For instance, Ockham opens the *Logica* with the definition: "The conceptual
term is an intention or passion of the soul naturally signifying or
consignifying something, produced to be a part of a mental proposition, and produced to supposit for that thing."[47] The mental term is a
signum in the sense that it substitutes in the mind for something
outside of the mind. But while it is "produced naturally" (*nata natu-
raliter*)—because it is not imposed artificially by convention—it both
fills an absence created by something once present and yet simultaneously completes the process of adding to what is already there. In this
act of "producing," fabrication artificially competes with the natural
and spontaneous "growth" and "birth" present in Ockham's participle
of action, *nata*, which remains rooted in *nascor*, "to be born, originate,
grow."[48] The natural growth of signifying interferes with the artificial
producing, adding, and completing of the sign. *Suppositio*, like *nascor*,
thus betrays the boundaries it would otherwise insist on; it satisfies a
vacancy by substitution but adds "naturally" to what is already present
in the mind. In this sense the word fulfills yet another meaning with
which it is associated, namely, to "falsify" or "counterfeit."[49] The term
is not used by Ockham to convey this meaning explicitly; but, when
he turns from natural to conventional signs, the generative process of
natum supponere (produced or born to supposit) fulfills the definition
of its exact opposite, those signs which are "added in a proposition"
and "those parts of speech [in written or spoken discourse] which do
not have finite signification."[50] *Natum supponere* is here made to "counterfeit" for both categories—natural and artificial, mental and material.

SIGNIFICATIO

The complication of this point in Ockham's theory of supposition
should not be underestimated. He is credited with effecting an unprecedented revision by separating "personal supposition" (*suppositio
personalis*) from "simple" and "material" supposition (*suppositio simplex*
and *materialis*). But whether or not his conclusions can be called "revo-

---

[46] Lewis and Short, *A Latin Dictionary*, s.v. *suppono*; Du Cange, *Glossarium*, s.v. *super-
ponere, superpositio*; Baxter and Johnson, eds., *Medieval Latin Word-List*, s.v. *supposit*.
[47] *Logica* 1.1.7.
[48] Lewis and Short, *A Latin Dictionary*, s.v. *nascor*.
[49] Lewis and Short list occurrences of *testamenta falsa supponere*.
[50] *Logica* 1.1.9.

lutionary" deserves to be reconsidered.[51] Ockham attempted to redefine these categories by maintaining that only the first, personal supposition, is an actual instance of *significare* ("to signify") in the strict sense, whereas simple and material supposition are nonsignifying modes.[52] That is, a noun serving as the subject of a proposition carries out its significative function when it supposits or stands for something other than itself; and the significate can be something either inside of the soul or outside of it: "universally, supposition is personal when a term supposits for its significate, whether that significate is a thing outside of the soul, or is the voice, or an intention of the soul, or is written, or anything imaginable; so that whenever a subject or predicate of a proposition supposits for its significate and is understood significatively, the supposition is always personal."[53] But the significate in these remarks plays the role of something fundamentally nonlinguistic, and thus the supposition is proposed as a *verbum-res* (word-thing or word-individual) relation, instead of simply a relation of terms.[54] The subject supposits for something different from itself, which is the predicate; it is an individual and not simply a concept or word synonymous with the subject of the sentence: in "every person is an animal," person supposits for its significate because person is not imposed except for signifying actual persons; and in "every vocal noun is a part of speech," the noun does not signify unless for individual voices.[55]

"Significative" claims emphasis because Ockham maintains that there are also "non-significative" propositions. The division is related directly to the conventional medieval separation between *terminos categorematicos* and *syncategoremos*. "Categorematic terms" are signs that take the place of their significates, as "man" is finite and has determinate signification—all men.[56] But "syncategorematic terms" are not finite or definite and do not supposit for distinct individuals; they only qualify or determine them. For example, "every," "no," "some," "all," and "except" do not signify as "man" does, but each could qualify "man"; therefore, they only "signify with" ("con-signify"—*consignifi-*

---

[51] Leff, *William of Ockham*, p. 139; cf. Loux, *"Significatio* and *Suppositio,"* pp. 414, 418, 423, 425–26.

[52] See Boehner, "Ockham's Theory of Supposition," pp. 236–48; Leff, *William of Ockham*, pp. 131–36; Henry, "The Early History of the *Suppositio,"* pp. 205–12.

[53] *Logica* 1.64.195.

[54] As Loux argues in *"Significatio* and *Suppositio,"* p. 425.

[55] *Logica* 1.64.195. So it is not enough to say, as had William of Sherwood, that supposition is personal "when a term supposits for a thing," but only when "it supposits for its significate significatively" (ibid.).

[56] *Logica* 1.4.15.

care) a categorematic term. *Omni* must be added to *homo* in order for "every man" to supposit.[57]

In short, only categorematic terms are proper to personal supposition. The nonsignifying mode of syncategorematic words compares with, if it does not determine, Ockham's revision of simple and material supposition, for neither of these modes signifies in the strict sense. "Simple supposition," he says, "exists when a term supposits for an intention of the soul, but is not held significatively."[58] In the proposition, "vegetable is a species," vegetable supposits for an intention or concept of the soul, because that intention is a concept, the species; an individual is not signified by vegetable or by species in this sentence. And furthermore, Ockham says such a word as vegetable does not properly speaking signify that intention; rather the *vox* and the *intentio* are signs subordinated in signifying the same thing—species.[59] To put the point differently, the subject of the proposition refers back to itself metalinguistically.

As this example attempts to illustrate a theoretical split between supposition and signification, so does the third category, "material supposition."[60] It too is nonsignifying, according to Ockham, because the term supposits only for the spoken or written word itself. "Supposition is material," he maintains "when a term does not supposit significatively, but supposits for voice or for writing."[61] Thus in "wine is a noun," wine supposits strictly for itself, the word in writing or in speech; but it does not "signify" itself. Similarly in "wine is written," wine supposits metalinguistically for what is written in the proposition, the material letters, w-i-n-e.[62]

SUPPOSITIONAL LOGIC

Ockham did not, as already mentioned, invent these distinctions. Rather, he defined and applied them in new ways. If a term is to represent something other than itself, the supposition must be personal; for then alone can it be verified in experience. His position has been received in scholarship as an unprecedented breakthrough into the fundamen-

[57] Ibid. Thus "consignification" is not equivalent to "connotation," as Adams suggests (*William Ockham* 1:320).

[58] *Logica* 1.64.196.

[59] *Logica* 1.63.196.

[60] Though four more categories of supposition were discussed in logic, Ockham's contribution to the split between signifying and nonsignifying modes is built principally around the three discussed here. See Kretzmann, Kenny, and Pinborg, eds., *Cambridge History of Later Medieval Philosophy*, p. 196.

[61] *Logica* 1.64.196.

[62] Ibid.

tal opposition between supposition and signification. As one critic writes, "This recognition by Ockham, more than anything else, transformed virtually the entire philosophical and theological vocabulary of scholasticism."[63]

But the instability of the word *suppositio*—as the substitution and yet completion of the sign, the presence and postponement of representation, the natural and artificial function of language—has left its mark on the integrity of Ockham's tripartite division of supposition. He maintains that these three modes have little if anything to do with their names: "personal" specifies nothing specifically personal about a knower's supposition, nor is "material" indicative of a necessary materiality in this mode.[64] He would prove, moreover, that no mode has priority in the determination of divisions by the illustration of writing down the following propositions: "Man is an animal"—personal: "man" supposits for an individual; "man is a species"—simple: "man" supposits for a concept; and "man is a written expression"—material: "man" supposits for the letters on the page.[65] If the materiality of writing does not determine how the third example, *homo est dictio scripta*, is to be distinguished, then this writing must exist in the mind in an immaterial form. Indeed it does, he goes on to say, for in the language of the soul, "a concept can supposit for what it signifies, for itself, for voice, and for writing [pro se ipse et pro voce et pro scripto]."[66] The writing of the mind is not material; nor is it writing; and yet it distinguishes how we are to construe concepts and individuals. The individual precedes the concept and the written or spoken word, and still a writing that is not writing differentiates both individuals and concepts. Although Ockham assumes the primacy of an immaterial and unmediated mental language, it both "stands for" and "counterfeits" the material supposition it is intended to produce. The "man" who exists exclusively as a *dictio scripta* of parchment has already differentiated his "origin" in the real individual and in the concept produced by it. And the undecidability of his status is witnessed by the ambiguity of Ockham's Latin phrase, which, of course, does not mean that "man" is the product of writing as we know it in the silence of writing and reading; for his form as *scripta* is simultaneously a *dictio*—a spoken,

[63] Leff, *William of Ockham*, p. 139. Cf. Courtenay, *Schools and Scholars*, p. 217, and "The Reception of Ockham's Thought in Fourteenth-Century England," p. 107. Leff's claim is not engaged by Adams, though it would corroborate her conclusions (*William Ockham* 1:341–42) about the fluid boundary between material and simple supposition, as John Buridan realized in Ockham's time.

[64] *Logica* 1.64.197.

[65] *Logica* 1.64.196.

[66] *Logica* 1.64.197.

audible expression—heard before it was written and written as it was spoken in the situation of classroom and scriptorium of the fourteenth century.

It may appear that this critique of Ockham does not grant him a certain leeway with terms which he says are used "equivocally" (*aequivoce*).[67] But the issues at stake here do not concern "plurivalent" meanings, "equivocal" terms, or "ambiguity." I am suggesting, instead, that despite Ockham's leeway with mental and real orders, natural and artificial, present and prior meanings, he assumes that a definite logic determines these oppositions and, what is more, resolves them into a hierarchical order descending from the *mentalia verba* present in the mind. As every reader knows, the logic of noncontradiction is Ockham's "really invincible weapon."[68] However, it might be better to say that a "suppositional logic" takes precedence as the materiality of signs determines an assumed immateriality of concepts. It has been observed by at least one scholar that Ockham's ontological principles determine his linguistics because he relocates being from the Platonic and Aristotelian orders of transcendent forms and categories into the real existence of the individual thing and because he argues that personal supposition alone has the power to signify from mental to real.[69] Such a formulation would appear to answer Ockham's questions about the *fictum* as an impediment to the immediacy of the act of knowing. Personal supposition would seem to perforate the representationality of human understanding because it can only be posited of individuals evident in reality. Thus a new ontology of the individual, as recently proposed, arises to replace the older scholastic priority of the concept. But the *intellectio* of the individual is simultaneous with the presence of *vox* in the mind, an immediacy identified by appeal to the word actually spoken *hic et nunc*.[70] As narrowly as such an assumption might appear to close the gap between the sign knowable only as a repetition of a past sign, it remains a definition of the spoken or written word, which is always a sign and always—as Ockham would be the first to

[67] Ibid. Spade has drawn similar attention to the problems of extending the three modes of supposition to spoken, written, and mental language ("Synonymy and Equivocation in Ockham's Mental Language"). Adams calls Ockham's move "a careless blunder" (*William Ockham* 1:349), following from his assumption that a mental term "presents itself," when in fact it only renders mental language "systematically ambiguous" (p. 351).

[68] Adams, *William Ockham* 1:68. On the sources of *verbum* for the principles of identity, noncontradiction, sufficient reason et al., in Aquinas and Aristotle, see Lonergan, *Verbum*, pp. 33 and 219.

[69] Leff, *William of Ockham*, p. 134.

[70] Loux, "*Significatio* and *Suppositio*," p. 427: Ockham's "theory of meaning shows the meaning-structure of terms to involve a non-eliminable reference to the propositional form of discourse."

say—imposed artificially by convention. The *signum*, in general "the representation of the other," is delayed before it starts; it arrives late on the page of the mind which tries to close an opening that can only be called "closed" in the recognition of its irreconcilability with habitual knowledge. Whether of the mind or of the page, language functions with the palpability of evidence he would validate in *res*, and they are knowable, finally, as conventional words. Others have argued that Ockham is not, as was once believed, a nominalist, since he does not reduce universal categories to empty words or deny the ability of language to signify the concepts of real individuals. But my argument has moved in a different direction, toward the materiality of language (the *dictio scripta* or oral form of writing) that is denied even as it forms propositions in the soul.

The Materiality of the Sign

This suggestion about Ockham's linguistics has a certain resonance, as distant as it is, in modern discussions of the "materiality of the signifier." As Saussure maintained, the signifier is said to be "material" by virtue of the acoustical or visual image which is identifiable by its difference from other images, rather than by any natural identity with a concept in the mind.[71] Accordingly, the displacement of identity by difference is forestalled as soon as the materiality of the "sound-image" is thought of as correspondent with and identifiable by an originary concept.[72]

Although the linguistics of Ockham does not figure in Saussure's discussions, a certain similarity appears to exist between both theoreticians. As Saussure argues that signification depends on the difference of one sound-image from another, rather than on a putative "natural" link between it and a concept, so does Ockham move away from the priority of transcendent categories and concepts and toward linguistic differentiae, the various modes in which a word like "man" can supposit. But here the parallel stops, except for the fact that the same contradiction that works its way back into Saussure's theory of signification also returns to complicate Ockham's. For a definite principle of identity informs their linguistics and determines—in the case of Ockham—distinctions among signs by appeal to the individual "man" which is synonymous and instantaneous with the natural sign or "word of man" in the soul. From this primal sign, other distinctions

---

[71] Saussure, *Course in General Linguistics*, p. 66.

[72] As Derrida has pointed out in *Of Grammatology*, pp. 30 ff. Cf. de Man, *The Resistance to Theory*, pp. 11 ff.; Miller, "The Triumph of Theory."

follow in Ockham's logic, as in many other theories of the word in medieval tradition. He is surely not a nominalist as that label may include Abelard and his teacher, Roscelin. Rather, Ockham is closer than he would seem to Augustine and the scholastics in the priority he grants to *verba mentalia*, since the ontology of words comprehended *de praesenti* is indistinguishable from the being of things in his philosophy.

In the broader context of the intersection between oral and written modes in the later middle ages, the contribution of Ockham might at first appear to urge an emphatic priority of the written word and of textual analysis. Consulting earlier written treatises, puzzling over their relevance to his own arguments, deriving meaning out of the scrutiny of sentences written down, and above all, assuming the discrete separation of mental, spoken, and written categories for *vox*— these activities of high literacy were his provenance as a professor at Oxford in the early fourteenth century, and his popularity was considerable, though not unchallenged.[73] Yet he composed no comprehensive "system" for all knowledge; he wrote no *summa*, no encyclopedia, in the high scholastic mode. He denied the organic teleology of knowledge and even rejected venerated notions of the "progress" and "purpose" of history. For he opposed such medieval syntheses, insofar as they depended on the unity of the universal essence or species; only the numerical unity of individuals was possible for Ockham, and from that premise he had to acknowledge the necessary inconsistency and confusion of things in the world—whether they arose in the natural universe, from interactions among persons, or within the institutions of church and state. But, as I have suggested, Ockham's conception of the evident intuition of individuals, defined as it is through habits of analysis scarcely possible without writing and texts, is constituted by an understanding of the word that finally will not remain confined by the margins of separation he so carefully articulates.

Although Ockham begins with the absolute priority of intuition to knowledge, the representation of that intuition is not simply its *supposition* but its *signification*, since the word of thought simultaneously *represents* and *is* the specific knowledge of things. The individual postulated as the origin of understanding remains caught in the regress of representations about it, and knowledge is mediated by the repetition of signs in the moment that they are thought to be representative of reality. If the old view of Ockham as a nominalist who reduced the categories of being has been replaced by an appreciation of his ontol-

<hr>

[73] See, e.g., Tachau, *Vision and Certitude.* Cf. Courtenay, *Schools and Scholars,* and the essays in Hudson and Wilks, eds., *From Ockham to Wyclif.*

ogy of individuals, it appears, instead, that he is situated somewhere in between—surely not as a thinker who did not know his own mind or who allowed a certain equivocal slippage in his use of terms. To the contrary, he illustrates—as Saussure does centuries later—that the conditions of signifying which he sought to qualify and contradict return to configure and even determine the kinds of conclusions about experience he tried to draw.

I do not imply, of course, that Ockham perpetuated without realizing it the hierarchical relation of word to individual thing formulated by the scholastics. Rather, I suggest that Ockham carries with him more of the past than he realizes when he makes *voice* play a critical role on both sides of the margin between language and reality. He is not shadowed by the past of scholastic realism per se, but more generally by its language—by Latinity. For literacy in Latin—as every schoolboy knew on the authority of his Donatus—insisted on the centrality of the spoken word in the assessment of written language. *Vox literata* is the proper subject of study, and it was learned through the *dictio scripta* of classroom and manuscript. Ambrose's adage proclaimed at the dawn of the Latin middle ages, that hearing is the "guarantee" of sight, is entirely pertinent to the educational scene one thousand years later; for that old hierarchy is still to be observed in Ockham's logic. He obviously does not preserve it without modifications; but he does reinscribe its most distinguishing orientation when speech and writing function in his epistemology as two expressions of the same communicative act, the "spoken writing" of academic discourse.

In this assumption—that writing is inscribed speech—the *dominion* of Latin literacy, as I have called it, is very much in evidence in Ockham's work (not to mention in some of his modern commentators). It accounts in large part, I would estimate, for the importance of *vox mentalia* in his identification of the individual thing. Yet the vacillation of the margin between these two categories is not simply an effect of late medieval literacy and logic. It is an epistemological debate precisely because it was a fact of life in manuscript culture—not only in the production of script but in the conjunction between oral custom and written skill negotiated in marketplace and court during the early fourteenth century in England.

Other areas of Ockham's philosophical work could be explored for evidence of the dominion of literacy operative in the logic. But the treatises in which it would appear readily at hand are Ockham's political writings, which take up explicitly the question of power in church and state. He embarked upon this terrain after arriving in Avignon in 1324 to answer charges about his philosophical teachings.

It has often been assumed that with his departure from England, Ockham parted ways once and for all with the philosophical projects of his early career. As one recent critic concludes, "Between Ockham's earlier and later thought, it seems clear that a straightforward deduction of one from the other is not to be expected."[74] Perhaps not. But the exploration of possible connections is a gaping hole in the modern scholarly assessment of this great philosopher. For someone who spent the last twenty years of his life thinking and writing about power, it seems unlikely that the way had not been prepared by his early work, especially since his thoughts about the sign are themselves shaped by the structure of dominion in language.

Section II
THE SEMIOLOGY OF DOMINION

If the first parents had not sinned,
then there would be no power of appropriating.
—Ockham, *Opus Nonaginta Dierum*

INTRODUCTION

It is not difficult to surmise, as many have, that when Ockham left England for France in 1324, he also left behind the scholarly interests of his Oxford career. For it is obvious that he had come face to face with deeply serious political problems about his personal circumstances, not to mention the commitments of his religious order. Doubtless he must have been concerned for his future as a professor of theology and philosophy, since he had traveled to Avignon to defend his teachings before a papal commission—established at the instigation of John Lutterell, his former chancellor at Oxford. But it must have become apparent to Ockham that he was not fighting on academic and moral grounds alone. He may well have felt himself "a pawn in Lutterell's game of chess": in all likelihood, Lutterell had come to Avignon primarily to seek his own professional advancement at the papal curia, rather than to try a case against an English friar, whose reputation hardly merited the kind of attention it was getting.[75] Moreover, while Ockham waited for an evaluation by the commission—perhaps over three years in coming and never finally consequential—he

[74] McGrade, *The Political Thought of William of Ockham*, p. 199.

[75] Kelley, "Ockham: Avignon, Before and After," p. 9; Tachau, *Vision and Certitude*, pp. 207–208. Cf. Courtenay, *Schools and Scholars*, pp. 194–96.

had to deal with the political difficulties facing his brotherhood. He stood firm with the head of the Franciscan order, Michael of Cesena, in 1328 against Pope John XXII at Avignon over the commitment of one sector of Franciscans to ecclesiastical poverty. The details of the outcome and of Ockham's remaining days in Avignon are still sketchy—as are the reasons for his hasty departure from the city. But we do know that he and Michael fled Avignon in May of 1328 for Italy, where they received the protection of Ludwig of Bavaria. Shortly thereafter Ludwig took them with him to the security of the imperial court at Munich, and eventually both Ockham and Michael were excommunicated by the papacy and by the Franciscan order.

No one would deny that these are compelling reasons for becoming a political writer in the fourteenth century. But, if we are to avoid oversimplifying Ockham's "departure," we may begin by recalling that his primary interest throughout the so-called political writings of his remaining years is about the nature of power. It is, of course, self-evident that Ockham is not a writer of political criticism in the manner of Wyclif during the second half of the century. He is a philosopher determined to get to the bottom of the kind of dominion wielded by those who have it, both pope and emperor. This means that Ockham did not in these years write primarily as a political apologist in the service of a specific cause, as sometimes imagined.[76] Rather he takes an unprecedented look at the tradition fortifying two major issues, the pope's "plenitude of power" (*plenitudo potestatis*) and the "universality" of the church (*ecclesia universalis*). Both of these investigations, as scholarship has noted, have something to do with the priority granted to the individual in Ockham's ontology of evident knowledge.[77] But if, as I have proposed, Ockham's "individual" assumes from the outset the mediating *vox* of mind and speech, we may very well ask whether a similar mediation is involved in his attempt to refine a concept of dominion as uncorrupted or pristine. The question is not without import since the whole matter of the location of power is in the balance: does Ockham identify it with an origin that he would restore to purity, or does he recognize its "origin" in the images of representation itself—leaders and institutions of this world?

Although there is an enormous fissure in the intellectual work of Ockham, it is too simple to divorce the treatises of his Munich period from his earlier pursuits at Oxford, as is typical in modern scholarship. And it is equally mistaken to conclude, with those who have looked

[76] E.g., by Boehner, "Ockham's Political Ideas," p. 444. For a dissenting view, see Kelley, "Ockham: Avignon, Before and After," p. 11.

[77] E.g., Leff, *William of Ockham*, pp. 614–16; Coleman, "*Dominium* in Thirteenth- and Fourteenth-Century Political Thought," pp. 93–97, and *Ancient and Medieval Memories*, pp. 530 ff.

for a connection, that there is nothing in the early work that would lead one to anticipate his critique of dominion in the later treatises.[78] Ockham was surely provoked, as Wyclif was later, to curb papal infallibility because he was convinced of the pope's heresy; but he took aim from positions well known to him already, those based in previous explorations about the capacity of signs to signify in language and society. Earlier he had questioned the adequacy of language to represent thought. Now he asks how well does the sign of the papal office and person represent the power with which it was endowed. As the priority of the spoken form of the sign determined to some extent his answer in the logical treatises, we now want to know whether or not it shapes his thoughts about power as well.

Representative or Individual

"The highest pontiff is of such power because he is that spiritual man who judges everything and is himself judged by no one." With this remark, Egidius Romanus opens the *De Ecclesiastica Potestate*, a work epitomizing contemporary respect for the long-standing belief that the heart of the papal office consists in its power to judge.[79] Ockham came to have less and less patience with this premise and gradually undermined the arguments of a host of writers who had corroborated it, including Guido Terreni, Alvarus Pelagius, and Augustinus Triumphus. All of them regarded the pope as the human representative of God in this world and thus *ille spiritualis homo* who had jurisdiction over all things, secular and sacred. The vertical organization of power from God as applied in this concept of dominion was totalizing: the exercise of jurisdiction outside of the limits of the church was not possible, since the pope was *fons et origo* ("the fountain and origin") of everything that came from God through Christ, the apostles, and the genealogy of Peter. For most writers, such as Egidius, analogies paled before the absolute "fullness of power" embodied in the person of the pope—though not if they ultimately confirmed his dominion, as did the "analogy of the body" (Rom. 12.4–6); according to commonplace interpretation, as the "head" (*caput*) controls the "body" (*corpus*), so does the "head of the church" control the *corpus* of Christendom.[80]

---

[78] See McGrade, *Ockham's Political Thought*, pp. 9, 28–43; and Leff, *William of Ockham*, p. 615. NB the exception of Coleman, *Ancient and Medieval Memories*, p. 502.

[79] Egidius Romanus, *De Ecclesiastica Potestate* (henceforth, Egidius), pp. 6–9.

[80] Egidius, pp. 190–93, uses the phrase *totum posse* for the total power contained within the person of the pope. Cf. James of Viterbo, *De Regimine Christiano*, pp. 267–68. On ecclesiastical power, see, e.g., Ullmann, *Principles of Government and Politics*, pp. 19–26; Wilks, *The Problem of Sovereignty*, pp. 15–63; McGrade, *Ockham's Political Thought*, pp. 82–83, 140–49.

Opposing views of dominion were argued in the fourteenth century, most notoriously by Marsilius of Padua, who was with Ockham at Munich. Marsilius conceived of power not vertically but horizontally, because he located its origins in society and stressed that rulers must be subject to the people who elect them. Ockham had a similarly secular view, and the critique of universals and of Neoplatonic "appearances" which he had launched in his philosophical works is to be noted in his politics. In one of the earliest treatises of his Munich period, the *Opus Nonaginta Dierum* (ca. 1332), Ockham's attention is on the actual individuals who make up the community of the faithful. It is "ridiculous" and "erroneous," he argues, to assume as so many do that the church is a spiritual appearance; for we need only recall Exodus (32.6) or the text of Paul mentioning that the "people sat down to eat and drink" (1 Cor. 7). A member of this early community of either Israelites or Christians is not "an imaginary or representative person" because that individual performs a "real act"—sitting down to eat and drink. And therefore it is absurd, he insists, to think of the church as *imaginaria et repraesentata*, since it is a "community which can exercise many real acts." It can judge and defend and do many other things that no imaginary or representative *persona* can do.[81]

As Ockham qualifies the "mask" or "fiction" of this assumption about the church, so too does he undermine the "analogy of the body" as it was used traditionally to validate the dominion of the "mystical body" of Christ. In the *Dialogus* (ca. 1338–1346), Ockham reduces the two sides of this metaphor to one material church of this world. The notion of the church as the "mystical body," he argues, does not really have an adequate "similitude" (*similitudo*) in the "body of man"; for the body of a person cannot survive without a head, whereas the mystical body can survive through time without one, since that head is Christ who is in heaven. Indeed, the mystical body of Christ in heaven can exist without many members; but the "particular church" (*ecclesia particularis*) on earth is simply one of those members without which the mystical body would continue to exist. And what is more, however much the Roman church became the principal member of the church after the pope, still—Ockham concludes—"without that principal member the church would continue to be."[82] The church of Rome itself is unnecessary.

These are dangerous words in the fourteenth century, but since they were composed from behind the protection of the imperial walls at Munich, Ockham obviously felt that he could risk them. His sight is directed toward the concrete or *particularis* church of this world, that

---

[81] *Opus Nonaginta Dierum* 1:6.365.
[82] *Dialogus* 1.494.

is to say, toward the individual souls who make up the *communitas fidelium* ("community of the faithful"). While a specific *persona* of that body, such as John XXII, may be a poor representation of the faithful—as he obviously was for the English Franciscans—Ockham's complaint is ontological and linguistic: *representatio* itself involves distortions of power and identity. In order to expose them, Ockham attempted to penetrate through the *imaginarius* of dominion as an unnecessary intermediary in order to arrive at its genuine and originary form. The question of mediation in Ockham's political theory—as in his linguistics—is crucial to the course of his ongoing critiques against church and state.

PLENITUDE OF POWER

For this reason, his central target is the doctrine of *plenitudo potestatis*. It occupies his concerted attention in many documents from the *Contra Benedictum* of ca. 1337 until the *De Imperatorum et Pontificum Potestate* of ca. 1347. As scholarship has customarily maintained, Ockham's politics differ prima facie from many conventional medieval theories of government because of the utilitarian or functional cast of his arguments. Egidius or Augustinus, for instance, would never have thought of criticizing the doctrine of *plenitudo potestatis* because for them dominion in this world—however tarnished—originated in a metaphysical order that could not be dislodged. But Ockham's departure from such political idealism is apparent as early as his defense of Franciscan poverty in the *Opus Nonaginta Dierum*, where he contests the whole foundation of the papal claim to possession and dominion. And in this critique, he argues in the line of such theorists as John of Paris and Godefroid of Fontaines, who bequeathed to the early fourteenth century a new approach to the concept of *dominium*, away from "lordship" and toward individual "ownership" and possession of property.[83] For instance, in opposition to John XXII, Ockham maintains that the account of Adam and Eve before the fall does not establish the right of possession and dominion. For the first parents had "perfect power" over the fish of the sea and birds of the air only in the sense of "ruling and governing rationally the things of this world without any violent resistance from them." Their perfect power could not be called total "ownership" (*dominium*) of everything in Eden. To the contrary, the vegetables and animals of the garden were at their disposal: they

[83] See Coleman, "*Dominium* in Political Thought" and *Ancient and Medieval Memories*, p. 537.

simply had "the power of using" what God had provided.[84] Nor can their power be defined as "common" ownership either before or after their sin, as the papalists had argued; for in any strict sense, "no one could appropriate anything for himself without common consent"— which hardly describes the action of Adam and Eve.[85] The decisive shift toward possession and dominion came with the fall; for "if the first parents had not sinned, then there would be no power of appropriating."[86] What, then, is the origin of *potestas appropriandi*? It is, says Ockham, "from corrupt nature," from the "speech of natural reason" which convinced Adam and Eve that they could defy divine prohibition because they had the power of taking for themselves what they desired; from that moment on, dominion was one with possession of property, and that is why they are regulated by positive law.[87]

As Ockham takes up the theory of *plenitudo potestatis* directly a few years later in *Octo Quaestiones de Potestate Papae* (ca. 1340–1342), he begins with the customary opinion that "the pope has such fullness of power in spiritual and temporal affairs that he can do all things which are not explicitly against divine law or the law of nature, even though those things may be against civil or canonical law."[88] Ockham's stern objections to this doctrine of unlimited papal dominion are based on a germinal principle of law, which he—apparently—is the first to apply to the question of papal power: "The law of the gospel is a law of freedom [lex evangelica est lex libertatis]."[89] But the full context of Ockham's legal arguments proceeds from certain semiological differentiations, the unavoidable incompatibilities between the pope as "vicar" and Jesus Christ, between the "plenitude" of papal dominion and the real presence of God's power, and between the individual soul as "servant" under the "New" law and as "slave" under the "Old" Mosaic law. Christ's law, says Ockham, "is a law of freedom with respect to Mosaic law" because it liberated mankind from his former "servitude." Accordingly, "if the pope had such plenitude of power from Christ and gospel law, that law would be one of intolerable servitude, far greater than Mosaic law. Indeed under it everyone would be made servants of

[84] *Opus Nonaginta Dierum* 14.432.
[85] Ibid. 14.435.
[86] Ibid. Cf. Coleman, "*Dominium* in Political Thought," pp. 94–95.
[87] Ibid.
[88] *Octo Quaestiones* 1.2.17. Cf. *Contra Benedictum* 6.2 in *Opera Politica* 3.273, where Ockham uses the phrase "potentia absoluta" for papal power. Also relevant: *Imperatorum et Pontificum Potestate* 1.455
[89] *Contra Benedictum* 4.4 in *Opera Politica* 3.275. See McGrade, *Ockham's Political Thought*, p. 141, and Kelley, "Ockham: Avignon, Before and After," pp. 12 ff.

the pope, because he would have power over all Christians. . . . Therefore the pope does not have such plenitude of power."[90]

The argument here is not exactly that the pope claims a power greater than Christ's; Ockham does not attack him for the sin of pride. Rather, Christ claimed no power whatsoever in worldly affairs and disavowed all possessions: he was the preeminent Franciscan ideal of the *pauper*; and his *lex libertatis* encouraged moral freedom by prohibiting the subjugation of other people. How, therefore, could the representative of Christ, the pope—"cuius est vicarius"—claim for himself what Christ repudiated?[91] The representative "vicar" not only presumes more for himself than his heavenly exemplar, but appropriates a plenitude explicitly denied at the source. The sin, as Ockham argues, is nothing less than "heresy," because those entrusted to protect the *lex libertatis* have used it to make all people *servi*. In accusing John XXII of this sin, Ockham is obviously pointing out that Christ would never have instituted the law of freedom to bind all Christians; such an "incomparably greater servitude than the Mosaic law" would be an intolerable contradiction.[92] And he is also suggesting that the pope has grasped, like Satan before him, for the dominion only God the Father himself possesses. Ockham, in short, regards the doctrine of papal *plenitudo potestatis* as merely an unnecessary appearance or ornament of the essence of power, and he moves backward through the seemingly infinite regress of *repraesentata* in order to purify the lineage of dominion by unveiling its untainted source. By virtue of this analysis, however, Ockham has implied that power is not ornamental at all, but that it arises from the semiological process itself, from representing effectively the *imaginarius* of dominion where there is none. Through the appropriation of absolute rule, the image of the papal *vicarius* exceeds itself but guarantees its own dominion in the process. Ockham's thinking on this subject will be recognized for its comparison with the attempt earlier in his logical theory to penetrate the universal for the individual, the linguistic sign for evident knowledge. As mediation was his focus in linguistics, we see it determining his political theory also.

Although in the passages under discussion thus far Ockham clearly contrasts those medieval theorists who would discuss political dominion only in terms of metaphysical ideals, he is, nonetheless, markedly similar to them by defining *plenitudo potestatis* in terms of its putative origin. The "functionalist" Ockham cannot accept the inadequate im-

---

[90] *Octo Quaestiones* 1.6.29–30. Cf. *Dialogus* 3.776–77.
[91] *Octo Quaestiones* 1.6.31.
[92] Ibid. 1.6.30.

age for the fullness of the exemplar, but still his procedure has already been determined by the priority he sets out to question. He does not vacillate on the question of "who has the power," Satan or Adam, God or pope. But his method of questioning the delineation of power aprioristically leads him to bypass the "discovery" of his own inquiry—the situation of dominion in its various dissimulations. If there is a connection between Ockham's early discussion of papal possession in the *Opus Nonaginta Dierum* and the later theoretical explorations of papal dominion, I suggest it is established semiologically by the similarity between the rationalizations for the seizure of property in Eden and the appropriation of images of power in the fourteenth-century papacy.

A Solo Deo

During 1341 or 1342 Ockham once again pondered the subject of papal dominion in the *Breviloquium*. Ridiculing contemporary ecclesiastical corruptions and theological contradictions with the *lex libertatis*, he points his critique specifically at the scriptural roots of the pope's claim to power, and his answer this time is that it can only derive "from God alone" (*a solo Deo*).[93] As other political theorists had turned to the Petrine commission, so does Ockham; but the mind of the linguist is unmistakable in the determined movement backward to the unmediated presence of authority. "Jurisdiction," he argues, may be understood to be "from God alone without any ordination, election, or human ministration" in the case of Peter, for "he received power directly through the words of Christ, 'feed my sheep'."[94] Some power, he continues, can be understood to be "from God alone" through the "ministry of men," such as in administering baptism or dispensing the Eucharist, but "papal power is from God alone in every highest pontiff after Peter. . . . Although Christ conferred papal power on Peter without any human ministry, still does he confer such power on Peter's successors with only the least canonical election. Yet the electors contribute no power at all to the highest pontiff himself. God alone gives power to him."[95]

This argument is, paradoxically, nothing if not absolute. Descending from a fixed origin, power in this estimation compares with various contemporary fourteenth-century accounts of the metaphysical roots of government, and at least one recent commentator has labeled Ock-

---

[93] *Breviloquium* 4.5–6. Cf. *Octo Quaestiones* 2.3–6.
[94] *Breviloquium* 4.5–6.
[95] *Breviloquium* 4.5.150.

ham's explanation of it "formal," rather than functionalist.[96] The assessment states explicitly what Ockham questioned in other treatises, that no created image could represent *plenitudo potestatis*. In this case, power not only exists in the physical world; it was actually conferred *per verba Christi* on Peter. As Ockham's linguistics bears the trace of the formalism he rejected through the continuing primacy of *vox* in his theory of knowledge, his politics reinstates the immanence of papal power— however diminished in Peter's successors—in spite of his determination to cut his ties with formalist ideals of government.

That a conflict between formalist and functionalist elements emerges in Ockham's political writing may not be surprising in view of the problem posed by representation in his earlier work on sign theory. But the political problem has not been explored semiologically, and that factor may account for the present confusion in scholarship about it. For instance, the conflict between absolute power and utilitarian circumstances has been regarded as an "impasse" that Ockham never overcame;[97] as a separation necessary for his defense of Ludwig of Bavaria's independence from papal rule;[98] and as a crisis that Ockham resolved through his arguments for the centrality of "expediency" in government.[99] The last point is of particular relevance here, since it attempts to reconcile the absolute power of one ruler with the larger needs of a community demanding expedient solutions. In *Dialogus* 3 Ockham argues: (1) that it is "expedient" (*expedire*) for a community to be under one head rather than a multitude of judges, who may disagree among themselves about a decision; (2) that many judges may err, whereas one is more "expedient" since all reference can be made to a single person; (3) that a community of several leaders, who might feel no sanction on their behavior, would find it more "expedient" (*expediat*) if one supreme and faithful head had power over all.[100] Despite the functionalist orientation of this explanation of political order and its interest in circumscribing the boundaries of government, it would be incomplete to assume that Ockham's remarks on dominion

[96] Lagarde, *La naissance de l'esprit laïque* 5:126: "Ockham croit que l'ordre du Christ instituant la primauté est formel."

[97] Ibid.

[98] Leff, *William of Ockham*, p. 643: "The whole of Ockham's intent was to vindicate the *status quo* in temporal affairs so far as the emperor was concerned and to undermine it in the church so far as the pope was concerned. . . . The absence of a natural law binding upon a ruler's actions contrasts with the omnipresence of divine law circumscribing papal actions and the means it provided of enforcing it. The opposition between them was the focus of Ockham's political philosophy." Cf. Lagarde, *La naissance de l'esprit laïque* 4:247.

[99] McGrade, *Ockham's Political Thought*, p. 155 ff.

[100] *Dialogus* 3.806–808.

do not have ideal or metaphysical bases. The argument in favor of one ruler who resolves all conflicts, although set in the context of expediency, has obvious ties to the premises of Ockham's ecclesiology, which have already been noted: the *communitas fidelium* is one *corpus* with one head; more than one head makes the church a monster. In *Dialogus* 3 Ockham says outright that the leader must be more than spiritual; he must be actually present to the faithful—"there must be one leader as vicar of the church, who is corporally present to it [*praesens eidem*]."[101]

THE RULE OF THE FATHER

But Ockham's argument, which is interested in establishing monarchy as the best form of ecclesiastical government, has other roots—notably in Aristotle's *Politics*. With reference to secular communities, such as the *civitas* and *regnum*, Ockham cites Aristotle's points that the model for forms of order in the state is the "household," the "family," and the rule of the "father."[102] As Aristotle begins with paternity because he recommends monarchy as the preferred kind of political rule, Ockham makes the same recommendation for church government, but for a slightly different reason: the rule of the "father," he argues, is a more "natural" (*naturalis*) form of dominion because it is like art—it imitates nature.[103] Family and household—not as precisely organic as the *corpus* of the church—nonetheless constitute a powerful assertion of formalist theory, the rule of one man, one order, and one word in the affairs of the *communitas fidelium*.

Ockham's use of Aristotle's *Politics* may seem misleading, since the secular model only goes so far in justifying church government. He is primarily interested in the arguments against tyranny and thus in the rule of a leader who is *superexcellens* in all aspects of character, such as morality and sapience. But it should not be overlooked that monarchy had other than classical manifestations during Ockham's life in the first half of the fourteenth century, and he enjoyed the privileges of working at the court of one of the most prominent in the world. Yet another element informing Ockham's theory of monarchy must also be recalled since it is implied rather sharply in the recommendation for the more "natural" regime of the family. As the father is present to the household in word and deed, so also—says Ockham—must the church have a vicar who is "corporally present" to the faithful. Mediacy versus immediacy, the problem of long standing in Ockham's linguistics, has

---

[101] *Dialogus* 3.788.
[102] *Dialogus* 3.792–93.
[103] *Dialogus* 3.796.

surfaced at this crux in his political theory, and according to the recommendation of *Dialogus* 3, monarchy in the church is preferred especially because it resolves the problems of separation and difference between *rector* and *communitas*. The leader of the church is Christ, but the rule of an invisible head is not expedient. He must be physically present, says Ockham, in deed and word: the claim is yet another version of the argument that papal *potestas* is *a solo Deo* and delivered originally *per verba Christi*. Monarchy, in other words, adopts not only a familial analogy but a semiological one as well: it is more "natural" that the power of rule be constituted in the spoken words of one man.

The connection between language and monarchy might be less pressing were it not for the fact that Ockham's theory of ecclesiastical government is so intricately connected with his arguments for separating it from secular dominion. Scholars addressing this issue, however, are by no means in agreement. Some see a striking theological positivism at the core of Ockham's theory of secular rule, a world theocracy comparable to Dante's, with claims for the legitimacy of lay power documented in the Bible.[104] Another study maintains that Ockham brought forward a new "laicist" interpretation of government completely desacralizing the tradition of papal supremacy to empire and grounding secular polity, somewhat like Marsilius of Padua, in popular sovereignty.[105] A third group, seeking a reconciliation between these two, recognizes that Ockham is nowhere decisive or complete on the subject of secular rule; for he at once documents lay authority in Scripture, thus directly embarrassing the papists, and yet never maintains in any work that the origins of rule spring from the popular consent of the governed.[106] He recommends, according to this assessment, the government of a wise and good emperor, who is superior in secular affairs to the pope but who remains his subordinate in spiritual matters. The pope, on the other hand, has no power at all in secular affairs. Based on what both realms of dominion, secular and sacred, cannot do, this position ultimately advances a minimalist politics. But it would be incomplete to conclude that it is the result of entrenched utilitarian assessments about the workings of government. Ockham's problems with representation in language have again found their way

[104] E.g., Boehner, "Ockham's Political Ideas," p. 446: "Ockham's political ideas in their great outlines could have been developed . . . from any of the classical metaphysics of the thirteenth century." Cf. Scholz, *Wilhelm von Ockham als politischer Denker*, pp. 1, 21–22.

[105] Lagarde, *La naissance de l'esprit laïque* 4:223. "Au nom de la foi, on a justifié un activisme anarchique et désordonné de tout le corps ecclésial, et la logique du système interdit qu'une institution quelconque puisse le contrôler efficacement" (ibid. 5:164).

[106] Leff, *William of Ockham*, p. 643; McGrade, *Ockham's Political Thought*, pp. 45–46; Coleman, *Ancient and Medieval Memories*, pp. 531–32.

into his politics at this point; for as some studies have noted, mediation is again at issue in his discussion of lay order.[107] The observation, I suggest, is well taken, for mediate versus immediate power not only appears in the discussions of lay government; it is an opposition at the foundation of his bold separation of church and state.

MEDIATE OR IMMEDIATE

"Supreme rule is from the pope" ("imperium est a papa"), said Alvarus Pelagius in defense of the traditional curialist position on the origin of power.[108] Ludwig of Bavaria, of course, was outrageously offensive to this tradition when he did not wait for the papacy at Avignon to elect him before he seized rule in 1328. And in 1345 he still had to face challenges from the papacy to depose him, since his "rebellion" had precluded his reign from any claim to legitimacy. Writing within these years at Munich, Ockham was questing for sources of authority in lay government on a day-to-day basis, and *imperium est a papa* was his point of departure. But political exigencies notwithstanding, the principle in itself must have bothered Ockham the logician and linguist. For the notion that the emperor rules only at the pleasure of the pope, who crowns and authorizes him, assumes a priori that the pope is the embodiment of the ultimate source of power, *plenissima potestas*.[109] That such a category could have ontological status (*ens*), from which its being in the world (*esse*) as a real person would be derived, goes against everything Ockham wrote about universals. But he does not handle this critique of rule in explicitly philosophical terms. Rather, in the *Breviloquium* he moves in a different direction—paradoxically— seeking a divine origin for secular empire by considering its possible foundation in Holy Scripture.[110] Finding none, he rejects the idea but does not concede, therefore, that imperial power is mediated by Rome or Avignon. To the contrary, says Ockham, "Supreme lay power is from God alone."[111] The principle looks perfectly consistent with Ludwig of Bavaria's opinion, set forth in *Licet iuris*, that the emperor embodied power directly from God alone, not through the intermediary of the papacy.[112] Yet the context of Ockham's arguments in both *Breviloquium* and *Octo Quaestiones* suggests a different conception from Ludwig's notion of immanent power. It has been remarked that Ockham meant

[107] Leff, *William of Ockham*, p. 630, and McGrade, *Ockham's Political Thought*, p. 99.
[108] *De planctu ecclesiae* 18.32–33, 37.42–58.
[109] *Dialogus* 3.786.
[110] *Breviloquium* 4.10.
[111] *Breviloquium* 4.5–8; *Octo Quaestiones* 2.3–6.
[112] Cf. McGrade, *Ockham's Political Thought*, p. 99 n. 55.

72   CHAPTER TWO

by this formulation only that the emperor was not *subject* to anyone in
the affairs of state, not even the pope;[113] but the separation from theological assumptions is far less clear.

The distinction belongs to the "third mode" in which temporal
authority is related to God. In the first, as already noted, temporal
authority is bestowed on people without any mediation, as when
Moses received authority at Sinai or Peter received it from Christ; in
the second, power is conferred through an intermediary as in the case
of baptism when grace is conferred through the ministration of a
priest.[114] But the third mode presents complications. Regarding it Ockham says, "A certain jurisdiction or power can be understood to be
from God alone not when it is given or conferred, but after it has been
given, so that, for instance, when it is given it is not from God alone
in either the first or second sense, but truly given and conferred indeed
by another [*ab alio*] rather than by God; yet after it has been conferred,
it thus depends on God alone, because discharging such things he [the
conferee] ordinarily recognizes it [power] from no other than from
God, just as from a superior."[115] We might be led to conclude from this
passage, as one commentator has noted, that the third mode is altogether separate from the first two because it identifies the people as
the source of power: it is conferred *ab alio* upon a ruler.[116] But the
distinction is by no means self-evident;[117] for once power is conferred
on a leader, it "depends" on God for its continuation—he is its conserving cause. And in the final twist of the argument, Ockham says
that those who confer power ordinarily recognize that what they
discharge is not original with them but "from no other than from God."
Thus in the third mode, secular power is *immediate a solo Deo*.

Commenting on this problem in another place, *Octo Quaestiones*,
Ockham cites the example of Christ's words, "Render unto Caesar the
things which are Caesar's" (Matt. 22.21). "By these words," says Ockham, "Christ did not give anything specifically to Caesar, but ordered
those things be given to Caesar which first had been given through
human ordination; and therefore he did not say, 'Give something to
Caesar,' but 'Render unto him those things which are his,' namely,
which had been conferred upon him by men."[118] Christ is not institut-
ing a new source of power, but confirming what has already been
conferred by human institutions—the ability to appoint rulers or de-

[113] Ibid.
[114] *Breviloquium* 4.5.
[115] *Breviloquium* 4.5.150.
[116] McGrade, *Ockham's Political Thought*, pp. 105 and 150.
[117] Cf. Leff, *William of Ockham*, p. 631.
[118] *Octo Quaestiones* 2.6.77.

pose them. The words illustrate what Ockham says in *Breviloquium* 6, namely, that God is conserving the *imperium* held by Caesar through reiterating what has already occurred. But the ultimate origin of temporal power—Ockham goes on to say—does not come *ab homine* or *ab communitate*. If supreme lay power were possessed by people, it could be assigned by no one other than the pope, which means that he would possess it.[119] Such a circumstance is patently impossible, since ancient pagan emperors did not possess temporal power from the pope. Nor could temporal authority originate ultimately among the community of Romans, who are, finally, "inferiors and vassals of the emperor": no one "can be both vassal and lord." Therefore, Ockham again concludes, supreme lay power in the third mode comes *immediate a Deo*.[120]

As Ockham refers to the reign of Caesar, so also does he include several situations mentioned in Scripture and subsequent histories which illustrate that imperial rule was permitted and even supported by God. His aim, of course, is to sever the tradition that empire is subject to papacy. But none of the examples proves an unmistakable dominion *immediate a solo Deo*, as Moses received it at Sinai. Ockham refers to the kings of Egypt and Sodom in the history recorded in the Old Testament and to the rulers of Rome mentioned in the New Testament.[121] Paul acknowledged that he was a Roman citizen, and John the Baptist respected the jurisdiction of the empire.[122] Nero, Domitian, and Julian—from the early years of the church—are noted as emperors by Augustine and Ambrose.[123] Ockham's conclusion is that true *imperium* not only preexisted Christianity but was not even abrogated by the persecutors of the early church or by apostates like Julian. He has announced unquestionably a separation between rulers in the order of grace and those *extra ecclesiam* and thus has made his case for the independence of Ludwig of Bavaria from the papacy in temporal affairs. But on the other hand, he has not implied in the *Breviloquium* or in the *Octo Quaestiones* that the power of rule originates from the people alone. He never even recommended a political order constituted by popular vote. At most what we can say of the third mode of supreme lay power is that the emperor has authority "immediately" in his "dependence" on God who granted it in the beginning, but that the lay ruler is only the mediator of that origin. The whole existence of secular dominion within the *societas Christiana* depends on that mediation, for without it, the emperor would be, like Pharaoh of old, the

[119] Ibid. 2.6.78–79.
[120] Ibid. 2.6.79. Cf. Coleman, *Ancient and Medieval Memories*, p. 530.
[121] *Breviloquium* 3.2.110–13.
[122] *Breviloquium* 3.3.113–18.
[123] *Breviloquium* 3.4.119.

immanence of absolute divinity, and God himself would have ordained pagan Rome just as he bestowed the papacy on Peter.[124]

Yet even in attacking papal *plenitudo potestatis* by appeal to the
legitimacy of such *imperatores* as Pharaoh, Ockham's attempt to desac-
ralize secular office is not as final as we might expect it to be. He
invokes the Bible for examples of secular legitimacy because, he says,
"the testimony of God is greater than the testimony of men."[125] And
his third mode clearly suggests the religious nature of lay office in the
ruler's dependence on God's conserving hand in the affairs of empire,
however remote and mediated the origin of that power. Furthermore,
his whole conception of empire is not that it circumscribes certain
pockets of the *communitas fidelium*; it is hardly "secular" in any modern
sense; quite the reverse is the case, since the *societas Christiana* includes
within itself the order of empire. In the end, we must acknowledge, as
a few studies have, the conflict that Ockham both sacralizes and de-
sacralizes lay dominion.

Language and Dominion

But the fact that he does not resolve the problem conclusively is itself
instructive: for his politics is preoccupied with situating power in a
specific origin, in the same way as his linguistics is interested in
locating the evident knowledge of the individual in the "voice" of the
mental sign. Both political power and the individuating word are
explicitly identified by appeal to the "presence" of the sign—be it the
rector to a *communitas* or *vox* to mental language. Explaining language
and dominion thereafter becomes a process of unveiling the *repraesentata* of their sources: the mediation of the ruler, like the intermediary
status of the mental sign, seems caught in an infinite regress in which
the validity of authority or experience is identifiable with an origin
always out of reach. As "voice" supplements for experience which is
in turn supplemented by "voice," the immediacy of the "fullness of
power" is ultimately deferred rather than differentiated. The logic of
suppositio—in which one term adds to what it is supposed to replace—
determines as well Ockham's politics of immediate power: it is possessed by the emperor from its origin with God, but mediated ever
after as a likeness or representation, and all too often a diminished or
corrupt one. To transpose the point into the terms of Ockham's linguistics, the emperor's dominion is not "categorematic," for it does not

[124] See *Breviloquium* 4.6–7 for Ockham's argument that the Roman Imperium is not *a
solo Deo* in the first or second modes.
[125] *Octo Quaestiones* 4.3.

"signify"—as Ockham defined the term—by carrying out a totally differentiated sense of power; rather, a ruler "consignifies" a dominion original in God but meaningful only as a modification in the temporal affairs of society. The order of this world must necessarily be the syncategorematic "qualification" of a dominion whose "substantive" form is always out of reach.

That Ockham leaves us with such blurred distinctions about the immediacy of both dominion and individual cognition once led a scholarly tradition to label him a skeptic—an "apprentice sorcerer."[126] Recent studies of his work are gradually changing that opinion, and I concur with the conclusion that to perpetuate the notion of Ockham as a skeptic is an unprofitable line of inquiry. But I do not conclude that we abandon the very real conflicts which remain in Ockham's linguistic and political theory. For these two areas of his work—far from being divorced as widely in his thought as Oxford from Munich—are bothered by the same problem, the undecidability about the immediacy of both cognition and power. If this problem cannot be resolved (and we shall have to wait for compelling argument that it can), I suggest we look at it for what it may indicate about the historical context in which Ockham was working.

From the outset, both of these realms of inquiry bear the stamp of the terminist logician. Ockham is relentless—brilliantly so, need I say—in questioning the adequacy of the linguistic sign to represent thought or meaning and the political sign to represent dominion. He situates himself in the opposition between sign and referent, and for the moment he looks very much like a medieval deconstructionist, accepting the equivocation of signs in the aftermath of a philosophical realism and transcendentalism that had anchored them in the universality of substantial forms—whether they be the concept of the individual or the source of power. But even as Ockham questions the adequacy of linguistic and political *repraesentata*, he ultimately assumes that some signs are self-evident, that the mental term or concept will "present itself" in differentiation from conventional language and that the ruler of this world (pope or king) will be self-evidently different from the source of power in the Godhead. This move, as already noted, is much more subtle in the logic than in the politics, where Ockham comes right out and says that the vicar of power must be present to the community of the governed. In the pragmatic order of daily affairs, such an opinion is doubtlessly valuable political advice. But Ockham is not offering

---

[126] Gilson, *History of Christian Philosophy*, p. 498. Contrast Adams's conclusion, *William Ockham* 1:629: the notion of Ockham "as the chief of medieval sceptics is largely misguided and highly misleading and should, accordingly, be abandoned."

such advice. He is defining the nature of immediate power, and it is here tied up with its sign in such a way that it compromises the aim of his argument, which is to differentiate mediate signs of power (all too mired in heresy, so he thought) from their true source. Ockham clearly assumed the same principle of noncontradiction in his linguistics, when he claims the self-evident differentiation of mental from conventional language. However, the problems which trammel that assumption bear recalling for the dilemma about mediated power in the political treatises.

Let me repeat that although Ockham questioned the ability of conventional language to represent thought, he never questioned in any systematic way the capacity of writing to represent speech. Instead, both speech and writing are expressions of the same communicative act, and when they refer to themselves in "material supposition," they are inevitably subordinated to the controlling "self-presence" of mental language. Metalanguage as understood today is thus stillborn in the material supposition of medieval logic. The "inscription" of language, its form as *scripta*, is subsumed within its spoken form, its *dictio*. And yet, the situation could hardly have been otherwise, given the oral circumstances of producing manuscripts, reading, lecturing, and notetaking in the fourteenth century.

Speech is prerogatory in Ockham's attempt to control the metalanguage of mental language, and that prerogative comprehends the writtenness of language as a marginal form; or—what amounts to the same thing—inscription was trusted and valued insofar as it was received as a kind of speech. There are powerful illustrations of this assumption about written communication in the world of marketplace and court during the late thirteenth and early fourteenth centuries in England. But what is remarkable is that they resonate as well in the higher reaches of philosophical speculation about such notions as "material supposition" in the university. No less than the prerogative power of oral language in the social order, the "voice of books"—as Thomas à Kempis put it—has a mind of its own.[127]

I do not want the point here to be misunderstood. Certainly Ockham of all people realized the equivocality at stake when both conceptual and conventional forms of language were self-reflexive. But he presumed, as it were, vertical control in the signifying chain, in which *vox mentalis* would present itself a priori as different from speech and writing. There is nothing unusual about this structure in medieval language theory, and that is precisely my claim: the perception of the difference of writing is occluded by the sense that voice dictates its

---

[127] *Of the Imitation of Christ* 3.43.188.

inscribed form. The sign, in other words, has a "voice"—silent as it may be in the mind or in the reading process.

Because the voice of the sign asserts its own prerogative, it also assumes its own dominion as the "discourse" of conventional and mental language. It is small wonder, therefore, that when Ockham vacillates on the *imaginaria* of dominion in the political order of church and state he is caught once again in an either-or situation: the vicar is not to be confused with the origin of power in God, and yet it is only by virtue of the governed that leaders have dominion in the first place; the church of this world is only a tainted form of the universal church for which all Christians pray; and still, without an established church, Christendom could never have developed. Although Ockham sets out to reject Neoplatonic ideals of government which had come down from Augustine and the scholastics, nonetheless he repeats a typically medieval anticipation when he identifies power with models of language that are traditionally oral—received *a solo Deo* or comprehended in the speech of the father of a household. He is manifestly removed from Augustine in assumptions about both government and language; but he still has not broken with the tradition set in motion by his predecessor, that writing is the inscription of voice.

As the social order became the scene of many collisions when old oral expectations engaged sophisticated forms of literacy and textuality, so also do Ockham's political and linguistic projects: they exemplify the crisis of representation in language through the highly refined conflict between *vox* and experience, *repraesentata* and the knowledge of *res* per se, the mediated power of rulers and the *plenitudo potestatis* of God. To the extent that his distinctions between sacred and secular, voice and individual, text and experience elide into each other, Ockham's project testifies to the uncertain margin between oral and written tradition in his time: as the priority of one term in an opposition (the source of power or the privilege of *vox*) takes hold, the representation of the other as a diminished likeness of the first, a fall away from it, is inevitable. Though conflict within the hierarchy of this descent may be momentarily deferred, it has by no means been voided simply because it has been suppressed.

The suppression of conflict by representation surfaces in the central preoccupations of Ockham's major work: papacy against empire, the voice of rule against the high literacy of his own written challenges, the discovery of power in the act of seizure in the garden of Eden against the origin of power in the Godhead. These conflicts were real in the life of Ockham, and the veil of representation was torn on several occasions, some of which were never redressed, such as his refusal to the end of his life to confess submission to the pope or return

to the Franciscan order its seal—its signature of authority—which he
and Michael of Cesena had taken with them to Munich from Avignon
in 1328.[128] Mediation, as I have suggested, is far more than an airy
academic dilemma in Ockham's linguistic and political theory. To the
contrary, it is a semiological problem specifically because it is a political one—the site of a struggle between volatile oppositions in the social
history of the later middle ages. His philosophical project realizes those
conflicts in a most unlikely way as it witnesses the crisis of opposition
that persists when familiar oral customs attempt to prevail over changes
urged from the sophistications of an expanding literacy and textuality.

[128] See new evidence provided by Gàl, "William of Ockham Died 'Impenitent' in April
1347."

Chapter Three

"REAL LANGUAGE" AND THE RULE OF THE BOOK IN THE WORK OF WYCLIF

Section I
ON "REAL LANGUAGE"

> The modern generation seeking signs looks for them
> precipitously in Scripture, but it does not have
> them. For the writing they read is little more than
> the line of the hand in chiromancy or the figure of
> punctuation in geomancy—indeed no more than the
> trace of a comb upon wool.
> —Wyclif, *De veritate sacrae scripturae*

Introduction

If William of Ockham's work suggests the delicate balance between voice and writing in the first half of the fourteenth century, the project of John Wyclif in the second half tips the scale much more decidedly in the direction of familiar traditions—in philosophy toward ties with realism from the "ancients," and in the world of religious affairs toward support for the orality of language (both vernacular English and vulgar Latin). Scholarship on Wyclif, and on late medieval thought in general, has not taken up in any systematic way the possibility that these two topics, realism and spoken language, are related to each other.[1] But they clearly invite consideration within the framework that has organized my inquiries in this book—how to account for the claims of oral tradition in a world making increasing use of written documents and texts.

For Wyclif there is never any doubt about the value of realism in philosophy; nor does he slight the importance of oral language to

---

[1] On Wyclif's realism, see, e.g., Robson, *Wyclif and the Oxford Schools*; Kenny, *Wyclif*; Kenny, "The Realism of the *De Universalibus*"; Kenny, "Realism and Determinism in the Early Wyclif"; Leff, *Heresy in the Later Middle Ages*, vol. 2. Orality in Wyclif's work is confined largely to his interest in vernacular English: see Aston, "Wyclif and the Vernacular" and *Lollards and Reformers*, chs. 4–6; Hudson, "Wyclif and the English Language"; Mueller, *The Native Tongue and the Word*, pp. 40–55.

religious doctrine in his time.[2] Unlike Ockham, his philosophical positions develop within a context of embattled religious reform, and he
relates the two explicitly in his work. For instance, realism is preeminently responsible for his position on the nature of the church as a
transcendent form (or universal); and it is clearly the philosophical
principle upon which his trenchant critique of the Eucharist rests. With
respect to the question of orality, it will become apparent that Wyclif
assumes some kind of bond between realism and models of spoken
utterance in the revealed Word of God in Holy Scripture as well as in
various elements of doctrine, such as the Annunciation and Incarnation. A modern perception of medieval Latin as a written, textualized,
and even "dead" language must not get in the way of appreciating
how Wyclif searched through it for vital wellsprings of orality. As for
vernacular language, conclusions must be constrained by the fact that
we do not know with certainty anything written specifically by Wyclif
in English.[3] But recently it has been demonstrated that the evidence
for his "vernacular initiative" or "impetus" is quite strong;[4] and the
activities of his followers in and around Oxford, including the Lollards,
confirm his continuing charge to tell important details about the faith
in a language the faithful could comprehend.[5]

The immediate context for this influence is unmistakable, flagrant
abuses in many of the religious orders during the second half of the
fourteenth century, principally the friars.[6] The larger context for his
philosophical commitments to realism is less accessible. Surely these
derived from his perception of the weaknesses in nominalist trends at
Oxford, where Ockhamism still echoed fifty years after the departure
of its master. But, as the philosophical positions of Ockham do not

[2] Courtenay, *Schools and Scholars*, p. 352: "His was the most compelling and extensive
realism that had been presented at Oxford for many generations." Aston, *Lollards and
Reformers*, p. 105: "Literacy was the preserve of the minority. . . . The church had developed in a society whose culture was predominantly oral."

[3] McFarlane, *John Wycliffe and the Beginnings of English Nonconformity*, p. 118: "That he
ever wrote anything in the vernacular is open to question." Hudson, ed. *Selections from
English Wycliffite Writings*, p. 10: "None of the English texts can certainly be ascribed to
Wyclif himself, despite the desire of modern critics to associate him directly with many
of them." Accordingly, unlike Mueller (*The Native Tongue*), I have not offered "Wycliffite"
English texts as evidence for Wyclif's positions. For editorial problems with Latin
treatises, see David Thomson, "The Oxford Grammar Masters Revisited."

[4] Aston, "Wyclif and the Vernacular," p. 328; Hudson, "Wyclif and the English Language," p. 102.

[5] On Lollardy, vernacularity, and Wyclif's reformism, see Hudson, *The Premature
Reformation*, pp. 82–93, 103–19, 185–87, 512, and *Lollards and Their Books*, chs. 1, 2, 5, 11;
and Aston, *Lollards and Reformers*, chs. 1 and 7.

[6] Szittya, *The Antifraternal Tradition in Medieval Literature*, p. 153: Wyclif was "the most
prolific antifraternal writer of medieval England."

arise simply out of the thin air of the classroom, so too is the project of Wyclif conditioned by its larger cultural context. Exactly how it influenced his work deserves more detailed scrutiny than it has received. We have yet to see refined application of the conclusion drawn decades ago about Wyclif's era: "Christianity in the fourteenth century was still an oral religion."[7] In the following pages I pursue this proposition through two vital aspects of his work—his critique of language (Section I) and dominion (Section II).

As I indicated in the last chapter, the relation between Ockham's linguistic and political writings is much more than accidental, since his critique of the sign challenges both the traditional sources of knowledge as well as the authority of ecclesiastical and lay dominion. Wyclif also begins with a critique of language and specifically those teachers who study it at the expense of traditional metaphysics. His departure, like Ockham's, involves him directly in the real historical world; but even more than the treatises of Ockham, Wyclif's theories of the word and the universal—which dominate his thought from one end of his career to the other—lead deliberately and powerfully toward some of the most provocative statements about dominion formulated in the later middle ages.

THE UNIVERSAL

Wyclif never abandoned the perspectives and interests of a thinker trained, as he was, in terminist logic.[8] But he did not cotton well to its vocabulary. Indeed, he repudiated in no uncertain terms the obscurity and irrelevance of formulations that tended to reduce to mere signs or artifice the "real being" of things and ideas. His project was to decentralize language as the matrix for studying the universal: rather than seeking it *post rem* in linguistic events, he sought a return to the classical *universalia ante rem*.[9] Because of the remarkable consistency of his stance, we may begin with a passage from relatively late in Wyclif's career included in the *De universalibus*, probably his most important philosophical treatise: "Metaphysicians," he argues, "know that a common nature [i.e., a universal] is understood naturally by God as imparted to many suppositions before it is actually shared by them. And thus universality or metaphysical truth does not depend on the created intellect, which it precedes, but on the uncreated intellect, which pro-

[7] Manning, *The People's Faith in the Time of Wyclif*, p. 70.

[8] Cf. Courtenay, *Schools and Scholars*, p. 350: "In that broad and stylistic sense Wyclif was as much a 'terminist' as any of his contemporaries or predecessors."

[9] See, e.g., Robson, *Wyclif and the Oxford Schools*, pp. 171–95; and Kenny, "The Realism of the *De Universalibus*" and "Realism and Determinism in the Early Wyclif."

duces everything from eternal intellectual knowledge. Ignorance of this understanding made Ockham and many other sign doctors, from infirmity of intellect, deny the real universal."[10] The *doctores signorum* are disparaged in this passage—and elsewhere in this treatise—in favor of *antiqui* like Augustine whom Wyclif commends to us because he knew that true being exists outside of time. But the *moderni*, as Wyclif complains earlier, look in a different direction: "How vain are the ambiguities they look into, those who—attending only to signs— say that genus is a term or concept which . . . is in itself predictable correctly and essentially of many terms signifying distinct things specifically."[11] The Ockhamism of the position represented here is obvious, and Wyclif vigorously disapproves of it. He prefers the metaphysics of Robert Grosseteste, first chancellor of Oxford, to the philosophy of the *magister* still commanding attention among some of the faculty. For Wyclif, Grosseteste deserves continual praise as the perfect amalgam of Christian and classical philosophy—a vivid illustration of the extent to which Aristotelian empiricism was read through the eyes of Plato and Augustine in the later middle ages.[12]

In the second chapter of *De universalibus*, Wyclif cites Grosseteste for the purpose of subscribing wholeheartedly to his theory of the universal. It is a *locus classicus* of the chain of being descending from on high in five essential links: the first universal "is the exemplary idea or reason eternal in God. The second kind is the common reason created in superior causes, such as the celestial intelligences and spheres. The third kind of universal is the common form established in its individuals . . . the genera and species of which Aristotle speaks. The fourth universal is the common form located in its accidents. But the fifth mode of the universal—signs as acts of intellect—is dismissed by Grosseteste as irrelevant."[13] The Aristotelian categories of being, we notice, are not represented in their own right as self-subsistent entities, but in the highly qualified context of a Platonic-Augustinian First Cause from which all being stems; it infuses the celestial intelligences and spheres, Aristotle's categories, the form of individual things, and ultimately the accidental properties of individuals. Below them, on the last link of the chain of truth, we come to *signa*. For Grosseteste, it is futile to study universals through "signs." Wyclif assents without hesitation and enlists Aristotle once again to his purpose, since he (in Wyclif's opinion) locates logic "midway between grammar and meta-

[10] *De universalibus* 2.65.

[11] *De universalibus* 2.44.

[12] Cf. Robson, *Wyclif and the Oxford Schools*, p. 25: "It is hard to think of any century . . . more soaked in Augustine than the fourteenth."

[13] *De universalibus* 2.59.

physics": it is principally concerned with "things" (*de rebus*) and only secondarily with "signs" (*de signis*), which are the province of grammar.[14]

There is no question, for Wyclif, of which has "priority," language or reality. For he asks, "How could there be priority at all, unless the truth establishing that order existed to be signified?"[15] *Veritas*, he insists, is the "common thing" (*res communis*) we are seeking; what signifies it is merely "artificial." Even if all *signa artificialia* were destroyed, *talis prioritas* would remain; and that is why "priority"—without which nothing can be "prior"—is the determining origin of all thought.[16] The point forces his rejection of those whom he calls the Oxford "sign doctors": "how can a term or concept," he protests, "be called universal, if not because of what it signifies? From that alone, and not from a term or concept, does knowledge achieve its universality, its species, and its dignity."[17] To deny universals in the real world (*universalia realia*)—as do the *doctores signorum*—is to deny truth itself. But Wyclif maintains, with reference to Augustine, Anselm, and Grosseteste, "that no proposition is true if not because of the truth that it primarily signifies."[18] He calls that truth *prioritas originis* (the "priority of the origin"); it is a first principle of his metaphysics, and by comparison with it the languages of human institutions pale into mere artificiality.[19]

NATURAL OR ARTIFICIAL

Wyclif holds out for the "priority of the origin" as a transcendent ideal in the mind or in God with the same rigor that Ockham exercises in the opposite direction when he stresses the priority of the individual thing known intuitively. Both philosophers attempt to move beyond the mediation of language, and yet—as I have indicated—Ockham leaves us with a mental language still obedient to the conventional language it is supposed to distinguish. Wyclif, on the other hand, begins with the same premise, that language is artificial or invented; but he also argues mightily to separate it from what he calls, somewhat paradoxically, "real language." How successful he is in this division must now be considered in the text devoted to it, the *Tractatus de logica*.

His intention of getting to the truth of things is set forth with the

<hr />

[14] *De universalibus* 2.56.
[15] *De universalibus* 7.144.
[16] Ibid.
[17] Ibid.
[18] *De universalibus* 7.138.
[19] *De universalibus* 7.130.

first sentence, when he says that his treatise is compiled ultimately "for declaring the logic of Sacred Scripture."[20] He begins, as had many of his predecessors, by turning to the logic and linguistics of everyday discourse, along with some examples from the Bible, and he demonstrates in the process that *universalia ante rem* determine his conclusions about language in much the same way as they shape the course of his metaphysics. The linguistic "term," he argues, "is an utterance artificially invented for the composition of propositions; and thus any such term that is an utterance in grammar is a term in logic."[21] Ockham, and even Anselm in the eleventh century, would not have assimilated one discipline into another so swiftly, preferring instead to treat *grammatica* per se. But Wyclif's project is more conservative, as he subordinates *grammatica* strictly to logic. Although he speaks of *termini* as "artificial" and "invented," he does not establish a rigorous separation between spoken and written signs: one simply does the work of the other in convenient hierarchical order. A categorematic term in writing, for instance, "corresponds to an intention in the soul, signifying for it and convertible with that same term; for instance, the term *homo* in writing or in speech corresponds to the intention, *homo*, in the soul" and vice versa. A "substantial term," he continues, "signifies the nature of a thing without the connotation of accidental property; . . . [for instance] the term, *Angelus*, principally signifies angelic nature or essence without extraneous connotation."[22]

Although Wyclif acknowledges the medieval linguistic principle regarding the artificiality of language, his remarks on the topic of "propositions" (*proposiciones*) in chapter 5 of the *Logica* compromise, if they do not bypass, the import of the distinction. He opens by saying that *oratio* ("speech") is *artificialiter inventa* ("artificially invented") and that signification is "artificial" (*artificialis*) in a proposition that "signifies the truth as it is or is not from the imposition of a peculiarity of expression." For instance, the proposition "Deus est" ("God is") signifies "from imposition the truth itself, namely, that God exists"; so also the proposition "nullus Deus est" ("no God is") signifies "from imposition neither what is nor what is possible to be."[23] Linguistic determination in this discussion depends crucially upon a universal or intelligible species assumed a priori of any "imposition" by the *idioma* of language. As in the example cited previously, the inscription *a-n-g-e-l-u-s* is comprehensible because of the identity between the word and the universal essence or intelligible species of angelic nature contained in the

[20] *Logica*, "Proemium," 1:1.
[21] *Logica* 1:1.2.
[22] *Logica* 1:1.2 and 3.
[23] *Logica* 1:5.14.

mind of God. The signification of a term or proposition flows down
from its celestial origin, controlling the hierarchy of linguistic meaning.
It does not depend, we should note, on what has become known in
modern theory as the "material" properties of discourse, in which the
identity of a term proceeds not from a signified concept but from its
acoustical and visual difference from another term.[24]

If *angelus* signifies something different from *homo* because of the
given concept informing each word, artificial signification, in Wyclif's
discussion, begins to fulfill the same functions of what he describes as
its opposite category, "natural signification" (*significacio naturalis*). He
defines this form—all too briefly—as a proposition that does not depend upon any *imposicio idiomatis*, but rather that "signifies itself naturally."[25] "Angel" signifies itself when the idea of angelic nature is
understood; so too with the propositions "God is" or "man is"; their
intelligible species, their being (*esse*) existing naturally from the beginning in the divine mind, is comprehended because of the bond between expression and concept. Wyclif does not address the properties
of that bond in this section of the *Logica*. But it is apparent that his
appeal to the tradition of linguistic "artificiality" and "convention" is
played out to fulfill the demands of the natural order of *universalia*: as
they come before the *res* of language in this discussion, so does the
discipline of logic prevail over grammar. The paradox of this situation
in the *Logica* is not unlike the elision of categories in the *De universalibus*. Wyclif denies that "a priority of nature" belongs to logic; instead,
it is governed by the "priority of origin," which, he says, is "like that
between the Father and the Son in the Trinity."[26] If there is a categorical
difference here, one is compelled to ask how it is articulated through
a simile of paternity.

Wyclif proceeds next to assume a difference between propositions in
the mind and those expressed in speech or writing. A "mental proposition," he says, has no less than four designations: it may refer to the
"intentions" and "inclinations" (*intenciones, inclinaciones*) in the soul,
the various "acts" (*actibus*) composed from those intentions, the "complex act" (*actu complexo*) corresponding to a total proposition, or finally
the soul itself.[27] Wyclif does not press a sharp division between this
category and the next two kinds of propositions, written and spoken,
but it becomes apparent that they have subordinate status. A "vocal
proposition" (*proposicio in voce*), he argues, "is composed from words

[24] See ch. 2 above, s.v. "materiality of the signifier."

[25] *Logica* 1:5.14.

[26] *De universalibus* 7.130. On the *verbum* in relation to the Trinity in earlier scholasticism, esp. Aquinas, see Lonergan, *Verbum*, pp. 45, 206.

[27] *Logica* 1:5.14–15.

successively pronounced [and] . . . exists as long as any of its parts";
it is a function of a speaker's intentions, but, like the successive elements of time, it lasts no longer than the moment of speaking. A
"written proposition" (*proposicio scripta*) is somewhat different; it is
"composed from written terms, with their own complex signification";
thus it fulfills what is spoken, but with one salient exception: if writing
does not signify to us, "still it continues to signify itself to God."[28] Some
written propositions, we may conclude, are autonomous: their meaning depends neither upon a speaker, a reader, or an author, since God
himself can read them.

Real Propositions

The obviously ambiguous status granted to *proposicio scripta* as both
artificial (like all human language) and yet autonomous is not without
purpose at this point in the *Logica*. Since both values cannot hold
simultaneously, Wyclif hedges his bets in view of the demands of his
next category, "real proposition" (*proposicio realis*).

> A proposition, such as that man or that stone, is real because just as in a
> certain statement there is a subject, predicate, and copula, so in *that man*
> there is rendered that person which is the subject part of the human
> species and which is like the subject; and there is rendered similarly
> human nature, which essentially consists of that man like the predicate,
> and really predicated of that man. Then there is rendered the essence of
> that man, which is the real copula joining that man with his own nature.
> Just as the predicate is said of the subject in the artificial proposition, so
> in the real proposition, *that man*, it is essentially and really human na-
> ture.[29]

The use of *realis* in this category specifies a word-thing relation, insofar
as the artificial subject directly signifies an individual person, the
predicate his or her intelligible species, and the copula his or her
specific essence. According to this formulation, invented discourse can
correspond immediately to the reality of *universalia ante rem*.

Even though Wyclif discredits the status of language as artificial or
invented and disparages, as we have seen, "sign doctors" like Ockham,
still he maintains that some propositions can be synonymous with the
natural order of universal being. He would exhort us to begin at the
beginning—with the *prioritas originis*—but his own theory of real being
depends fundamentally on language, on the natural roots of artificial

[28] *Logica* 1:5.15.
[29] Ibid.

signs, and ultimately on the venerated medieval premise that language and nature obey the same laws. In this last category, the reality of language—or what amounts to the same thing, the language of reality—may be either spoken or written; the form of the example, *iste homo*, loses nothing to artifice since it is *essentialiter et realiter* human nature. Although Wyclif speaks in the *Logica* (ch. 2) of "representing" universal reality in the breath of speech or the inscription of documents, he has effectively erased the margin of distinction between them at this crucial stage of his sign theory. It may seem that he would fix his vision on ideal Platonic forms and leave the world of appearances to those who care to waste time with mere artifices of eternity, but his sense of the word in either speech or writing as the real presence of universal signification finally closes the transcendental gap: language for Wyclif is the realization of being.

This principle, as I have suggested, is less a matter of explicit commentary in the *Logica* than it is a controlling assumption. But in the *De universalibus*, Wyclif is quite plain about it. Despite his repeated disdain of "signs" as the end of grammar and logic, he maintains that truth would not be real for a logician unless it were "actually" (*actualiter*) "in the soul as in a sign."[30] Yet, he continues, there is a more metaphysical way of regarding the truth: "as the adequation of a thing with a word, as Augustine speaks of it." Truth exists not just within the soul but has "real being" outside of it in the mind of God and also in the truthful propositions of ordinary communication.[31] Such statements can signify both *in quale* and *in quid* (qualitatively and essentially) the nature of universal things. And therefore, Wyclif concludes, "the properties of universals are everywhere to be explained in a realist sense."[32]

The bond between the word (spoken or written) and reality that emerges first in Wyclif's *Logica* and later in *De universalibus* led him ineluctably to conclusions in several other areas which sooner or later met with heated contention. One of the initial battles he had to face in defense of his theory of the "real word" concerned the status of language in the Bible. He eventually set forth his thoughts on divine writing between 1377 and 1380 when he composed *De veritate sacrae scripturae*. But he surely had taken up the subject about six years earlier when he incepted for the doctorate in theology at Oxford between 1372 and 1373 and lectured on the *Sententiae* of Peter Lombard and on the Bible in fulfillment of the requirements for the degree. His notions about the language of Scripture did not go unnoticed, to say the least.

[30] *De universalibus* 2.56–57.
[31] *De universalibus* 2.57.
[32] *De universalibus* 2.58.

John Kenningham, an East Anglian Carmelite who was master of theology in the school of his Order at Oxford, took Wyclif to task on the subject of the "presence" (*praesencia*) of the word and of the Biblical text. Stemming from the *Logica* as well as the *De universalibus*, Wyclif's position always assumes that existing things (language included) are constituted in their intelligible species, which, as an aspect of the uncreated intellect of God, has neither past nor future but only an eternal "present." As the divine word, the literal text of Scripture is the material form of an eternal exemplar and therefore is true in every part. Kenningham, a shrewd—and patient—critic of this metaphysics of presence, launched his attack on several fronts. First of all, he contested Wyclif's notion of "present" as inconsistent and imprecise. *Praesens*, for Kenningham, could mean something understood in the mind or actually existing outside of it at a specific moment: he says that "presence . . . is called that which is understood clearly and immediately, not abstract but intuitive cognition. . . . The present is called what exists now, in the time of the present [*in tempore praesenti*]."[33] Wyclif does not object to any of these points; they are simply tertiary to the central matter of the debate. His Platonism shines through as he insists that real existence is the effect of an eternal exemplar informing—in the most basic sense of the word—things with being and meaning: their presence in the mind or in the hand is simultaneous with their existence in God. Kenningham acknowledges the position, but with surgical precision draws a distinction between what is present to God as understood by him and as actually existing in him. Wyclif objects summarily, resorting to sarcasm for want of an adequate response: "More than that does the Doctor of Presence distinguish—conceding that a thing is present to God, and yet does not exist. But in fact, neither grammar, logic, nor physics can grasp that interpretation."[34]

If Kenningham suggested what language cannot apprehend, it is not because he has "distinguished" his own ignorance. The bolder *doctor de praesenti* is no secret in this debate. Concerning the status of language in Holy Scripture, Wyclif's theory of being controls his argument fully. At the outset he insists that since God's word is present to him, the literal sense of Scripture is true in every part, and furthermore, it is eternal. On the other hand, Kenningham, recalling that written and spoken words are invented and transcribed by people, poses the unavoidable question of how a text can exist prior to its author. But

---

[33] Wyclif, *Fasciculi Zizaniorum*, p. 11. See Robson, *Wyclif and the Oxford Schools*, pp. 161–70.

[34] *Fasciculi Zizaniorum*, p. 465.

Wyclif has the answer: if truth, he argues, is the adequation of a thing and its divine exemplar, God's *verbum* and the *verba* read by individuals are interchangeable, and what is more, they are indestructible. Since the words of the Bible have a natural origin in God, they are not subject to time. But Kenningham does not let this equivalence between the sign and timelessness pass so easily. If time is a specific point, a unique occurrence at a single moment, then Wyclif cannot speak of it as something that has *ampliatio*, "amplification" or "extension," as do the signs of language. Indeed, Kenningham continues, the postulation of an "extension of time" is contradictory; it is "much less an extension than a confusion of terms."[35] For "the whole strength of such an expression exists in signs"; Wyclif has "amplified the signification of the word 'is'; [but] time does not expand beyond. . . . Therefore only the sign, with respect to signification, receives such expansion, and so my Master injures himself when he vituperates against the sign doctors."[36]

The last remark could stand as the *terminus ad quem* of the debate: how could Wyclif simultaneously ridicule the *doctores signorum* and yet turn around to reduce time to a mere term? Still, his insistence on the "fullness" of significance in the letter of Scripture was exposed on even more obvious grounds, and Kenningham pointed them out. What, for instance, is to be made of the radically inconsistent and contradictory statements in the Bible itself? A fundamentalist of the letter, says Wyclif's opponent, will find his hands tied before many such comments—for instance, the statement from the prophet Amos: "I am no prophet."[37] Metaphysical realism of the sort defended by Wyclif will have difficulty with such a "rhetorical" and "artificial" use of terms.

BIBLICAL AUTONOMY

But the lessons of the debate—such as they were—after 1373 had only minimal impact on the version of Augustinian Neoplatonism that surfaces again when Wyclif turned, a few years later, to writing *De veritate sacrae scripturae*. No book is quoted with greater frequency in this treatise than Augustine's *De doctrina Christiana*. While Augustine begins his text by separating the timelessness and immateriality of the divine *verbum* from the temporal limitations of the written word in the Bible, he advises strongly that readers will have access to the mysteries of Scripture if they become skilled at studying the similitudes, analo-

[35] Ibid., pp. 26–27.
[36] Ibid., pp. 64.
[37] Ibid., pp. 458–59.

gies, and symmetries between the two modes of language. The advice
was not misspent on Wyclif: in his hands, the gap between what God
originally spoke and what people read on the page remains insuper-
able only to the unregenerate heart. Interpreters of God's word, he says
at the outset of his treatise (with an assist from Augustine), should
"imitate the authors of Holy Writ as their humble disciples"; readers
should not simply appeal to their "authority," but "explain their plain
speech."[38] If their "logic" and "eloquence" cannot be imitated, their
simple utterance can, and it should guide our speech in many areas,
not just in explaining the Bible; for "the form of utterance in Scripture
is the exemplar of every other mode of probable speaking."[39] The
disciplines of the trivium, such as grammar, are not quite sufficient for
grasping the fullness of the divine utterance because the Bible has its
own "new grammar and new logic."[40] The meaning of that language,
which is *una racio*, was not written by Christ and the saints, except "in
the book of the heart, when it is without sin."[41] The sense of the letter
is all important for Wyclif; he by no means dissolves it into immateriality, but emphasizes its palpability, its status as a *tabula cordis*. For this
reason he goes on to say that the authority of Sacred Scripture consists
in the "verbal, literal sense," in the *forma verborum* and *modus loquendi*,
"the form of its words" and "mode of speaking."[42] And the closest he
comes to discussing its special "logic" is the remark that Scripture itself
teaches its own logic. For example, when Christ speaks against taking
oaths, he advises us to say, "est est, non non."[43] This is the logic, says
Wyclif, of verbal communication that can effectively oppose the "false
duplicity" of those who use human logic too cleverly; it drives straight
"to the ultimate end without the tumultuous ambiguities" such as we
find at Oxford University, where one logical system replaces another
"every twenty years."[44]

The no-nonsense pragmatism of Wyclif's comments on the study of
the Bible are oddly mixed at times with an idealism of almost mystical
proportions. Scripture obeys, he says, a "celestial logic" (*celestem logi-
cam*); it never errs; rather, human interpretation is the cause of mis-

[38] *De veritate sacrae scripturae* 1:1.4. Wyclif's most condensed explanation of his theory
of the Bible is found in *Trialogus* 3.31.238–43. See Smalley, "The Bible and Eternity," pp.
73–89; Leff, *Heresy* 2:511–16; Kenny, *Wyclif*, pp. 56–67; Keen, "Wyclif, the Bible, and
Transubstantiation," pp. 1–16.

[39] *De veritate* 1:1.6.

[40] *De veritate* 1:3.41–42.

[41] *De veritate* 1:3.44.

[42] *De veritate* 1:3.52.

[43] *De veritate* 1:3.53; Matt. 5.37.

[44] *De veritate* 1:3.54.

takes.[45] A "similitude" obviously "made up" (*ficta*) in the Bible is not to be taken literally, but still it can "signify the truth mystically"; in fact, the pages of Scripture contain "many fictions and yet they are true"; and finally even the parables obey the law of celestial logic: "the parabolic sense is literal and authentic."[46] The quasi mysticism of these statements is hardly unique to Wyclif in the later fourteenth century, though he gives it extraordinary emphasis by combining it with the realism of the letter and text of Scripture.[47]

For instance, it accounts for the belief that meaning streams down from on high touching every book, chapter, and verse of the *sacra pagina*: "If a part of Scripture is true, then every imperative statement, syllable, and letter must be true."[48] As the exemplar of meaning present in God informs this totalization of the text, the pragmatic realism of some of his remarks may seem less incongruent. For his sense of the seamlessness of the whole, dictated as it is by his metaphysical conviction in the priority of the universal, is yet another manifestation of the unity of being. And as he had earlier described the "five steps" of the philosophical universal in the *De universalibus* (ch. 2), here in the *De veritate* he delineates in vertical perfection the "five steps" ("quinque gradus") of the Bible descending from on high: first is the "book of life" mentioned in Apocalypse 20.12—the celestial text existing in a visionary realm; second is the "truths written in the book of life according to their intelligible being"; third is the truths for believing written in the book of life according to their actual "existence or effect"; fourth is the truth "as inscribed in the book of natural man as the soul"; and fifth is the book composed of "codexes, vocal expressions, or other artificial means, which are the signs of remembering prior truth."[49]

While the most immediate source for the *quinque gradus* of the Bible is the descent of being in *De universalibus*, it is appropriate to note that Wyclif's vision of the book also participates in a much wider medieval context. The idea, for example, that sacred things exist in vertical structures reaching to the heavens is something of a commonplace cultural form by this point in the middle ages. It is an informing principle of what may be called the "mythology" of sacred space manifested, for instance, in the intricate organizational motifs of sacred

[45] *De veritate* 1:3.58, 59.

[46] *De veritate* 1:4.66, 75, 83.

[47] Smalley, "The Bible and Eternity," p. 80: "Wyclif . . . in his own mind connected his realist metaphysics with Scripture"; and his inspiration was the Neoplatonism of Plotinus, as exemplified by the metaphor of the Bible as "mirror" of eternal truth.

[48] *De veritate* 1:4.86.

[49] *De veritate* 1:6.108–109.

art and architecture.[50] Wyclif was not uncritical of such forms, as we
learn from his qualifications about the mystical hierarchies of the
pseudo-Dionysius, and from his reservations about the use of certain
images in religious ritual.[51] And yet his own notion of the Bible as a
sacred form descending in five steps from a celestial origin conserves
the familiar medieval association of the sacred with the vertical. He
would have little appreciation, presumably, for the imitation of bejeweled reliquaries or Gothic facades on the covers of holy books; but his
own sense of the holiness of inscription in the Bible is reminiscent of
"the sacred aspect to letters" apparent in a variety of forms during his
time.[52] Here the difference and artificiality of writing are overcome by
comprehending it as a form subsequent to speaking on the "stairway"
descending from above, and thus a mythologized view of sacred things
intersects momentarily with the apparently distant pursuits of *grammatica* and *dialectica*.

We have seen in the *Logica* that, notwithstanding remarks on the
artificiality of signs, Wyclif locates "natural" properties in them whenever he insists on the "priority of origin" for signification. In chapter
6 of *De veritate*, the "fifth step" of the Bible, which belongs to his
category of *artificialia*, becomes the occasion for him to rail once more
against the vacancy of "the sign," but this time he identifies it with
"writing." The modern generation of "sign seekers," he protests, looks
in vain in Sacred Scripture, because the "writing" they seek is no more
than the "line of the hand in chiromancy or the figure of punctuation
in geomancy—indeed, no more than the trace of the comb upon wool."
However, the faithful know better. They are "led as if by the hand to
a knowledge of celestial scripture."[53] It is "aggregated," he notes later
in chapter 9, "from codex and sense or from the sacred *sentencia*." It
composes a "mental understanding" that is "a truer writing than the
letter on the manuscript page"; inscription is "not scripture, unless it
is clothed in such understanding, nor is the writing of the mind sacred,
unless it too is from objective writing . . . for that is first sacred in
which all Catholics communicate."[54]

[50] Explored in my study, *The Idea of the Book*, chs. 2–3.

[51] For his critique of the pseudo-Dionysius, see *De ecclesia* 15.349, and Luscombe,
"Wyclif and Hierarchy," pp. 233–44.

[52] Clanchy, *From Memory to Written Record*, and Stock, *Implications of Literacy*, discuss
illustrations of sacred books prior to the fourteenth century. The quotation is from a
unique study of sacred letters in the age of Wyclif by Aston, *Lollards and Reformers*, p.
108.

[53] *De veritate* 1:6.114–15.

[54] *De veritate* 1:9.189.

From remarks such as these, it is apparent that Wyclif is not dena-
turing voice and writing, nor is he valuing only their ideal, transcendent counterparts. To the contrary, his commentary on the fifth step is
that, while it can signify various things, the "artificial" *codex* and
lineacio signify "personally and concretely . . . the *sensum dei.*" "In this
way," he argues, "I understand Sacred Scripture as perceived by the
senses."[55] For this is the understanding that Christ himself took for
granted when he said: "The scripture cannot be discarded, which the
father sanctified and sent into the world." And furthermore, Wyclif
adds, as Christ was "formed and made" *sanctus humanitus* (*sic*), so he
was *illum librum* which God the father sent into the world; "that book
cannot be discarded, since divinity and humanity are joined indissol-
ubly in that same person."[56] *Copulantur*, the verb joining subject and
predicate in that sentence, foregrounds Wyclif's point: as the person of
Christ does not simply represent but "is" *deitas*, so also voice and
writing are not shadowy appearances; they are the "fleshed" *persona*
of Christ; he is "literalized" in word and text which Wyclif receives
personaliter et concretive. Thus he does not speak metaphorically but—in
his use of the term—"really" when he says, "the whole body of the
Bible . . . is one perfect word."[57] In the same way, he declares—in a
later work—that "the whole of the created world is a natural book [*liber
naturalis*], saying to us how we must love our God and neighbor."[58]

The Immediacy of the Letter

Because of the personal nature of the encounter with the text that
Wyclif recommends, he does not propound a doctrine of interpretation
in which readers are free to understand passages in any way they wish.
Everyone, he exhorts, should be a student of Scripture; but the principle that "scripture alone" (*sola scriptura*) is all that is necessary, such as
it became in the renaissance, appears only vaguely, if at all, in his
discussions.[59] Although the commonplace designation of Wyclif as "the
morning star of the Reformation" applies in some respects, it is not
quite appropriate to the author of *De veritate sacrae scripturae.* As ap-

---

[55] *De veritate* 1:6.109.

[56] Ibid. Cf. John 10.35.

[57] *De veritate* 1:12.268 (further discussion of this point to follow in Section II). Cf.
Aston, "Wyclif and the Vernacular," pp. 314–15.

[58] *De officio regis* 12.163. He goes on to say (p. 164) that this *sentencia* "is written in
man, who is a microcosm."

[59] Leff, *Heresy* 2:511: "There was too much of the scholastic in Wyclif to dispense with
the impedimenta and the authorities of a millennium"; cf. pp. 512–14, 523.

parent in several passages, he advises that every person should be a *theologos*, which is to say, a learned reader who knows what commentaries of the *auctores* to refer to for accurate understanding.[60] He disdains extravagant glosses compiled by the ecclesiastical institution, especially those of the recent past; indeed he says that Scripture should never be confused with interpretation, which is merely its "herald or servant."[61] While he does not banish the traditional levels of reading (allegorical, tropological, and anagogical), neither does he put much faith in them because they are removed from the literal sense. He prefers the "immediacy" of the letter to the "mediated" meaning of the other three senses. The "literal sense" alone is the ordinary "catholic sense," he insists, because it is "immediately drawn out of scripture"; moreover, the other three senses too "are literal" if they are "immediately" derived.[62]

Far from abandoning readers to arbitrary responses, Wyclif's theory is single-minded and highly controlled. *Sola scriptura* for him is a fundamentalist doctrine in which every part of the book has the same absolute authority; for the truth of Scripture, he says (repeating a formula from the *Logica*), is the "adequation of the thing and the divine intellect."[63] That truth will make a "personal and concrete" impact through the "flesh" of the word, which is the *corpus biblie*. Such a theory is certainly individual and private, but it does not hold out to readers the freedom of response to a script recognized as a thin, artificial appearance. Quite the reverse is the case: "from the voice and sense" of the text the "catholic inscription" is written on the soul; that is "scriptura"; if it "is inscribed in a sacred mind, then that scripture is sacred"; but if "it is the utterance of a sinner, scripture is false."[64] Rather than sanctioning the relativity of interpretation, Wyclif's theory of the text depends profoundly on the conditions of reception, and they are prepared by the moral state of the reader. Meaning cannot be discovered by someone wandering around in sin; it preexists the language

[60] E.g., *De veritate* 1:15.378.

[61] *De veritate* 1:15.386.

[62] *De veritate* 1:6.123; he adds: "But if they are mediately derived, then the allegorical, tropological or anagogical senses are not literal" (pp. 123–24). See Evans, "Wyclif on Literal and Metaphorical," pp. 259–66, for the literal status of figurative language in Wyclif's commentary.

[63] *De veritate* 1:15.392. Evans, "Wyclif on Literal and Metaphorical," p. 266: the divine intention "modifies the rules of ordinary usage and makes the figurative literal." Leff, "The Place of Metaphysics in Wyclif's Theology," p. 224: "The truth of the Bible was . . . metaphysical. . . . It represented an ever-present state of reality, eternally true in God. . . . Wyclif accordingly reinforced the self-sufficiency of Scripture."

[64] *De veritate* 1:12.287.

of the text which ultimately enacts it as the catholic writing in the *tabula cordis*—but only for the pure of heart. The same text read by a sinner has no significance; it is artificial.

To a conservative thinker like Wyclif, a reception theory of reading is anything but arbitrary. From his point of view, such an objection would be more appropriately launched against the extravagant glosses of certain Biblical commentators. For him Scripture is the *liber vitae* spoken in the beginning by God, inscribed as the intelligible species in his mind, recorded in human souls, and present as the literal sense of the text. Reading, therefore, was not a process of exploring the possibilities of signification, but of rediscovering what was already written. Some people could never recover it, so long as they remained in sin; but those in grace possessed it from the start, since the book of the soul and the visionary inscription of God were synonymous in the letter. The autonomy of such a textuality will be self-evident, to the extent that meaning is constituted as the form of the book, totalized and contained within it. But Wyclif's challenge to the authority of the institution of conventional interpretation is perhaps matched only by his more subtle presumption of authority in the literal sense. It is not a casual appreciation of the spirit of grace shining remotely through the veil of words, such as we find in some versions of fourteenth-century mysticism. The claim to authority of Wyclif's *sola scriptura* is nothing less than tyrannical: it is the self-sufficient and autonomous embodiment of the divine will. In this theory of the word, "spiritual" is not essentially separated from "real." But such an autonomy goes hand-in-hand with an authority that may be hardly less monolithic than the institutional forms Wyclif spent much of this time attacking.[65] For the person who actually possesses the grace necessary to receive the correct reading is, finally, unknown—or what amounts to the same thing—known only to God. And in this sense, the power ordinarily attributed to God is assimilated to the book as real object. All-knowing and yet unknowable *in esse*, this vantage of power is established by its own unimpeachable guarantee. Wyclif, perhaps, knew not how close he was in this theory to a totalitarianism of the word when he situated the absolute authority of the Bible in "the form of its words and mode of speaking."

---

[65] On the "determinism" implied by this theory of the text, see Kenny, "Realism and Determinism in the Early Wyclif," pp. 165–77, and Leff, "The Place of Metaphysics in Wyclif's Theology," pp. 217–32.

Section II
THE RULE OF THE BOOK

Just as a pope gives empire to a king, so also does
an earthly king make his bishop pope.
—Wyclif, *De officio regis*

INTRODUCTION

It has come to the fore in scholarship recently that Wyclif's political project, specifically his critique of authority in church and state, took an irreversible turn when he encouraged using vernacular English for discussing doctrinal issues traditionally reserved for Latin alone. By means of this daring new venture, says one commentator, "Wyclif contributed to the vernacular breaching of *arcana eucharistie*."[66] His attacks on similarly sensitive doctrines created the most radical departure in the English church in this century: the Lollard movement would have been the first successful heresy before Protestantism, if it had not ended abruptly in the early fifteenth century. But Wyclif was a key player in the "premature reformation" of his time.[67]

That the reforms of the Wycliffite movement and Lollardy can be construed in terms of an opposition between English and Latin deserves more attention than it has received. Surely there is much to be said for the shift in the structure of power encouraged by the growth of a genuine *literacy* in the English vernacular, since it was, needless to say, gaining provocative momentum from other quarters, notably politics and poetry. Furthermore, it would appear that the historical moment of Wycliffite reform bears witness to the opinion that literacy conserves a source of power all its own, and that it may well be far more consequential to change in history than orality. We need only look for further illustration in subsequent centuries when the reformation in England was accomplished in fact—well after the new technology of literacy, movable type, was already securely in place. This paradigm for cultural change has many supporters. But I have been arguing in a different direction, to suggest that the notion of a sudden "epistemic break," like the theory of the "great divide" between orality and literacy, leaves too many questions unanswered. With respect to the fourteenth century, I am skeptical of equating Wyclif's religious reform with a new source of power in "vernacular literacy." My sense is that Wyclif's effectiveness, such as it was, cannot be explained by

[66] Aston, "Wyclif and the Vernacular," p. 328.

[67] Hudson, *The Premature Reformation*. Cf. Aston, *Lollards and Reformers*; Kenny, ed., *Wyclif in His Times*; Leff, *Heresy*.

the assumption that "literacy is power."[68] A subtler combination of factors is at hand in his use of language.

Part of the problem stems from the fact that scholarship has tended to think of Wyclif's Latin work as belonging on the "literate" or "textual" side of the fence, whereas his vernacular initiative or impetus remains on the "oral" side. This binarism, I submit, is based on an illusion. For many aspects of Wyclif's reformulation of topics from the textual tradition of Latin appeal directly to models of language that are oral. And, moreover, his influence on the vernacular was clearly made in the interests of inspiring ongoing work in written English. In short, it is time to look more carefully at the status of voice and writing in Wyclif's reformism. In the remainder of this chapter I suggest that the resource of power in Wyclif's project arises from neither the strength of voice nor the power of the written word per se, but rather from the capacity of speech to disguise itself in the form of writing. Clearly he sought reform in both Latin and English. Which language was the more successful is finally beside the point. The strength of assertion is not generic. It consists in the act of displacement that occurs when writing mimes the properties of speaking. The mimesis of language was already firmly in place for Wyclif in the customs of producing the written word on the manuscript page. But it was also fortified when Wyclif set forth his critique against keystones of doctrine in the English church by appeal to ideals of language and society which derive from oral tradition.

We may begin by reconsidering Wyclif's search for the "pure form" or "original version" of religious principles or practices in the primitive church—both their prefiguration in the Old Testament and their historical existence during the first few centuries after Christ. He is interested, to be sure, in the "fundamental" forms of the faith, those which existed putatively in *illo tempore*, before chance and history obscured them. But in view of the fact that such a frame of reference is to a spiritual, prelinguistic order and to a historical period before records and books, it is appropriate to note that his Christian fundamentalism rests on an ideal of language both mental and oral, whereas writing is relegated to the farther shore of the confusions wrought by "history."

DOMINION

From about 1376 when he finished *De civili dominio* until his death, Wyclif was preoccupied with arguing against the wealth and corruption of the church and in favor of evangelical poverty, illustrated by

---

[68] See ch. 1 above for consideration of this assumption in the the work of Pattison, Street, Lévi-Strauss, Goody, Stock, Clanchy, McKitterick et al.

the life of Christ and the apostles as the worthy exemplars for all
ecclesiastics. But the moral basis of his propositions competes with, if
it is not overcome by, his determination to subvert customary foundations of dominion and particularly to disprove the need for the papacy.[69] In *De civili dominio* the subject of discussion is the relation of
iusticia ("justice") to *dominium* ("dominion," "lordship"); yet it is apparent throughout that Wyclif is building a case for determining who may
claim the right to rule. At the outset he states that justice is a *donum
dei* ("gift of God") which cannot be possessed by anyone in sin. On the
other hand, those who have such gifts of grace, possess God's *bona*
("goods"); without them, a ruler has no claim to power: "the foundation of dominion . . . is justice."[70] And dominion can only come from God:
"No creature can be a lord of someone unless God endowed him."[71]
The argument, in its bare outline, is unexceptional in medieval political
theory; in fact, Wyclif had the gist of it from Richard FitzRalph. But its
explanation by Wyclif takes a unique turn insofar as the ground of
dominion involves the ultimate inscrutability of God's Word, and we
can only know it from its revealed form in writing.

Therefore, it is only through God's special communications in "grace"
that the right of rule is conferred for civil dominion.[72] The "just person"
(*iustus*) possesses this right because he or she lives in communication
with God through charity. However, since that virtue is the privilege
of those who are predestined to be saved, the legitimate claim to rule
is finally something known only to God.[73] For instance, God might
allow an evil leader to rule tyrannically as a means of persecuting
sinners and testing the righteous; furthermore, such a government, in
spite of its oppression, could still illustrate a political principle of no
little significance for Wyclif—the total autonomy of all lay dominion.[74]
The rule of a sinner, consequently, might be unfounded, but it could
nonetheless serve the ends of God.[75] We may not know what they are
in each instance, but we can know the general principles of right rule
since they are set forth in the Gospel, which is the exemplar of "the
whole body of human law" manifested in the spoken words of Jesus
and in the life of his Word during his ministry.[76] As a result of this

[69] See McFarlane, *John Wycliffe*, pp. 59 ff.; Wilks, "Predestination, Property and Power,"
pp. 220–36; Leff, *Heresy* 2:546–48; Kenny, *Wyclif*, pp. 42–55.
[70] *De civili dominio* 1:1.6.
[71] *De civili* 1:6.39.
[72] *De civili* 1:2.15.
[73] *De civili* 1:7.47.
[74] *De civili* 1:6.43–44.
[75] *De civili* 1:3.24.
[76] *De civili* 1:20.139.

argument, Wyclif is led eventually to the conclusion in another work, *De potestate papae*, that true dominion not only comes from Christ but also that even a virtuous "layman can be pope."[77]

Thus tracing his ideal of Christian dominion to the primitive church and to its foundation in what Jesus actually said to Peter and his disciples, Wyclif writes off virtually in one fell swoop the entire tradition of *auctoritates* which had validated the centrality of the pope to Christian society. Using the textual procedures of exegetical authorities against themselves, Wyclif notes sharply that there is no mention of *papa* in the entire Bible.[78] He does not deny that a commission was given to Peter when Christ said, "I give to you the keys of the kingdom of heaven" (Matt. 16.19), but those words, in Wyclif's opinion, cannot be taken as a Scriptural foundation for the papal curia; the power of the keys was given only to Peter "in the person of the priesthood of the church"; the spoken words of Christ give no special privilege to the Roman pontiff for the salvation of souls.[79] Similarly, Peter showed great courage and boldness in walking on the sea (Matt. 14.29), yet this suspension in the laws of nature is no sign of special privileges conferred by God on the "vicar of Peter."[80] Such a conclusion, he implies, is mere interpretation; indeed, the papacy has no foundation whatsoever in any words spoken by Christ or other Biblical figures. It was created—he recalls sardonically—when Constantine was blessed with empire by his bishop, only to turn around and make that bishop head of the entire church. It evolves, in other words, from a willful and arbitrary decree by a secular ruler, and most certainly not from divine ordinance.[81] But Wyclif goes on to emphasize that the illegitimacy of the popes, cardinals, and other members of the ecclesiastical hierarchy is witnessed by even more obvious factors—namely, their vulgar, worldly institutions and habits, which constitute an egregious betrayal of Christ: the papacy is "an abomination of desolation standing in a holy place."[82]

De potestate papae, probably one of Wyclif's most well-organized Latin treatises, asserts his bitterest criticism yet in identifying the church as Anti-Christ with the pope at its head. For him Anti-Christ quite literally means opposition to Christ: as he says summarily, "he who is not of Christ, is of Anti-Christ."[83] His category includes not only heretics—the customary members of Satan's body—but all those persons

[77] *De potestate papae* 11.272.
[78] *De potestate* 7.165.
[79] *De potestate* 5.97, 7.135.
[80] *De potestate* 7.142.
[81] *De officio* 6.146. See also *De potestate* 9.215.
[82] *De potestate* 12.321.
[83] *De potestate* 9.217.

who in any way live in imitation of the wealth and lure of worldly institutions. The primary defect of the faith, he insists, is demonstrated in the sin of the first parents in Eden, "concupiscence of the eyes" (*concupiscentia oculorum*).[84] But the sins of priests and bishops go far beyond such illicit desire: they are "priests of Caesar" (*sacerdotes Cesarei*) who imitate the vainglory and power-grabbing vices of the world. The sins of Anti-Christ, Wyclif continues, are nowhere more in evidence than among ecclesiastics "today in England," where they are "signified in the forehead sign of the beast." Because they do homage to Rome (or Avignon), these *sacerdotes Cesarei* are heretics—"really Anti-Christs."[85]

Wyclif does not foreground his own semiology in this denunciation, perhaps because it was self-evident to him. But we cannot fail to note his association of the sins of the eye with paganism (a very old typology going back to the "blindness" of the "synagogue"), and both of these in turn with the ostentatious artificiality of "signs" worn by the clergy. That the deformity of the sign is linked to the distortion of "writing," as opposed to the "voice" of Christ, becomes apparent when he turns typically medieval etymological analysis against itself: the origin of Anti-Christ, he says, must be from the clergy. Lucifer, once closest to God, is *magnus Antichristus*; the same is true of Judas Iscariot and the whole generation proceeding from Cain. They fall within the category established by Christ himself when he said: "For many will come in my name, saying, I am Christ. And they will seduce many" (Matt. 24.5). These people, Wyclif concludes, were later named by Christ *pseudochristos*, "from which it is apparent that they arise from the clergy."[86] The spoken word of Jesus has demonstrable priority here against the false etymologies of exegesis: the word *papa*, be it recalled, originates from the books of the ecclesiastics, whereas only God himself can make a pope through the mystery of grace.[87]

From one point of view, Wyclif's procedure in sifting through *auctoritates*, both from Scripture and tradition, for textual evidence repeats familiar medieval practice. But his radical deviation from tradition on the subject of the legitimacy of power is not, for him, a matter of pitting his own way of reading exegetical sources against the authorities of the past. It is not, finally, a matter of opinion. His fundamentalism emerges from the larger self-understanding of his project, which validates the authority of reading without ever having to justify it as his own particular account. As we have seen in *De veritate*, he is against

[84] *De civili* 1:2.62.
[85] *De potestate* 9.217, 218.
[86] *De potestate* 6.119.
[87] *De potestate* 8.177.

interpretation in the first place because the words of Scripture proceed from the mystery of the divine "voice" which is synonymous with God's final inscrutability. It is not that Wyclif claims this point of view as his own, but rather that he bypasses the views of others—an enormous amount of exegetical writing—by appealing to what the *sacra pagina* says in itself. For him, the medieval custom of reading *sotto voce* by listening to "the voices of the pages" became something of a hermeneutical principle. He practices a formalism without reserves by assimilating to the text the absolute dominion of the divine will: the pope has no legitimacy because we cannot know who is saved or damned; God grants his power without visible signs; *iusticia* is a divine gift that no one can claim to possess; Christ opposes Anti-Christ just as the voice of the Bible contests the distortions of written exegesis. In each of these conclusions, Wyclif is more than a fundamentalist of religious ideals from the primitive church, in which something like "documentary history," the evidence of inscription per se, has priority. To the contrary, the spoken form of the written has privilege, and it is the foundation of a dominion legitimated in the autonomy of the book as oral object. Its dominion consists—quite literally he would say—in the fact that it is *Vox Dei*, "God's Voice."

MONARCHY

Although scholarship has often explained Wyclif's critique of ecclesiastical authority according to his view of divine revelation, we must confront the fact that the subject of grace alone cannot explain the shift in his later thinking, when he argues for the supreme lay power of the king over the pope. By the time of *De potestate papae*, "royal power" assumes far more prominence than grace in his discussions, prompting some commentators to conclude that Wyclif was moving toward a "second theory of dominion" in which grace was no longer prior.[88] We should note, however, that Wyclif once again bases his apology for royal power on references to the primitive church, and—as before—his appeal is to models which exist in an order untainted by history, the timeless realm of mental language and the oral world of Old and New Testament leaders. The interpretation of his semiology can be easily oversimplified, if we assume one-to-one correspondences between the contemporary fourteenth-century context and Wyclif's "allusions" to Biblical rulers. But if we are prepared to see that Wyclif never abandoned the strategies of terminist logic, as noted earlier, we may con-

---

[88] Wilks, "Predestination, Property and Power," p. 236. Independently, Leff draws the same conclusion in "The Place of Metaphysics in Wyclif's Theology," pp. 228–30.

tinue exploring how his "historical" categories are first and foremost semiological. For he launches his critique against wealth, church, monarchy, and the eucharist ultimately through a theory of dominion based upon the Bible as the language of God. And while the importance of Biblical foundations for his reductions of these doctrines has been well-recognized from his earliest interpreters, what has not been appreciated is that Wyclif does not really shift away from grace and toward some unspecified new "source" for royal power. Grace, for him, was always a means of talking about the mystery of God's voice in human affairs, and in this case he has not changed directions. The Bible is still his foundation, but in his special sense of it as an autonomous whole, as a *modus loquendi* that assumes its own self-sufficiency in the moment of utterance.[89] The dominion Wyclif identifies in the secular order of monarchy is not found like a sign "in" the Bible, but rather is assimilated to it "as a whole," as a self-subsistent oral event.

For instance, when Wyclif addresses corruptions in the English church, his arguments for disendowment of property and authority are obviously motivated by the desire to excoriate indulgences.[90] But, as in his critique of the papacy, his arguments bear the traces of his larger interest in the authority of the Bible beyond its mere inscription. As he disqualified the papacy, so too does he subvert the foundations of the church: both contradict the omnipotence of the divine word. It is perhaps no accident that among Wyclif's many protests, the argument against church endowments is one which we know he made (as he tells us) "in lingwa duplici"—in Latin and in spoken English.[91] The medium in this case was of a piece with the Christian fundamentalism of his appeal to the poverty of the primitive church and the simplicity of its rule.

But such purity is not to be found in the contemporary world. Indeed, priests could be of the devil's party without knowing it, and laypersons could be blessed. This point, from *De eucharistia* (ca. 1379), is the fulcrum of disenfranchising the entire priesthood. In *De officio regis* (completed in 1378) Wyclif makes a similar claim: being a priest offers no certitude of God's approval; intermediaries are not necessary for access to God; even prayer is not essential for salvation.[92] What, he asks finally, is the purpose of the church? In *De civili dominio* he says

---

[89] Cp. Leff, "The Place of Metaphysics in Wyclif's Theology," p. 229, for the view that Wyclif shifts the grounds of dominion away from grace. Wilks, "Predestination, Property and Power," p. 236, traces dominion to Aristotle and Aquinas, noting the role of voice.

[90] E.g., see McFarlane, *John Wycliffe*, pp. 37–57; Leff, *Heresy* 2:516–45; Kenny, *Wyclif*, pp. 68–79.

[91] *De veritate* 1:14.349–50.

[92] *De officio* 6.142.

that its mission is to the saved, and since Christ is the sole source of apostolic nature, ownership and authority assumed by the church have no legitimacy.[93] Property must be forsworn completely, although the use of possessions without ownership is permissible.[94] As he insists elsewhere, private property contradicts utterly Christ's life of poverty.[95] It will be apparent that the meaning of *ecclesia* in these discussions is quite restricted. It is surely not the whole body of the faithful, since their will alone has nothing to do with predestined election; nor does the church consist of the priesthood or the ecclesiastical hierarchy, however much they may avoid sin. According to Wyclif, *ecclesia* most properly refers to "the whole body of those predestined" for salvation, and that is why it is called the *corpus Christi mysticum*.[96] This definition of the church as the elect has nothing to do with the visible form of it in this world. For the true church is "founded on the faith of Christ"; its walls are made of "hope" (*spes*); its roof is "charity" (*caritas*); and it has no "continuing city" (*manentem civitatem*) here on earth.[97]

It is possible to read the extremity of this description of *ecclesia* as a rhetorical stratagem aimed in satire against the stronghold of ecclesiastical worldliness in fourteenth-century England.[98] But his rhetoric also springs from the larger issue of dominion which, as we have seen, can have no implementation in the written or spoken word of the church. In *De officio regis* Wyclif takes up at length the issue of who has the ultimate right to power. It is a treatise that must have confirmed the political patronage he had obviously enjoyed when he entered the service of the Crown in 1371 and when he was protected ten years later on the eve of crisis by John of Gaunt and Joan of Kent, widow of the Black Prince. For the treatise is designed to explain the king's superiority over his kingdom, which in principle includes all humankind, even the church.

With a title disrespectfully reminiscent of ecclesiastical office, Wyclif calls the king "God's vicar" (*dei vicarius*), and he insists—with more satiric bite—that the honor and service one owes to God rightfully belongs to this vicar.[99] To take the charge one step further, it is even sinful to resist serving the king, since all the power of the secular branches of government are ordained by God.[100] And lest anyone think

---

[93] *De civili* 1:39.288, 1:43.375.
[94] *De civili* 3:14.242, 3:21.441.
[95] *De ecclesia* 16.371–72.
[96] *De civili* 1:39.288.
[97] *De civili* 1:39.288–89.
[98] *De civili* 1:39.289 ff.
[99] *De officio* 1.4.
[100] *De officio* 1.7–8.

it spurious to maintain that a secular (rather than religious) head deserves such homage, we are referred to one of the church's most sacred mysteries: as Christ combines two natures, divinity and humanity, so the king is the "image of Christ's divinity" and the priest is "the image of his humanity."[101] Therefore, a priest must be ruled by a king on the authority of both Melchisedech, whose kingship was prior to his priesthood, and of Christ, whose kingship was far more absolute than his priesthood.[102]

It is difficult to define specifically what literary critics would call the "tone" of such readings as these. But we can be sure that Wyclif is torturing hermeneutic convention when he parses the political difference between Christ "the king" and Christ "the priest." In the interests of a truth beyond written authority alone, Wyclif makes a devastating point. And in *De officio regis*, he carries out the consequences of it.[103] With virtually absolute power over his realm, the king as *deitatis Christi* was sovereign over the church, possessing the *potestas* to condemn evil ecclesiastics, disendow the church of its property, and mandate reform in the behavior of the clergy.[104] If need be, he had the right to use churches as fortresses for protecting the kingdom from attack; and similarly he was obliged to protect theology by removing threats to it, even when it came to prohibiting the teaching of civil law.[105] Not only was he sovereign over the whole realm and the visible church, including the pope, but also over those who were elected for salvation while they resided on earth.[106] Nearly all that Wyclif denied to the church in wealth and power he turned around to grant and even praise in the administration of state—so long, of course, as the king ruled in conformity with divine law. For his duty, Wyclif observes with reference to Augustine, is to constrain his people in the service of God, which necessarily involves a ruler in the worldly affairs of wielding power, demanding obedience, and accumulating possessions.[107]

Wyclif's "text" for such broadsides as these is, once more, the spoken words of Jesus—this time on the question of civil obedience: "Render therefore to Caesar the things that are Caesar's" (Matt. 22.21).[108] But Wyclif does not really single out one passage from Scripture as authoritative above all others for the kind of *dominium* and *potestas* which he

---

[101] *De officio* 1.13.
[102] *De officio* 1.14.
[103] Cf. *De officio* 4.66. And see Leff, *Heresy* 2:543–45.
[104] *De officio* 4.68, 5.97, 8.207.
[105] *De officio* 7.185, 188.
[106] *De officio* 6.133.
[107] *De civili* 1:26.188, 189.
[108] *De civili* 1:26.188.

vests in the king. As in his discussions undermining the sovereignty of the papacy, Wyclif's support for royal power has more to do with his theory of the self-sufficient integrity of the *sensus literalis* in general than with particular textual citations or metaphysical tenets.[109] Surely they inform his judgment, as in his proposition for the preexistence of the church or the Bible as universals comprehended in the eternal mind of God. But the dominion he speaks about does not call for a new theory of dominion in which grace is no longer prior. To the contrary, his argument is that "grace" as manifested in the institutions of this world is no longer recognizable. And that is why he approaches the subject of power negatively and satirically. His trump card, as it were, is a firm conviction in a dominion beyond the reach of written tradition and contemporary practice—the grace of God's inscrutable will revealed as the *modus loquendi* and *forma verborum* of the Bible. It is entirely fitting, therefore, that Wyclif ends *De officio regis* with emphasis specifically on a "writing" subsumed completely within the logos of God's creative act and its continuing manifestation in moral behavior: the whole of the created world, as noted earlier, is a *liber naturalis* uttering the love of God, and this "sentence" is *inscribatur* in the "little world" of the individual.

Unlike Ockham, who declared his radical departures in politics under the protection of Ludwig of Bavaria, Wyclif—several decades later—published his challenges to the church and papacy from a far more vulnerable platform. As a professor at Oxford, he was open to censure at any time, though no actions were taken against him until nearly the end of this life. The Crown offered little security, since by 1375 it was anything but stable. Edward III was in his dotage; the Black Prince, having just returned to England, was sick and near death— which came in 1376. Thus weakened in leadership, the order of the realm was in the hands of a council led by John of Gaunt. After a concordat with the papacy was sealed at Bruges, England could not afford to incur the displeasure of Pope Gregory XI over the radical politics of a governmental representative. Gregory, clearly disturbed by the attitudes of Wyclif toward the church, had bulls of censure against him drawn up and ready for execution. But the pope's unexpected death in 1378 and the ensuing confusions of papal election derailed the charges. When Urban VI was elected at Rome and Clement VII at Fondi, the resulting Great Schism of 1378 left the authority of the papacy in shambles and the case against Wyclif was virtually forgot-

---

[109] As argued by Leff, "The Place of Metaphysics in Wyclif's Theology"; Wilks, "Predestination, Property and Power"; and Kenny, "Realism and Determinism in the Early Wyclif" and "The Realism of the *De Universalibus*."

ten. Initially, he threw his support with all of England behind Urban—
primarily because of fear of the French pope; but his fundamental view
of the two rival popes simply confirmed his more general sense of the
modern church as the incarnation of Anti-Christ, in this case rearing
itself as a beast with two heads.

EUCHARIST

His motivations for turning in the next year (1379) to challenging the
traditional doctrine of the eucharist cannot be traced specifically to the
political circumstances of profoundly weakened authority at home and
in Rome. But Wyclif's power had yet to be tested: he had earned a
great deal of respect from the Crown and from curialists abroad; he
had not been silenced before, and the time was opportune for him to
bring to conclusion the force of his philosophical and theological critique. Whether or not he calculated in advance the reaction that would
follow cannot be determined. But when he finally touched this most
sacred mystery, he brought down upon himself after 1381 not only the
ire of Rome but of Oxford as well. His own university spearheaded
the immediate attack against its radical professor, and he had little to
count on this time from political powers in England who had helped
him before. Yet Wyclif did manage to stem the worst of the tide against
him through the good offices of the Duke of Lancaster and Joan of
Kent, who were of some help in securing for him a post in the parish
of Lutterworth where he had to endure the censure of silence from
teaching imposed upon him until the end of his life, which came in
1384. That the eucharist became the target of his attack and the preoccupation of much of his work throughout his remaining years was not
a particularly tendentious move against an institution which had lost
all respect in his eyes. But he was nothing if not rigorous, and the
doctrine of transubstantiation offended his realism—not only his philosophical premises but even more his objection to the obscurity of its
traditional formulation. His objections, as represented in *De eucharistia*,
De apostasia, and *Trialogus*, deserve brief attention here insofar as they
illustrate exceptionally well the convergence of his philosophical commitments with his emphasis on the priority of spoken language.[110]

"Beasts can eat the consecrated host which is the bare sacrament,
and not the body and blood of Christ."[111] With these shameless words,

---

[110] Scholarship centers primarily on realism, as in McFarlane, *John Wycliffe*, pp. 94 ff.;
Leff, *Heresy* 2:549 ff.; Keen, "Wyclif, the Bible, and Transubstantiation," pp. 1–16; Kenny,
Wyclif, pp. 80–90. An exception is Aston's study of the vernacular, "Wyclif and the
Vernacular."

[111] *De eucharistia* 1.11.

Wyclif opens *De eucharistia*, proceeding immediately to attack a fallacy in the orthodox understanding of the "real presence" of Christ during the celebration of the eucharist. To those who may imagine, he continues, that in "breaking the body of Christ" the priest is breaking his "head, neck, arms and other members," we must say that a priest breaks him no more than he does a "ray of sunlight."[112] Wyclif's hyperbole is energized, first of all, by its urbanity, which is particularly cutting since he is writing in Latin. We do not know, unfortunately, what in particular he said about the eucharist in English. But anything at all at this point in ecclesiastical history would have been similarly outrageous, since a mystery of this sort was not discussed by the laity in Latin and surely not in the vernacular. That Wyclif did say something about it, however, is certain, at least on the authority of his remarks in *De eucharistia*: "I elected to tell the lay public in plain speaking that the sacrament figures the body of Christ, and that it is consecrated, worshipped, and eaten for the purpose of remembering and imitating Christ."[113]

The key word in that statement is *figurat*. In Latin or English it amounts to a demythologizing of scholastic theology; for Wyclif seeks to expose the aura of secrecy which had descended upon the words of the priest, hiding and obscuring the real nature of the consecration. Instead, he would offer "in plain English," as it were, an explanation the public could understand, even if it had to be made in Latin. Thus he begins by targeting those scholastic theologians who are responsible for obfuscating the sacrament in a technical argot which neither priest nor populace really comprehends. "In all of England," Wyclif protests, there are not "two priests who know what the sacrament of the altar is." They may be able to administer the office and number the various sacraments, but "they do not know how to distinguish one from another. And when a lay person asks out of simple ignorance whether to believe that the round, white thing . . . is the body of Christ," they are forced into a position of explaining what they do not understand— that it "is *not* Christ's body, but only an accident without a subject."[114] Wyclif's target here, as we might guess, is the argument about the eucharist put forward by Duns Scotus and Ockham. They had argued that the substance of bread and wine was annihilated in the words of transubstantiation, and that act created a new being, the body of Christ now present under the appearance of the accidents. For a thinker who maintains, as Wyclif does, that every *res* is constituted by an *esse*

[112] *De eucharistia* 1.12.
[113] *De eucharistia* 9.305.
[114] *De apostasia* 4.57.

intelligibile eternal in God, the destruction of a substance or essence is simply not possible. For Wyclif, annihilation of the substance of bread and wine could not occur because it would involve the death of a part of the divine intelligence, which would, in turn, involve the destruction of essence in general.

In another context, he cites Aquinas for the opinion that the external forms of bread and wine remain intact as "extensions" of the "universal of quantity"; although prima facie the accidents appeared to be unchanged throughout the "transubstantiation," they received from the act of the priest's words a new "substance" or "being," which is the "essence" of Christ. Thus they ceased to be *panitas* and *vinitas* and became the true presence of Christ. But for Wyclif, this change too was impossible because a substance can never be separated from its accidents, and for the same reason that it cannot be annihilated. The whole physical and spiritual order—as Wyclif saw it—was in the balance if scholastic arguments about the eucharist prevailed. To forestall such an apocalypse, he eventually attacked contemporary eucharistic theories as forms of idolatry because they encouraged the worship of mere signs and accidents as the immanence of divine nature.[115]

Although Wyclif had to repeat current terminology in order to refute explanations of the eucharist, it is always obvious that he has little patience with the technical vocabulary of Latin, and that he would install in its place a "plain style" closer to spoken language—whether it be in English or Latin.[116] We have seen him make such a shift before in discussing dominion, the church, and monarchy. In this case, the terms of understanding the eucharist (*transubstanciacio, impanatio, quidditas*, etc.) are mere "novelties," as he called them, without any foundation in the spoken words of Jesus in the Gospel.[117] Once again, the confusions in contemporary thinking are associated with a writing that

[115] *De eucharistia* 1.14 and *De apostasia* 10.129. His opposition to "images" is related to his repudiation of signs. The subject has not been studied in relation to the binarism of voice and writing in his work. On iconomachy in Lollardy, see Aston, "Lollards and Images."

[116] Wyclif's typical phrase is *planum locucionem* ("plain speaking"), e.g., *De veritate* 1:1.4. NB he does not refer to *plana scriptio* ("plain writing"), nor do his commentators on this point, e.g., Hargreaves, "Wyclif's Prose"; Auksi, "Wyclif's Sermons and the Plain Style"; and Aston, "Wyclif and the Vernacular."

[117] E.g., *De eucharistia* 8.229: "Because the law of scripture revealed to us enough about the eucharist for belief, it is obvious that it is presumptuous stupidity to add novelties to its foundation." Cf. *Trialogus*, p. 350. NB Aston, "Wyclif and the Vernacular," p. 314: Wyclif assumed a "relationship between plain speaking—which could include scripture—and the faculty of common sense that controlled the belief of ordinary people."

has blurred and hidden what should be plain for all to hear at Mass or in the lecture room.

For Wyclif the real presence was never in doubt, in the same way as the "literal sense" of Scripture was the "mode of God's speaking." Accordingly, the notion that the bread and wine of the eucharist are annihilated offended not only his philosophical realism but even more so his sense of the purity of the spoken word. These two issues are often interwoven in his commentary, as when he identifies distortions of the eucharist with deformations of speech: "Let us not rest," he complains, "with the stuttering of the blasphemer, for whom there is whiteness without something white, the figure without something figured and quantity without how much."[118] The host signifies the whiteness of bread;[119] it does not disappear into a mere "accident," for no accident can exist apart from its essence. And therefore to argue that a change in essence occurs at the consecration means that the host must take on the actual form and behavior of a person, or that Christ's blood itself would spill from the altar if the chalice of the eucharist were accidentally knocked over during the Mass.[120]

What, then, is the nature of the "change" as Wyclif saw it? In *De eucharistia* he mentions two sources, one from Scripture, the other from tradition. Citing Matthew (26.26), "this is my body," Wyclif argues that the reference is to the bread on the altar as the host, not as the physical body of Christ. Second, he documents his position in the arguments of Berengarius, who in the eleventh century opposed orthodox opinions which held that through the consecration the body and blood of Christ were conveyed "sensibly" (*sensualiter*) onto the altar as the bread and wine. Wyclif opposes a similar animism in his own day and regrets how Berengarius was forced to recant his teachings at the council of Rome in 1059.[121] In truth, Berengarius was pointing in the right direction: the eucharistic elements placed on the altar before the consecration retain their substantial identity after it.[122] He seems to see Berengarius as the representative of a simpler moment in the history of the eucharist, one closer to the spoken words recorded by Matthew; for Wyclif ultimately grounds his own position on this sacrament in the practices of the primitive church.

And, therefore, his appeal to Jesus as *verbum Dei* has special bearing on his argument: the eucharist has two natures in the same way as

---

[118] *De apostasia* 16.230.

[119] *De eucharistia* 7.202. Cf. *Trialogus* 4.2.249.

[120] *De apostasia* 14.185–86 and *De eucharistia* 1.24.

[121] *De eucharistia* 2.34 (and cf. 2.230, 4.98). For Berengarius on the eucharist, see Stock, *The Implications of Literacy*, pp. 275–77.

[122] *De eucharistia* 2.32.

Christ himself combines divinity and humanity. There really is no "transubstantiation" in essence, just as the words of the priest do not change the host into the presence of Jesus: the bread retains its own essence. However, the body of Christ also exists simultaneously in the same "place or form as the bread."[123] It is not a question of the "accident" of one element combining with the "substance" of another, but of appreciating how Jesus is both man and divine "word": thus the eucharist is two things simultaneously, in the same way that the words of conventional language can have "equivocal" signification. "Christ is two substances, namely earthly and divine, so this sacrament is, by virtue of its equivocation, the sensible body of bread, which is created from the earth, and the body of Christ which the word begot in Mary."[124]

Unlike Aquinas, Wyclif does not regard the consecrating words of the eucharist as a repetition of the divine speech act responsible for the Incarnation. That moment exists in *illo tempore*, in the mystery of God's language and in the purity of Gabriel's oral utterance to Mary. The words of the priest at the altar, on the other hand, are like the writing of the church, necessarily equivocal: the terms *corpus* and *verbum*, he argues, are merely words; *panis* is called *corpus Christi* only "tropically according to the signifying [word] or figure."[125] This is not to say that as tropes or figures of speech, the words of the consecration are arbitrary, fictitious, or void. At the instant of the consecrating words, *panis* loses nothing as bread, nor does *corpus Christi* become a mere fiction of the real presence. To the contrary, the words of the priest refer to both substances really, but we must appreciate the difference between "the mode of being the sign of Christ's body and the other mode of being truly and really . . . the body of Christ."[126] The difference here is not between appearance and reality, but between the host as a sign of the natural Christ (which can only be seen in heaven) and the sign of his spiritual presence. Realizing the dual nature of the eucharist, therefore, should be no more difficult—but no less either—than appreciating that Jesus is of humankind and "of the word begot in Mary."

That the host *figures*, rather than *is*, the body of Christ drastically challenged the conception of the priest's role in the liturgy of the eucharist. Without attempting to lessen the importance of the priest,

[123] *De apostasia* 16.210.

[124] *De apostasia* 9.106. Cf. Mueller on the English "Wycliffite" sermons (*The Native Tongue*, pp. 43–45): the "oral" prose style of these sermons reflects "Wyclif's Christocentric and communicative sense of Scripture."

[125] *De apostasia* 9.106. Cf. Evans, "Wyclif on Literal and Metaphorical," p. 260, on the obedience of "equivocality" to *gramatica scripture* (*sic*).

[126] *De apostasia* 9.117. See also *De eucharistia* 4.109, 5.121.

Wyclif says that "we priests make and bless the consecrated host which is not the body of the Lord but his efficacious sign [*efficax eius signum*]."[127] In several places his arguments are quite technical, but only because he is arguing with professional peers about their own terminology. His aim, however, is to emphasize the plainness and simplicity of the consecrating words, and thus to appreciate the plain speech of Jesus at the Last Supper. That Wyclif explained the "figure" of the host to the laity is perfectly in line with the more sophisticated reach of his theological critique, but even more so than we may be able to realize. For the first time, or very close to it, people were able to hear in their own native tongue a basic fact of their faith explained in a vocabulary as simple and familiar as the terms of any daily meal.[128] But whether in English or Latin, Wyclif's aim was to bridge the gap created by a terminology that he thought had separated terribly the real presence of Christ from the faithful.

The vocabulary of scholasticism, if not Latinity itself, had become a barrier to the wellsprings of faith in the oral language of the primitive church and in the life of the faithful in fourteenth-century England, most of whom knew no Latin. The vernacular was the catalyst for dissolving that barrier. But the force of change did not issue simply from the difference of another tongue.[129] It was challenged by Latin as well when Wyclif showed how the traditional language of religion had hardened into a form no longer able to convey life to the faithful. It was as encrusted and closed to them as writing was to the illiterate. His project, therefore, was hardly to move directly into the vernacular or to detract writing itself. Rather, his criticism associates writtenness with obscurity, secrecy, and lifelessness. If he does not explain this factor explicitly, nonetheless, inscription takes on this signification by virtue of its sharp contrast with oral models of language, ranging from theological mysteries like the Incarnation to the language actually spoken in contemporary England. For vernacularity, too, is finally less a "historical" reference in his arguments than a semiological one, generated for the purpose of purifying the religious values of an apostate church.

It is difficult to estimate the nature of the reaction that Wyclif had to face from his critics. But it must have been severe. In fact, ten years

[127] *De eucharistia* 1.16 (and cf. 2.34).
[128] Mueller, *The Native Tongue*, p. 48: "The Word says all, and that plenum of meaning can be comprehended and articulated in the vernacular for the people." Aston, "Wyclif and the Vernacular," p. 292, says vernacular preaching about the eucharist began about 1380.
[129] Cp. the conclusions of Hudson, "Wyclif and the English Language," p. 90, and Aston, "Wyclif and the Vernacular," p. 305.

later some commentators would look back on the Peasants' Revolt and blame it on Wyclif for spreading heretical religious teachings among the laity.[130] Clearly he had mounted nothing less than a stupefying rebuke of the role of the clergy in the heart of its office. For a priest was no longer one whose words could "call down God from heaven." No one could pretend to such powers. Wyclif's demythologizing criticism was carried out in the name of the absolute sanctity of God and in full recognition of the limitations of human language. That the council charged with investigating his theory of the eucharist saw the whole situation differently probably did not surprise him, for he had obviously stirred up enough attention among his peers in the academy as well as among the residents outside of it that the meeting of the Blackfriars Council in May 1382 was marked by a procession through the streets of London and was attended by both clergy and laity. The vernacular initiative of his teaching had apparently found its mark. As one commentator has observed, "the vernacular . . . was here on trial."[131]

But what was it exactly about the vernacular that was so threatening to the formulation of sacred doctrine in Latin? Was it another version of lay versus clerical prerogatives? Plain as opposed to technical vocabulary? One thing is certain, the openness of understanding occasioned by the use of English exposed pointedly the secrecy of professional language for what it was. The challenge was aimed immediately at the nature of Latin literacy itself; for the vernacular—which already had its own literacy—confronted the older language with a differentiation of no little consequence within the walls of the church and the academy. From their point of view, the writtenness of Latin was synonymous with its oral form: there was no difference, or none of substantial import, between them. But the priority of that bond could no longer be taken for granted when challenges to doctrine were set forth both in written and spoken forms of the vernacular. English engaged Latin literacy with a difference that Latin itself had quite forgotten, the disclosure that the priority of voice was not necessarily given; it could be taken over by the writing of another tongue; it was, therefore, separable from writing and possibly even arbitrary in its preemptive control over what could be taught about sensitive topics. By virtue of its diglossic separation, therefore, the vernacular dislocated the traditional subordination in the structure of Latin by making obvious a split between voice and writing long since suppressed within the assumption that one was simply the imitation of the other—as evident as the scribal imitation of spoken dictation. English, in short, co-opted the

[130] E.g., Walsingham, *Chronicon Angliae*, pp. 281–83.
[131] Aston, "Wyclif and the Vernacular," p. 298.

voice of Latin. And since that voice was identified with the form of the written, the vernacular threatened less a breach than a complete displacement. English could become what Latin had always been, the mother tongue of doctrine.

The term "vernacular literacy" has been used by scholars unilaterally with reference to Wyclif's recommendations for spreading reform by teaching in *English*. But I have been suggesting that the oral interests of his *Latin* reform is "vernacular" as well. For he tried to slough off the accretions of Latin terminology in explaining sacred mysteries; he exposed the nonfunctional literacy of ecclesiastical Latin—its "dead letter," so to speak. Moreover, he sought models for teaching Scripture and governing the realm in "pure" forms which existed, he maintained, in the world of ideas or political contexts presumably untouched by the taint of an unnecessarily complicated textual history. His "vernacular literacy," in other words, is the articulation of a strikingly traditional oralism—not, of course, the reassertion of anything like "primary" orality, but a return to spoken forms of the inscribed word. And if he found it in English writing (because it was so close to the language of the people), he also found it buried in the history of an ossified Latinity. He did not, need I say, dislike Latin. He spent most of his time (all of it, on the basis of present historical knowledge) writing in the language. It was his lingua franca, as "vernacular" to him as English to the laity.[132]

Although it is apparent that in advocating the vernacular Wyclif was counting on the spoken form of language, the strength of change, to repeat, did not come exclusively from the advance of English per se. It issued from the inscribed form of oral language, and in this development Wyclif's project remained committed to the most basic assumptions of manuscript culture. Indeed, he did no less than imitate the church's own historical relation to vernacular language. For it, too, as scholarship is very well aware, rejected an excessive and confusing Latinity in the early centuries, such as the high literacy of Roman eloquence, in favor of the simple, spoken forms of everyday conversation.[133] Augustine is the preeminent advocate of the new possibilities of the *sermo humilis* in reaching the multitudes of society for whom the Latinity of high culture had become an empty shell. Wyclif never tires of citing Augustine at crucial moments of his opposition to barnacled formulations from the scholastics or other *auctoritates*. He would find in his predecessor, presumably, the spirit of new life and breath issuing

[132] That he writes a "base" style by comparison with "purer" models in antiquity (e.g., Loserth's "Preface" to *De civili dominio* 1:xviii) exemplifies the orality-literacy standoff.

[133] See Auerbach on *sermo humilis* in *Literary Language and Its Public*, Curtius on Roman literacy in *European Literature and the Latin Middle Ages*, and evaluations of both in Pattison, *On Literacy*, pp. 61–103.

from oppositions to the "dead letter" of Ciceronian oratory, criticized in such texts as the *Confessiones* and *De doctrina Christiana*. And Wyclif, without saying so precisely, echoes his master. He too offers a "plain style" for religious teaching, and whether in Latin or English his hope is the same—to deploy a writing as closely wedded to oral language as humanly possible. He found that bond, I estimate, in the language of Augustine in the same way as he found it in the spoken words of Jesus. Wyclif thus put his finger on the nerve of evangelical reform in the history of the church. For the power he touched consisted in neither voice nor writing, oratory nor polemical document. It sprang from displacement, the capacity of oral language to present itself in the form and habit of writing.

Voice or Writing

But there is another side to this page of Wyclif's criticism, and it is already obvious in the fundamentalism of his return to the primitive church. It is a well-attested fact in the history of medieval language theory that one year's practice prefigured another year's reform. It was not long, for instance, after Augustine that his own style, however humble, was swallowed up by the larger institutional interests of exegesis to become an exemplar of an authoritative literacy in its own right.[134] Such a development, so it seems, was inevitable. At certain moments in the early middle ages, the effort to close the widening distance between literacy and spoken language took the form of actual institutional controls. The Carolingian reforms of the eighth and ninth centuries, as recently studied, are a case in point. Written and spoken competence in Latin may have existed in a larger sector of society over a longer period of time than heretofore realized, and the reasons are to be found in the sociopolitical pressures exercised over the language for many years.[135] Wyclif's project of reform in language is different

[134] Pattison, *On Literacy*: "The society was rooted in speech, but the Church had gradually adopted another literacy of formal procedure and written texts" (p. 79); the church emerged from the first Christian millennium with an attitude toward language "almost diametrically opposed to that with which it began" (p. 82).

[135] McKitterick, *The Carolinginans and the Written Word*: "Latin may not have been the foreign or learned second language of the Franks, but their native tongue in its regular-ized and conventionalized written representation" (p. 13). Although reforms created a "diglossia" between written and spoken registers of Latin, linguistic unity was "con-sciously promoted by pressure for a nationally understood and correct language in its written or high form" (p. 21). But contrast Auerbach's argument about the difference between the "text" language of Latin and "popular idiom" (*Literary Language and Its Public*, p. 254), a difference compromised in the interests of a "correct" standard, as I am suggesting.

insofar as he encouraged the development of English. But he also sought, like the Carolingians, to preserve the oral form of an increasingly institutional literacy, and in the long run he contributed to the same paradigm of control he would revise.[136] Writing is still theorized as an imitation of voice; letter is subordinate to speech; dictation, in every sense, has the last word. Within this hierarchy, Wyclif's project of "vernacular" reform perpetuates, however paradoxically, the most basic structure of institutional dominion in Latin literacy.

At least one place where we might have expected Wyclif to open up the margin between voice and writing is in his explorations of the difference between "artificial" and "real" propositions. But, in one form or another, a hierarchical logic organizes his repudiation of *signa*, be they the signs of ordinary discourse, the Bible, the liturgy, or the church itself. His realist preferences were not in and of themselves unique; any medieval Platonist, even one with Aristotelian commitments like Aquinas, would have made them. What is striking, however, is that Wyclif returned to them so tenaciously in the wake of well-worn arguments in terminist logic. The realism for which he opts, like the representation Ockham could not circumvent, thus presents itself in a new light, not as an account of what William Wordsworth would one day call "the real language of men." The "real language" of John Wyclif is not, finally, an imitation of the vernacular or of experience in itself. Rather, it is more complete to suggest that realism in the texts of Wyclif is an *interpretation* of language. However strenuously he opposed ecclesiastical tradition, he also leaves in place the paradigm of dominion at the core of its literacy. This repetition, in my judgment, goes a long way toward explaining why his "reformation" was "premature."

My point is not that Wyclif made the mistake of writing in the Latin of the traditional church. It is, on the contrary, that "real language" and the "real text" become assimilated to an essential "speaking"; and in seeing his choices in terms of this binarism he was led inevitably to perceive any talk about the artificiality of language as a necessary degeneration into mere "signs." He negotiated the margin between voice and writing, in effect, by denying it, and that is why he found Ockham such a bitter pill to swallow. It is predictable, too, that as Wyclif would erase the artifice or writtenness of Scripture, he would illuminate the reality of the *liber vitae*, suspended from on high. Spoken by God, the "celestial grammar" of this text is self-subsistent. Noncanonical writing can also illustrate a similar autonomy, insofar as it may be impenetrable to human readers but "read" by God, like certain

---

[136] McKitterick, ed., *The Uses of Literacy*, p. 324: literacy was "a potent instrument of power" for the Carolingians.

figures and signs on the towers of medieval cathedrals. The church of
the modern world is also such an artificial sign, in Wyclif's opinion,
not only because it had betrayed Christ but because no one finally
knows who is elected for salvation: the universal church is a self-subsistent entity to which no one in this life may secure access through
personal volition, even in acts of penitence and prayer. So too the grace
of the eucharist: its efficacy is known self-sufficiently in God alone. In
the order of government, neither the church nor any secular agency
has the power of the king: to him alone is granted the real sovereignty
over the kingdom which God the father has over this universe.

In each of these reductions, "reality" is claimed for something beyond "mere language," but not without projecting in the process specifically linguistic structures for establishing truth and authority. Wyclif's formalist defense of the *sensus literalis* in the Bible is the most
vivid example of this doctrine of a real and autonomous discourse.
Insofar as its validity is guaranteed ultimately in the unfathomable
purposes of God, his argument for the letter alone professes to solidify
an unimpeachable bond between language and power. The dominion
of the book consists in its autonomy, which in turn dictates Wyclif's
claims about authority and rule in the social order. This argument for
the reign of the book would suggest that his defense of "real" language
and realism in general is less a reduction of false appearances or of
deceiving signs (and thus less an indictment of Ockham) than it is a
systematic relocation of the text and of language beyond the reach of
time and place.[137] Although Wyclif argues on many fronts for anchor-
ing language and text in what he calls *realitas* and the mother tongue
of England, his textuality and linguistics are generated autotelically
out of themselves; they are grounded, finally, neither in reality as he
understood it nor in the spoken language of English society.

The import of this paradox for his social theory should not be
underestimated. A vivid instance of it surfaces, toward the end of his
career, when he vests absolute and self-subsistent dominion in the
king. What is more, Wyclif vests a version of it as well in society when
he advises that every reader should become a *theologos* of the Bible. He
does not exactly recommend, as I have noted, the specific principle of
sola scriptura that was to dominate hermeneutics in the protestant
reformation. But the autonomy of Scriptural discourse has surely influenced a new sense of the individuality of the reader in Wyclif's
advice for confronting the letter alone. Nor is his advice for personal
reading an explicitly revolutionary plea for the power of the individ-

---

[137] Cf. Leff, *Heresy* 2:511: Wyclif's "conception of both [the church and the Bible] as
independent of time and place" fulfills the determinations of his realism.

ual. Wyclif never forgot in his own commentaries the assistance of authorities—where they corroborated, be it noted, his specific purposes. Still, his theory of language and of the Biblical text cannot help but foster a sense of private, if not silent, reading and thus the emergence of an autonomous self; for as divine speech is synonymous with written word in Scripture, so also his notion of "real" language closes the gap between truth and error, reality and appearance, the breath of utterance and the evidence of meaning. It is pointless to look for distinctions between voice and writing in such an idea of language, and that is why Wyclif does not argue any. Language no longer mediates artificially for experience but organizes it "as it should be." Kings and princes, said Wyclif, should maintain the state by virtue of their words, which must always obey divine law. But the reign of power in the secular world could only have taken shape in Wyclif's politics because of the more abiding autonomy of his linguistics, the bond between oral and real which he heard in the individual voice from the outset.

OCKHAM AND WYCLIF

Although Ockham and Wyclif begin their logical investigations with the medieval tradition that the origin of language is convention, rather than nature, and that words and texts are artificial forms, I have been suggesting in Part One of this book that this opposition is too simple to explain prima facie either their theories of language or their ideas about power. On the one hand, both thinkers count heavily on the convention of written analyses and intensely textualized habits of thought; yet they also appeal ultimately to models of language that are oral: Ockham assumes the priority of "mental language" as the *vox* of the soul that is simultaneous with the identity of an individual *res*; and Wyclif much more boldly argues for the "real language" of truthful communication and for the "priority of the origin" of God's voice in the Bible. This transformation of a written into an oral object, in spite of the rigorous textual maneuvers in which it occurs, is not as surprising as it may appear. Medieval linguistic history offers many similar instances, as we have seen, of literate practices learned from textual analyses and then recycled according to familiar habits of oral culture.

This development may well have been motivated—and surely was sanctioned—by the rich medieval mythology of the *liber praesentiae Dei*: "the book of the presence of God" was the consummate representation of writing as speaking, the physical text of Scripture presented as the speech of God at creation and reiterated in countless manifestations—consuming the eucharist, accepting the words of prophecy, and receiving the nourishment of books. As the spoken word is associated with such physical activities, it is no wonder that the act of reading *sotto voce* in the schoolroom or monastic cell was mythologized as eating the words and leaves of texts.

But I have also suggested that Ockham and Wyclif were not only writing about language theory in their logical treatises. When Ockham departed from England in 1324, it is hardly the case, as was once believed, that he left behind *dialectica* to take up the banners of politics. In the case of Wyclif the connection between linguistics and politics is much more explicit, but for him also the relation of the two disciplines is deeper than may be observed merely from textual cross-referencing. On the contrary, the *grammatica* of both writers involves a metalanguage about the origin and efficacy of power. The priority of the "individual" for Ockham is synonymous with its being "spoken" in the mind. From this linguistic principle, his entire theory of ecclesiastical and lay dominion emerges. Because of his commitment to the ontology of *res* and *vox*, the question of "representation" in knowledge is a problem throughout the *Logica*; and the matter surfaces later under a different form in the political tracts as Ockham attacks the pivotal doctrine of papal *plenitudo potestatis*. Consequently, the same problem that besets his philosophy of language bothers his politics as well: because he situates power in a fixed origin and the linguistic sign in the evident knowledge of a specific thing, he is caught in an infinite regress of representations in which the validity of dominion is identifiable with a source always out of reach.

The position of Wyclif is somewhat less complicated. As he addresses the notion of the autonomy of Scriptural language and the location of truth in its literal "form," the text of the Bible emerges as the sole authority for dominion in church and state. Denying papal sovereignty over the secular order and reserving absolute dominion for the king, Wyclif justifies his theory of power not strictly on Scriptural grounds or metaphysical tenets. Rather, his theory of lay rule has its closest analogue in a linguistic formulation, his notion of the unquestioned will of God realized as the *modus loquendi* and *forma verborum* of the Bible. While the argument for the absolute authority of writing—to all appearances—has little to do with politics, it still accounts semiologically for the realization of unlimited power in the word of the sovereign. That neither Ockham or Wyclif argues distinctions between writing and speaking is clearly predictable in view of the privilege granted to voice in their linguistics. Existing on a par with "evidence" for Ockham and with divine "authority" for Wyclif, the status of the oral as originary does not initiate questioning the written for its adequacy as representation. And neither does logic suggest itself as a metalanguage of political dominion until the speech of writing becomes a problem for study in its own right.

Such an exploration, as we have seen, is not the immediate concern of the philosophical inquiry undertaken by Ockham and Wyclif. As different as these thinkers are, they compare on the apparently simple point that they do not make much of the distinction between spoken and written. It is not that they do not perceive the difference between them, but rather that a penetrating theoretical inquiry into their separation is occluded by an assumption that voice is prior and foundational to any inscription. The split between spoken and written is thus governed by what I have called a *discourse* which resists and even denies the significance of their opposition. The dominion of literacy arises from that denial, from conserving the traditional subordination that the letter, as Aristotle said, is an indivisible unit of sound. Medieval theorists did not look into this problem, and that factor indicates why fourteenth-century philosophy is as much the product of the history of thought as it is influenced by time-worn assumptions about *literacy* in general.[138] As odd as it may seem, the philosophical project bears out how deeply rooted the written word remained throughout the middle ages in the experience of its audible form.

Insofar as the approach to diglossia in theoretical linguistics involves the question of control and dominion, it leads, as I have argued, to reconsidering the link between language and political theory in the fourteenth century. But, since both of these ventures in philosophy remain tied to assumptions about literacy, we must confront the fact that the philosophical enterprise does not arise ex nihilo out of rarefied academic speculation. We are obliged to see that the direction of philosophy is part and parcel of the functions of literacy in the social and political context of the time. And that context, needless to say, was far more committed to the oral past than anything occurring in the high culture of medieval academic life.

The affairs of government were still caught in the vestiges of a feudalism that located the power of rule in the person and word of a lord. While it is impossible to find archaeological evidence for such an ephemeral and transitory phenomenon as the dominion of the spoken word in the fourteenth century, we do have written records in the chronicle histories of the time; and by means of close, critical reading of them, we may begin to take a new look at how they represent the

[138] The "dominion" of this model may be noted in recent claims that literacy is the foundation for "rationality," "civilization," and "culture"; e.g., see the concluding pages of Goody, *The Logic of Writing*, Stock, *The Implications of Literacy*, and McKitterick, *The Carolinginans and the Written Word*. The rebuttal of Street, *Literacy in Theory and Practice*, to this model for literacy is reviewed above, in ch. 1.

margin between oral and written traditions at this point in British history. Negotiating between those modes in fourteenth-century philosophy takes shape specifically around the vested interests of the marginal orality of manuscript culture. In a genre of writing far less committed to accounting for its own procedures, we are even more likely to find that the linguistics of oral and written elements is not only present, but that it constitutes in the form of chronicle the historicization of political interests in the life of the times.

PART TWO

Politics

Chapter Four

ORALITY AND RHETORIC IN THE CHRONICLE
HISTORY OF EDWARD III

> Writinge of poetes is more worthy to preisynge of
> emperoures þan al þe welþe of þis worlde, and
> riches þat þey welde while þey were alyue. For
> storie is wytnesse of tyme, mynde of lyf, messager
> of eldnesse. . . . Dedes þat wolde be lost storie
> ruleþ; dedes þat wolde flee out of mynde, storye
> clepeþ aʒen; dedes þat wolde deie, storye kepeþ
> hem euermore.
> —Trevisa, *Polychronicon*

INTRODUCTION

A transition from philosophy to political writing is assisted by familiar
scholarly categories about the kind of history composed in fourteenth-
century England: it was an age that produced an unprecedented number of philosophical histories, works that approach the past as a record
of "universal" truths and "exemplary" morals necessary in the present.
Such works represent the "shape" of history as the expression of
specifically medieval modes of perceiving the natural and supernatural
universe.[1]

But the fourteenth century was also a time in which a new sense of
the past as different and separate from the present also emerged to a
certain extent.[2] When the Dominican friar Nicholas Trivet turned to the
study of Livy's *History* at Oxford in the early years of the century, he
produced a serious appreciation of antiquity, and he was read avidly
at home and at Avignon. While history had no discipline in the university curriculum comparable to grammar and logic, still the older
anachronistic sense of the past was gradually being severed in academia. Moreover, chronicle histories of monastic and aristocratic prove-

---

[1] Taylor, *English Historical Literature in the Fourteenth Century*, pp. 90 ff.; Brandt, *The
Shape of Medieval History*, pp. 65 ff. Cf. Southern, "Aspects of the European Tradition of
Historical Writing" (1970, 1972); Chenu, *Nature, Man, and Society in the Twelfth Century*,
ch. 5; Momigliano, *Essays in Ancient and Modern Historiography*, ch. 8.

[2] See Smalley, *Historians in the Middle Ages*, pp. 190 ff.

nance demonstrated a new interest in recording the details of events, particularly contemporary deeds of war and politics.[3] An appreciation of the past, both recent history and distant epochs, as distinct from contemporary society was at hand.

But *how* distinct remains an open question in scholarship. For instance, moving from the thirteenth-century chronicles to those composed in the fourteenth, one finds the old models for organizing information about the past still in place. Ranulf Higden and Thomas Walsingham do not give us a new genre for their projects. Each author organizes his chronicle as a "universal history," following the periodization of the ages of the world emphasized by the fifth-century Spanish monk Orosius. God's voice in human affairs is the motive of this historiography, and Geoffrey of Monmouth's *Historia Regnum Britannie* or Vincent of Beauvais's *Speculum historiale* are well-known, magisterial examples of it.[4] But as manifestations of universal history, the chronicles will be judged "very bare, promising a doctrinal fullness that is never given."[5] Such a criticism is inevitable when it is assumed that the chronicles are "reportage, eyewitness accounts . . . based on oral evidence and on documents, put together piecemeal in chronological order to create a serial episodic narrative."[6] The "purpose" of history is elided with an unusual interest in "the facts," and the result is that the pastness of the past has still not emerged in its own right. Such a consequence did not apparently bother Caxton, who was extraordinarily well read in medieval chronicles. When he ended the *Order of Chyvalry* with the injunction, "Read Froissart," his point, presumably, was that the chronicles are intended to inspire virtue: they are hortatory history. And that is one reason why they became important to historians in the sixteenth and seventeenth centuries.[7]

A similar vacillation between factual and purposive history is to be

---

[3] On twelfth-century efforts at historical accuracy, see Southern, "Aspects of the European Tradition" (1971), pp. 159–79. An early British example is Gerald of Wales' *Descriptio Kambriae*, which Bartlett, *Gerald of Wales*, pp. 11 ff., describes as an ethnography based upon a "new naturalism."

[4] Funkenstein, "Periodization and Self-Understanding," p. 9: "In the language of Bonaventura, 'Faith moves us to believe that the three periods of law, namely that of natural law, of the Scripture, and of grace followed each other in the most harmonious order.' The succession of periods manifests the well-ordered divine providence, not the independence and spontaneity of human history." Cf. Smalley, *Historians in the Middle Ages*, pp. 95–105.

[5] Partner, *Serious Entertainments*, p. 228.

[6] Gransden, *Historical Writing in England* 2:458–59.

[7] See Keen, "Chivalry, Heralds, and History," in Davis and Wallace-Hadrill, eds., *The Writing of History in the Middle Ages*, pp. 393–94.

noted when we consider the question of the past from the point of view of philosophical debates about the knowledge of "universal substance." According to a recent study, realists like Duns Scotus fortify an appreciation of the "presence" of the past because they maintain that a knowledge of the universal is immediate in the mind.[8] A sense of history as a record of timeless truth follows directly from this justification of the real universal. But in his dispute with Scotus and the scholastics, Ockham introduced a radical shift in assumptions about the past. Since for him knowledge of the universal was first of all knowledge of terms and propositions about it, we do not know the universal in itself but only through "habitual" acts of knowledge about the substance of things. Accordingly, knowledge of the past is not a knowledge of its timeless edification, but of the temporal act of interpreting propositions and texts. In the long run, Ockham became the "turning point" for a "Renaissance confidence in the uniqueness of the past as past."[9]

It would seem that this argument about Ockham demonstrates sharp differences from his scholastic forebears on the subject of history. But, as a harbinger of a new historical consciousness in the remaining years of the fourteenth century, he occupies a rather uncertain position. If he gives us a historiography based upon texts, a textualized history, how is it that he also brings us closer to "the past as past," so that "we can understand the present and the past in all their individuality and uniqueness?"[10] The presumption here is that textual analysis perforce introduces a sense of the distance from the object of interpretation in other times.

But even if Ockham so acknowledged the temporal distance of interpretation, his own arguments about the knowledge of propositions do not constitute a thoroughgoing nominalism, splitting mental understanding sharply away from experience of the individual in the past or present. For he argues that the "voice" of the concept in the mind, as I have suggested (in chapter 2), is at once a representative "sign" of something other but also synonymous with the intuitive understanding of its object. A concept is both the product of past understanding because it is "habitual," yet also immediate and present in the mind because it is an "act." *Vox* is the red herring in this epistemology, as it acknowledges the past status of understanding and its present identity in the language of the mind. When the act of

---

[8] Coleman, *Ancient and Medieval Memories*, chs. 21–22.

[9] Ibid., p. 526. Cf. Funkenstein, "Periodization and Self-Understanding," pp. 15–16.

[10] Coleman, *Ancient and Medieval Memories*, p. 537.

understanding remains thus qualified, so also must the possibility of
knowing the past *as past* in all its idiosyncrasy.[11]

It is true that Ockham sought access to the past through textual
analysis, but so did staunch realists like Wyclif, for whom the past was
an illustration of timeless truth. In order to see this problem in a
different light, I suggest we recall the medieval commonplace of history as an expression of the *vox Dei*. Within that category, it is apparent
that the *writing* of history remained, as Ockham and Wyclif always
assumed, subordinated to what someone said. Writing was the extension of its origin in speech, and accordingly its capacity to become
something different and apart was forestalled. The "writinge" of history, as Trevisa put it, was "wytnesse" and "messager" of deeds from
the past. His metaphors are not incidental. They reflect the much more
broadly based notion from the later middle ages that the text is an oral
and visual object. It may have been intended for silent or audible
recitation, but its writing was imagined as the speech of its author, who
might pose as writer, performer, or scribe.[12]

Scholarship on the arts of memory in the middle ages confirm these
assumptions about writing as the instrument of speech. Popular medieval images for memory as "book" and "tablet" call attention to the
special place of the memorial arts in medieval society.[13] They lead one
recent commentator to regard the medieval book as the product of
"memorial composition," rather than speech or writing per se, since
the language of the mind is not material.[14] But whatever these figures
may signify about memory, they assume the persistence of the familiar
medieval hierarchy about spoken and written language. Because the
language of memory has affinities with the monastic practice of *ruminatio*, speaking in *sutto voce* the words of meditation and digesting
them, the emphasis is on the orality, not the inscription, of the act of
recollecting.[15] If the letters of a page, as Isidore said, are the "voices of
the absent," a book is the memory of what someone spoke.[16] Assuming

[11] Cf. Funkenstein's conclusion, "Periodization and Self-Understanding," p. 16: "For
all the instances in which the middle ages approached our search for contexts, it never
reached the methodological consciousness of placing such a search in the first order of
priorities. . . . It could not really overcome its view of history as governed by transcendent structures and of historical facts as given rather than made."

[12] See Huot, *From Song to Book*, pp. 336–37 and passim. Cf. Scott, "Design, Decoration,
and Illustration," p. 47.

[13] See Yates, *The Art of Memory*.

[14] Carruthers, *The Book of Memory*, p. 194.

[15] See Leclercq, *The Love of Learning*.

[16] Noted by Carruthers, *The Book of Memory*, p. 111, though she insists on the separation of memory from writing and speaking. Cf. the orality of the figures cited on pp.
221–22.

the same origin for speech as for writing, such metaphors of memory unify the two channels of language into one. And thus although memory may be approached as a category discrete unto itself, it assumes the same priority in the order of material language that we have seen in the philosophical tradition. Typical medieval commonplaces about memory do not encourage a sense of writing as a differentiated mode of discourse.

I mention these problems because it would seem that the uncertain sense of the past in late medieval chronicles is part and parcel of the ambiguous status of writing, its role both as speech and inscription. We become aware of the speech of these texts in such figures as Trevisa gives us, but much more so in the appropriation of commonplaces from the arts of oratorical practice. We may think of them merely as efforts to dress up the bare bones of historical events. But I suggest that they are much more important to the "rhetoric" of chronicle, the determination to breathe life into the dead letter of the text. Although these documents have served long and well as encyclopedias for looking things up, they also contain an embedded orality in their rhetoric. They may be less demonstrably oratorical than their sources and analogues from the twelfth century, which were the production of a much more explicit "oratorical history."[17] For in the fourteenth century, the recording of events was an unequivocally *literary* act. But the reliance on oratorical commonplaces from rhetoric has a *use*, and we would do well to look into it.

Scholarship has long recognized that the chronicles of this time were composed in response to political interests and patronage. Some would see the entire project of history writing as a defense of the "national prestige" damaged in the aftermath of the Norman Conquest.[18] Be that as it may, the chronicles do not constitute "official history," but they definitely represent the vested concerns of their monastic or aristocratic affiliation; that they often verge on propaganda is commonly recognized. In light of such factors, I suggest that these documents have a "voice" (or several voices, as the case may be), and that a literary criticism of them is in order. Looking specifically at the chronicles written about the reign of Edward III, I will explore how the voice of record is linked up with the *dominium* of the king: the "word" of history is coordinated semiologically with the "property rights" of monarchy.

---

[17] On rhetorical history in the twelfth-century, see Coleman, *Ancient and Medieval Memories*, pp. 275–99 (and pp. 300–18 for John of Salisbury as "historian-orator"); and Ward, "Some Principles of Rhetorical Historiography in the Twelfth Century," p. 148: the "reality" of an event resides in its "re-telling" rather than in getting to the facts. Cp. Ray, "Rhetorical Scepticism and Verisimilar Narrative," p. 69.

[18] Gransden, *Historical Writing in England* 2:456.

Certainly the historian is concerned with memorializing "the facts." But he is also negotiating the subtle and volatile problem of the king's dominion. Foregrounding the speech of the king is of a piece with rhetorical strategies for giving the text itself a voice. The writtenness of chronicle thus remains, as the philosophers repeatedly said, a sign of the spoken word.

But in this context, the subordination of writing has striking implications. One of them is political, insofar as the voice of rule takes precedence over all others, including written precedent. The other is theoretical, since the notion of writing as speech written down continues the old historiography of the past as an edifying timeless record. Although the chronicle histories of Edward III make unprecedented ventures in the recording of details, a new historicist appreciation of the pastness of the past is occluded in the same way that writing remains an occluded instrument of speaking. The persistence of this factor in the chronicles suggests, perhaps for the first time in the fourteenth century, that the possibility of change in historical consciousness was tied all along to the status of writing within the text: a new awareness would have to await the unqualified acknowledgment of a writing distinct from speech, emerging in its own right and for its own sake. The rhetoric of chronicle, therefore, deserves close reading, not only because of its political valence but also because it will help us answer the question of why orality continued in spite of the advance of writing and books.

THE RHETORIC OF HISTORY

The great political histories of the fourteenth century had a very limited circulation outside of their provenance, but Higden's *Polychronicon* is an exception: it was widely known beyond the walls of the author's own religious house, St. Werburgh's, and it was read not only as a reference work but "for the story."[19] In the preface, Higden opens specifically on the point of finding a proper rhetoric so that the memory of past deeds will not die. With the familiar trope of affected modesty, he apologizes that he may not possess the great voice of past *auctores* to enunciate properly the fruits of history, and therefore he will proceed *stidulo* and *sibilo* ("gruntynge and whistelynge").[20] If he lacks

---

[19] Taylor, *English Historical Literature*, p. 56. See also the same author's invaluable volume on the *Polychronicon*, *The "Universal Chronicle" of Ranulph Higden*, esp. ch. 3. On the possible readership of the work, including Usk and Chaucer, see Edwards, "The Influence and Audience of the *Polychronicon*," pp. 113–14.

[20] *Polychronicon* 1:10–11, trans. Trevisa (who continues to the year 1360; he made the translation in 1387).

the power of oratory, he will humbly follow Horace, who replied—
when upbraided for stealing lines from Homer: "It were wel greet
strengþe to wreste a mace out of Huercules honde." So, Higden continues, if I come with only "soond and askes," at least I will—as Horace
says—become the "whetston þat makeþ yren sharpe and kene."[21] Borrowed directly from the *Ars poetica*, the analogy betokens the basis of
Higden's approach to historical writing in the arts of eloquence, in the
same way as Horace founds his own defense of poetry in the decorum
of Roman oratory.[22] With other famous poets and rhetoricians on his
mind, notably Virgil, Seneca, Jerome, and Gregory the Great, Higden
worries repeatedly about speaking without sufficient "sotilte of sentence, noþer faire florischynge of wordes"; he wants to be sure that the
"swetnesse of deuocion of þe matire schal regne in þis book."[23] And
lest there be any confusion about when he speaks in his own voice
rather than in the words of others, he closes the preface with the
assurance that he will signify his voice by inscribing the letter *R* in the
manuscript: "for my self and for myn owne name I write þis letter."[24]

In order to look closer at the voice of the letter in this and other
chronciles, let us start with representations of the Black Prince, Edward
of Woodstock, at age sixteen in the battle of Crécy (1346). An early note
of this event in Higden's history (as translated by Trevisa) simply
records the occurrence: "At Cressy in Pycardie, kyng Edward glori-
ousliche overcome the kyng of Fraunce, and slough kynges of Beem
and of Majorik, the duke of Lothorynge, tweie bisshops, eighte erles,
many noble lordes, two thowsand knyghtes, and other men with oute
noumbre, chased the people that fligh awey on lyve."[25] The military
fame that later chronicles report about the prince at such a young
age—and that was to become proverbial—is conspicuously absent in
Higden's chronology.

Walsingham surely had a copy of the *Polychronicon* for reference in
his assiduous efforts to follow in the footsteps of such scholars as
Matthew Paris and develop chronicle writing in England while he was
precentor of St. Albans (1380–1394). In the *Historia Anglicana*, Walsingham also mentions Crécy and includes a comment on Prince Edward,
saying that he fought with his father "constantly and valorously."[26]
That Walsingham has high regard for the prince is obvious from

---

[21] *Polychronicon* 1:12–13.

[22] See Trimpi, *Muses of One Mind*.

[23] *Polychronicon* 1:14–15. NB Higden authored two works on public oratory, the *Speculum curatorum* and the *Ars compendi sermones*.

[24] *Polychronicon* 1:20–21.

[25] *Polychronicon* 7:341–42.

[26] *Historia Anglicana* 1:268.

remarks on later battles and from the eulogy of his death, in which he calls him "another Hector."[27] But the report on Crécy, where his reputation is supposed to have started, is rather spare. This factor is set in relief when we consult an account composed probably twenty-five years before Walsingham's, Geoffrey le Baker's chronicle, dated ca. 1357–1360. "In this very fierce fight, the great Edward of Woodstock, the king's first son, sixteen years of age, demonstrated his admirable prowess against the French in the first guard of the battle line by charging through horses, prostrating horsemen, shattering helmets, lopping off lances, avoiding shrewdly the blows from flying objects, and at the same time protecting himself, helping his fallen friends, and setting a fine example for everyone."[28] Baker goes on to observe that in the press of battle, word was sent to King Edward that the prince was in great danger and in need of help. The king responded by sending twenty knights to his son's aid; but on arriving, they discovered the prince and his men "leaning against their lances and swords upon mounds of the dead."[29]

In another example, from the chronicles of Jean Froissart, we find a much more elaborate account. Book one, which contains the report on Crécy, was probably composed between 1370 and 1371, about fifteen years after Geoffrey le Baker and twenty-five years after the battle. It is assumed that Froissart not only had his own firsthand evidence of the events but also had at his disposal the oral testimony of witnesses as well as other chronicles of the time.[30] With regard to one engagement of battle at Crécy, a Saturday morning shortly after the feast of John the Baptist in 1346, Froissart tells us that his sources for the story are English, specifically the testimony of people attached to Sir John Hainault.[31] For example, he reports that the French outnumbered the English by eight to one on that day; prior to battle the king and the prince heard mass, received the eucharist, and then prepared to fight; the English army, divided into three battalions, was heartened by the king's address of encouragement to them before battle. But, Froissart continues, when the French king looked upon the English spectacle for the first time, "he began to sweat blood" ("se li mua li sans"), and he cried out, "order the Genoese to march forward and begin the battle in the name of God and St. Denis."[32] He notes the fifteen thousand

[27] *Historia Anglicana* 1:321.

[28] *Chronicon*, p. 84.

[29] Ibid.

[30] On the difference between literary and historical origins for discourse in the chronicles of Froissart, see Nichols, "Discourse in Froissart's *Chroniques.*"

[31] Froissart, *Chroniques* (ed. Lettenhove) 3:174.

[32] *Chroniques* 3:175.

Genoese mercenary crossbow soldiers; their cowardliness in battle; the rebuke of them by the Earl of Alençon ("It serves us right for hiring such ribalds"); and the various signs and portents appearing at the initial stage of engagement: "A heavy and fast rain fell from the sky, with much loud thunder and many horrible eclipses . . . before this rain, a great flock of crows without number hovered in the air above all the battalions, and created a violent commotion. . . . Later the skies began to clear and the sun became bright and sharp." So that we do not miss the significance of this final "signe," as Froissart identifies it, he observes that "the French had it directly in their eyes, and the English on their backs."[33] Compared with Geoffrey le Baker's account, one of the fullest we have, Froissart's report surely exercises the advice of the rhetoricians "to amplify" discourse with such material as direct address, provocative signs, and narrative suspense. When the prince is in trouble in the heat of fighting, Froissart embroiders the king's response in a series of lengthy conversations with the messenger, ending with an aphorism that enjoins lessoning the boy and yet ensuring that he will have military glory for the day: "I command," says the king "that they let the boy earn his spurs."[34]

Other sources are equally affirmative of the exploits of Prince Edward, such as the poem written by the Chandos herald. Although this account of Crécy (composed ca. 1376–1387) is far less developed than Froissart's, both reports clearly realize some of the qualities already implicit in the less elaborate chronicles, as they employ language rhetorically to amplify details for dramatic emphasis and for persuasion, in this case to convince audiences of the prowess of Edward's son—the auspicious heir apparent of England until he predeceased his father by one year. Conventional generic distinctions, as drawn by Isidore, between *fabula* and *historia* come to little point with regard to materials of this kind, since narrative, dialogue, suspense, symbolism, and moral *sententia* compose the substance of history from the point of view of these writers.[35]

To appreciate the rhetoric of these documents is, first of all, to recognize that they are motivated by an ethos—not specifically the realization of God's voice in the affairs of this world (*gesta Dei*) or the hero's voice in the deeds of conquest (*res gestae*). Rather, the organization of these accounts, as fragmentary as they are, is disposed decidedly toward a particular outcome, and no one was more aware of it than medieval chroniclers themselves. Walsingham, for instance, con-

[33] *Chroniques* 3:175–76.

[34] *Chroniques* 3:183.

[35] Isidore, *Etymologiarum* 1.38, 40, 41 (*PL* 82, 117, 121, 122). See Partner, *Serious Entertainments*, p. 195.

ceals nothing of his dislike of Wyclif and the house of Lancaster, at the same time as he expresses praise for the Yorkist interest in preserving the monarchy when it is toppling in the final years of Richard II's reign. On the other hand, Henry Knighton, writing at the same time, is pro-Lancastrian, favoring the takeover lead by John of Gaunt's son, Henry of Hereford. And Froissart is perhaps most telling of all, since he at first supports the efforts of Edward III and the prince to secure the Aquitaine and then in the later sections of his narrative takes a more critical stance toward England. In a word, editorializing is as common to chronicle as speaking publicly in *amplificatio* with invented conversation and symbolic details. However, narrative self-interpretation of this sort is manifestly different from the larger textual interests that I have been suggesting. To the extent that these texts purport to be *historia* and to list events "as they occurred," they bypass recognition of their own rhetoric—what medieval linguists would have called the "consignifying" or modifying properties of their discourse.[36] *Historia* rarely has more affinities with *fabula* than in the chronicles. Both modes are functions of consignification, suppositing an image of reality rather than becoming the transparent vehicle of it. But because the chroniclers assume a categorical difference between these modes, we may characterize the emergence of historical writing as the result of successfully concealing and suppressing the function of rhetoric and consignification. While these texts may editorialize and interpret, they do not acknowledge their own *fabula*: the "fiery dragon" reported by Knighton *de re* in 1388 is listed next to accounts of a proposed tournament at Calais and of alarming increases among the Wycliffites.[37] The accomplishment of this kind of credibility about chronology constitutes a rhetorical power rather more pervasive and consequential than any explicit editorial aside, political slant, or exegetical intention.

THE VOICE OF HISTORY

As admiring and sympathetic observers of the deeds they describe, Froissart and the Chandos herald develop narrative *personae*, not unlike the fictional voices of poetry. And Walsingham, who has almost no comparable development as a speaker, still comes off as an omniscient newscaster whose descriptive styles attempt to persuade through a seemingly benevolent didacticism. As these historical styles are the achievement of narrative instead of the individual voices of it, we may recognize that the accounts of society presented by the fourteenth-cen-

[36] See *consignificatio* in ch. 2, above.
[37] Knighton, *Chronicon* 2:260.

tury chronicles are less interested in news, entertainment, and edification than they are in the dominion of the text of record: although
chronicles assert their political allegiances rather explicitly, their more
subtle and unexpressed interest is in maintaining the authority of their
own speaking. And by this gesture, they testify to the importance of
the context that motivates the writing of this history in the first place—
the oral witness of being on the scene of battle, of creating its color and
suspense, of becoming the credible and realistic "voice" of the past.
The import of such narrative effects is that the rhetoric of the account
takes precedence over the text as documentary evidence: the "facts"
have credibility by virtue of the significance given to them.

These documents, as will now be apparent, involve a conflict that
they themselves do not confront, and it provides us with a consideration of fourteenth-century France and England that is not available to
us when the chronicles are consulted in the customary way as encyclopedias for looking things up. Insofar as the conflict concerns the
difference between rhetoric and the putative "facts," the consignification of syntactical events and the signification of real ones, then it
recalls the opposition between textuality and orality negotiated in
various other contexts of society. As the chronicles report on the suc-
cesses of the Prince of Wales and King Edward III in securing their
territories in France, they also show us—quite aside from the chronology of events—a cross-section of a larger dilemma facing the English
Crown. The textual problem is assimilated to the political problem by
virtue of the ambiguous status of voice in both domains: what the text
takes for granted—the evidence and authority of its own speaking—is
also under siege in the political arena, the displacement of the king's
sovereign word from his property in France. The oral basis of textual
authority thus participates in the question of the king's claim to patrimony.

In attempting to assess the value of the chronicles as history, scholarship has largely ignored such metalinguistic factors.[38] For instance,
"It is probable," one commentator remarks, "that England's resounding victories provided an incentive to historical composition."[39] It is
observed that a number of the chronicles end with military victory and
that their "historical intention" is obviously commemorative. The point
is argued further with reference to the facts that only one-half of the
chronicles (of eleven) continue beyond 1360, the date of the Peace of
Brétigny, which concluded the victories at Crécy (1346), Calais (1350),

---

[38] Brandt, *Shape of Medieval History*, is an exception, as an early approach to "literary"
matters in these histories.

[39] Gransden, *Historical Writing in England* 2:60.

and Poitiers (1356); two of the chronicles end in the 1360s; the Chandos herald's life of the Black Prince terminates with his death in 1376; and only Froissart's narrative continues through the end of Richard's reign (1399). However, to conclude that these dates tell the story of a connection between the genesis of chronicle and military history obviates consideration of other influences, particularly the increasing literacy of the nobility and the dependence of English chronicle writing on the literary tradition of France.

For instance, it is true that the fourteenth century does not produce a corpus of chivalrous chronicles in the English language. But the reason is not necessarily because of a decline in chivalry or feudalism per se. Rather, French as a literary language was disappearing from England, as we may note when the French tradition of the prose *Brut* terminates in mid-century. And yet the cult of chivalry continued to flourish at the court of Edward III and in such institutions as the Order of the Garter. Perhaps we have no chivalrous history of Edward in English because the king never appointed a court chronicler.[40]

My point is that the evidence of feudal and chivalric values must be sought in the form and structure of the chronicles we have. Geoffrey le Baker, the Chandos herald, Froissart, Walsingham, and Knighton— all stage the problem between England and France as a chivalric contest arising from the breaking of a promise when the French "usurper," King Philip, seized the lands inherited by King Edward and the Prince of Wales. These are well-worn paths in the conventional histories of England and France, and not least among them in the chronicles is the rhetorical commonplace of commemorating the hero.

ORALITY AND PATRIMONY

What is unmistakable in the accounts, as noted earlier, is that the chivalric protection of patrimony goes hand-in-hand with the assertion of the ruling lord's presence to the feudal host in his spoken word.[41] One of the more pointed instances of this connection is contained in the account of the siege of Calais by Geoffrey le Baker. The Prince of

[40] See Taylor, *English Historical Literature*, p. 174; and Gransden, *Historical Writing in England* 2:80.

[41] On the oral nature of documents for the indenture of retinue between lord and retainer, see Bean, *From Lord to Patron*, p. 13. NB p. 143: "Through this whole period the word 'retained' was generally accompanied by 'demore' (literally, 'stay with'), a word that had its roots in the notion of physical presence at the lord's side. . . . In this sense the indenture of retinue of late medieval England was a remodeled survival of bonds that went back to the warbands of centuries before when a lord's familia and his warrior following were synonymous."

Wales and King Edward conceal themselves from the enemy and from
their own men by hiding in the precincts of the castle. The French,
under siege for many months, presume that they have a strategic
advantage and mount a charge against the English. In response, Edward, who remained unknown to his own retinue, assaulted the fugi-
tives with fewer than sixteen armed men and an equal number of
archers.[42] In this grim situation, with soldiers "sinking in the mud," the
king heartened his men; "Drawing himself near with enticing words,
he addressed them courteously: 'Do your best . . . archers, and know
that I am Edward of Windsor.'"[43] A certain amount of rhetorical *copia*
is to be expected in chronicle accounts of impending victory, such as
at Calais; but, in this instance, Edward's spoken word—whether or not
a transcription of what was said—is connected directly with the power
of *regis presencia* in recovering the land under siege: "Recognizing then
for the first time the presence of the king and the necessity of fighting
well, the archers bared their heads, arms and chests, and each one
pressed his strength not to waste one arrow; they received the advancing French bitterly with an intense salvo of sharp arrows. . . . Without
doubt the king with his men around him and his archers on either side
killed or captured the French, resisting them powerfully until the
arrival of the Prince of Wales forced the rest to flee."[44]

In his account of Calais, the Chandos herald does not report nearly
as many details, emphasizing instead the objective of the siege as
"illoeqes la piece de terre" ("a piece of ground") and the means by
which it was taken, "by the strength and by the power / of the noble
king and his son the Prince, / who was so valiant."[45] With just as much
influence from the French tradition as the Chandos herald demonstrates, Froissart recounts the events with his usual *copia* and *amplificatio*, which in this case have distinctly oral manifestations. Introducing
the detail that the Calesians, whose city was under siege for some time,
attempted to save themselves from further famine and illness by sending out of the city six sacrificial victims "with ropes around their
necks," Froissart narrates a standoff between the king who receives the
prisoners and his queen, who is also present and attempting to save
them from beheading.[46]

The matter is resolved because of the chivalric generosity of the king,
which is elicited by means of the confrontation or flyting typical of oral

[42] Geoffrey le Baker, *Chronicon*, p. 106.

[43] Ibid.

[44] *Chronicon*, pp. 106–107.

[45] Chandos herald, *La vie du Prince Noir*, ed. Tyson, ll. 400, 408–10. Cf. *The Life of the
Black Prince*, trans. Pope.

[46] *Chroniques* 4:59.

circumstances: the queen proceeds not by analyzing the situation or by appealing to law or justice; she prevails by the force and gesture of her pleading: "Ah, gentle sir," she cries, "since I have come to this side of the sea with great peril to be with you, I have never requested or demanded anything from you. But now I humbly request to ask you as a favor, for the son of Saint Mary and for your love to me, that you will have mercy on these six men." The king, regarding her quietly, responds, "Ah, lady, I would prefer that you had been any place but here. You have beseeched me so keenly that I do not dare refuse you; thus . . . I give them to you, for you to do with them as you please."[47] Froissart goes on to report the detail, included in Baker, about the king's secret intrigue at the castle of Calais, but with snatches of conversation embellished at the crucial moments of signaling victory. Making his identity known only to Sir Walter Manny, he remains with Prince Edward incognito, fighting under Manny's banner; but at the instant of the enemy encroachment, the king bursts out of his hiding place shouting with his men, according to Froissart, "Manny, Manny, to the rescue! . . . Do these Frenchmen believe that they can conquer the castle and city of Calais with so few men!"[48] Preserving an exact quotation of the original pronouncement is less important than cementing the link between the royal patrimony and the king's power, emphasized by Froissart in the *amplificatio* of giving the king's words the oral force of a slogan ("Manny to the rescue!") shouted subsequently by the advancing English soldiers in overtaking the castle and the land.[49]

Other accounts of the incidents at Calais between 1347 and 1350 contain far less dramatic narrative and conversation than Froissart's chronicles. But even the abbreviated entries in Higden's *Polychronicon* and Walsingham's *Historia Anglicana* are notable for some of the literary styles included, such as a "compleynt" to the Virgin, as it is designated by Trevisa. It is spoken by King Edward in response to adverse weather experienced while crossing the channel back to England. Trevisa's translation preserves the telling rhetorical balance, common to the genre, of Higden's Latin: "My goode lady seynt Marye, what is it, and what bodeth it, that in my wendynge into Fraunce I wynde have weder and al thing at my wille, and in my comynge agen toward Engleond I have tempest and many hard happes."[50] Walsingham, writing later and following the *Polychronicon* closely in places, feels no need to quote the "compleynte" verbatim; his modest *amplifi-*

[47] *Chroniques* 4:62.
[48] *Chroniques* 4:76.
[49] *Chroniques* 4:77.
[50] *Polychronicon* 7:345.

catio, like Froissart's and Trevisa's, answers to its oratorical tradition, expanding amply where emphasis is possible.[51] Moreover, the literary quality of this speech becomes a structural principle, since the portent of the king is fulfilled by Higden, who goes on to list the "hard happes" of English history in subsequent sentences—noting such catastrophes as "a grete reyne" lasting for many months; a "grete deeth of men in all the world wyde . . . so that unnethe lefte half the peple onlyve" (the Black Plague); the death of Pope Clement; the "grete derthe of thinges" (a famine) followed by runaway inflation of prices; and finally "the see and the lond gan to wexe more bareyne than they were to forhonde."[52] To look at such entries as skeletal chronology is to ignore what amounts to their fictional plot, which in this entry and in Walsingham's record as well is an interpretation prompted by the force of the king's spoken "compleynte."[53]

These documents provide "evidence"—manifest in many more instances than those cited here—of a most unlikely kind, since any one event is reported differently in each of the accounts. But the apparent confusion as to "what actually happened" may well be more of a problem for modern readers than for fourteenth-century chroniclers and their audiences. For what commands their attention is the storial quality of the information, the conversation among important figures and the causal sequence of events centered around them. Validating the authenticity of deeds and words is manifestly not the first item on the agenda of the medieval student of the past. Yet that factor hardly prompts us to conclude that the chronicles are an impoverished species of more advanced historiography or a bastard form of poetic fiction. That there are inconsistencies among these documents about what the king or prince may have said on a certain occasion is all to the point, insofar as these gaps in the report locate the juncture at which the putative "facts" in a sequence give place to the *propriety* of describing them. Thus the rhetoric of a document is not a deformation of history but rather its affirmation.

To the extent that the propriety of telling the past was indebted to the oratorical skills of *amplificatio*, *copia*, and *narratio*, it witnesses the embedded orality within the written tradition that preserved them; it testifies to the power of speech to transform the consignification of syntactical events into a realistic account of the past; and most of all, as these proprieties of language attempt to ground discourse in reality, they also forge a significant link to the ground or property of the king's

[51] See *Historia Anglicana* 1:271–72.
[52] *Polychronicon* 7:345–47.
[53] See *Historia Anglicana* 1:272–73.

patrimony, the territories he is seeking to recover in France and preserve in England. The embellishment of oratory and the ornament of
fictional ordering—rather than distorting the "content" of history—
constitute its content by virtue of establishing voice as the essential
force behind the claim of England to its past. When Edward III first
arrives at Crécy ready to do battle against Philip of France, Froissart
accounts for the event by attributing to the king rousing words spoken
to his army gathered around him: "I am now on the land of my
mother's inheritance, given to her in marriage." His men want nothing
more, says Froissart, to seal their obedience.[54] The propriety of language has everything to do with the property of the king's demand:
both appeal to the orientation of so much medieval thinking in what
Wyclif calls the "priority of the origin"—in this case, the unimpeachable origin of discourse in voice and of inheritance in the land given
by ancestral promise.

The semiological relation between literary propriety and political
property in the chronicle accounts of Edward III does not depend, as
I have indicated, upon a standard of verisimilar correctness between
text and history. Rather, the form of chronicle constitutes evidence in
its own right, irrespective of the accuracy of historical reference. In this
regard, it manifests what economic historians of the middle ages think
of as the "ideology" of feudalism, when that term is used to signify a
social order in which "surplus" (money, goods, labor) is appropriated
by a ruling nobility in either church or state.[55] Although this paradigm
will be recognized as a classic formulation of feudalism per se, not only
its medieval phase, it is worth noting briefly that the control of surplus
in the economic sphere bears directly upon the political control of
property in the fourteenth-century chronicles. Because the claim to
property appeals specifically to the commonplaces of rhetorical embellishment, the form of chronicle becomes evidence, in the most basic
sense of the term, of feudal ideology. What is critical here, however, is
that the appropriation of surplus is an accomplishment of what I am
calling the "orality" of the account, the capacity of rhetoric to assert
itself over the status of text as document. This assertion, to repeat, is
aligned with the accumulation of political property by the royal demesne. In the next chapter, I will take up again the economy of
feudalism and the deferral of crisis.[56] For now it is appropriate to
consider primarily how crisis is contained by the persistence of oralism
in the writing of history, and therefore I return to the link between

[54] *Chroniques* 3:165.

[55] See, e.g., Hilton, *Class Conflict*, ch. 20.

[56] For the economic argument about the crisis of feudalism, see Hilton's essays in
Class Conflict, chs. 19 and 22.

rhetoric and property in the campaigns of King Edward and the Prince of Wales during the conflicts immediately following Calais—those at Poitiers between 1355 and 1356.

The accounts of this battle are unanimous in stressing the impossible odds faced by the English army, a mere eight thousand led by the prince, now aged twenty-six, against approximately sixty thousand French soldiers headed by John II. The suspense leading up to battle— stretched out over weeks and months—is also extenuated by Geoffrey le Baker, the Chandos herald, and Froissart; and each author takes advantage in his own way of the narrative tension in the moments preceding the engagement. Turning first to Baker, we cannot miss the thrust of rhetorical *inventio* again controlling the order of events as it did earlier in the account of King Edward facing the raid at Calais; but this time the author invents two speeches by which Prince Edward heartens and encourages his archers. Their basis, which at least one scholar has already noted, is not military history but literary tradition stemming ultimately from Roman eloquence and probably from Livy.[57] The oratory of the moment is elegantly captured in a renaissance translation of the second speech, rendered by John Stow:

> Your manhood (saith he) hath bin alwaies known to me, in great dangers, which sheweth that you are not degenerate from true sonnes of English men, but to be descended from the blood of them which heretofore were under my fathers dukedome and his predeccessors, kings of England, unto whom no labor was paineful, no place invincible, no ground unpass-able, no hill (were it never so high) inaccessible, no tower unscaleable, no army impenetrable, no armed souldiour or whole host of men was for-midable. . . . Wherefore followe your antientes and wholy be intentive to follow the commandement of your captaines, as well in minde as in body, that if victorie come with life, we may still continue in firme frendship together, having alwayes one will and one minde: but if envious Fortuene (which God forbid) should let us at this present, to runne the race of all flesh, and that we end both life and labor together, be you sure that your names shall not want eternall fame and heavenly joy . . . to have wonne the nobilitie of France.[58]

The effect of the speech is not this time dramatized in the bearing of helmets and chests, but in what is doubtless a fact of military history during these campaigns, the strategic advantage of the English long-bow archers over the crossbowmen deployed by the enemy. The en-gagement is told with unusual attention to details: the English archers

[57] Barber, ed. and trans., *The Life and Campaigns of the Black Prince*, p. 61.
[58] Ibid., pp. 74–75. Geoffrey le Baker, *Chronicon*, p. 146.

were safely positioned in a marsh where the French cavalry could not reach them; but their position came to little purpose since their arrows either broke upon the steel plates and leather shields of the French front guards or "scaled toward the skies, descending in uncertain paths on both enemy and friend."[59] The occasion for *copia* in such details takes on its own force in the narrative, particularly at instances of editorializing: "The horrible madness of war continued, with Warwick and Salisbury fighting it out like lions to prove which of them could make the land of Poitou drunk with the most French blood, and each man gloried to stain his own weapons with hot blood."[60] The fear of being outnumbered is explicit in this narrative, but it is challenged rhetorically at several points. An English knight cries out from the field of combat, "Alas! we are defeated!" And "the lord prince retorted with faith in Christ and the Virgin Mary mother of Christ: 'You lie, vile wretch,' he said, 'you blaspheme if you say that I can be conquered as long as I am alive.'"[61] The narrator is just as resourceful with the oratory of his own realistic descriptions: "Then the threatening Prince of Wales raged forward, mutilating the French with his biting sword, snapped off lances, deflected stabs, annihilated advances, supported the fallen, and taught the enemy what desperate fury was like under the pale of war."[62] Parallelism, balance, opposition—the orator's customary props for holding the attention of listeners—are all here; and in order to make the reading experience simulate more emphatically the appearance of a listening experience, the narrator feels not the least hesitation about shifting on occasion from prose to verse: the prince "threw himself into the middle of the enemy forces,

> And whirled about savagely
> His sword everywhere;
> He slashed those in his way,
> And killed others;
> He ruined all things
> In the path of that sword."[63]

As the odds of sixty thousand in the French army are countered by the rhetoric of this English report, the narrator does not abuse the interests of chivalric balance. It is captured by yet another commonplace of oral narrative, parataxis, found frequently in the details of the story, such

[59] *Chronicon*, p. 148.

[60] Ibid.

[61] *Chronicon*, p. 150.

[62] *Chronicon*, p. 151.

[63] *Chronicon*, p. 152. For borrowings from Lucan's *Pharsalia* in these passages, see pp. 151–52.

as "the English fought, the French fought back" ("Pugnant Anglici, repugnant Gallici"); or "with the wheel of fortune spinning precipitously, the prince of Wales plunged into the enemy forces and, like a lion of raging courage, he subdued the proud, pardoned the wounded, and received the capitulation of the usurper."[64] But the parataxis facilitating oral performance also functions to some extent as the organizing principle of what happened at Poitiers, for example, when the narrator in all chivalry gives the final words of his account to the captured King John—soon to be deported as a prisoner back to England. Seated at dinner as the guest of his English captors, he addresses the group:

> "Although we have met with an inevitable and sad fate, at least we have come to it worthily; for although we have been conquered in battle by our noble cousin, at least we were not captured like a criminal or cowardly fugitive hiding in a corner, but, like a stout-hearted soldier ready to live and die for a just cause, we were taken on the field by the judgment of Mars, where rich men were held to ransom, cowards fled ignominiously and the bravest of all gave up their lives heroically."[65]

In offering the equivalent of narrative relief after the "killing," "cutting," "bruising," "gutting," and "beheading," this closing oration also effectively punctuates what the French encroachment has signified all along—a threat to the origin of English political power through a semiological severing of the king's word from his property. In protecting this bond of language and land through the propriety of oral elements, Geoffrey le Baker's chronicle uncovers what is not "reported" in his story of the French wars, an infrastructure or myth of dominion crucial to the English kingship.

The *amplificatio* of voice is not unique to Baker's account of the battle of Poitiers. We find it also in the reports of this engagement written approximately twenty years later by Froissart and the Chandos herald, both of whom conjoin the authority of speaking with the recovery of land as they had in their reports of Crécy and Calais. Like Baker, Froissart also mentions a speech delivered by Prince Edward in the moments before advancing on the enemy; but it is not a speech to the archers, and it differs in content. Here again, whatever is not preserved of the prince's actual words appears to be of less concern to the chronicler than dramatizing the authority of an oration in the record: "My good men, we are a small band against the power of our enemies, but we must not be discouraged for that, because victory does not go with a numerous or great people, but where God wants to send it. . . .

---

[64] *Chronicon*, p. 153.
[65] *Chronicon*, p. 154.

So I beseech you to press yourselves forward together this day in good combat, for it pleases God and St. George that you shall see me today a true knight."[66] The formulaic phrases of the discourse ("un petit contre le poissance" or "la victoire ne gist mies ou grant peuple") testify rather suggestively to the context of this account in conversational language. And so too with other axiomatic pronouncements and slogans scattered throughout the story about Poitiers.

For instance, Froissart records cries of "Saint Jorge! Giane!" on the English side, while the French shout, "Monjoie! Saint Denis!"[67] Such pronouncements, commonplaces of battle literature in the middle ages, are also synecdochic echoes of their circulation in what amounts to an "oral chronicle" of the times, since they have the force of gesture tantamount to military advance. Formulaic phrases of this sort are, accordingly, of a piece with other instances of language as gesture, such as sounding and flyting—a vivid illustration of which is mentioned by Froissart. Appropriately included immediately prior to battle, the exchange between Sir John Chandos, Prince Edward's right-hand man at Poitiers, and Lord John de Clermont of the French army serves as a provocation of action powerful enough to threaten the existing truce, rather than a communication in any textual sense:

Clermont:	"Chandos, how long have you been wearing my emblem?"
Chandos:	"You have mine . . . for the emblem is as well mine as yours."
Clermont:	"I defy that . . . and were it not for the truce which is between our forces and yours, I would show you immediately that you have no right to wear them."
Chandos:	"Ha! . . . Tomorrow you will find me all dressed to defend and prove by force of arms that the emblem is as well mine as yours."
Clermont:	"Chandos, Chandos, these are the big boastings of you English, who do not know how to devise anything new; whatever they look on, theirs is beautiful."[68]

The history of oral narrative is rich with such exchanges—Roland against Ganelon, Beowulf against Unferth, the Green Knight against King Arthur, and so forth.[69] In Froissart's rendering, "boastings" are provoked by insults about martial "emblems," but since they are worn as signs and symbols of military victory over disputed property in

[66] *Chroniques* 5:33.
[67] *Chroniques* 5:38, 40, 44.
[68] *Chroniques* 5:28–29.
[69] See Parks, *Verbal Duelling in Heroic Narrative*.

France, linguistic conflict is explicitly assimilated to territorial displacement.

BETWEEN ORAL AND TEXTUAL

Although verbal confrontation in Froissart's account is a prelude to military combat, the function of language as an agonistic instrument also demarcates the border between oral cultural practices and textual determinations to analyze, explain, and transfer meaning. Because of the recording into text of such oral conflicts as those between Chandos and Clermont, Froissart's account participates in the larger cultural tension between orality and writing. And that is one reason why it shows such flexibility in adopting both spoken and written proprieties—as if to make one set of practices familiar to the other. It is apparent, as recently observed, that in the chronicles Froissart is a writer of texts, whereas in his poetry he is much more concerned with the "oral performance . . . he is engaged in: reading his works out loud." But the separation is not as clear-cut as this assessment would have it.[70]

In the role of objective reporter, for instance, Froissart stands on the side of text, explaining and describing, though analyzing and testing very little. But, breaking out of this posture and entering into the immediacy of oral circumstances, he editorializes at the most telling moments and with the most emphatic responses. Amid the charge of horsemen and foot soldiers, the prince orders his banner bearer, Sir Walter Woodland, to advance into the melee, and Froissart stops the narrative to address us on the subject of the danger of being unhorsed in battle: "You must well realize that whoever fell was not able to pick himself up again, nor could he be very well helped by others."[71] Froissart never ventures so far into empathy that he allows historical persons to speak directly to the audience, for example, as do fictional characters in Dante. But perspectival shifting is frequent, insofar as the narrator apparently feels no need to keep his opinions and feelings out of the account. They appear in his approbation of both the Prince of Wales, "who was like a lion fierce and merciless," and the enemy King John, who "showed himself a very good knight; in fact, if one-fourth of his people had fought as well, the day would have been won."[72] At such junctures the rhetoric of the author attempts to overcome the

---

[70] Huot, *From Song to Book*, p. 241; on the chronicles, p. 314.

[71] *Chroniques* 5:39.

[72] *Chroniques* 5:55, 5:47.

mere writtenness of the text, as he gives voice to the moment at the same time as he is deoralizing it into written record.

The persistence of the spoken is also significant to the matter of inheritance in the account of Poitiers rendered by the Chandos herald. Because he composed his biography in vernacular French verse, speeches and conversations tend to be even more formulaic and axiomatic than in the prose documents. Like other chroniclers, the herald emphasizes the impossibility of the odds against the English, a textual strategy serving not only military drama but the importance of conflict between what is claimed or spoken and the territory denied. The agonism of impending battle comes to a head—after papal negotiations fail—in a verbal taunt from the French camp when two English reconnoiters, Sir Eustace d'Abrichecourt and Lord Courton, are taken prisoner: "All the others will come after."[73] The account of the English response follows directly—not with a counter boast but with action in the field. The little conversation we hear is gestural and formulary: "Advance! gentlemen," the Earl of Salisbury shouts, "by the grace of God; / since it has pleased Saint George / that we were once last but now we will be first, / let us have all the courage to do it!"[74]

Unlike other reports, the herald's account notes the absence of the prince from the initial stages of engaging the enemy, and his awaited appearance is marked by his astonishment at seeing the French divisions. He responds with a prayer followed immediately by a call to arms: "Almighty Father, / as I have always believed / that you are King over all kings / . . . for your holy name, / please protect me and my people from evil / . . . Advance, advance banners! / Let everyone think of his honor."[75] Perhaps in sharpest contrast with Geoffrey le Baker, the herald describes action in generalities, avoiding the biting details of sword and battle ax in preference for naming who was present or absent; the language of the text, therefore, stands out all the more as pronouncement, rather than as realistic detail; and yet the conjunction of such formulary orations with the recovery of territory, as we note in the following remarks of the prince, cannot be overlooked. "Advance gentlemen! said he, for God's sake, / let us take this place and this position, / if we value our life and honor."[76]

As this text is preoccupied with extreme contrasts in military power and hopes for victory, so also are oral pronouncements set in relief against a highly textualized record of events. The conflict is particularly apparent in the editorialized remarks of the narrator who, like

[73] *La vie du Prince Noir*, l. 1120.
[74] *La vie*, ll. 1175–79.
[75] *La vie*, ll. 1263–65, 1270–71, 1276–77.
[76] *La vie*, ll. 1339–41.

Froissart, breaks in on the scene of a conversation to say, for example, that all men at once cried out "Guinne! Saint George!" And then the herald himself enters the scene to tell us, "What would you want me to tell you? / The great division of Normandy / was defeated on that morning."[77] The force of the narrator's own rhetorical question contributes to the orality of pronouncements and formulary phrases elsewhere, as well as to the sense that the entire account is an extension of what the herald has heard over the years. The battle of Poitiers draws to a close on this note, situating the report between text and speech: he has written, he says, "as I have heard it recorded / . . . Pardon me if I have spoken it briefly, / for I have passed over it swiftly."[78]

And the remark is not only relevant to the story of Poitiers: the poem as a whole offers abundant evidence that, while relying on what may have circulated by word of mouth, the narrator intends surely to deliver his biography orally before an audience present and listening.[79] He opens the text observing that the composer of "beaux ditz" ("poems," "songs," "fables") has been often referred to as "aucteur" ("author") and "amenteveur" ("recorder"); but rather than a "jangelour," that kind of author well known for performing songs before an audience with grimace, buffoonery, and lies, the narrator of these "beaux ditz" will do more than "imitate the snail" ("contreferoit le lymache").[80] That is, he will follow those who speak about virtue and put their songs or poems "in a book" ("en livre mettre"), so that a "just record" ("juste recort") may be made, "because it is alms and charity to speak of the good and true."[81] Thus he commences "to record" ("recorder") his "beaux ditz," which "you" will "hear" if you "listen with a good heart."[82]

Attention-getting devices of this sort are frequent: not since the time when the Lord God was born has there been a more valiant person— "as you will hear in my records, if you will listen and attend to my material." And reminders such as "I do not lie to you" underscore the fiction of the recorder as public speaker who is preventing stories from being forgotten within the silent pages of a book. "So must this material not be forgotten under any circumstances. Now is it most fitting

---

[77] *La vie*, ll. 1234–37.

[78] *La vie*, ll. 1400, 1409–10.

[79] On heralds as minstrels in late medieval France and England, see Taylor, *English Historical Literature*, p. 167.

[80] *La vie*, ll. 1–4, 17–20.

[81] *La vie*, ll. 32, 34–36.

[82] *La vie*, ll. 41, 48, 53–54.

for me to tell it to you."[83] At one point he even allows his preoccupation with addressing an audience to carry over into his approach to his subject matter: "Now is a good time for me to address myself to . . . my material."[84] Otherwise a mere formality of style, "addressing the material" has a particular relevance in this poem, insofar as the author is not making a story out of old books but "recording" a living body of information, the unwritten oral chronicle about the deeds of the king's first son in France and Spain. The Chandos herald contributes to information commonly circulated by word of mouth, and thus he apologizes at times, for example, with "Why should I make you a lengthy record about what men must already understand?"[85] Small wonder he wrote in vernacular French.

Other poets make eloquent satirical use of such topoi of authorial apology, but the herald has more modest ambitions. His poetry is simple, in some passages overstylized and repetitious; yet in view of his ambition of keeping alive the memory of the prince's prowess for recovering the English patrimony, he chose the medium of public performance he had doubtlessly witnessed at court as herald of the Chandos family. Like the jongleur, he would preserve from the past the living presence of his hero by virtue of the performative qualities of his text. But the inevitable deoralization of his medium is also involved in his undertaking, although the conflict of this factor hardly ever surfaces as a problem of textuality in its own right. One instance of it closes the poem, when the narrator describes the prince speaking, as it were, from beyond the grave through the inscription on his tomb. Without someone passing by to read it—as the herald has been saying about his own delivery from the start of his poem—the prince's last words (and thus the poem as a whole) remain dead letters etched in stone: "Listen to what I shall say to you, / just as I know how to say it."[86] Had he explored the possibilities of this conflict between voice and writing, the Chandos herald, presumably, would have composed a very different poem. As it is, his "record" documents the phenomenon I have been exploring, that the crisis of orality in textual history is very much a part of the crisis of dominion in political history.

A final example from Froissart deserves mention in this connection, because he too assumes that his *Chroniques* are in large part an extension of the oral history about Edward III and the French campaigns. He opens the "Prologue" by observing that in order to "rejester" for the present and future the glorious deeds of this time, he will "put into

---

[83] *La vie*, ll. 104–106, 268, 454–56.
[84] *La vie*, ll. 80–81.
[85] *La vie*, ll. 1583–84.
[86] *La vie*, ll. 4255–56.

prose only the true information which I have had [i.e., heard] from villeins, knights, esquires and those who have helped them."[87] And he closes the "Prologue" with a similar effort to resuscitate his written words with the immediacy of a listening experience when he addresses audiences "in times to come" ("temps à venir") who will want to know the author of "ceste hystore"; as if stepping before an audience in the fourteenth century, he steps forward for us: "My name, for those who wish to credit me, is Sir John Froissart, born in the county of Haynau and in the good, beautiful, and fresh city of Valenciennes."[88]

Many sections of his book commence with "you have heard before" and "I must now tell you," or "I can never tell you." When Froissart turns to comment on his own writing—as he often does—there is hardly an occasion in the entire *Chroniques* when he does not appeal to verbs of speaking like *dire* or *parler*. Such expressions, as noted earlier, effect the same participation in the narrative as editorial commentary. We see the conjunction of editorial and emotional responses especially in accounts of momentous events, such as the death of Sir John Chandos in battle, which inevitably elicit asides from Froissart. When that knight is run through on the battlefield, those around him cry out, "Oh! gentle knight, flower of all courage, Sir John Chandos, may evil befall the forging of the lance which pierced you and sent you into the peril of death"—to which Froissart responds with his own anguished prayer, "May God have mercy on him for his graciousness."[89] In some instances, we can be sure that Froissart had no firsthand information, and thus could only offer a version of what had obviously circulated by word of mouth, as he does for an engagement during the Spanish campaign in 1372. Narrating with a fair amount of detail, he assures us the English showed themselves well, "by what I have heard from those who were present at the engagement of La Rochelle."[90] But his aside is not simply autobiographical. As we have seen in the many aspects of orality in this and other chronicles, the effort to vitalize speaking, whether it be through the *amplificatio* of conversation among historical persons or through the poetics of the text as performance, is tied up with the English claim to political power in France. The threat to that power—as we see it in the chronicles— consists in the displacement of the king's voice from his promised patrimony. The struggle with writing in these documents witnesses the political dilemma of forestalling that displacement by preserving the

---

[87] *Chroniques* 1:1.
[88] *Chroniques* 1:7.
[89] *Chroniques* 7:206.
[90] *Chroniques* 8:38.

dominion of the English Crown through its roots in late medieval orality.

THE CRISIS OF POWER

These documents tell the story of the insult to the national pride in the loss of the French territories and the slow, uphill struggle of the English to vindicate their history and their hegemony on the Continent. But they do not tell quite so plainly the story of the crisis of power that is at stake simultaneously in the moments of victory over France. That story is available beyond the "facts" or, rather, within the conflicting narratives about what happened abroad under the kingship of Edward III. The weakening of political rule is surely apparent in the desperate sickness of the once valiant Black Prince during the middle 1370s and in the gradual decline of his father into dementia. But the narratives of their ventures in France and Spain witness a decline of a different order, a more general crisis in the fabric of society during the later middle ages.

Insofar as the chronicles illustrate the conflict between oral and textual habits occurring on other fronts during the fourteenth century, it becomes apparent that the effort to affirm the power of voice is also evidence of the impending erosion of the centuries-old validation of the bond of the word in a ruler's claim to land. These documents demonstrate, without explicitly saying so, that this tradition could no longer be sanctioned by appeal to its origins. The story of victory in France compensates for the displacement of power from the spoken word and from its historical roots in property. In economic terms, the "ideology" of feudalism was slipping from the grip of seigneurial control. The upset of this balance becomes evident in the economy of chronicle, in its repeated appropriation of oral models for recollecting events within a context that would eventually become the source of questioning and validating them.

Wyclif surely contemplated this eventuality as he attacked doctrines of church ownership of property, but he never capitulated the secular arm of power, which remained for him the epitome of rule. Moreover, any possible displacement of speaking by writing was flatly abrogated through his vigorous commitment to the oral basis of *proposicio realis*, to the location of power in the spoken *forma verborum* of the Bible, and even more radically to reading, writing, and teaching in the English vernacular. Ockham, on the other hand, is closer to the displacement of rule that we witness in the conflict of voices in the chronicles. For his defense of Franciscan poverty and his attack on the *plenitudo potestatis* of the pope arise through his dislocation of essence from the universals of being to the words of everyday discourse. Yet even in this move, Ockham does not assume that writing is an empty cipher of the universal; it remains for him the representation of the "spoken" language of the mind. The subtleties of such philosophical approaches to the margin between oral and written become much more prominent in the chronicles written under Edward III, particularly those in the vernacular.

They witness, to begin with, what has been said about literacy in general during the middle ages: "The writer remained a visual artist and the reader a specialist in the spoken word. . . . The laity were gradually coaxed toward literacy by ensuring that it changed the old ways of hearing and seeing as little as possible."[91] The orality of reading finds its notation in the rhetoric of the chronicles. As the voice of *dominium* in these documents would make writing echo the old ways of seeing and hearing, the chronicle form also participates in the larger cultural hesitation about the reception of writing. As paradoxical as it may seem, chronicle history manifests a resistance to its own writtenness.

And yet such resistance is not a phenomenon associated exclusively with literacy. It does not surface out of some sort of endemic skepticism toward new things or out of an incipient disdain for the *via moderna*; nor is it a matter of deliberate choice. Rather, it eventuates from distinct cultural conditions of the time which are grounded in a "mythologic" that resolves or mediates conflict. The resistance to writing in the chronicles—their tendency to vitalize rhetorical forms—is aligned with the assertion of dominion in the social order: both proceed from the same myth that grounds discourse in the assumed priority of voice. It is not that writing is a vacant form cut off from its author and thus an intrinsically inadequate vehicle, but rather that writing confronts orality with an illusion it does not countenance—that it would seek to be proliferated as an absolutely undifferentiated mode.

It has been noted of pre-chirographic society (not without oversimplification) that the oral mind is not inclined to analyze.[92] Yet even in the developed literacy of the fourteenth-century chronicles, the attempts to "explain" social history are remarkably unanalytical. What we see, instead, are the customary oral habits of the affirmation and aggregation of information apparent in such tell-tale commonplaces as *amplificatio*, *copia*, and *narratio*. The accounts of battles, if not all campaigns, from 1345 to 1357 do not explore and expose the opposition

---

[91] Clanchy, *From Memory to Written Record*, p. 230. Cf. Huot, *From Song to Book*, pp. 2–4.

[92] Ong, *Orality and Literacy*, p. 37; for oral expression as "additive rather than subordinative" and "aggregative rather than analytic," see pp. 41, 43, 44, 47, 49.

but bolster by and large the politics of British hegemony; they are like their heroes, agonistic, insisting on the authenticity of their own speaking, and thus affirming the political status quo.[93] Chronicle writing manifestly avoids accounting for its own rhetoric and consignification, and that is why it does not question and test its representation of the past or establish the kinds of departures that were to mark historical consciousness in subsequent centuries.

Accordingly, this resistance to writing in the chronicles of the time constitutes, in effect, a resistance to history itself. We observe, particularly in England, a society still in the grip of a nostalgia for the political ideals of feudalism and its anachronistic myth of the power of a ruler in his presence and word.[94] As language in this context is an instrument of opposition, to engage and provoke rather than to exchange and communicate, so also does it betoken a cultural infrastructure that does not favor change but equilibrium and homeostasis. The economy of this ideology is fortified powerfully by a historicism designed to accommodate literary proprieties (the "surplus" of writing) to the familiar koine of oral custom. However, at the same time as the embedded orality of chronicle would underwrite a victorious future for the dominion of England in France, it also signifies—rather unwittingly—a genuine uncertainty at the heart of the old locations of power in voice, property, and the past. Excluding the threat of the letter and the challenge of history could only succeed for so long before the representation of writing as a form of speaking would be recognized as a problem in itself.

As the chronicles written about Edward III do not engage that problem in order to weigh its theoretical and historical consequences, neither is it confronted explicitly in the documentary history of his successor, Richard II. The orality of writing remains a fact of the times, no less a feature of the historical record through the end of the century than a problem at the heart of Richard's dominion and his ultimate deposition.

[93] Cf. Ward, "Some Principles of Rhetorical Historiography," pp. 147–48: "In the twelfth century . . . rhetorical history functioned, like liturgy, to close out doubt and encourage and create certainty." For the fourteenth century, see Aston on the "vocal letters" of devotional literature ("Devotional Literacy," p. 114).

[94] See Bean, *From Lord to Patron*, p. 235, for comparisons with pre-Conquest England; Catto, "Andrew Horn," in Davis and Wallace-Hadrill, eds., p. 391, on the *Liber Horn* as "very nostalgic" about the Anglo-Saxon past; and Taylor, *English Historical Literature*, p. 3, for the opinion that the entire century was "still profoundly medieval."

Chapter Five

THE POLITICS OF LITERACY IN THE REIGN OF RICHARD II

"You will swear that you will not assent nor suffer,
as far as you are capable, that any judgment,
statute, or ordinance made or rendered in this
present parliament will be in any way annulled,
reversed, or repealed at any time in the future. . . .
So help you God and his saints."
—in Parliament, 1388

INTRODUCTION

Chronicle histories through the end of Edward III's reign (1377) present us with a paradox: on the one hand, authors are concerned—in a modern idiom—to "get it in writing," so that a report fleetingly circulating by word of mouth did not evaporate; and yet on the other, they perpetuate one of the oldest commitments in medieval tradition when they borrow the styles and strategies from the arts of eloquence to vitalize and validate the written record. The rhetoric of history writing under Edward III throws light on the general inquiry I have been pursuing into why orality persisted in a culture making unprecedented use of documents and books. It is obvious that writing was engaged to replace a precedent oral history; but, by recuperating the older model, the new venture in historiography compromised the border it might have otherwise fortified. The *discourse* of voice, as I have called it, occluded the theoretical and historical difference of writing, and that is one reason why the record of Edward III is so fraught with nostalgia for the vanishing world of feudalism.

The reign of his successor, Richard II (1377–1399), is marked by a similar nostalgia, not just in the historians but in the king himself. And as writing proceeded more or less in the shadow of England's political interests under Edward, it was also manipulated during the reign of Richard. Scholarship has duly noted that the sovereign power of Richard is illustrated by the success and failure of his word; but it has not studied the political machinations surrounding his reign in relation to the status of written and spoken language toward the end of the middle ages.[1] In this chapter, I suggest that this relation is crucial to understanding both the trials of the king and the trials of literacy.

Like the rhetoric of orality embedded in the text of Edward's history, literacy is a sign in a complex semiology about the distribution of power in the government of England during the last quarter of the fourteenth century. From the king to the commons, the use of written documents and the power of the spoken word figure prominently in the records about the political and economic collisions of this time. The bloodiest pages in this history are written for 1381 when peasants and townspeople rose up in furious protest against the authorities and laws keeping them in "servage." But other instances are equally violent: Richard sat in parliament during the purge trials of 1388 without any voice of authority to save his friends and advisers as the appellants ran roughshod over the entire textual history of written precedent to bring in verdicts of capital punishment against them. And, finally, the deposition in 1399 is justified by parliament and chronicler alike on the grounds that the king had arrogated "into his own mouth" the written law of the land. As such circumstances illustrate the wanton political appropriation of both written and oral authority, they inevitably point to the delicate balance of these two traditions in the literacy of the time; and yet simultaneously literacy functions in the historical record as a sign of the delicate balance of political power between king and lord, aristocracy and peasantry, learned and unlearned at this stage in English history.

In order to explore the sign-like status of literacy in the text of Richard's history, I will proceed in the same way as I considered rhetoric in the chronicles of Edward. If literacy represents how people communicated, it does so metalinguistically by exposing the overlap of oral and written modes. Because of its split allegiance to two traditions, its diglossia, literacy was ready for exploitation by the torn allegiances of dominion in contemporary political affairs. The uncertain relation of voice to writing, which, as we have seen in other contexts, typifies manuscript culture, reached the breaking point in the politics of the time. Historical forces brought to the surface the "politics" within the structure of literacy itself: the old hierarchy in which writing was the subordinate echo of voice was challenged with unprecedented force. That structure had been recognized before—par-

---

[1] E.g., Figgis, *The Divine Right of Kings* (1896); Oman, *The Great Revolt of 1381*; McKisack, *The Fourteenth Century*; Steel, *Richard II*; Hutchison, *The Hollow Crown* and "Shakespeare and Richard II"; Galbraith, "A New Life of Richard II," and "Richard II in Fact and Fiction"; R. H. Jones, *The Royal Policy of Richard II*; Sayles, "Richard II in 1381 and 1399"; Tuck, *Richard II and the English Nobility*; Mathew, *The Court of Richard II*; Given-Wilson, *The Royal Household and the King's Affinity*.

ticularly by Ockham and Wyclif—as a resource of enormous power. And now others were aware of it too, as they moved onto the floor of parliament and into the city streets with very dangerous agenda.

THE RISING OF 1381

No one was more aware of the precarious balance between social order and the old hierarchy of language than those who set out to record the events of the revolt during the summer of 1381. The chroniclers, on whom we rely principally for details about what happened, were members of the high literate culture of the middle ages—for example, Thomas Walsingham from the scriptorium in the Abbey of St. Albans in Hertford, or the anonymous author of the *Anonimalle Chronicle* from St. Mary's Abbey in York.[2] They felt immediately the danger to their own survival at the hands of the masses protesting indiscriminately against lay and ecclesiastical authority. The cultural diglossia of four-teenth-century England was never more sharply evident than in their satiric disdain for the rebels as *rustici*. Chroniclers use the word, on the one hand, to suggest that the whole body of those who rebelled were of "rustic" origin, and thus at the bottom of the social scale with "bondsmen," "natives," and "people of the soil."

But on the other hand, *rusticus* dates from early in Roman antiquity as a commonplace for characterizing the archaic speech habits, man-nerisms, and vocabulary of people who live in the country. Cicero and Quintilian so use the term to derogate a discourse that lacks the politeness and refinement of individuals familiar with *urbanitas* ("city life");[3] and Macrobius in the fifth century identifies the barbarous practices of people with their *rusticus* language.[4] In later medieval Latin, the term is regularly used in opposition to *litteratus* as a desig-nation of someone whose speech does not obey grammatical principles and who has no ability to read simple Latin.[5] *Rusticus*, accordingly, appears in conjunction with *laicus* ("layperson") to specify an individ-ual who is *illiteratus*, in contrast to a *clercus* ("clerk"), who could read, write, and perhaps even speak Latin. So *rusticus* has linguistic, not just agricultural, signification with reference to the rebels, as in Walsing-

[2] For a review of the scholarship, see Taylor, *English Historical Literature*. A handy thumbnail sketch of the events is in Hilton, *Bond Men Made Free*. Dobson, *The Peasants' Revolt of 1381*, has translated some of the accounts.

[3] *De oratore* 3.12.44; *Institutionis oratoriae* 1:6.3.7.

[4] *Commentariorum in somnium Scipionis* 2.10.6.

[5] See Parkes, "The Literacy of the Laity," pp. 556–63; he cites (p. 560) Walter Map for reference to the unlettered tongue of peasants. See also Clanchy, *From Memory to Written Record*, pp. 175–201.

ham's report about their violent exclamations as they burned the books and records of the authorities: "This exclamation pleased the rustics immensely, and once they were incited to even greater extremes, they shouted that all court rolls and old records be given to the flames, so that once the memory of ancient things had been destroyed, the lords could have no power to vindicate any law at all over them thereafter."[6]

As *rusticus* articulates the split in social class between lettered and ignorant, bondmen and free, it carries forward another powerful connotation, that the rebels thought of themselves as a new "affinity" gathered under King Richard. And although this notion may be explained politically as an expression of the rebels' program to do away with the ruling class in church and state, leaving no dominion except the king's, the claim is rooted ultimately in a social ideology reinforced by the hierarchy of language in medieval England, specifically by the priority of oralism in both Latin and vernacular literacy. It reflects at once the disdain of literate historians against the violence of illiterates raging in the streets, as well as the ambition of the mobs to imagine themselves as a new feudality answerable exclusively to the voice of one lord.

For instance, the *Westminster Chronicle* notes that the rebels held themselves out as "defenders of the king and the welfare of the realm against their betrayers."[7] The *Anonimalle Chronicle* reports similar descriptions of the crowds as they marched from Kent and Essex to Blackheath outside London in a band said to number 110,000 on either June 12 or 13. Demanding the heads of the Duke of Lancaster and fifteen other lords of the realm—including the Archbishop of Canterbury, Simon Sudbury—the protesters maintained their solidarity by a "wache worde en Engleys" directed to all newcomers:

"With whom haldes yow?"
"Wyth kynge Richarde and wyth the trew communes."

The penalty for failure to respond correctly was beheading.[8] Walsingham provides a link between this new fellowship of the "trew communes" and its Latin equivalent when he reports the rising of the inhabitants near his own abbey. Observing that his abbot was called upon to respond "to the commons" (*communibus*), he specifies that there was for them "no name more honorable than the name 'community'; for according to their stupid estimation, there would soon be no lords, but only the king and the commons."[9]

[6] *Historia Anglicana* 1:455.
[7] *Westminster Chronicle*, p. 2.
[8] *Anonimalle Chronicle*, p. 139.
[9] *Historia Anglicana* 1:472.

COMMONS

From the opening of twentieth-century scholarship on the revolt, it has been recognized that the people involved were not only "peasants."[10] The rising was, as recently remarked, a "plebeian affair"—including in the great majority peasants, tenant farmers, and serfs, but also a certain number of townspeople, such as members of the craft guilds, laborers, poor clergy, clerks, and even some members of the lesser gentry.[11] Although none of the London patriciate took part, some civil authorities from the outlying towns were apparently involved. The line of demarcation has been drawn somewhat vaguely between the ruling class (civil authority and landed gentry) versus individuals from all social categories below them, mostly peasants. Hence the word "commons," which occurs throughout the chronicle histories and court rolls, has been taken to mean the third estate.

Although the chronicles insist variously on John Wyclif and John Ball (the "mad priest") as principal instigators of the rebellion, no one has maintained that this vast and diffuse movement was organized by a central committee or a single outlook, let alone a specific individual.[12] From the many groups who took to the streets, a number of demands have been identified: freedom from homage to the lords; an end to policing by the gentry elite (to be replaced by popular policing, supposedly established by the Law of Winchester in 1285); the distribution of church property to the commons (the clergy to have property necessary only for their own subsistence); the abolition of church hierarchy (only one bishop to rule the church); tithes to be paid to a priest only if he were poorer than the parishioner; freedom from the poll tax; freedom from all serfdom to landlords (from "villeinage"); the replacement of all old law by a new law; direct access to the king—the only lord of the land.[13]

Although each of these demands arises from very pragmatic concerns in the third estate, their articulation at Mile End and Smithfield by Wat Tyler and at other points by John Ball have been taken to be representative of "naive monarchism."[14] With the erasure of written statutes—which had mandated taxes in the form of cash payment,

---

[10] Oman, *Great Revolt of 1381*, passim.

[11] The phrase is Hilton's in *The English Peasantry*, p. 216. See also Hilton, *Bond Men Made Free*, pp. 184, 221; and Dyer, "The Social and Economic Background to the Rural Revolt of 1381," p. 17.

[12] Oman, *Great Revolt of 1381*, p. 12.

[13] Hilton, *The English Peasantry*, p. 221. On protest against the cost of war see Kaeuper, *War, Justice, and Public Order*, pp. 349–58.

[14] Blum, *The End of the Old Order in Rural Europe*, p. 335.

goods, or labor—the masses thought of their king as a revered and benevolent guarantor of their liberties, a lord to whom they could appeal without any intermediary. This picture has been rejected by at least one scholar, who calls attention to the cynical politics of the rebel leaders.[15] But it is also possible to follow the lead of others who point out how frequently the peasants throughout southern England called for the sole lordship of the king and direct access to him. The peasants' idea of kingship, as expressed by Tyler, has a good deal of "illusion" in it; but still the masses "thought of the monarchy as an institution standing above individuals and classes, capable of dispensing even-handed justice."[16] This ambivalence toward government may be considered in terms of a recent economic argument that there was a growing alignment between laborers and lords, an increasing dependency on each other to sustain a developing market of goods and services.[17] From this point of view, peasant protesters had no "politics" to express their new and confused dependency, none except the naive veneration of monarchy.

Archaism and Vernacularity

However, that this veneration was simultaneous with contempt for law was not as "naive" as it may appear. The socioeconomic ambiguity is understandable in relation to the *archaism* of peasant protest. When Tyler and Ball preached that no lordships should exist but the king's, they echo a model of rule from the time of ancient kings.[18] Ball looks back as far as the beginning of history for his idea that the lordship of the aristocracy should be abolished on the model of the common parenthood of all people: "Whan Adam dalf and Eve span, / Who was thanne a gentilman?"[19] But the protest is archaic in an even more fundamental sense: it appeals to a time before writing, books, and the intermediary of recorded history, an ideal time—*illud tempus*—when God spoke, and the first parents listened; when a lord spoke, and his host responded. The appeal is to an oral ideal of language untrammeled by lawyerly qualification in the "fine print" of a document or the readerly experience of ambiguity and connotation "between the lines" of a story. Perhaps the most significant fact about the politics of

[15] Faith, "The 'Great Rumour' of 1377 and Peasant Ideology," p. 69.

[16] Hilton, *Bond Men Made Free*, p. 225. Cf. Kaeuper, *War, Justice, and Public Order*, p. 366.

[17] See Mann, *The Sources of Social Power* 1:409–12.

[18] On the archaism of peasant politics in the "magical" and "mythological" substrata of medieval culture, see Graus, "Social Utopias in the Middle Ages," pp. 3–19.

[19] *Historia Anglicana* 2:32–34.

the rebel speeches is that they were rendered in a language that the masses could understand, without the mediation of written documents or translations from another tongue. The *vernacularity* of peasant protest is one of the most obvious facts about it, and yet it remains one of the least appreciated factors in scholarship on the English rising. Ball, Tyler, and whoever else tried to rouse the peasants in that year were successful preeminently because they appealed to the vast illiteracy—or at best, semiliteracy—of their audiences, who lived in an oral world almost completely uneducated in the bookish history of government, contractual negotiations, and so forth.[20]

The closest that commentary has ventured toward the oral customs evident among the peasants is the attempt to explain why poor priests and clerks were counted among the rebels. According to one argument, since England had not seen an expression of heresy for over two hundred years prior to the Lollard movement in the late 1400s, the popular preaching exemplified by people like Ball gave vent to religious discontent that was swiftly fueled by the rebellious behavior in other sectors of society.[21] Those clergy who took to the streets may well have felt, according to this argument, that the other social orders had abdicated their divinely ordained roles, and Tyler and Ball were articulating this sentiment: the two of them suggest the existence of a period of unrecorded heretical preaching in England from the twelfth to the fifteenth century.

This opinion is especially suggestive with respect to the role of Wyclif's followers and the Lollards. Although there has been much uncertainty, for lack of historical record, about the origin and affect of Lollardy in the last two decades of the fourteenth century, we must not ignore the obvious connection that the movement has with the vernacular life of the peasants and commons: Lollards were notorious for protesting against the same diglossia as the third estate, the linguistic barrier of a mandarin elite in church and state who garnered authority in a written language that was no longer the mother tongue of the people. In order to press legal complaints, people had to hire lawyers who were compelled to represent them in a foreign language—pleading court cases in French and recording them, more often than not, in Latin.

But the commons in 1381 were certainly not ignorant of the politics of their situation. And the archaism of their political "ideal" is a specific

---

[20] Hilton, *Bond Men Made Free*, p. 214, comments that only "a sprinkling of the literate" were involved. Faith, "The 'Great Rumour' of 1377," p. 60, notes the illiteracy of the peasants. Kaeuper, *War, Justice, and Public Order*, pp. 373 ff., assumes greater literacy among "middle class" rebels.

[21] Hilton, *Bond Men Made Free*, p. 225, and *The English Peasantry*, pp. 209–13.

illustration of the vernacularity of their protest. The relation of these two factors, suggested in the speeches of Ball and Tyler, is explicitly established in the historical record of the connection between the agenda of 1381 and the so-called "great rumor" of 1377. As the earlier event has been studied recently, it shares several crucial points with the 1381 revolt, including the demand of special privileges for tenants on Crown lands, the validation of local traditions in ancient rights, and the veneration of charters as warrantee of those rights.[22] The similarity between the two events, as pointed out years ago, was the claim that peasants were exempt from services due a lord because of their residence on "ancient demesne."[23] They pleaded that they were "sokmen" or residents of property once owned by the Crown and thus entitled to all the rights and privileges formerly attached thereto by the king himself. Although "ancient" may be qualified to signify simply "former," the record indicates that the peasants of 1377 were seeking to circumvent heavy taxation by appealing to an ancient tradition of property rights.

DOMESDAY BOOK

The relevant detail of the pleading for amnesty from service or payment due is how it was appealed through legal channels. As we may surmise from a parliamentary statute passed in 1377, there was concern among the authorities that a general movement of civil uprising was afoot because of cases moved in the king's court by villeins and tenants who sought to be "discharged of all manner of service"—taxation in any form due a landlord. The pleadings appealed to the special privileges attached to ancient demesne as verified in "exemplifications from the Book of Domesday concerning those manors and vills where these villeins and tenants live."[24]

The use of the Domesday Book as a real estate record proved to be far more disappointing to the peasants than the parliamentary statute of 1377 suggests, since the verdict commonly reached in court was: "Domesday does nothing for them."[25] But such decisions did not stop peasants and tenants from pressing their cases. They continued to believe in Domesday, in spite of the fact that they could not read it,

[22] See Faith, "The 'Great Rumour' of 1377," pp. 62–63.

[23] Oman, *Great Revolt of 1381*, p. 10. Faith, "The 'Great Rumour' of 1377," reviews relevant scholarship on this issue.

[24] Recorded in the *Rotuli Parliamentorum* 3:21–22, and translated by Dobson in *The Peasants' Revolt of 1381*, pp. 76–78.

[25] See Barg, "The Villeins of Ancient Demesne," pp. 213–37; and Faith, "The 'Great Rumour' of 1377," p. 50.

and those who could told them that the citation sought was not to be found in its pages. Scholarship has been stumped on this inexplicable peasant veneration for the book, and all the more so because of the fierce hostility to documents and books during the destructions of the rising in 1381. But at least one scholar has pointed in a promising direction by suggesting that we pay less attention to the Domesday Book as a historical source and look instead at its role "in the popular imagination." The custom of "vouching Domesday," it is concluded, reflects "that the book itself had its own charisma."[26] And for this reason people continued to appeal to it, however mistakenly from a legal point of view, because therein was their hope for freedom.

This paradox is less mysterious once we bear in mind the oral fringe on which peasants lived in 1381. Unable, in the great majority, to read or write, they knew about a written text in their own language which provided final answers on various problems. It was even known in English as "Domesday" for at least two hundred years, as we learn from the *Dialogus de Scaccario*, which verifies its reputation among the populace. "This book is metaphorically called by the native English, Domesday, i.e., the Day of Judgment, . . . not because it contains decisions on various difficult points but because its decisions, like those of the Last Judgment, are unalterable."[27]

Whether or not the book contains information on the "difficult points" of the law is less important, from the perspective represented here, than the reverence generated out of the status of the text as a symbolic object. The "inscription" of the text is of little consequence to someone who, without the ability to read, simply believes that its pages "speak" about freedom in some mysterious way, above and beyond what the writing actually verifies. Regarding a book that lacks details about specific points to be nonetheless "final" in its decisions can only be appreciated on the oral side of the diglossic divide. Domesday was for the popular mind what Apocalypse was for the exegetes, a mythology, not a "legend" or "fiction" but one of the faiths people lived by. The myth of the book is based upon an unequivocal sense that its writing is a sign language of speaking.[28] And Domesday represents what ancient kings had spoken to the people. It is a profoundly archaic political basis for a belief that was alive and powerful in the vernacular life of fourteenth-century England.

It is difficult, if not impossible, to prove the existence of a myth with such wide cultural proportions by appeal to the historiographical model

---

[26] Faith, "The 'Great Rumour' of 1377," pp. 50, 51.

[27] *Dialogus de Scaccario*, p. 64.

[28] This cultural mythology is explored in my study *The Idea of the Book*, chs. 1–3.

of statistical evidence. At most one can only point to patterns of behavior in society, and that is what we find in the habitual leaning toward the oral side of literacy among those who rebelled in the fourteenth century. The events at St. Albans are a case in point. On June 14, a number of residents from the town and farmland around the abbey were apparently under the leadership of William Grind-cobbe at the Mile End conference, and heard that the king was providing charters of their liberation; but instead of waiting for them, they raced back to the abbey, a remarkable distance of thirty miles, to claim their own freedom from the abbot and specifically to take over the privilege of hunting and fishing in his warren. They were driven by the belief that they had been granted a charter of freedom in the misty past by King Offa, but that the monks of the abbey had stolen and suppressed it. According to subsequent records in the chronicle history of the abbey, the residents were provoked into rebellion by "the lies of certain old men" who told the younger generations about a beautiful document with illuminated and decorated letters hidden somewhere in the abbey.[29] Unseen and unread, the charter was "recorded" in the oral memory of the ancients of the village, who passed it on by word of mouth—like Domesday Book.

First taking possession of the abbey woods, they engaged in a distinctly mythological reunion with ancestral lands by the ritual exchange of verbal promises and the distribution of symbolic objects. They offered each other an oath of fealty, joined right hands, exchanged twigs and sticks from the warren, slew a rabbit from the fields, and displayed it as a sign of their reunion.[30] This ritualistic identification of the spoken word with objects from the woods is reminiscent of the practice of attaching to a manuscript page a piece of property deeded by its inscription. The orality of the whole affair is carried over subsequently when the crowds demand the abbot to produce the mythical charter of King Offa from the scriptorium; but failing that, they accept charters in its place guaranteeing them access to the abbey lands.[31] The documents invented by the abbot's scribes are as symbolically linked to peasant dominion as the next event at the St. Albans cloister. The people break open the doors and tear up the floor in which a previous abbot had cemented the millstones he once seized in repudiation of the peasant practice of using their own hand-mills, instead of paying to mill grain at the abbey. "They took the stones outside and handed them over to the commons, breaking them

[29] Walsingham, *Gesta abbatum monasterii Sancti Albani* 3:365.
[30] Ibid. 3:303.
[31] Ibid. 3:308.

into little pieces and giving a piece to each person, just as the consecrated bread is customarily broken and distributed in the parish churches on Sundays, so that the people, seeing these pieces, would know themselves to be avenged against the abbey in that cause."[32]

Like the symbolic orality of exchanging objects from the abbot's warren, the pieces of millstone are here explicitly linked by the contemporary recorder with the symbolic word of the eucharistic bread. Even a peasant totally unlearned in the host as divine logos would have understood fully that the piece of millstone in hand was identical with the spoken promise of liberty given in ancestral times variously by King Offa and his successors, if not God himself. Denying that tradition on the authority of statute was an act of stealing the spoken word out of its written representation, which is exactly what had circulated in popular legend around St. Albans about Offa's charter. But to someone from the scriptorium of the abbey, such an attitude was preposterous "illiteracy," and that is precisely what Walsingham and others said of the crowds who participated in the 1381 rising.

BOOK BURNING

The record of what happened at St. Albans is especially helpful in clarifying the attitude of the commons toward books and documents throughout many episodes of the rebellion. Scholarship has not really acknowledged, let alone explained, the ambivalence of this attitude—that the crowds both venerate documents and summarily burn them in fury.[33] The myth of the stolen letter and the ritual repossession of the warren and millstones signify, first of all, what has been noted of inscription in many other cultural phenomena of the later middle ages: it is speech written down or else it is merely artificial and deceitful. The burning of records in the streets, which is referred to frequently in the accounts, has been regarded too simply in scholarship as an unambiguous hatred of the law. But the burning of books is itself symbolic, perhaps the most symbolic act next to beheading in the historical records. It signifies, quite plainly, the anger of betrayal that arises specifically from the theft of spoken promise—what peasants took to be their natural right—out of the venerated symbol of it on the inscribed page. They felt cheated by the political diglossia of a scriptorium and court which alone had the power to confirm what history had always said and what the king was now saying about their com-

[32] Ibid. 3:309.

[33] E.g., Harding, "The Revolt against the Justices," studies hatred of law as a protest in "civil rights," rather than a reflection of the cultural implications of literacy (pp. 174 ff.).

plaints. Official writing had stolen their voice, and now they were reclaiming it. The historical record, needless to say, has in part stolen it too, by virtue of its compromised politics on the side of the authorities; and thus we need to look more closely at such peasant "signs" as book burning.

From an oralist's point of view, trusting the written was only possible if it ventriloquized its author. Herein do we find the basic structure of what is sometimes called the "lay literacy" of the middle ages. It explains, for instance, why the rebels were first inclined to believe the king when he promised letters of manumission for them, but then turned around to repudiate him when he requested from them letters listing their grievances. This ambiguity has everything to do with the marginal orality of manuscript culture at the time.

According to the *Anonimalle Chronicle*, on June 13 as the rebels stormed the Tower of London where the chancellor, archbishop, and members of the royal family remained in seclusion, Richard climbed out on to a turret and shouted to the crowds below that they should disband and that he would pardon them. "In one voice" ("a une voice"), the commons cried out that they would not disburse until they had captured the traitors within the Tower and had "charters" freeing them "from every kind of bondage."[34] Richard forthwith instructed a clerk to write a bill in their presence, signifying that they were pardoned and that they should go home to put "in writing" (*en escript*) all of their complaints. After putting the seal of his signet ring on the letter "in their presence" and delivering it to the peasants outside the Tower, Richard "had it read to them."[35] Although the peasants call for "chartres," they do not take the letter into their own hands and read it among themselves, nor do we know anything about what they may have put in writing to him. Presumably some in their midst could have composed responses, but the vast multitude surely could not have described each of their grievances *en escript* and almost certainly not in French or Latin.

The chronicler goes on to explain that they were incensed upon hearing the letter read, not only because—one assumes—it contained no reference to the liberation from *servage* demanded but also because it obviously mocked their illiteracy by imposing on them an even more sweeping servitude than labor law—obedience to the "King's English." They wanted a sign of promise and freedom synonymous with his spoken presence and word. In return they got a demand for qualification, verification, and reference—the unfamiliar habits of the literate

[34] *Anonimalle Chronicle*, p. 143.
[35] Ibid.

world. They wanted, as Wat Tyler put it, a "proper covenant"—not necessarily one they could read in every letter and clause, since the vast majority of them could not read at all.[36] In response, they got what they called "nothing but a trifle and a mockery" ("ne fuist forsqe traefles et mockerie"), and that is why they tore off to London to have it "cried about the city that all lawyers, all men of the chancery and exchequer, and *anyone who could write a bill or a letter* should be beheaded wherever they might be located."[37]

Walsingham provides similar evidence about the ambiguity of literacy among the peasants. He hyperbolizes peasant "voice" as an unforgettable example of their hatred toward the law. Narrating the abduction of Archbishop Sudbury from the Tower on June 13, he calls the mob "doomed rebels and whores of the devil" seeking out "the common father of the whole people."[38] At Sudbury's beheading, the chronicler describes "the most horrendous clamor" which went up out of the masses as "the wailings of the inhabitants of hell." He says that "no words were uttered during the horrific noise; their throats resounded with the bleatings of sheep, or to be more precise, with the devilish voices of peacocks."[39] From such oral bestiality, it is a short step for Walsingham to conclude his account of the revolt by linking hatred of law to the repudiation of all things written. And his position as an eminent member of the St. Albans scriptorium more than colored his rhetoric in this detail: in those times, he remarks, "It was dangerous to be known as a clerk, but even more dangerous if an inkpot should be discovered near one's elbow; for such people rarely or never escaped from the hands of the rustics."[40]

It is not difficult to see why a literate would so hyperbolize voice and writing among illiterate rebels. But we have no explanation of how this peasant attitude squares with the fact that they also venerated the written word and even communicated in it. The answer, as I have been suggesting, may be found in the marginal literacy of the times. If the law was no longer the "voice of the commons," their protest was stated *in amplificatione* as a hatred of writing in general, or—what amounts to the same thing—the spoken expression of sedition. Wat Tyler, says Walsingham, planned to kill all lawyers not only out of vengeance but in order to eradicate the existing law of the land: 'Thereafter, all the laws of England would emanate from his mouth and from his lips'

[36] Ibid., pp. 144–45.
[37] *Anonimalle Chronicle*, p. 144 (emphasis added).
[38] *Historia Anglicana* 1:459.
[39] *Historia Anglicana* 1:460.
[40] *Historia Anglicana* 2:9.

("de ore suo et labiis").[41] John Ball was similarly seditious because of what he said, and also because of what he wrote in the English language.

JOHN BALL'S LETTER

Following the entry of Ball's speech at Blackheath in the *Historia Anglicana*, Walsingham quotes a "letter full of enigmas" ("litteram aenigmatibus plenam") which Ball allegedly dispatched to the commons of Essex and which was apparently read as an act of treason.[42] Writing in English and calling himself "John Schep," once a priest of St. Mary's in York, Ball addresses a certain "Johan Nameless, Johan the Muller, and Johan Cartere" and bids "that thei ware of gyle in borugh, and stondeth togiddir in Goddis name, and biddeth Peres Ploughman go to his werke, and chastise welle Hobbe the robber, and taketh with you Johan Trewman, and all his felaws, and no mo:

> Johan the Muller hath ygrownde smal, smal, smal;
> The Kyngis sone of hevene shalle pay for alle.
> Be ware or ye be wo,
> Knoweth your frende from youre foo,
> Haveth ynowe, and seythe 'Hoo':
> And do well and bettre, and fleth synne,
> And seketh pees, and holde therynne.
> And so biddeth Johan Trewman and all his felawes."[43]

The treason here is reported to be in the provocation of insurrection. But one of the telling phrases, "ware of gyle in borugh," as one scholar has noted, throws a different light on the situation.[44] It echoes an archaic fear that tenant farmers and peasants had of towns and cities, as places where freemen ostracized people of the soil as well as "villeins." And thus it aligns the solidarity of those who protested the government with those who communicated in the vernacular and were wary of city law and literacy as enforced by abbey landlords and civil authorities. From the point of view of literates, the medium itself—written or possibly spoken English—is a threat as much for its suggestions of rebellion as for its difference from the official language of law.

Scholarship has pointed out for years that the line in the letter,

[41] *Historia Anglicana* 1:464.

[42] The political poetry concerned with the revolt has recently been reviewed by Taylor, *English Historical Literature*, pp. 243–46.

[43] *Historia Anglicana* 2:32–34. See Dobson, *The Peasants' Revolt of 1381*, pp. 381–82, for variatons in Knighton's account.

[44] Hilton, *The English Peasantry*, p. 76.

"biddeth Peres Ploughman go to his werke," is an allusion to Langland's poem and that it expresses unity of purpose among the rebels ("obedience to one leader").[45] Perhaps Ball and the few other literates among the rebels knew the poem and its satire against governmental and ecclesiastical abuses. Perhaps solidarity of purpose was galvanized by Langland's swelling sympathy for the downtrodden and his romanticized ideal of the plowman. However, it is highly doubtful that the great majority of those who rebelled had such a literary appreciation of a poem, even one in the vernacular.[46] The sedition reported, therefore, is more likely an expression of literate fear in the historical record than an indication of the secret messages that preaching and writing in the vernacular were able to convey at the time. The representation of Ball's letters in the chronicles of the rebellion—specifically the identification of vernacular literacy with sedition—betokens the challenge of English to the official literacy of the realm. It is seditious to the chronicler because it demonstrates how the written representation of the voice of the land could be appropriated so arbitrarily by people from across the diglossic border.

The bond between authority and law once fortified by the subordination of letter to voice in the high literacy of court or scriptorium was no longer on firm foundations. And thus the danger to the realm of England posed in the popular sentiment of protest illustrated by the circulation of Langland's poem, Ball's letters, and no doubt other documents did not stem simply from the oral roots of the English vernacular. Needless to say, English had already found acceptance, minor though it was, in some proceedings of government. The threat to political solidarity was posed by the manifest *literacy* of these writings, by the "gyle" of poetic allusion, elliptical names, clever references, innuendo—in short, all the tricks of the trade familiar to shrewd authors seeking to disguise voice in writing.[47] Walsingham and Knighton express an unsubtle disdain because of the *suggestiveness* of the vernacular epistles they quote, and that attitude speaks volumes about the hierarchy of language which was shuddering in the daring literacy of rebel leaders like Ball and Tyler. English was succeeding in co-opting the voice of a literacy that had always held writing in tow, and now the tail was wagging the dog.

[45] Oman, *Great Revolt of 1381*, p. 44; Hilton, *Bond Men Made Free*, p. 215. Cf. Middleton, "William Langland's 'Kynde Name,'" pp. 67–69.

[46] Medcalf, "*Piers Plowman* and the Ricardian Age in Literature," p. 687, draws attention to the problem of how a poem about the quest for peace became an instrument of rebellion.

[47] See Middleton, "William Langland's 'Kynde Name,'" pp. 75–76, on Langland's improvisation of identity as "transgression" of the "syntax" of social relations.

Just how dangerous vernacular literacy became is obvious from the editorial arrangement in several of the chronicles that cite Ball's writings in conjunction with the punishments delivered on him. For composing the letter and for *plura alia* ("many other things"), Walsingham reports that Ball was "accordingly drawn, hanged, and beheaded near St. Albans . . . in the presence of the king; and his cadaver was then quartered and sent to four cities of the realm."[48] The *plura alia* are not identified; instead Walsingham repeats the dangers of Ball's abuse of language, the *placentia verba* of his oratory and the *aenigmata* of his writing.

TRANSLATION AND SEDITION

The complaint against a descent from higher to lower literacy apparent in Walsingham's account is developed by Knighton into a full-blown theme about how the revolt arose in the first place. Scholarship has scoured his claim that Ball was a follower of Wyclif, who was the real violator of *ecclesiasticae unitatis* and the sower of discord *inter clerum et laicos*.[49] For want of documentation about a genealogy, however, the connection has remained superficial, and so has Knighton's correlative point, that Wyclif's interest in translating Latin doctrine into the tongue of the people was a primary cause of rebellion. But there is much more to Knighton's interpretation than a simple link between the uprising of the commons and Wyclif's influence on the legitimacy of their language. For Knighton leaves no doubt about the consequences for both social class and gender that would ensue from collapsing the traditional diglossia protecting the high literacy of religion and government from taint by association with the vernacular. By translating Holy Scripture "from Latin into the English, not the angelic, tongue" ("de Latino in Angelicam linguam non anglicam"), Wyclif "was to make vulgar for illiterates what was open to the wise and for women to read for knowledge what was only to be for the good of the understanding of clerks and literates; and thus he cast evangelical pearls before swine." Moreover, Knighton continues, what was dear to clerks was tossed to the "laughter of the commons" ("jocositas communis"); "the gem of the clerks was exchanged for the play of illiterates."[50]

Since women did not have the advantage of formal education, it is not exceptional for a clerk like Knighton to list them among the

[48] *Historia Anglicana* 2:34. Cf. Knighton, *Chronicon* 2:150.

[49] See Hilton's review of the problem in *The English Peasantry*, pp. 218–26.

[50] *Chronicon* 2:152. Cf. *Eulogium Historiarum sive temporis* 3:355 for similar oppositions to English translation.

illiterates. But the semiology connecting English speech and the tongue of women with the habits of "swine" registers a typical clerical misogyny as the sign of collapse in the diglossia stabilizing language and society. The *lingua angelica* has only one acceptable imitation, the high language of literates competent in Latin. Although Knighton could not be clearer about his disdain for English translation, his terms of rebuke, *jocus* and *ludus*, also tell in another direction, against the hierarchy of voice which had subordinated the letter of writing in the literacy of the scriptorium for centuries. English mocks that literacy by virtue of the randomness and playfulness which its imitation introduces into the traditional subordination. The point is not that *lingua anglica* is a far cry from the purity of *lingua angelica*, but that it is too close for comfort, a difference of no more than one letter, as Knighton himself suggests in his play on the words. His indictments of peasants and women bespeak the suppression of a political crisis within a linguistic one; or to put the matter differently, the raid of the commons against all structures of the establishment—what the rebels called the "hurlying time" of June 1381—carries out a social conflict latent in the order of language for as long as imitation held sway over the discourse of voice in literacy.[51] The *lingua anglica* was most certainly *non angelica*, and any attempt to equate them was bound to collapse class and gender distinctions in place from time immemorial.

But Walsingham, too, had a final thing to say about the teachings of Wyclif and the genesis of social conflict. Hyperbolic in the extreme, Walsingham's "literary portrait" of Wyclif's dying moment is not simply clerical outrage against the betrayal of one of its own. How Walsingham reports the stroke that Wyclif apparently suffered while preaching at Lutterworth on December 28, 1384, completes the semiological pattern of the precarious balance in the structure of traditional literacy posed by the new challenge of the vernacular. "Diabolical instrument," Walsingham begins as if writing an epitaph:

> enemy of the church, confusion of the illiterate, idol of heretics, mirror of hypocrites, inciter of schism, disseminator of hatred, fabricator of falsehood—John Wyclif. . . . On the feast of St. Thomas while in the midst of the sermon which he had prepared to deliver, he wanted to vomit up orations and blasphemies; but suddenly having been struck by the judgment of God, he felt a paralysis seize every member of his body all over. His mouth, which had spoken such monstrosities against God, his saints, and the church, and which had been miserably distorted out of its shape,

---

[51] The phrase is documented as a Middle English expression of the commons in the prose *Brut, or the Chronicles of England* 2:336. It refers to hurling down buildings and structures as well as hurling forth words.

exhibited a horrendous spectacle to those who were watching; his tongue, having been made mute, was denied the eloquence for confessing or testifying; and as the Divinity fulminated condemnation upon Cain, his shaking head demonstrated what had been pronounced upon itself just as evidently.[52]

The satire here aligns Wyclif's mouth with the countless references to the distortions of voice in the chronicle history of the revolt. Wat Tyler, we recall, wanted all law to originate *de ore suo et labiis*. The cadaver of John Ball was quartered in punishment for the *placentia verba* of his orations. The voices of the commons are the *horrificos strepitus* of bleating sheep and peacocks sent from the devil. English translation is pig Latin for the ears of women. The discourse of voice, once sole arbiter of dominion in church and state, is no longer recognizable. Mutilation and bestiality, therefore, are as much the historical "evidence" of social crisis in 1381 as an interpretation of the revolution in lay literacy taking place at the time.

Sovereign Voice

That the threat to the sovereignty of voice would not have the last word in the history of that year becomes apparent in the unusually detailed account of King Richard at Mile End and Smithfield on June 14 and 15.[53] Richard is depicted by the majority of contemporary reporters in the one moment of his life (aged fourteen) when he filled the shoes of his redoubtable father. In a startling—not to say romanticized—moment of strength, Richard intercepts on June 15 the standoff between the mayor of London and Wat Tyler which had come to bloody knives as a result of Tyler's failure to observe the proprieties of civil "speech" befitting a subject before his king. Insulted by his plain and rustic *sermonem*, his "base indiscretion and indiscrete baseness" ("temeritatem improbam et temerariam improbitatem"), the mayor attempts to arrest Tyler, and violence quickly follows.[54] But Richard rode suddenly into their midst shouting to the crowds: "What is this my men? What are you doing? You do not want to attack your king, do you? . . . I will be your king, I will be your captain and leader; follow me into the fields."[55]

[52] *Historia Anglicana* 2:119–20.

[53] For a list of the various representations of Richard's behavior on this occasion, see Duls, *Richard II in the Early Chronicles*, pp. 13–28.

[54] *Westminster Chronicle*, p. 10. Cf. similar accounts of Tyler's roughness *ab ore* in the *Historia Vitae et Regni Ricardi Secundi*, p. 66, and *Eulogium Historiarum* 3:153–54.

[55] *Historia Anglicana* 1:465. Cf. *Westminster Chronicle*, p. 12. The *Historia Vitae Ricardi* is singular in representing Richard as cowardly before the crowds (p. 65). See Steel, *Richard II*, p. 42, for the opposite opinion.

With Tyler wounded, Richard is represented in most reports as the new leader of a dubious affinity, successfully convincing the mobs to quiet down and assemble at Clerkenwell Fields a short distance away.[56] The *Anonimalle Chronicle* describes the commons as falling to their knees in Richard's presence after Tyler's execution and the impalement of his head upon a pole.[57] But the letters of manumission and amnesty probably drawn up at Mile End came to little effect. Walsingham is perhaps the most dramatic of the chroniclers in registering the utter repudiation of any written guarantees. And his sentiment is unequivocal in the relish he takes in reporting Richard's response to the envoys who came to the door of Waltham palace inquiring if the king would allow the commons their promised liberty equal to the lords. In *propria persona*, says Walsingham, Richard gives them an answer that both condemns them and mocks their demand as an assault on his royal literacy: "O you wretched people, hateful on land and sea. . . . Rustics you were and rustics you are still. You will remain in bondage, not as before but incomparably harsher."[58]

In this chronicle history, as we have seen, *rusticus* is a synecdoche for the privileges of cultural diglossia in fourteenth-century England. Giving letters in one breath and taking them away in the next may indicate something about the youthfulness of the king in 1381, as biographies of Richard have often noted; yet his action also signifies that the dominion of the moment is an expression of neither voice or writing per se. Rather, one mode can simply be *displaced* by the other, and therein is the "source" of power. Walsingham clearly appreciates the strength of mockery in this instance, just as he does in excoriating elsewhere how the vernacular mocks the literacy of Crown and church. But without saying so, he has noted the importance of displacement to the structure of literacy. In this sense, the social history of his report "explains" the politics of literacy just as much as the report explains history.

---

[56] E.g., the *Historia Anglicana* (1:465) and the *Westminster Chronicle* (p. 10) indicate that Tyler died in the fight with the mayor; the *Anonimalle Chronicle* (p. 149) says he was executed at Smithfield. None of the accounts claims that Richard was in total control of the situation at Mile End or Smithfield; see *Historia Vitae Ricardi*, p. 65, and nn. 99 and 100 (p. 185).

[57] *Anonimalle Chronicle*, p. 147.

[58] *Historia Anglicana* 2:18. The report in the *Anonimalle Chronicle* (p. 51) showing Richard as a hero of the masses and victor of the day in spite of the betrayal of the lords appears to be confirmed by the subsequent parliamentary rescission of the letters of manumission which had disinherited landowners by denying them their property rights. Such a reading of the accounts would seem to be denied by the *Historia Vitae Ricardi* (p. 64), which represents the king as a "sheepish" deceiver who would no sooner make good on his written promises to the rustics than allow himself to be taken in by the "wolves."

Propaganda

A history written so clearly in the interests of specific purposes sur-
prises no one familiar generally with the remaining years of the Ricardian monarchy. But the question which this record raises is: *why*
does history writing in the first place take up the banners of political
propaganda instead of trying harder to "get to the facts"? It is obvious
that altering the historical record was not done in response to the truth
of what actually happened but to the political pressures of the time.
And although those forces may have been severe, it is also apparent
that a well-entrenched tradition of the written record was not stable
enough to override the influence of politics on how the history of
Richard II should read.

The explanation of propaganda in the historical record has thus far
been weighted far too heavily in terms of the political forces of the
time. It is true that they were complicated, and they were vicious. But
language, too, must be factored into the problem, both how historians
used it and how it was used by the historical players. It is a general
yet nonetheless valid question to ask why the medieval chronicler was
so ready to "trim his sails," as one recent commentator puts it, to the
political winds of the time.[59] I submit that the conflict between history
and politics is yet another manifestation of the difficulties of accom-
modating writing to a tradition formed by oral habits of communicating and thinking.

In the remainder of this chapter, I explore a few prominent moments
in the history of Richard's reign when a movement toward and away
from the law was provocation for "editorializing" the historical record.
My aim is to continue looking at linguistic and cultural diglossia for
the light it may shed on the prevailing problem of the monarchy
through the end of the century—the assertion of the royal prerogative.
To the old question of how politics determined history, it is now
appropriate to ask how the orality of literacy may have prepared the
way for chroniclers to slant their story about politics, and for the king
and the magnates to slant their attitudes toward the law.

Medieval scholarship has proceeded with a general awareness of the
fact that the writing of history in the middle ages is not the product
of a formal discipline taught in the university, like grammar or logic.
The chronicle form does not assume, as argued in the previous chapter,
the foundation of history in a sense of the text as an empirical process
for testing, qualifying, conjecturing, and refuting. As these qualities do
not prevail in the documentary history of Edward III, neither do they

---

[59] Stow, "Richard II in Thomas Walsingham's Chronicles," p. 102.

distinguish the record of politics in the last quarter of the fourteenth-century, even when influence from ethnographical and philological projects, such as those of Gerald of Wales, is acknowledged. And thus to reflect on the "limitations" of historical understanding during this time is to assume the primacy of a "text" which had yet to develop as an historiographical model. The one area which scholars ordinarily have in mind for comparison with documentary history, as the chronicles illustrate widely, is the accounts of *res gestae* in medieval romance. But even this comparison does not go very far as a significant influence for the loose and diverse form that documentary history took in this period. The vagueness of its genesis out of a well-defined textual tradition suggests that we look instead to what I have called the "oral chronicle" of the times, the stories about political affairs circulating by word of mouth in the popular imagination.

If the evidence for such an "influence" is not a text, it is nonetheless embedded in the texts about Richard as one of their more prominent features, the unqualified *bias* in assembling details about what the king said or did on certain occasions.[60] A writer like Adam of Usk is exemplary since his *Chronicon* represents such a sharp indictment of the king following the deposition. He is manifestly not writing from a commitment of fairness to the facts. His document is forensic or agonistic, and its model is the persuasion of rhetoric before a listening audience entirely attendant upon the new political party in office under Henry IV. Usk's project is caught between two competing orientations about the purposes of history, and they bespeak the diglossia of the times, in this case manifested as the split between truth to the letter of the text and obedience to the sovereign word of Henry.

But Usk obviously does not worry too much about the delicate balance of his historical literacy, and this feature of his document aligns it with his subject matter. He would qualify the kingship of Richard by bringing to the surface the archaism, illiteracy, and illegitimacy of his political circle of friends and associates. For instance, he explains the deposition through the accusation that the former king "debased the noble and exalted the ignoble"; he made various "other low people

---

[60] The bias of the records has marked modern scholarly assessments of why Richard failed as a leader. E.g., Oman, *The History of England from the Accession of Richard II to the Death of Richard III*, 4:151: "No sovereign was ever more entirely the author of his own destruction than Richard II." Steel, *Richard II*, p. 41, considered him a schizophrenic weakling. Galbraith, "A New Life of Richard II," maintained that Richard was the image of his father and followed traditional ideas about kingship. Jones, *Royal Policy*, p. 2, argued that he followed a "deliberate policy" of autonomous rule badly out of place in its time. Tuck, *Richard II and the English Nobility*, pp. 203–204, opposed Steel and Jones to claim that Richard followed no specific policy except exerting his own will above the law.

magnates" of the land, and he even exalted the "unlettered [*ydeotis*] into bishops."[61] Usk does not say that Richard acted out of idiosyncratic willfulness, which might be associated with an impetuous, insecure leader. To the contrary, he would justify the fall of Richard by echoing phrases from the accounts of other fallen monarchs, notably the ancient king of Britain, Arthgallo, described by Geoffrey of Monmouth as one who also sought "to debase the noble and exalt the ignoble."[62] When Usk moves to disenfranchise Richard, he describes him as an impostor in the Plantagenet genealogy, not the son of the Black Prince at all but the bastard of an adulterous wife, Joan of Kent. Richard, Usk concludes, was given to exalting the base because he himself was baseborn: "Thus it happened with all things concerning this Richard; many an evil story was circulated among the illiterate regarding his birth, namely, that he was not born from a royal father, but from a mother given to a lubricious way of life."[63]

Affinity and Oral Fellowship

Although Usk names among the *infimi* the knight William Bagot, his generalization is intended to blanket the whole of Richard's career.[64] From the earliest of his appointments, such as the elevation of Michael de la Pole to the chancery in 1383, the general outlines of Usk's judgment can be documented. But explanations of Richard's prerogative in those appointments go far beyond the slant of Usk's propaganda that the king debased the aristocracy because he was baseborn. It is true that de la Pole was not connected by blood to the Crown; but Richard's appointment of him does not per se demonstrate a repudiation of the gentry by a willful young leader. At the time of assuming the chancellorship, de la Pole was in his fifties and already a baron (since 1366); he was the son of a well-to-do merchant from Hull, had served Richard's father in 1359 and 1370 as well as John of Gaunt in 1371 and 1372, and had married an heiress from Suffolk. Although he was serving as one of Richard's guardians at the time of his promotion to chancellor, he did not have much experience as an administrator of government, and he had no social standing equivalent to the people

---

[61] Usk, *Chronicon*, p. 29.

[62] Geoffrey of Monmouth, *Historia Regnum Britannie*, 50.42: "nobiles namque deponere, ignobiles exaltare." Cf. Usk, *Chronicon*, p. 180.

[63] Usk, *Chronicon*, p. 29.

[64] On Richard's court and appointments in the early 1380s, see McKisack, *The Fourteenth Century*, pp. 427 ff.; Steel, *Richard II*, pp. 92 ff.; Hutchison, *The Hollow Crown*, pp. 81 ff.; Mathew, *Court of Richard II*, pp. 110 ff.; Jones, *Royal Policy*, pp. 20 ff.; Tuck, *Richard II and the English Nobility*, pp. 58 ff.

he served. Since Richard was sixteen years old at the time of making the appointment, he was probably not rewarding a crony but trusting the management of England to an elder whom he knew on a day-to-day basis.[65]

The case of Robert de Vere is similar. He has passed into the pages of history with the tarnished reputation of Lancastrian propaganda. Many of the chroniclers besides Usk cast de Vere as the wastrel of the English treasury and a cohort of the king's debauchery. Walsingham, in a notorious passage, strongly suggests that he was the king's homosexual partner, and that "fact" has stuck to the history of the times with a predictable tenacity, until it was pointed out recently to be an interpolation Walsingham went back and made in his record well after the winds of politics had changed in favor of Henry IV.[66] The facts are that de Vere was the ninth Earl of Oxford and related by genealogy to the royal court. Four years older than Richard in the first years of the new monarchy, de Vere was too young to take over as chamberlain, his office by hereditary right, and so his uncle, Aubrey de Vere, acted in his capacity to run the affairs of the king's chamber. That body, as recently analyzed, was changing drastically from its earlier role as the inner unit of the king's *familiae*: it was becoming an office of state in its own right, with as many as eleven chamber knights by 1385.[67] Richard was apparently constructing it as a center of political power in the 1380s, and until the parliament of 1388 halted his efforts, it was on its way to financial independence as well.

De Vere was a familiar participant in these developments, and Richard rewarded him lavishly for his service. When he was made Marquis of Dublin in 1385, the new title bestowed upon him a respectability and dominion comparable to the magnitude of John of Gaunt. But in point of fact, he had only the appearance of power, since he probably could not have depended on the subordination and obedience of Ireland to his will.[68] Moreover, Richard had been equally generous the previous year with his uncles, advancing Edmund of Langley to the dukedom of York and Thomas of Woodstock to the dukedom of Gloucester—grants netting them lands or income worth at least £1,000

[65] On the foundation of affinity in reward for service, see Taylor, "Richard II's Views on Kingship," p. 191; in the "bond" of the lord's word, Bean, *From Lord to Patron*, p. 235; in payment for service, Given-Wilson, *The Royal Household*.

[66] Stow, "Richard II," p. 86. Typical previous views of the "effeminate" de Vere, e.g., McKisack, *The Fourteenth Century*, p. 444, and Mathew, *Court of Richard II*, p. 138.

[67] See Tuck, *Richard II and the English Nobility*, pp. 59 ff. Cf. Given-Wilson, *The Royal Household*, on the enormous costs of keeping the growing *domus* of the king—e.g., 800 marks for ten days (p. 34).

[68] See Tuck, *Richard II and the English Nobility*, p. 82.

each.[69] If we believe the accusation of the lords in their appeals of
parliament during 1386 and 1388, that Richard's associates were ac-
croaching the royal prerogative and ignoring the security of the realm
from potential threats from France, one could conclude that the nobility was justly alarmed. There must be some truth in the charge, but it
is not very well established through recent assessments that Richard
only appointed "favorites" and "parasites" like de Vere, whose "effemi-
nacy" and "king-like" status were suspect.

That the lords objected to Richard's inner circle of associates because
of political jealousy, personal insult, and governmental mismanage-
ment, as modern evaluations maintain, can be read both in the chronicles and in the articles of indictment delivered in the parliaments of
1386 and 1388. However, what the chronicles do not include and
probably suppress is evidence justifying Richard's exercise of his royal
prerogative. As we are not blind to the Lancastrian propaganda in the
charges against Michael de la Pole in 1387 and against the king's
associates one year later, so also must we look into the indictments for
the suppression of a concept of loyalty that was alien and threatening
to the aristocracy. The threat was certainly no secret, as a recent commentator indicates: "A new courtier nobility was coming into existence
which took precedence over the established aristocracy."[70] But in what
sense, one may ask, was it "new"? The evidence points in the opposite
direction—to the past, to previous models of kingship in Edward II,
whom Richard venerated nearly into canonization, and before him to
models of royal *communitas* shared by ancient kings predating *Magna
Carta*, to Arthgallo and very likely to the legendary leaders beyond
written record.[71]

When Richard began to develop the royal chamber into a governmental body, the foundation of his apparent effort to create a new
group of loyal servants throughout the realm can be referred to a
model of service with a very long history and with enormous respectability. It offended the nobility, to be sure, but it did not ignore blood
ties entirely and it did not pander to the young. Richard chose people
with whom he was immediately familiar. His *familia*, the chronicles say,

[69] *Westminster Chronicle*, p. 140 and n. 3.

[70] Tuck, *Richard II and the English Nobility*, p. 86. Cf. Mathew, *Court of Richard II*, pp.
144–45.

[71] Cf. evidence of Richard's "medievalism," e.g., the caparisons of royalty, old books,
refined dress, elaborate cuisine, the building of Westminster Hall (with its statues of
kings at the south end), the patronage of painting (the Westminster Abbey portrait of
himself in majesty and the Wilton diptych), as cited by McKisack, *The Fourteenth Century*,
p. 497; Jones, *Royal Policy*, p. 128; Mathew, *Court of Richard II*, pp. 23 ff; Given-Wilson,
The Royal Household, pp. 70–74.

was foremost in his attention, and from it he made appointments he could trust in the ancient way of Arthgallo. He may have bypassed bloodlines among the princes, but they were not sacrosanct in the *comitatus* of former leaders: obedient service in exchange for protection and reward is the cardinal virtue of the older fellowship. Sir John Chandos and Simon Burley joined the retinue of the Black Prince not for his wealth but because of his heroic reputation as a formidable leader. Both men were like members of the royal family, because loyalty of this sort was synonymous with the sustenance and company of the household, where genealogical lines generated bonds of fellowship.[72]

These factors suggest that when Richard captured the chancery with de la Pole's appointment in 1383, he was acting out of an appreciation of an unwritten law of an archaic fellowship, and not out of childish impulse, or for that matter, the heavy political designs of bookish *auctoritates*. He was young, he had already heard the power in his own voice echoed back to him from the crowds at Mile End, and he surely had heard about the charismatic leadership of his father and grandfather. Loyal friends would have returned to him the same charisma in response to his royal beck and call.[73]

THE ROYAL SIGNET

Richard's creation of an inner circle of associates was an easy target for writers of Lancastrian propaganda, but that literary effect in the historical text may also be read as evidence of the politics of literacy in Richard's court. The use of the king's personal signet for the authentication of communications is a case in point. By the beginning of the 1380s, the chancellor of the realm formally carried out the duties of government upon instructions authorized by the Privy Seal (or great seal). Because its function had become so widespread, the business of the Privy Seal developed into an office in its own right within the

[72] Cf. Mathew, *Court of Richard II*, p. 145, on the significance of such bonds in the Ricardian court, which "collapsed not merely by treason but in the paralysis of conflicting loyalties." Cp. McFarlane, "Bastard Feudalism," pp. 173–75, and Mann, *The Sources of Social Power* 1:412, for a more pragmatic view of loyalty.

[73] On Richard's "voice," McKisack, *The Fourteenth Century*, p. 423, says that at Mile End the populace accorded him the "almost mystical power inherent in his sovereign word"; Jones, *Royal Policy*, p. 126, notes that his "word" proved to be all-powerful before the rebels; Steel, *Richard II*, p. 90, observes that the reprisals ordered by the government gave Richard "the clearest possible proof how little his word was worth"; Tuck, *Richard II and the English Nobility*, p. 106, and Hutchison, *The Hollow Crown*, p. 107, see his subordination to the commission of governance during 1386–87 as suppression of his royal "voice."

government. Consequently, another seal was necessary to authorize the king's personal communications, and precedent for one already existed in the reign of Edward II. The usual path for orders of state originated with a signet letter from Richard to the Privy Seal office and thence on to the chancellor for action. But it was also common for Richard to send signet letters directly to his chancellor for execution, since they were received as warrant of Privy Seal matters. The use of the signet for both private and governmental business thus put the king in immediate control of the execution of his orders, insofar as he bypassed the possibility that his instructions might be intercepted in the office of the Privy Seal.

When de la Pole came to office in 1383, he continued this practice, and the officer of the Privy Seal, Walter Skirlaw, did not object. In fact, in 1385–86 more than three hundred signet letters were directed to the chancellor for various requests, including drafts from the exchequer for payments to Burley or appointments to the king's chamber, both of which were usually ordered only through the Privy Seal. Richard had obviously discovered the royal prerogative in the exercise of his personal signet. It became the extension of his voice in the affairs of government, as one commentator remarks, "the most potent instrument of Richard's personal power."[74] Needless to say, it was an assertion of royal prerogative which the lords would not tolerate for long from the young leader, and when de la Pole was removed by parliament in 1386, the new chancellor, Thomas Arundel, Bishop of Ely, no longer would accept the king's signet as the equivalent of Privy Seal authentication. Richard's voice in the affairs of state had been silenced, as Arundel accepted his signet henceforth only for personal wishes.

But the suppression did not stop with the disregard of signet letters in the chancellor's office. As Usk remarks on the commission of governance charged with managing the realm at the end of the October parliament in 1386, "The king [was] indignant that the due freedom of his majesty was being bridled by his own lieges."[75] The opinion of the nobility that Richard's ministers were mismanaging the realm must be set in the context of the evidence that his word to the *communitas* of his associates in such vehicles as the signet letter had become a power equal to that of the magnates of the realm. When John of Gaunt left the country in 1385 on his Spanish campaign, a contest with other nobles was imminent, but it did not originate with the king. Richard Earl of Arundel, Thomas Earl of Warwick, Thomas Bishop of Ely, Thomas Duke of Gloucester and William Courtenay began their press

[74] Tuck, *Richard II and the English Nobility*, p. 67.
[75] Usk, *Chronicon*, p. 4.

against Richard's increasing power, and their scapegoat was Michael de la Pole.[76]

They came before Richard with reference to the "law" that the king had to hold parliament once per year and attend in his own person; but their source, *quod ex antiquo statuto*, was of highly dubious currency at the time.[77] Richard refused to listen, saying he would seek help from France against those plotting "rebellion" in England.[78] Responding with unmistakable allusions to the fate of Edward II in 1327, the lords told him that on the basis of "ancient statute and fact experienced not very long ago," it was "lawful for them with the assent of the commons and the consent of the people of the realm to depose the king from his royal throne."[79] Without a well-entrenched textual tradition of law, Richard was left with no alternative but to allow the prosecution and sentencing of de la Pole. His prerogative had been silenced, but the proceedings testify amply to the strength of his power base, rather than to the corruption of his chancellor, since parliament closed with the creation of the regency commission, made up of his opponents among the lords, who took over the control of every aspect of the royal chamber and the administration of the realm for the next year.[80]

Knighton, Walsingham, and the other chroniclers tell us precious little about what Richard said or felt in response to this humiliation. And their silence is an expression of their own agenda to disenfranchise him. But his struggle to communicate his personal word continued in another form. In a ritual of oath-taking—archaic in a time of written contracts and indentures of retainer—Richard urged individuals of the outlying districts "to swear that to the exclusion of all other lords entirely they would join with him as their true king, and he gave them badges of livery, made of silver and gold crowns, so that they would come to the lord king with their arms ready whenever they were called."[81] The attempt to organize a retinue of followers—which Richard generated much more elaborately in the next decade—was recognized by the regency commission for what it was, a serious threat to power. Richard was now using his own propaganda, the potent promise of royal patronage, and it doubtlessly found its mark in

[76] Cf. Jones, *Royal Policy*, p. 31: "Now for the first time royal authority had been entirely sidestepped in the prosecution of an officer of the state."

[77] Knighton, *Chronicon* 2:216–17. Jones, *Royal Policy*, pp. 29–30, says the statute was no longer in existence.

[78] Knighton, *Chronicon* 2:218.

[79] *Chronicon* 2:219.

[80] Until November 1387; for the commission's charge, see Knighton, *Chronicon* 2:225–33; *Westminster Chronicle*, pp. 166–76.

[81] *Westminster Chronicle*, p. 186.

districts on the fringes of the literate world where symbols of agreement were far more efficacious than the textual evidence of law—as
the reputation of Domesday Book amply demonstrates. The potential
of a growing affinity under the banners and signs of King Richard
must have loomed on the horizon of the magnates, for they wasted no
time in dealing with the sergeant entrusted with issuing the badges:
outside of Cambridge he was arrested and imprisoned.[82]

The events which follow are familiar in the biography of Richard,
beginning with the purge of the king's circle by the appellant lords in
the 1388 parliament, followed by his gradual move into despotism in
the late 1390s, and ending in the Lancastrian coup in 1399. Although
the role of law—both its function for Richard and the magnates—needs
no summation in this history, it bears reconsideration in certain details
of "precedent" or "legal opinion" where oral attitudes are apparent in
the way documents were used.

LAW OF THE JUDGES, 1387

For instance, we may note the uncertain status of the opinion of the
justices which Richard sought in 1387. He asked them to look into the
law on the right of the lords to execute the statute and ordinance
passed in the October parliament of 1386 (which had convicted Michael de la Pole), and specifically to consider whether those two meas-
ures "derogate from the regality and prerogative" of the king.[83] The
judges brought back the unanimous answer that they do indeed so
derogate the royal prerogative, "especially because they were made
against the will of the king."[84] They also declared unanimously that
the king alone sets the agenda for parliament, controls the proceedings,
and dissolves the assembly. Lords and commons do not have the
authority to impeach officers appointed by the king; nor does reference
to the deposition of Edward II have any bearing as precedent in the
October parliament. Accordingly, the impeachment of de la Pole was
erroneous and revocable. Throughout each of the ten articles of their
disposition, the justices maintained that those who urged the petitions

---

[82] Ibid. Richard was eventually reproved, through accusation of treason against his
ministers, during the Westminster parliament of 1388 for the practice of soliciting a
following through the "power of the badge" (ibid., p. 256).

[83] *Westminster Chronicle*, p. 198. See Knighton, *Chronicon* 2:237–40, for the so-called
"questions to the justices."

[84] *Westminster Chronicle*, p. 198. Chrimes, "Richard II's Questions to the Judges," has
established that the decisions returned by the judges were valid in law. Cf. Taylor,
"Richard II's Views on Kingship," p. 198.

in parliament or who were otherwise involved in bringing them about were "traitors" (*proditores*) deserving of capital punishment.[85]

Not mistaking the portent of this decision, the appellant lords turned the tables against the king by representing his ministers as fomenting rebellion in the realm. They had a letter read publicly throughout the city streets of London that Richard's ministers "were false traitors each and every one to the king and the realm" and that they were bound to disinherit the Crown and dismember the realm of England.[86] The letter is spectacular propaganda, since not a word of it was factual. But it illustrates exceedingly well the forensic success that the nobility was to have by manipulating written declarations.

The appellants charged that Richard's associates, as one commentator puts it, "literally bewitched the king" into willingly granting to them the sovereign dominion of England by taking advantage of his "tendresce del age" and "accrochantz a eux roial poair."[87] We know from the parliament rolls that Richard referred their appeal to yet another panel of justices for consideration of its legal status. In view of the fact that this panel was appointed by the nobles, not by the king, their opinion, as others have not failed to note, bears heavily on what was about to transpire: they delivered the verdict that treason could not be appealed before parliament; there was no foundation in law for such a procedure; the Court of Chivalry could entertain the process of appeal, but certainly not for the alleged crimes. Under the aegis of the chief justice, Sir Walter Clopton, who was a retainer of the Duke of Gloucester, the judges stood their ground against the lords, declaring, in effect, that civil and common law was simply not able to judge cases of the gravity charged by the appellants in parliament.[88] However, the lords proceeded anyway, insisting that crimes involving the person of the king, the realm, and the peers must be tried in parliament. In such high crimes, the lords proclaimed they themselves would become the judges and be guided by no other law than the "law of parliament" ("ley du parlement"), which is to say, what they discussed on that occasion.[89]

It must be recalled that the justices who had deliberated the legality of the 1386 parliament and its regency commission had been deposed for rendering precisely the same opinion regarding the inviolability of the royal prerogative. Their successors (to repeat, not of Richard's

---

[85] *Westminster Chronicle*, p. 200.

[86] Knighton, *Chronicon* 2:246.

[87] Jones, *Royal Policy*, p. 48.

[88] *Rotuli Parliamentorum* 3:236. See, e.g., Jones, *Royal Policy*, pp. 44 ff.; Tuck, *Richard II and the English Nobility*, pp. 121 ff.

[89] *Rotuli Parliamentorum* 3:236.

party) were remaining faithful to precedent, to the laws on the books, and to the integrity of textual tradition. While we could conclude, with one historian, that the position of the lords was "little better than lynch law," there were certain precedent situations that might corroborate their determination to try state cases in parliament when the crimes were as serious as treason.[90] But the possibility that they were acting according to a specific precedent or that their process was otherwise the reflection of a documented policy is abrogated by the record of their own strategies in the prosecution of the appeal. The thirty-nine articles of accusation do not reflect any particular order; their explanations follow no acknowledged process; the appellants shift from one basis of justification to another; they authorize the body of the whole assembly and then individual groups within it in seeking the intended verdict. And not once do they put forth a written opinion in the law, citing chapter and verse, to document the authority of their action.

"Ley du Parlement," 1388

The fate of law in the notorious parliament of 1388 is well known as a story of political machination and strong-arm tactics. But I suggest that the actions of that assembly are also an indication of the "literacy" of government: if the use of precedent and opinion were more firmly entrenched in a stable textual tradition, the propaganda and persuasion of the lords may not have taken hold so easily. The law was vulnerable to appropriation because literacy itself was still uncertain about the relation of oral and written channels of language. We may note this vulnerability, for instance, in the conflict between the validation of documents presumed in the records of parliament and the sworn oaths or oral covenants presumed by various individuals.

Before the opening of the proceedings, the lords came to Richard (December 28, 1387) to protest his "failing to keep his personal oath to them"; they insisted that he was plotting their death and was continuing to defend his false, traitorous ministers. He must submit to them, or else understand that "his heir was unmistakably of full age" to assume the throne.[91] With irony laced in their utterance, they were saying Richard should not assume that his heir apparent was Roger Mortimer—next in line for the crown, though underage; the king should open his eyes to the fact that the Duke of Gloucester was in the wings and all too ready to submit to their instructions. Not succumb-

[90] Steel, *Richard II*, p. 152; rebutted by Tuck, *Richard II and the English Nobility*, p. 122. See Bellamy, *Law of Treason in England*.

[91] *Westminster Chronicle*, p. 228.

ing to their will, Richard is eventually forced to set the date for parliament, February 3, 1388, and his associates are called upon to respond *vivicater* ("in their own voice") to the charges at Westminster. The lords put their appeals *in scriptis* ("in writing") and Richard orders that they be read aloud so that he can hear them. To a certain degree, these requests are conventional, but they are also tendentious, because it was well known that the king's ministers had fled and that they would add contempt of parliament to the charges against them if they failed to attend and speak *in viva voce*. Moreover, specifying that the lords dutifully respected the practice of putting their charge *in scriptis* gave the patina of legality to a proceeding which had already circumvented the law of the justices.

But the evidence of oath-taking figures much more prominently in article 2, which alleges that Richard's ministers "made him swear and assure them that he will maintain and support them to live and die with them." The objection here, presumably, is that the ministers denied the king, as the article reads, his "free condition above every other person in his realm" by holding him "in service" to them. But the article stands contradicted by the very procedures undertaken in the appeal; for the appellants, too, were in the process of denying the king his *franc condicioun* by silencing his royal prerogative in passing judgment on how he chose to exercise it with regard to the "honor, estate, and regality" purportedly defended in this article.[92]

Additional counts in the indictment contain similar inconsistencies regarding legal process. Item nine stipulates that de Vere, de la Pole, Tresilian, and others impeded many people in the realm from enjoying their rights under "the common law of England" ("la comune ley Dengl'"); and yet the appellants themselves set aside that law in particular in order to pursue charges which had been customarily the prerogative right of the king. And even more to the point, count twelve indicts the ministers, naming specifically Nicholas Bembre (former mayor of London) for failing to be bound by "the great charter and other good laws and usages of the realm of England." The reference is to the *Magna Carta*, which protected individuals from being taken or imprisoned or put to death, as the article specifies, "without due process of law" ("sanz due process' du ley").[93] But what "process," one must ask, was being observed after the justices declared that the written laws of the land were incompetent to deal with the charges brought by the appellants? Invoking "due process" in this instance is a good

---

[92] Ibid., p. 242.

[93] Ibid., pp. 248, 249 and n. 2. For the relation of the French phrase to *per legem terre* of *Magna Carta* (ch. 29), see Thompson, *Magna Carta*, pp. 86 ff.

deal more forensic than specific to *Magna Carta*; for the entire case cobbled together by the appellants obeys no written process, as they themselves indicated, except for the "law" made up in parliament as they went along.

Items twenty-six and twenty-seven pointedly indict the ministers for "having drawn the heart and good will of the king" away from his nobles by assuring him that the opinion of the justices delivered in 1387 was correct and that the ordinance, statute, and commission set forth by the 1386 parliament were indeed derogations of sovereign regality and prerogative.[94] Count twenty-eight signifies that not only the ministers but the justices too were guilty of treasonous acts for establishing the ordinance in the first place. Although the appellants impeached the validity of their own ordinance through such accusations, as others have noted, they proceeded unopposed, with the "law" emerging quite obviously as a construction of those who held the floor of discussion.[95]

The case of Nicholas Bembre, the one person in the appeal who actually stood for trial, brings into focus unmistakably how textual referencing, documentary validation, and due process were superseded by the confrontational tactics of the appellants.[96] In the full audience of parliament, the charges against Bembre were read to him. He asked for counsel, but was denied "by the law of parliament" ("par ley du parlement").[97] When he "asked for copies of the articles and a day to respond," he was again refused and was forced to answer either "guilty" or "not guilty" to the charges. He responded: "Guilty of nothing" ("de rien coupable").[98] In one of the few remarks of Richard recorded during the hearings, the monk of Westminster indicates that "the king excused Sir Nicholas with many reasons, protesting that he never knew him to be a traitor nor . . . guilty or even answerable to the terms of the articles."[99] Still protesting his innocence, Bembre asked that he be allowed to defend himself in trial by combat. In response the lords appellant, before the king and the entire assembly, "threw down their gauntlets," insisting that the charges against Bembre were true, and a great many of peers, knights, and esquires (to the number of 305) followed suit.[100] But the trial did not go forward because of the

---

[94] *Westminster Chronicle*, pp. 258, 260.

[95] E.g., see Tuck, *Richard II and the English Nobility*, pp. 122 ff.; Jones, *Royal Policy*, pp. 49 ff.; Hutchison, *The Hollow Crown*, pp. 103 ff.

[96] His case is described both in the articles and by the chronicler: *Westminster Chronicle*, pp. 280, 282, 310, 312, 314, 364, 366.

[97] *Rotuli Parliamentorum* 3:236.

[98] *Westminster Chronicle*, p. 282.

[99] Ibid., p. 310.

[100] Ibid., pp. 282, 310.

technicality that combat would be applicable only when there were no witnesses to the alleged crimes.[101] Confronting a deadlock in how to proceed, the appellants did not produce documentary proof or evidence of any kind to persuade parliament, but instead turned the case over to committee, composed of members from their own ranks. The opinion delivered, however, was that the death penalty was not warranted for Nicholas Bembre, a verdict which elicited no little *indignacionem* among the appellants.[102]

Having failed in their own committee, the appellants approached representatives of the London guilds in parliament, but neither was that group able to reach a verdict. Finally turning to the mayor of London (Nicholas Exton), certain aldermen, and a recorder, the appellants asked if they believed Bembre was aware of his crimes. "They said that he more than likely knew about his crimes than not." *Scire quam nescire* was enough for the appellants, and so they turned to the recorder—in a virtual parody of textual documentation—asking, "What does that law of yours [*lex tua*] say in a case of this sort?" Looking up the penalty for concealing knowledge of a crime, the recorder read to them, "He would deserve to be punished by loss of life."[103] Bembre was executed the following day.

The "ley du parlement" versus "lex tua": the pronoun alone ("that law *of yours*") tells sharply against the written record suppressed in so many ways by the astonishingly successful manipulations of the appellants in public forum. Of the prosecutions pursued in a second tier of purges, the case of Simon Burley is especially pointed, since Richard's response is, once again, either not quoted or paraphrased into silence. And in this instance, what history has *not* recorded is very telling of what must have been an excruciating moment for the young king. He was present at the hearing and had to endure the charges, condemnation, and execution of this longtime family friend, tutor, companion, and father figure. Both the queen mother and the king asked that Burley be given a chance to respond to the indictments, but the request was denied because, it was insisted, he had already answered, and "his responses were perpetually in the final written record."[104]

The appellants proved indomitable in playing fast and loose with the textual tradition of law even as it stared them in the face from the audience of justices in attendance every day during the many long weeks of trial. And when the session ended and the last execution was carried out (several of the king's associates escaped), the lords insti-

[101] See Jones, *Royal Policy*, p. 49.
[102] *Westminster Chronicle*, p. 310.
[103] Ibid., p. 314.
[104] Ibid., pp. 290, 292, 328, 330.

tuted a prohibition against "precedent in time to come": everyone was absolutely enjoined from drawing upon any of the written records of the proceedings for use as examples in future cases. And they sealed their final act with an oath absolving all persons involved in the hearings from any potential accusation of wrongdoing. The lords had spoken. They had silenced the king. And now, by final oath, all could be assured that history would have no echo of what they had done. By swearing to their own righteousness, they would ensure that references in textual documentation could never be looked up and read against them, as they themselves had read the judicial opinion of 1387 and used it against the judges.[105]

ORAL OR WRITTEN PRIORITY

It is tempting to regard this situation as a standoff between a tradition of textual procedure versus the public demands of the moment, respect for written documents versus insistence on the persuasion of political talk. But I have been suggesting in this book that the binarism of such an assumption is more illusory than real. In such circumstances we are faced with a contested border between two attitudes toward language and two different ways of looking at the world: neither precedent nor present conventions have come to terms with each other, and the "text" remains a highly relative construction. Domesday Book was "read" by some people with a profoundly oral sense of the written word. They, of course, had little occasion on the margins of a literate culture to know otherwise. But the lords and lawyers of parliament did have such an occasion whenever the writtenness of the law (the "text itself"—we would say) was before them as previous opinion, and their ignorance of it or failure to engage it spells out the desperate moves of their decisions. As they subordinate precedent to the force of the moment, their attitude toward written record does not differ in kind from the peasants and townspeople a few years earlier yelling in the streets for justice and demanding it in writing. A profound historical blindness (or deafness) marks the attitude toward language in these events. By default of voice, the written is overridden in the moment of its veneration. The illusion of priority that organizes this hierarchy could have been perforated on any number of occasions during the cataclysmic moments of 1381, 1386, or 1388. But the difference which the written evidence of law or history could have made in those years was occluded by deeply entrenched ways of communicating and be-

---

[105] The oath is quoted as the epigraph of this chapter (*Westminster Chronicle*, pp. 304, 306). The lords also awarded themselves £20,000 for saving the realm from corruption, the same kind of political gift they had prosecuted; see Jones, *Royal Policy*, p. 53.

having from the past. That occlusion, I suggest, goes a long way toward explaining how dominion took shape under the magnates and also why it failed so miserably under Richard's hand in the last decade of the century.

Many reasons for his failure have come forward, beginning with Shakespeare's portrait of King Richard as both a weak despot and a victim of Lancastrian designs on the monarchy. The arrest in 1397 of Gloucester, Arundel, and Warwick and the seizure of their property have often been regarded as the king's revenge for the prosecution and execution of his ministers in 1388. Thus asserting his own will above the law has been understood as evidence of emotional immaturity or even "schizophrenia" and "madness." I suggest, however, that we take another cue from Shakespeare, who portrays the vulnerability of Richard as a function of his speech, which has commonly been regarded as empty, autocratic, and "fallen."[106] The basis for such an interpretation of the historical Richard is not difficult to locate in the chronicles, specifically in reports about the "signs" that the king used to represent his voice.

The Word against the Word

Perhaps the most notorious of such signs is the badge of "the white hart with a crown and a golden chain," which Richard distributed widely after October 1390, or thereabouts, in order to expand his livery.[107] It became ubiquitous among members of the king's affinity, as illustrated in the badges worn by the figures in the Wilton diptych. But it was also associated with the worst abuses of the king's word— for instance, when ministers of the Crown sought revenue for the sagging royal coffers by outrageous means. One of them was the use of the royal *blank charture* ("blank charter"), which, like the white hart itself, was recognized as an empty sign of the king's dominion in its own time. It is mentioned frequently in the chronicles, as in the prose *Brut*:

> And yn þe xxii yere of King Richardeȝ regne . . . were made and or-
> deyned blank Chartureȝ, and made ham to be selid of alle maner of riche
> men þrouȝout þe Reme, inso-moche þat þai compellid dyuers pepill to
> sette to her seeleȝ; and þis was so for gret couetyse; wherfore alle þe gode

---

[106] See Calderwood, *Shakespearean Metadrama*, pp. 173 ff. Cf. Porter, *The Drama of Speech Acts*. On Shakespeare's use of medieval sources, see Reed, *Richard II*; Siegel, *Shakespeare in His Time and Ours*; Ranald, "The Degradation of Richard II"; and Petronella, "Regal Duality and Everyman."

[107] *Historia Vitae Ricardi*, p. 132, is the only contemporary record to describe this badge. Taylor, "Richard II's Views on Kingship," cautions against the dissemination of the badge as the start of Richard's tyrrany, suggesting instead 1397.

hertis of þe Reme clene turned away from hym euyr eftir, and þat was
vtturli destroccion & ende of hym þat was so hygh and so excellent a
king. . . . Alas, for pite, þat such a king myȝt not se![108]

The lords and prelates who were pressed into signing these blank
letters were signifying their submission to the Crown as traitors and
thus were held in jeopardy until they made contributions to the royal
treasury. The author of the *Brut* looks back to judge Richard for not
"seeing" what was afoot among his counselors, but the blame is pointed
at the king as well for not "reading" what was written in the blank
letter of his order.

No less extorting was the institution in 1399 of the King's "Ple-
saunce," which imposed fines willy-nilly on the populace in order to
assure the good pleasure of the Crown. The money was used, Walsingham tells us, to fund the expenses of the *comitatus regis*, and many
people were exacerbated by the practice, complaining that their rights
under common law were being denied.[109] But Richard's affinity had
become enormous in these years (with two thousand Cheshire archers
alone by 1397), and members of his entourage often took liberties
among townspeople well in excess of their entitlements under the
king's "badge." We hear an echo of this conflict between town and
Crown in *Richard the Redeless*:

> So, trouthe to telle as toune-men said,
> ffor on that ye merkyd ye myssed ten schore
> Of homeliche hertis that the harme hente.[110]

It is a minor but historically relevant detail that the truth of "telling"
and "saying" is here represented as split away from the image on
Richard's sign: the hart of the sign is empty in the hearts of the
community, and this diglossia is the source of much harm. Richard is
"redeless" of this fact about his royal semiology. That is the reason for
his failure, in the judgment of this poem.

[108] *Brut* 2:356. On "blank charters," see Bird, *The Turbulent London of Richard II*; Barron,
"The Tyranny of Richard II," pp. 1–18; and Taylor, "Richard II's Views on Kingship," p.
201.

[109] *Annales Ricardi Secundi*, pp. 234–35. See Tuck, *Richard II and the English Nobility*,
pp. 197–208: people tried in the Court of Chivalry for failure to pay fines to the Crown
complained of being denied due process of law as set forth in *Magna Carta*, and the
articles of deposition so indict Richard for using the Court in this way (pp. 198–204).
Given-Wilson, *The Royal Household*, p. 41, lists yearly expenses for supporting the royal
household between 1360–1413: 2,250 quarters of wheat; 1,000 tuns of wine; 1,600 oxen;
20,000 sheep; the figures are higher between 1395 and 1406.

[110] *Richard the Redeless* (ed. Skeat), vol. 2, ll. 41–43. The poem may well have been
composed during or shortly after the crises of 1397–1399. See Taylor, *English Historical
Literature*, pp. 211, 248–50.

If Shakespeare suggests the same conclusion, it is because he was led to it by the historical records of the time. Richard may have learned a theory of sacred majesty at the knee of Simon Burley, who kept a copy of Giles of Rome's *De regimine principium* in his personal library.[111] John Wyclif, however, is closer to home, since he insisted that power in both temporal and spiritual estates resided in the person of the king, who was immune from positive law but always subject to divine and moral law as set forth in Sacred Scripture: the *forma verborum* of God's discourse was the formal cause of all acts by a monarch.[112] In Wyclif we find the most prominent articulation of the foreclosure of any gap between spoken and written manifestations of dominion. And it comes forward into the world of political affairs with the profound sanction of its origin in the theology of the spoken logos. That Richard simply counted, however anachronistically, on the dissemination of his power in badges, letters, and other signs was not an attitude of his own devising, and certainly not an expression of profligate youth or madness. He was appealing to an assumption about the subordination of signs and writing to the spoken word of dominion which had come down to him from the most distant reaches of the past. It is a fact of the diglossia of the times, however, that he failed to align his own word adequately with written law, for it was on the basis of the collapse of this differentiation that he was cited in the articles of deposition: "He said expressly," the record indicates, that the laws of the land "were in his mouth [*in ore suo*] and also in his breast, and only he could change or make the laws of his realm."[113]

In 1397 the Bishop of Exeter, Edmund Stafford, delivered a speech before parliament, in which he insisted that "the power of the king existed singly and wholly in the king himself and that those who denied or rebelled against it deserved the penalties of the law."[114] With the prophecy of Ezekiel (37.22) echoing through his utterance ("One king shall be king over them all"), the bishop was affirming the same connection between the theology and politics of the word articulated by Wyclif.[115] But what Richard did not hear in this tenet, or chose to

---

[111] Jones, *Royal Policy*, pp. 143–61, argues that any theory of sacred majesty Richard may have learned was ultimately stillborn in the absolutist politics of the late 1390s.

[112] See ch. 3, above. Figgis, *The Divine Right of Kings*, pp. 76–80, remains a useful source on the anachronism of a divine-right monarchy in fourteenth-century England, where magnates had as much or more power than the royal court.

[113] *Rotuli Parliamentorum* 3:419. Although an exact quotation of Richard on this point has not yet been documented, McKisack, *The Fourteenth Century*, p. 419, notes that the king lived the principle in several ways during his final years.

[114] Usk, *Chronicon*, p. 9. He reports that parliament took up forthwith ordinances to implement the principles of the bishop's sermon.

[115] *Rotuli Parliamentorum* 3:347.

ignore, was made desperately clear after it was too late for him. While he was in prison, the Archbishop of York preached a sermon at the proceedings of deposition on the Isaian text (51.16), "I have put my words in thy mouth." Wyclif would have approved, since he believed that when the monarch broke divine law, God could withdraw the royal prerogative from him. But Richard believed that the oath of coronation conferring dominion on him could never be removed, and he protested this claim in the Tower, according to some accounts. His royal word was like the symbolic oil he carried around with him in the belief that anointment (which, incidentally, he did not receive) would spiritualize him into a *persona mixta*, an indivisible unity of lay and clerical.[116] Therefore a king could never abdicate his oath of office.

The oil is no different from the badge of the white hart and the blank charter. They are symbolic images of a dominion that the king presumed to exist *in ore suo*, at the expense of written law or even his own promise. They occlude inscription by virtue of their status as symbols of sovereign voice. Although they are signs of the sovereign, they also illustrate the sovereignty of oral signs which we have seen in many other forms—letters of the king's signet, Domesday Book, and even the millstones and branches exchanged by the commons at St. Albans in 1381. The power of Richard's signs, in other words, capitalized on the subordination of written to spoken in traditional expectations of language. But Richard subordinated much more than writing, as the record of his final years shows. He willfully or blindly ignored the opposition which signs of his dominion returned to him repeatedly, and no one was more aware of this tragic diglossia at the heart of Richard's language and his monarchy than Shakespeare.

Alone with only his thoughts in Pontefract castle, Richard remarks that his better thoughts:

> As . . . of things divine, are intermixed
> With scruples, and do set the word itself
> Against the word. (5.5.13–14)

The documentary history of fourteenth-century politics gives us almost nothing to indicate that the Richard of history listened for evidence of how his own word was set against itself. But at the end of

---

[116] Taylor, *English Historical Literature*, p. 193, denies Richard's free resignation as a fabrication of the Lancastrian regime; cf. Taylor, "Richard II's Views on Kingship," pp. 194–95. Evidence of Richard's belief in the divine nature of kingship is in the accounts of his protest in the Tower and in the books and records of his personal library; see Rickert, "King Richard II's Books"; and R. F. Green, "King Richard's Books Revisited." Walsingham reports the story of Richard's discovery of the holy oil—see Sandquist, "The Holy Oil of St. Thomas of Canterbury."

his reign we know for certain that his prerogative was deeply divided against the words of the people, nobles and commons alike. And those political collisions betoken the highly unstable balance of language and power in the last quarter of the fourteenth century. Shakespeare's historicism, therefore, is not simply for the age of Elizabeth. It is Ricardian in every sense of the term. For Shakespeare identifies the language of dominion in Richard's time, both the king's and the lords', as a discourse fallen from political and oratorical prominence into a meretricious play with words.

The Richard of history may not have had such a capacity with words. For all we know, he may have been afflicted with the speech impediment of stuttering and stammering, as the Monk of Evesham records in his portrait of the king: he spoke with an "abrupt and stuttering tongue" ("lingua breuis et balbuciens").[117] But it is clear on the basis of wide documentary evidence that Richard was terribly blind and deaf to the difference that written records of all sorts were making in his society, from the letters demanded by the peasants to the blank charters issued by his own hand. Shakespeare has pointed precisely to the split discourse of the fourteenth century and the division of dominion that it signifies. The leaning toward oral priorities in the structure of literacy and government had grown top-heavy by Richard's time. Both he and the magnates assume the dominion of that structure in the face of far too many situations that opposed it. And yet if they remain judged by this historical blindness, they should be exonerated by it, too, once we acknowledge the occlusion at the core of medieval literacy which led them into it in the first place.

PHILOSOPHY AND POLITICS

The documents of parliamentary record and chronicle composition considered in Part Two of this book respond in general to the need to "get it in writing," and thus they testify to the advance of *literacy* unprecedented in the history of English government. But, as we have seen in the philosophical projects of the century considered in Part One, the *uses* of literacy reveal how contingent writing remained in oral customs still holding on to the way people thought and behaved. The pragmatic use of a technical skill thus gave way to more urgent demands from the sociopolitical context. Unlike philosophy, however, history exposes the politics of literacy in far more explicit, not to say shameless, ways. It is certainly true that literacy had much to do with

[117] *Historia Vitae Ricardi*, p. 166. This famous literary portrait of Richard is not found elsewhere.

changes in English government in the latter part of the fourteenth century. But change did not come about, as sometimes concluded, because of the *strength* of literacy in the hands of a "middle class" who were becoming the "mainstay" of government.[118] On the contrary, government was still an affair of the nobility, and the upheavals in parliament and finally in the kingship itself were the direct result of the *weakness* of literacy, of the increasingly destabilized relation between written and spoken channels of language which were all too ready for seizure by the powers that be.

I have indicated that those powers readily appealed to texts, written records, and promulgated documents as the "voice" of political process and authority during the reigns of Edward III and Richard II. And yet it is obvious that such appeals too often paid only lip service to the validation, analysis, and cross-referencing familiar to a readerly society. A preemptive agenda is not far beneath the surface of such written records, and it is legitimized by the custom of receiving the written word as the extension and imitation of speaking. That is an oral way of regarding inscription. It is plain in the evidence of the time, much plainer in history than in philosophy, but the two projects do not differ in this fundamental leaning of the later middle ages. It is not that the written word had no authority in its own right, but rather that "its own right" had been ruled out of play. Dominion emerged from a sense of the text as something actually spoken by an author, a product of "dictation" in every sense of the term. Although this is a statement about medieval literacy, it is also a comment on English politics in the fourteenth century.

The historical anachronism which marks the reigns of both Edward III and Richard II has frequently been traced to the economic and military interests of feudalism.[119] But the nostalgic feudalism of the times, which is obvious in so many cultural forms, has a much broader foundation in the discourse of literacy and in the dominion of societal bonds which it bolstered. For the politics of this vision of the past reveals itself at several critical junctures precisely by virtue of a deliberate historical occlusion of written law and precedent—if not on occasion by an outright destruction of all things written. To be sure, other moments in the medieval past illustrate a similar suppression; but none takes the form of the standoff between written and spoken dominion such as we witness in England during the second half of the fourteenth century. It is no wonder that chronicles side so dramatically

---

[118] Coleman's thesis, *Medieval Readers and Writers*, pp. 25–29. For a contrasting opinion, see Bean, *From Lord to Patron*, p. 235; Taylor, "Richard II's Views on Kingship," p. 191.

[119] Recently by Kaeuper in *War, Justice, and Public Order*, p. 388.

with the cause of one political patron or another. The oral form of such a narrative procedure speaks unmistakably to the point of what was going on in the houses of state. Anselm's dictum—"We speak, that is we think"—had an extraordinary longevity in the logical tradition perhaps because it corroborated so well the exercise of political dominion throughout the reigns of Edward III and Richard II.

To sum up: Parts One and Two of this book lead to the conclusion that although writing was certainly appreciated for its difference from spoken modes of communicating, a recognition of what was at stake in the difference is compromised or obscured by a discourse of voice as prior and originary. The historical consequences of this occlusion are germane at once to our sense of medieval literacy—that writing counted on the dictation of voice—and also to our understanding of medieval structures of power in church and state: so tenacious was the commitment to the priority of voice that its displacement of written opposition, even legal precedent, could proceed often without apparent fear of sanction, or at least none that could not be silenced by spoken oath, such as the one uttered by the members of parliament after the purges of 1388. We should hardly be surprised at the realization of power in such moments, for it arises from neither voice nor letter, office nor precedent, but instead from the act of displacement itself. As Ockham said of Genesis, "If the first parents had not sinned, there would be no power of appropriating."

In Part Three I will turn to another manifestation of the relation between orality and writing, its exploration in Middle English poetry. Because poetic composition does not pay the same kind of homage to the centers of learning or political power as philosophy or historiography, we may well expect to find that it does not negotiate the border between voice and text according to traditional assumptions about their subordination. Not only do the poets feel the difference of their enterprise because of its vernacularity; they reflect more deliberately and forcefully than any of their contemporaries on the implications of playing out the difference of writing in a culture long used to its foundations in the spoken word. I turn to *Sir Gawain* and the *Knight's Tale* because they are scrupulously attentive to this division in language, and because they explore it specifically to confront the problem of nostalgia represented in the chronicles.

PART THREE

Poetry

Chapter Six

THE SPELL OF THE AX: DIGLOSSIA AND HISTORY
IN *SIR GAWAIN AND THE GREEN KNIGHT*

> In his on honde he hade a holyn bobbe . . .
> And an ax in his other, a hoge and unmete,
> A spetos sparthe, to expoun in spelle who-so myght.
> —*Sir Gawain*

INTRODUCTION

The tension between orality and writing which I have explored thus far in philosophy and chronicle history is also a considerable factor in the genre of poetry commonly recognized for its ties to both of these projects of the fourteenth century, chivalric romance. Because the development of this genre in the so-called alliterative revival of the time has had a long—though contested—association with oral tradition, I turn now to the example of *Sir Gawain and the Green Knight*.

When Middle English scholars first suggested that the oral-formulaic character of Old English poetry was apparently "revived" in the mid-thirteenth century and then again in the mid-fourteenth, they made no mistake about the fact that the later poetry was composed by literates with pen in hand.[1] The problem was in explaining how an Old English tradition, that part of it composed by a *scop* in oral circumstances, could have survived to influence verse composition many centuries later. Some of the customary explanations for such a survival have not worn very well in a recent quarter of scholarship. For instance, more than one reader has found it hard to believe that a poetic style of the 1300s could belong to a "continuity" going back to Anglo-Saxon times, since manuscript evidence for it has not been documented.[2] Moreover, a poetry that is oral in composition may never have been written down, and so to think of it as part of the "lost literature" of medieval

---

[1] Waldron, "Oral-Formulaic Technique and Middle English Alliterative Poetry"; Baugh, "Improvisation in the Middle English Romances." Cf. Ker, *Medieval English Literature*, p. 35, developed by Chambers, "The Continuity of English Prose," p. lxvii.

[2] Turville-Petre, *The Alliterative Revival*, pp. 14–17; Pearsall, *Old English and Middle English Poetry*, p. 153, and "The Origins of the Alliterative Revival," p. 6; Lawton, ed., *Middle English Alliterative Poetry*, p. 6; Salter, "The Alliterative Revival."

England, as once argued, seems misconceived from the start.[3] Accordingly, the whole idea of a "revival" has prompted some readers to ask what exactly was being revived.

The case against orality in fourteenth-century alliterative poetry has been argued with particular reference to meter. The location of the metrical pause, for instance, occurs in medial position for a line in Old English, but in terminal position for Middle English. Since so-called formulaic expressions may be observed in many different metrical situations of Middle English verse—such as straddling a medial pause— then the idea of a formulaic phrase based upon a predictable and definitive rhythm is rendered almost meaningless. Instead, the repetition of such phrases in Middle English would be better described, according to one critic, as "collocations" or "grammetrical units," since they obey the demands of written standards for meter and grammar rather than the dynamics of oral performance.[4] Furthermore, if metrical norms are pressed further, one would have to note that the poetry of the fourteenth-century revival is a compound of strong stress and foot meter, whereas Old English poetry (notably *Beowulf*) combines strong stress, syllabism, and quantity; thus from the point of view of meter alone, Middle English appears to be "profoundly different" from Old English.[5] And in general one would do best to approach the entire alliterative corpus by regarding it as the most "clerkly, literate and essentially bookish" to be found in the fourteenth century.[6]

In other parts of this study, I have noted similar instances in which achievements in medieval literacy are assumed to have established a definitive break from orality. For Middle English alliterative poetry, the line of demarcation has received adamant defense; but it does not represent a unilateral opinion. Some readers would still accept, perhaps with modification, the formulation of several years ago, that *Gawain* "is deeply indebted to the tradition of oral verse."[7] Reactions against this proposition seemed to have assumed that it rests on the

---

[3] Wilson, *The Lost Literature of Medieval England*. Cf. Everett, *Essays on Middle English Liteature*, pp. 25–26, 46.

[4] Turville-Petre, *The Alliterative Revival*, pp. 53, 87–92. Cp. Matonis, "Middle English Alliterative Poetry."

[5] Cable, *The English Alliterative Tradition*, pp. 2, 5. Cp. Sapora, *A Theory of Middle English Alliterative Meter*, pp. 4, 14–15.

[6] Lawton, ed., *Middle English Alliterative Poetry*, p. 6. Cf. Lawton, "The Unity of Middle English Alliterative Poetry," p. 93, and "The Diversity of Middle English Alliterative Poetry," p. 152.

[7] Benson, *Art and Tradition in "Sir Gawain and the Green Knight,"* p. 120. Cf. Borroff, *Sir Gawain and the Green Knight*, pp. 58, 90; Spearing, *The "Gawain"-Poet*, p. 20; Sapora, *Theory of Middle English Alliterative Meter*, pp. 4, 24.

criterion of oral verse-making, of "composition *during* performance."[8] But scholarship on orality in the poem has not made this assumption. Moreover, even in a poetic tradition like Old English, with recognized illustrations of extemporaneous oral composition, it is apparent that some poems were created by writers following textual sources and rendering them in a formulaic style. In other words, the presence of formulas, as we have known for some time, does not demonstrate that a poem was produced orally; but neither does their existence in texts created by a writer from other written sources discredit the theory of oral composition or the continuity of oral tradition.[9]

To the contrary, we need a better sense of the "transitional" nature of an oral-formulaic style when it is carried over directly into written productions. Medieval Germany and Anglo-Saxon England offer a number of compelling illustrations of how "transitional texts" may result when oral and literate cultures adjust to each other.[10] But the case can also be made for the composition of poems belonging to the alliterative revival of several centuries later. For example, the poet who wrote the *Wars of Alexander* did not compose during the act of public performance, but it is very possible that he "composed like an oral poet," that is, with a "grammar of composition which enabled him to generate an almost endless number of phrases, clauses, and sentences which were also rhythmic half-lines of alliterative verse." And this process was not simply a matter of allusion to a specific traditional vocabulary; rather, the *Wars*-poet "wrote formulaically."[11]

ORAL CONTEXT

From this point of view, which is admirably sensitive to the larger oral context in which medieval writing often developed, a formulaic text composed with pen in hand "necessarily and invariably refers the reader to the oral-formulaic tradition"; and although that tradition may thus become "fictionalized" by the written work, a "literary" property of it, still it remains a "socio-historical index," for it is an author's "answer" to a real tradition of his or her own time.[12]

---

[8] Lord, *The Singer of Tales*, p. 129.

[9] Benson, "The Literary Character of Anglo-Saxon Formulaic Poetry," p. 340. Cf. Parks, "The Oral-Formulaic Theory in Middle English Scholarship."

[10] Curschmann, "Oral Poetry in Mediaeval English, French, and German Literature," p. 50. Cf. Benson, "Literary Character of Anglo-Saxon Formulaic Poetry," pp. 338–39.

[11] H. N. Duggan, "The Role of Formulas," p. 281.

[12] Bäuml, "The Theory of Oral-Formulaic Composition," in *Comparative Research on Oral Traditions*, ed. Foley, pp. 39–41.

Recognizing oral context as a cultural factor, not simply a technique of literary history, goes a long way toward strengthening the position of those who would want to assume some kind of "continuity" between Old and Middle English poetry, but who are leery of explaining it in the absence of a documented history. That the fourteenth-century revival is part of a lost tradition of unrhymed alliterative verse from the Southwest Midlands is far less dubious once orality is no longer dismissed as a "low" channel of communication—which makes "wretched what it touches."[13] To the contrary, we have seen plenty of evidence that the situation was easily reversible, with *writing* on the defensive and in need of apology, particularly work in the vernacular. In a manuscript culture where written and oral traditions were continuously assimilating each other, it seems far less difficult to assume that the two most distinguishing features of the revival—the reversion to the alliterative stress pattern of Old English and the rejection of rhyme— were attempts to embrace a formulaic style that had some kind of currency in an oral tradition extending back over the centuries. Thus the poets of the revival were not thawing out a "deep-frozen" style; they were representing a voice from the past, preserved for them either in oral transmission or in manuscript, but recognizable on a par with the many other cultural forms which had come down from oral history.[14] Their representation was, to repeat, *literary* because written on parchment for public recitation or silent reading. But its context was "transitional," in respect of the literate and oral diversity of the times.

If, as I indicated in Parts One and Two, academic philosophy and chronicle history suggest how oral assumptions about language could lay claim to writing, it seems that poetry would have far less to explain about its ties to orality, especially when it seeks to imitate the formulaic rhythm, phraseology, and diction of verse forms not dependent on written standards. For this reason several approaches to poems of the revival, including *Gawain*, have assumed parameters for orality much wider than versification. Ring structure, for example, is a "grammar" of oral telling just as significant as formulaic phrasing, and *Gawain* makes use of it manifestly in the binary repetition of challenge and fulfillment.[15] One aspect of this structure in the poem, the initial confrontation of the Green Knight, is derived from a commonplace of oral

---

[13] Pearsall, "Origins of the Alliterative Revival," p. 6. Cf. his more qualified view in "The Alliterative Revival," pp. 43–44.

[14] Cf. Spearing, *The "Gawain"-Poet*, p. 20; Parks, *Verbal Duelling in Heroic Narrative*, p. 136.

[15] Wittig, *Stylistic and Narrative Structures*; Ritzke-Rutherford, "Formulaic Microstructure," in Göller, ed., *The Alliterative "Morte Arthure*," pp. 73–75; Camargo, "Oral Traditional Structure," in Foley, ed., pp. 126–31.

narrative, the "heroic contesting" or "flyting" that motivates the challenges of Roland or Beowulf. But by the fourteenth century, the form is only a vestige from the oral past, now a "literate" element in tension with its traditional context.[16]

That *Gawain* exploits the tension between oral and literate may be noted in still another respect, the distinction which one critic draws between "sequential" and "recursive" rhetoric to be found in many medieval romances and language treatises. Like one of its sources (*Caradoc*), *Gawain* proceeds frequently in the oral way of "paratactic" sequencing, but not without extensive recursions or "intratextual" cross-references within the narrative, made possible by its refined literary character.[17] Such an approach to the "rhetoric" of the poem is not unlike the consideration of ring structure, formulaic phraseology, or archaic diction: "oral" elements assume a "context" quite beyond poetic history alone. To disregard that context for want of a manuscript history of alliterative verse traceable to Old English is to insist on a textual standard for language more befitting the age of the printed book than the manuscript culture of the fourteenth century.

DISPLACEMENT

My point here is not simply that "standards" about evidence were uncertain. I take that uncertainty—for instance in the records of chronicle history—as a sign of the times, as an indication of the adjustment going on between oral and written traditions. In this environment, we cannot assume that the written word or document had a power all its own, as an autonomous mode in its own right. The opposite was more often the case, as we see in the chronicles, where the record of "the facts" bespeaks the interests of a definite political affiliation. I have described this situation as evidence of the uncertain status of literacy in a culture still functioning largely by word of mouth: the "orality" of this context is apparent in the *displacement* of writing, the representation of it as a mode of speech. In the philosophical tradition this cultural underpinning has much to do with the limited "nominalism" of Ockham's project and with the persistent "realism" of Wyclif's. In the political arena, the displacement of writing is tied to the anachronistic feudal ethos proliferated during the reign of Edward III and to the justification of a multitude of ills in government during the reign of Richard II. Among these developments, writing does not exemplify a concept of the word as an autonomous entity, existing in its own right

---

[16] Parks, *Verbal Duelling in Heroic Narrative*, pp. 152–59. Cf. Griffith, "Bertilak's Lady."
[17] Troyan, "Rhetoric Without Genre," pp. 377–80, 387, 394–95.

and for its own sake; and the document does not demonstrate well-entrenched textual standards for evaluating and judging evidence. To be sure, such standards were in formation; but "literacy" was still taking shape between two competing channels of communication, and that context was most encouraging to displacement.

In this cultural situation, *Gawain* is particularly relevant for consideration. As a poem about the Arthur of legend, it is also keenly concerned with its own genre, as several studies have demonstrated in the "game-like" properties of the text.[18] The subject of poetry within the poem has led to scholarship on the "uncertainty" of language and the problem of making contact with historical context.[19] More recently, displacement has attracted critical attention, too, but only with reference to Arthurian myth: one reader regards King Arthur as displaced from the "sovereign centre" of Camelot; another sees Morgan la Faye as the displacement of magic and incest from the "ideology" of the Round Table.[20] Finally, an attempt to see the image of chivalry represented in the poem as a reflection of the times has not been ignored, though it has been understood in both early and later studies as an attempt to embrace a nostalgic feudal ethos, not unlike the political vision presented in contemporary chronicle histories.[21]

However, the possibility that two of the vital discoveries of this scholarship, metalanguage and displacement, are related to each other has not drawn critical response. In the remainder of this chapter, I consider situations in the poem which attempt to expose displacement by calling attention to the "diglossia" of language, as I have called it, the split between spoken and written, statement and meaning. Moreover, in exploring its own poetic language, *Gawain* reaches beyond Arthurian romance and into the heart of a problem about dominion in language long ignored by the philosophical tradition in England and long abused by the politicians in government. Matters of genre and theme certainly lead back into the poetic history of Camelot. But I submit that metalanguage and displacement are critical in this text be-

[18] E.g., Cook, "The Play-Element in *Sir Gawain and the Green Knight*"; Benson, *Art and Tradition*, p. 208; Davenport, *The Art of the "Gawain"-Poet*, pp. 149–50; Kaske, "*Sir Gawain and the Green Knight*," p. 32; Finlayson, "The Expectations of Romance" and "Definitions of Middle English Romance."

[19] D. H. Green, "Irony and Medieval Romance," p. 50; Ganim, "Disorientation, Style and Consciousness," pp. 378–80; Hanning, "Sir Gawain and the Red Herring," pp. 12, 15; Hanna, "Unlocking What's Locked"; Shoaf, *The Poem as Green Girdle*; Spearing, *Readings in Medieval Poetry*, p. 195; Stanbury, *Seeing the "Gawain"-Poet*, pp. 105, 111–12.

[20] Spearing, "Central and Displaced Sovereignty in Three Medieval Poems," p. 260; Kamps, "Magic, Women, and Incest," pp. 314–23. Cf. S. Fisher, "Leaving Morgan Aside" and "Taken Men and Token Women."

[21] E.g., R. H. Green, "Gawain's Shield and the Quest for Perfection," p. 121; Aers, *Community, Gender, and Individual Identity*, p. 176.

cause of the immediate historical context in which it was produced: the poet writes about Arthur's court with a sharp eye on England's, where dominion had a flourishing association with displacement. Whether or not the poem ratifies the nostalgic historicism of the times remains to be seen. Accordingly, we need to look more closely at the ways *Gawain* reflects on itself, in order to appreciate more fully the philosophical and political implications of questions about language in poetry.

LETTER AND TONGUE

Opening with the "Brutus bokez" of chronicle history and historical romance concerning the time of Arthur, the narrator speaks about transforming the "lel letteres loken" of his silent script into the well-known oral story "as I in toun herde, / with tonge" (31–32).[22] His posture is conventional, recalling, for example, the Chandos herald presenting himself before an audience of listeners to tell the life of the Black Prince. In both cases, the convention is not fundamentally bookish, though it is found in written sources; it appeals to popular history. The *Gawain*-poet says that among all that has been built here in England "of Bretaygne kynges," Arthur was the "hendest, as I haf herde telle" (25–26). If he has found Arthur's fame told by word of mouth, he has also found it written in the books of Brutus—perhaps the records of such chroniclers as Geoffrey of Monmouth, Thomas Walsingham, or Ranulf Higden. But the combination of oral and written which marks such histories has now been foregrounded for attention in its own right:

> If ȝe wyl lysten þis laye bot on littel quile,
> I shal telle hit as-tit. (30–31)

"Now" (*as-tit*) he will begin the public recitation of his script just as it has been told "with tonge," and thus he will avoid the hesitation or interruption always possible in silent reading. Yet his delivery will not be impromptu, like the performance of the *scop* in the mead hall; rather, he will speak:

> As hit is stad and stoken
> In stori stif and stronge,
> With lel letteres loken,
> In londe so hatz ben longe. (33–36)

"Locked" in alliteration, the narrator's words will also be the oral pronunciation of letters linked in cursive script; the spoken will have

---

[22] Tolkien, Gordon, and Davis, eds., *Sir Gawain and the Green Knight*, used throughout.

the quality of words "set down and fastened" in the text "firm and strong." That book is none other than the poem in front of us, the written object presenting itself as the voice of the narrator. So powerful is the narrator's fiction of his speaking that it once led critics to opine that this is a poem "for the ear rather than the eye."[23]

But ear does not supersede eye: the metaphor works both ways, as every metaphor must, except that in this case the narrator would appear to slant things his own way and anticipate response according to what is heard. There is nothing new in this subordination of the channels of language. We have heard it before, and specifically in the chronicle records the narrator himself invokes, where it frequently assumes an autonomy for language which is aligned with the presumed autonomy of political dominion. *Gawain* appears to begin, therefore, by figuring a narrator who is not unlike the chroniclers of the political scene. But shifting between the registers of language will tell another story.

And a subsequent division of categories—between fictional and factual—complicates shortly the authority his voice would assume. As Arthur lays at Camelot with his retinue during the holidays, he would not eat until all others were served (85), and "he wolde neuer ete" until he was told:

> Of sum auenturus þyng, an uncouþe tale,
> Of sum mayn meruayle, þat he myӡt trawe,
> Of alderes, of armes, of oþer auenturus. (93–95)

A strange tale or marvel—a *fiction* about arms and adventure—was the necessary prelude to serving the meal at the Round Table. But if not the fiction, then a joust would also be welcomed by the king—the arms and adventure themselves carried out right there in court.

> Oþer sum segg hym bisoӡt of sum siker knyӡt
> To joyne wyth hym in iustyng, in joparde to lay,
> Lede, lif for lyf, leue vchon oþer,
> As fortune wolde fulsun hom, þe fayrer to haue. (96–99)

As Arthur would have either the tale or the real thing, so also does his narrator appear to respond to him by offering to tell "an aunter in erde," an adventure that occurred "on earth" or "in reality," and yet also "a selly in siӡt" (a "marvelous vision") or an "ottrage" ("strange") adventure about the "wonderez" of Arthur (27–29). To all appearances the arrival of the Green Knight erases the boundaries between *tale* and

---

[23] Burrow, *A Reading of "Sir Gawain and the Green Knight,"* p. 1. Cf. Spiers, *Medieval English Poetry*, p. 227.

iustyng, as the fictional enters with all the force of the real. Arthur's call for story, although seemingly bypassed when the "first cors" of the meal is served (116) before any "laykyng of enterludez" (472), has been ironically fulfilled. As the narrator sardonically remarks at the opening of Fitt II,

> This hanselle hatz Arthur of auenturus on fyrst
> In ȝonge ȝer, for he ȝerned ȝelpyng to here.
> Thaȝ hym wordez were wane when þay to sete wenten. (492–94)

Arthur got what he asked for—he wanted "tales," and he received one much larger than life.

But the blurring of the border between fictional and factual is more apparent than real, since the narrator knows very well that the episode has been a trick motivated by Morgan la Faye and Merlin to embarrass the *surquidré* of the Round Table (2457). Arthur, of course, is totally unaware of the trap, and thus he speaks with an irony beyond his understanding when he is ironical to Queen Guenevere in "explaining" the beheading of the man in green as merely an illusionist's trick:

> "Dere dame, to-day demay yow neuer;
> Wel bycommes such craft vpon Cristmasse,
> Laykyng of enterludez, to laȝe and to syng,
> Among þise kynde caroles of knyȝtez and ladyez.
> Neuer þe lece to my mete I may me wel dres,
> For I haf sen a selly, I may not forsake." (470–75)

Is he encouraging his queen or himself? The truth is that he speaks the truth without knowing it.

Arthur would like to believe that his call for story has been answered with this *selly*; but the interruption bears too heavily on the "wonder" of it. The narrator would want to believe that his higher irony controls the situation, that he feigns successfully the discourse of chronicle histories about Britain in order to teach history a lesson about political fame. He would insinuate irony into the putative sovereignty of the Arthurian *surquidré*, just as the king is ironic about his own political fears when he patronizes his queen with an "answer." And as Arthur is ignorant of the truth he speaks, neither does the narrator know that he too is telling the truth: he says in the end that the plot of his story is only Morgan's trick (perhaps instigated by Merlin) and that history will go on as before when the members of court ceremonialize the weakness and failure of Gawain into an occasion for their own "re-noun" by taking up the green girdle as a banner of Arthurian victory (2519). But he does not indicate any awareness that his reading of the testing of Gawain is ultimately partial to the political interests of the court. Instead, he presumes quite simply the autonomy of his own voice, which he would validate at the end of the poem (as at the beginning) by appeal to the written history of Britain (2521–23).

However, there is more than enough evidence that the writing of this poem is not so easily subsumed within its speaking and that the denouement is inevitably exposed for what it is—a political capitulation which subverts the discourse of history it was designed to exonerate.[24] Merlin, the arch-magician who was also a writer, never comes to the surface in this narrative, nor does Morgan la Faye.[25] Yet they inhabit it still with their "magic," which tricks the sovereignty of political explanations, like Arthur's, and even the ironic reflections on them, like the narrator's. Magic, in other words, is a trope of errancy in this poem; it figures the conflict between speech and writing, sentence and sense, which are so much a part of the subversion of Arthur. It has, thus, an import considerably broader than exposing the displacement of Morgan; for if the Round Table cannot exclude that woman or erase the memory she carries, the magic of her return is not only in the trickery of masked characters but in the much more subtle and pervasive "magic" splitting the tongue and action of speakers, including the narrator, from the beginning of the poem. The interruption of Arthur's call for story repeats itself in the narrator's response; the irony of his ironic plot—that he speaks the truth and knows it not—is a linguistic trick within his role as historian; and the fiction of the story within the story is trickery, too, since it stages the history of England as merely a poetic tale which cannot get beyond echoing itself.

BATTLE-AX AND BEARD

In order to pursue this point further, we may observe that Arthur's misreading of the beheading scene is delivered in response to one of the most unforgettable figures of disembodied language in the poem. The king and all of those who witnessed the decapitation have just listened to the discourse of a head severed from its bleeding trunk and held out at arm's length to speak directly to the court. The magic of the action in this image, however, has immediate bearing on the semiology of voice and writing in the poem. And its role in this connection begins, as we might guess, with the first mention of the weapon of

---

[24] Cf. Harwood, "*Gawain* and the Gift," p. 492; and Kamps, "Magic, Women, and Incest," pp. 323–30. NB Kamps's critique of Fisher's opposite conclusion ("Leaving Morgan Aside," pp. 131–37), that Arthurian ideology ultimately prevails by displacing women.

[25] On Merlin as writer, see Bloch, *Etymologies and Genealogies*, pp. 1–6 and passim.

decapitation. Bearing the holly branch in one hand, the Green Knight carries:

> . . . an ax in his other, a hoge and unmete,
> A spetos sparthe to expoun in spelle whoso might. (208–209)

Too "formidable" (*sparthe*) to describe *in spelle* ("words," "discourse") because of its size (forty-five inches across the width of the blade), the *spetos* is also beyond words because it is linked to the magic of beheading. *Spelle* does not refer specifically to the "magic" or "charm" associated with the term in later English, and yet the beginning of that suggestion is signified in Middle English "night-spelle," the charm cast by the utterance of special words.[26] In this case, the *spelle* of the battle-ax cannot be "expoun" because it is an instrument of magical language, the "craft" of Morgan's silent revenge controlling the plot. And consequently the deferral of description spoken in *occultatio*—the feigned exclusion of the detailed explanation to follow (208–20)—links the weapon to what is excluded or silenced, the "written" suggestions bypassed or suppressed by the voice of narrative.

But the *spelle* of the ax is linked to the tension between written and spoken in yet another way. The scene following the Green Knight's first words and ending with Arthur grabbing the ax from him is a vivid instance of ritual combat carried out as verbal battle, a form of flyting such as we find in *Beowulf* or the *Chanson de Roland*.

> Þe fyrst word þat he warp, "Wher is," he sayd,
> "Þe gouernour of þis gyng?" (224–25)

Since the king is present, though not in his place at the table, the question is mockingly rhetorical: it renders him indistinguishable from his subordinates who are speechless "to answare" (241). They are "al stouned at his steuen and stonstil seten"—all "stunned" and "stone-still" in their seats at the power of his voice (242). "So slaked hor lotez" ("so lacking in words") are they that the narrator enters the text to apologize for their "sylence" (243–44) and ends up daring even his own audience—us—to a more courageous response:

> Bot let hym þat al schulde loute
> Cast vnto þat wyȝe. (248–49)

The Green Knight qualifies his challenge by noting that if he had come for blood battle, he would have brought armor and weapons, "bot for I wolde no were, me wedez ar softer" (271). His *circumlocutio*, however, does not disguise the fact that he has intruded on the Arthurian court

---

[26] E.g., *Miller's Tale* (2480).

with armor and weapons as consequential as the battle-ax in his hand, the verbal challenge suppressed in the understatement of the *softer wedez* and then delivered point blank in lines that force the moment to its crisis:

> "Bot if þou be so bold as alle burnez tellen,
> Þou wyl grant me godly þe gomen þat I ask
> bi ryȝt." (272–74)

Establishing the terms of the test that motivates the whole action to follow, this remark threatens the foundation of heroic *comitatus* by exposing a breach between what is *told* about Arthurian fame and what it actually is. *Bold* is the fighting word here, not because it is a moral indictment of vainglory or self-aggrandizement, but rather because a member of such a society secured place and dominion through the strength of what was said about him, through the boldness of his reputation as it was constituted by common talk. The "riȝt" by which the Green Knight mounts his challenge is not written in any text or assumed in common law, unless we regard that "law" as the preemptive right of oral contesting to put down an opponent by word of mouth. And that is precisely the green man's next move. If he is piqued by Arthur's tendentious dig in calling him "cortays knyȝt" (276), he registers it with the rejoinder that there is no one present in the famous court of King Arthur "bot berdlez chylder" ("beardless children"; 280): "Here is no man me to mach" (282).

This is no battle of wits, as conversation will later become in the bedroom of Bertilak's castle. It is a boasting duel in which words are hurled to *stowne* the king and his knights.

> If he hem stowned vpon fyrst, stiller were þanne
> Alle þe heredmen in halle, þe hyȝ and þe loȝe. (301–302)

If he "stunned" them into silence earlier, he is "still" doing so, rendering auditors of every court even more silent (*stiller*) than before. Adding insult to injury, the green man punctuates his assault with the taunt of waving his beard at those in front of him, *carping* the victory accomplished in oral society when reputation is stolen by words.

> "What, is þis Arþures hous," quoþ þe haþel þenne,
> "Þat al þe rous rennes of þurȝ ryalmes so mony?
> Where is now your sourquydrye and your conquestes,
> Your gryndellayk and your greme, and your grete wordes?
> Now is þe reuel and þe renoun of þe Rounde Table
> Ouerwalt wyth a worde of on wyȝes speche." (309–14)

It has been commonly noted that Arthur's response to this challenge is a failure of royal prudence, of the "cortays" behavior of a nobleman;

as one commentator has put it: "Arthur's failure in the challenge is a failure in manners."[27] He is not the image of the conventional king to be found in the sources of the poem. But neither is the green man a carbon copy of his analogues. The customs of oral culture which characterize this verbal onslaught are here in tension with the courtesy of Arthurian literary analogues, and the king responds in the only way he can, by mirroring his opponent gesture for gesture, word for word. The king throws back in the face of the Green Knight the ironic *gome* he has sought and follows it with his phrase: "þy grete wordes" will not undo any member of the Round Table:

> "Gif me now þy geserne, vpon Godez halue,
> And I schal bayþen þy bone þat þou boden habbes." (325–27)

Arthur has been baited, to be sure, but he advances in full knowledge of the fact: his reputation and power, at once undermined in verbal battle, are also constituted by it. Seizing and brandishing the ax are not, therefore, signs of hesitation at cutting into his opponent, nor are they evidence of a failure in manners; they are taunts, like waving the beard.

The Green Knight's response, a silence of mockery much louder than words, mirrors the *stowned sylence* of the court at his initial entry.

> Þe stif mon him bifore stod vpon hyȝt,
> Herre þen ani in þe hous by þe hede and more.
> Wyth sturne schere þer he stod he stroked his berde. (332–34)

The subtlety of this parrying extends even to the stroking of the beard, an outrageous mimicry of the king who, without a beard to stroke, must fulminate by brandishing the ax. The green man has no more response to the king's rebuke than he would to someone who had brought him a glass of wine (336–38). But here the graces of courtesy are obviously displacements for the chest-beating of a former age.

Accordingly, to say that Arthur fails in this encounter because of personal and political *surquidré* is to overlook the oral contesting invoked by the narrator. And yet the king remains very odd next to the Arthurs of the sources and analogues of the poem, not to mention the models of royal behavior in contemporary English society. If Arthur is anachronistic, the narrator makes no apologies for him. Rather, anachronism serves the developing interest in the king's surrogate, Sir Gawain, who will mediate between the older feudal ethos of the king and a newer social style.

Still the narrator's approach to this shift is anything but clear-cut, since Gawain is introduced in the scene of the challenge through a diction and syntax that do not affirm the refined formality of high

---

[27] Benson, *Art and Tradition*, p. 218.

courtesy. Although it may appear that Gawain's overture to take on the challenge is an effort to restore a courtesy lost by the king, the style of the speech is artificial in the extreme.[28]

> "Wolde ȝe, worþilych lorde," quoþ Wawan to þe kyng,
> "Bid me boȝe fro þis benche, and stonde by yow þere,
> Þat I wythoute vylanye myȝt voyde þis table,
> And þat my legge lady lyked not ille,
> I wolde com to your counseyl bifore your cort ryche." (343–47)

The courtesy of the subjunctive mood befits address to the king, especially when valor is at stake; but its extenuation in the remainder of this speech through a virtual labyrinth of subordinating qualifications creates a style exactly the opposite of the terse, daring engagement of the preceding exchange. And if that is the point, then the high literacy of these lines calls attention to a speaker who is not quite at home with his own discourse and perhaps not even with himself: "I am þe wakkest, I wot, and of wyt feblest" (354).

Affected modesty is hardly necessary in this tableau of self-effacements, since Gawain cannot afford to reduce himself—in arms or mind—below all the knights of Arthur's court on this occasion. The line, like the speech in general, betokens the kind of style we will hear more of later, one that, by virtue of its indirectness, signifies limitation and elegance simultaneously. For in spite of pointed differences from the language of Arthur, Gawain's address is marked by a misprision of its own—a suppression of hesitation buried in the justification of unhesitating readiness for combat. Confronting this split is the narrator's dilemma, and in the beheading episode he negotiates it, as he had in the opening stanzas on his own performance, in favor of yet another custom from oral culture, the reliance on the power of the spoken oath.

FORWARDE

When the Green Knight puts forth the challenge, the terms of the contest appear legalistic: one blow for another—"stifly strike a strok for an oþer" (287)—with the "giserne ryche" awarded to the first bidder and vouchsafed in "quit-clayme" (288, 293); "twelmonyth and a day" will be allowed to pass for "respite" before "þou wyl diȝt me þe dom to dele hym an oþer" (295–98). But attention to the terms of the arrangement does not obscure the forensic and boasting tone: if

[28] Cp. Benson, *Art and Tradition*, pp. 211–18, and Burrow, *A Reading of "Sir Gawain,"* p. 12, with Spearing, *Criticism and Medieval Poetry*, pp. 38–45, and Shoaf, *The Poem as Green Girdle*, p. 62.

any "freke be so fell" to "dar" strike blow for blow, then—the Green Knight cries out—"barlay" (287–96). It is likely that the colloquial sense of this term from the verbal contesting of children's games—to bid first claim on an option—is its significance in this context;[29] for he puts down opponents by taunting the power of their "steuen":

> "Now hyʒe, and let se tite
> Dar any herinne oʒt say." (299–300)

Although written contracts were common forms of authenticating agreements by this time in England, the vocabulary of the challenge is not "document," "text," or "law." It is called a *forwarde*, a *couenaunt* (377, 393); it is established in the context of the boast; and it is validated by what is sworn out loud between the two parties. Responding to the Green Knight's behest that they "refourme" ("restate") the terms of the agreement ("þou me telle truly"; 378, 380), Gawain first names himself and then recounts the details, even stipulating that no one else but the green man can stand for the exchange twelve months hence—apparently presuming that there will by "no wyʒ" in green "on lyue" after the first blow (384–85). But the irony is not out of place in a covenant made in flyting.[30] "Þat oþer onswarez" immediately that Gawain has "redily rehersed" the covenant completely, except for one last detail (387–93). And he proceeds to mirror Gawain's qualification with a counterboast of his own:

> ". . . þat þou schal siker me, segge, bi þi trawþe,
> Þat þou schal seche me þiself." (394–95)

The "douþe ryche" of auditors is called to witness that he must appear alone and endure what he deals out. Without even knowing the name of his opponent, Gawain seals the covenant with his spoken word, "I swere þe for soþe, and by my seker traweþ" (403). "Þat is innogh," the Green Knight replies, referring to the binding of the contract in Gawain's "true word," rather than in oaths to God or in written contracts.

As the power of the spoken oath is sufficient to bind the subsequent fulfillment of action, the *forwarde* of the participants becomes aligned with the narrator's own claims about the unfolding story—the literary language of the text. Though "warde" is pronounced differently from "worde," the verbal nature of the oath-taking appears to substantiate a basis for Middle English "forwarde" in the *worde* uttered *before* as

---

[29] Opie, *The Lore and Language of Schoolchildren*, pp. 135, 146–49; and Tolkien, Gordon, and Davis, eds., *Sir Gawain and the Green Knight*, l. 296 and note.

[30] Cp. Burrow, *A Reading of "Sir Gawain,"* p. 68.

promise or agreement.[31] It is this sense of the term that is suggested in the Green Knight's final words to Gawain before the beheading:

> "Þen may þou frayst my fare and forwardez holde;
> And if I spende no speche, þenne spedez þou þe better." (409–10)

Hold me, he says, to the "forwarde," and if I cannot utter any speech thereafter, all the better for you.

But the semiology of *for-warde*, dividing the contractual *worde* before its fulfillment, has already insinuated itself into this tricky agreement, as well as into the narrative contract. And its next most dramatic moment is the speech of the decapitated head, which is at once the "covenant" and "forward" to all that will follow. "Loke, Gawan," says the head in an imperative offensive to sight, "þou be grayþe to go as þou hettez. . . . I charge þe" (448–51). The "charge" of this speaker, while naming the points of the agreement, ridicules all expectations of realism and logic; yet it appeals to the language of written exactness in that same assault—"forþi me," "þerefore com," and "þe behoues" (455–56). But the final words tell all as the head dares Gawain with a cardinal rule of oral society: "oþer recreaunt be calde"—you will be called "coward" if you fail to appear.

The strength of this ethic of public shame was felt long before the editor who appended the line "hony soyt qui mal pence" ("shame be to him who thinks evil") to the end of the poem. All the members of Arthurian society, in one way or another, are motivated by it; but the first person to feel it was the narrator who told the story. The many properties of oral tradition which have found their way into the poem witness its impact, and not the least of them is the semiosis connecting the *forwarde* with the narrator's own speaking. What he has not counted on, however, is the inevitable complication linking his narration with the disembodied language of the talking head. It is this magic which is at once identified with the trickery of Morgan (perhaps Merlin, too) and simultaneously with the *spelle* of the ax. In one of the most cryptic images of the poem, Fitt I ends with the figure of the ax hung on a tapestry suspended on the wall behind the king's high table.

> "Now sir, heng vp þyn ax, þat hatz innogh hewen";
> And hit watz don abof þe dece on doser to henge,
> Þer alle men for meruayl my3t on hit loke,
> And bi trwe tytel þerof to telle þe wonder. (477–80)

Here indeed is the *spelle* of the ax, as it hangs to tell "the wonder" by its *doser* and *tytel* ("tapestry" and "inscription" or "evidence"). It has

---

[31] *Middle English Dictionary* (hereafter, *MED*), s.v. *for(e)ward*, 1 and 2: "oath"; 2a: "in front, at the front"; 4: "first and forward."

been transformed into text with rubric and chapter. The phrase "þi tytel," which occurs later in the long exegesis on the pentangle (626), suggests that the ax, too, has a tale to tell, though none is rendered except as the occluded "writing" of Morgan's revenge. She is the mysterious force behind the workings of this intrigue, and she is absent. But images like the tell-tale ax are displacements of her motivations, as are other similarly disguised inscriptions, like the final four lines of the Fitt.

> Now þenk wel, Sir Gawan,
> For woþe þat þou ne wonde
> Þis auenture for to frayn
> Þat þou hatz tan on honde. (487–90)

Sounding like one of his own characters, the narrator is the speaker of these lines, and we have heard him enter upon the action in this way before.[32] But the comparison is not to his earlier voice: it is to the Green Knight, who is the only one to address Gawain in this tone, and he has just done so as the talking head (448–51). The narrator, though he knows it not, has found his "forward" in that speech, and by echoing it here he has given voice to Morgan's revenge. If she is absent from this text, she is also present in the unlikely displacement of the narrator's own utterance.

Voice, in other words, enjoys no innocent vantage upon the action, no more so than the sight of the decapitated head. Vision and voice are dislocated in this scene as they are in many other episodes. In fact, more than one critic has noticed how lines of sight are figured frequently in the poem as strategies for interrupting the action and changing the scene. But shifting angles of sight are liminal also in the sense that they explore the difference in how people view the same scene: no single vision composes a monolithic or unifying perspective.[33] In this sense, liminal vision in the poem corresponds to what I have been calling the shifting registers of language: no voice has priority either, insofar as writing repeatedly interrupts a speaker in his or her utterance and without apparent supervision.

Pentagonal Discourse

The battle-ax hangs in Camelot as a sign of this interruption in the discourse of the poem. It is the mysterious *tytel* suggesting a split between what is spoken and what is meant. And thus it contrasts the

[32] Cp. Benson, *Art and Tradition*, p. 202.

[33] See Stanbury, *Seeing the "Gawain"-Poet*, pp. 99–112, 127, following Renoir, "Descriptive Techniques in *Sir Gawain and the Green Knight*."

narrator's typical way of treating signs, including the sign of his own
voice. For instance, shifting in Fitt II to the five-pointed star depicted
on Gawain's shield and armor, the narrator identifies it as a sign of the
knight's *trawþe* and of his nature in general: he is "pentagonal man,"
as one critic has noted.[34] The extended gloss on this image sets it apart
from the treatment of others in the poem: the explanation of its history
and import suggests that it is an obscure sign, but also that the narrator
is obviously anticipating the expectations of a listening audience, who
would need the information he offers.

Documenting the figure on the shield in the Biblical tradition of
Solomon, who established it "in bytoknyng of trawþe" (626), the narrator uses the Latin word "pentangel," identifying it as a term familiar
to people "with lore" (665), with a knowledge of texts. He acknowledges that the star is also known by the *illiterati*, by those who only
speak English:

> . . . and Englych hit callen
> Oueral, as I here, þe endeles knot. (629–30)

Proceeding step by step so that both lettered and unlettered will follow
the weave of this knot, the narrator's anticipation of oral reception is
also apparent in the sharp visual appeal of his discription. Listening,
as opposed to reading silently, requires such assistance, and the evidence of it in documents of the time is abundant. In this case, the figure
of "fyue poyntez"—"vche lyne" of which "vmbelappez and loukez in
oþer" (627–28)—composes an uninterrupted line and unbroken image.
The narrator paints the picture of an abstraction, so that "bi tytle þat
hit habbez," by the "evidence" of its "inscription," the pentangle betokens *trawþe*. Picture and truth are identical—unbroken, endless, perfect.[35]

To appreciate the narrator's effort at eliminating ambiguity from his
description, we should note that his exercise, up to this point, conforms
to what medieval logicians would have recognized as "simple supposition": the sign of the star stands for a "species," the idea of *trawþe*.
But he particularizes linguistic reference even further when he uses
"personal supposition," the identification of the truth or virtue represented by the sign with the real being of "þat prynce noble" (623).
Metaphors of binding reinforce the identity between the pentads of the
star and the virtues of the knight:

---

[34] Howard and Zacher, *Critical Studies of "Sir Gawain and the Green Knight,"* p. 161.

[35] On the pentangle as *signum naturalis*, see Burrow, *A Reading of "Sir Gawain,"* pp.
187–89; Arthur, *Medieval Sign Theory*, p. 46 and passim.

> . . . þyse pure fyue
> Were harder happed on þat hathel þen on any oþer.
> Now alle þese fyue syþez, for soþe, were fetled on þis knyȝt,
> And vchone halched in oþer, þat non ende hade. (654–57)

But an inevitable effect of such an exact alignment between star and man creates the illusion that the narrator, too, speaks in "personal supposition," that is, uses language to predicate the "individual being" of real things. Ockham understood such an event in language to be an instance of "signification," rather than "supposition," because it identifies the individual reality of something that can be verified by intuitive evidence. Gawain may enjoy such an identify with his star within the fictional world of the poem. But the voice of his narrator can only postulate a "suppositional" relation with real being because he himself is first and last a creation of words, a fiction. The narrator crosses that border momentarily when he gets caught up with the moral precision of his account: at that point his story makes a claim upon the "truth" of a "reality" to which he has no access. As he weaves and crosses *vmbelappynge* and *loukynge* each line of the pentangle, so also would he link each of the "lel letteres loken" of his text. The star becomes a sign of the text, at least in the "pentagonal discourse" spoken by the narrator.

That the narrator succeeds in linking sign and text may be tested by considering responses to Gawain's actions which have stressed his morality. One reader, for example, would evaluate him in terms of the "geometric absolutism" of the pentangle, and another would regard all of the "sign theory" in the poem as a moralistic system.[36] But I have been suggesting that the narrator's "geometry" is not so absolute, no more than the language of Arthur, Gawain, or the Green Knight. He would have Gawain proceed *sub specie pentaculi*, as it were, but the sign offers him little protection, and it is forgotten from the story almost as soon as it is introduced. The narrator, too, would proceed under the aegis of this sign as soon as its moral and political exactitude begins to elide the "suppositional" language of fiction into a "signifying" statement about the truth of an individual. But narrative voice enjoys no such autonomy "outside" of this poem. For it has already been qualified by alignment with the diglossia of other signs—the *spelle* of the ax, the *forwarde* of the exchange, and the speech of the decapitated head. And it is about to engage the most protracted figuration of split discourse in the poem, the fateful conversations in Lady Bertilak's bedroom. She poses quite explicitly a threat to the sign of the pentangle

---

[36] Burrow, *A Reading of "Sir Gawain,"* p. 51. Cf. Arthur, *Medieval Sign Theory*, pp. 12, 14, and passim.

but also a resistance to its "discourse," the oral prerogative of personal and political dominion.

The Book of the Body

That Gawain's reputation precedes him upon his arrival at Bertilak's castle is signified by the response of the company, when each man said to his brother:

> "Now schal we semlych se sleȝtez of þewez
> And the teccheles termes of talkyng noble,
> Wich spede is in speche vnspurd may we lerne,
> Syn we haf fonged þat fyne fader of nurture.
>
> . . . .
>
> I hope þat may hym here
> Schal lerne of luf-talkyng." (916–19, 926–27)

Though the poet had this commonplace about Gawain from legend, his noted reputation in the "skill" of "talkyng noble" proves larger than the man, and that disparity is the opening sought by Lady Bertilak in her effort to trick him. She sets the direction and style of their exchanges, and he follows. Yet she is a model of eloquence not by reputation but by performance, and she begins with one of the oldest topoi in the rhetorical handbooks, *circumlocutio* (or *periphrasis*), which she deploys variously to mediate the statement of her seduction.

Gawain would appear, on the other hand, to begin by avoiding rhetoric altogether, when he says to himself upon her secretive entry into the bedroom:

> ". . . More semly hit were
> To aspye with my spelle in space quat ho wolde." (1198–99)

But he knows not the suggestion in his *spelle*, for there will be more ambiguity (and magic) in what follows than he can anticipate. She sets in motion a vocabulary of contest and warfare when she observes, in a periphrasis that can only refer to herself, that he has been a sleeper so "vnslyȝe" that a "mon" could have slid behind the bed curtains undetected: you are "tan as-tyt" ("seized herewith"), she says, and unless a "true" ("truce") can be arranged between us, "I schal bynde yow in your bedde" (1209–11). Although he has had his eyes and ears wide open all along, he still cannot perceive the irony of her "bynde," which makes him the prisoner of a plot over which Lady Bertilak is finally sovereign. Rather, he complicates his misprision by imitating and extending her diction in what seems to be an exercise of his reputed linguistic skills. "Me schal worþe at your wile," he says, "for

I ȝelde me ȝederly" (1214–15), if you will only "deprece your prysoun, and pray hym to ryse . . . of þis bed" (1219–20). But as they *karp* together at this fiction of captivity, she widens the prison well beyond the bed: "I schal happe yow here . . . and syþen karp with my knyȝt þat I kaȝt haue" (1224–25).

He continues to duplicate her vocabulary from the warfare of courtly love, playing "servaunt" to her "soverayn," whereas she controls the irony of *circumlocutio* figuring sexual pursuit, in yet another convention, as merely idling away the "whyle wel, quyl hit lastez, / with tale" (1235–36). Deferring desire into a fiction about it is so much a part of this colloquy that even the direct statement of her intent cannot avoid being taken metaphorically: "ȝe ar welcum to my cors" (1237). The leeway of her *cors*—between "my body" and "me"—offers Gawain an escape clause, so to speak, but it unmistakably completes the whole purpose of *circumlocutio* thus far, to capitulate the fulfillment of passion to statements of it, to intensify desire by mediating it, and to figure her body as fictional *tale*—the text of the suppressed plot of Morgan's revenge.

A clever student of the "book" of her reference, Gawain responds:

> ". . . I be not now he þat ȝe of speken;
> To reche to such reuerence as ȝe reherce here." (1243–44)

He refers to her praise, that he is "Sir Wowen . . . þat alle þe worlde worchipez." But he also widens the separation of her *circumlocutio* by insisting that the Gawain who refers to himself when he speaks is not the Gawain who speaks. Though he says, in effect, I am not who I am, she is not fooled that he would "daly with derely your daynté wordez" (1253). In these exchanges, as one reader has observed, we cannot help but notice a certain amount of "bookishness";[37] but it is less about the literary history of Gawain than the metalanguage of intensifying desire, and Lady Bertilak calls him up short on the point by taking his denial one step further as she inches closer to the first kiss.

> "Now He þat spedez vche spech þis disport ȝelde yow!
> Bot þat ȝe be Gawan hit gotz in mynde." (1292–93)

The narrator says that with this remark she "stonyed hym with ful stor wordez" (1291), and the image—repeated from the Green Knight earlier (241–42)—"astounds" him because he interprets it to mean that his language has not been true to his reputation. The Author of all speech is called to witness that the man who speaks is clever, but he is not Gawain.

---

[37] Burrow, *A Reading of "Sir Gawain,"* p. 92.

Thinking he must have "fayled in fourme of his castes" ("words";
1295), Gawain is at once farthest from the lady in the order of discourse, but all the closer to her in desire, as she divides herself by
speaking in the third person and distances him into a figure of history.
The Gawain of legend, she says, would never:

> ". . . haf lenged so longe with a lady,
> Bot he had craued a cosse, bi his courtaysye,
> Bi sum towch of summe tryfle at sum talez ende." (1299–1301)

But is it really the knight of renown who seduces in this exchange by
a clever use of words? And does the reproof of "courtaysye" occasion
the kiss of the next sentence, or is it "craved" because desire is config-
ured by the *circumlocutio* of syntax and text in this poem—by staging
seduction as the grammatical dissimulation of "touching some trifle at
the end of a tale"?

Once the split between syntax and meaning has begun in these
scenes, it seems to ramify in all directions, as both knight and lady take
advantage of its implications. After the first visit, they negotiate this
gap, not as before by pretending that they understand each other, but
by the reproof that speech has not been true. "Sir, ʒif ʒe be Wawen,"
she objects on the second day, you have forgotten what I taught you:

> ". . . ʒisterday I taʒtte
> Bi alder-truest token of talk þat I cowþe." (1485–86)

Yet as an apology for telling the truth, "token of talk" is highly rhetorical, since she taught by an "example" or *token* which had little to
do with the truth: if she was the very "example" of honesty, her talk
was also its mere "token," and that is what she left him with—talk's
token—when she kissed him in bed.

After the second kiss (1505), the diglossia expands, when with "much
specie þay þer expoun" the pros and cons of loving (1506). She begins
to inquire about his experience, his "skylle"; but the syntax of her
question is distracted into a digression on the "lel layk of luf" ("beautiful entertainment of love"). Without completing her inquiry, she observes many lines later that although Gawain's "worde and . . . wor-
chip walkez ayquere" ("everywhere"), she has not yet heard one syllable
from him "þat euer longed to luf" (1521–24). The anacoluthon of this
passage might be resolved by trying to connect her initial inquiry
(1509) with her eventual return to his current behavior (1520). But such
a link in syntax is remote at best, and the anacoluthon remains—perhaps, as some would have it, to imitate the often interrupted patterns
of spoken discourse.[38] But a more local justification becomes apparent

---

[38] E.g., Tolkien, Gordon, and Davis, eds., *Sir Gawain and the Green Knight*, l. 1508, n.

if we consider this syntactical gap as a result of the division that has been the subject of the discourse all along—between experiencing desire and hearing about it in old books about Gawain.

Her digression, first of all, echoes the charge of her earlier rhetoric, that Gawain is not Gawain. She chafes him by observing that all "trwe knyȝtez" are known for their exploits ("teuelyng") in love—for what they have "auntered" or "endured" in "dulful stoundez" and how they have "broȝt blysse into boure" (1514–19). But the diction of this rejoinder draws so elaborately on the semiology of writing and reading that the strategy of validating the "truth" of knightly behavior as the "lettrure of armes" ("doctrine" or "code" of knighthood) also has the opposite effect, of rendering it as merely a story made up of "letters" (1513). While she insists that love is the experience of all true knights—the very "tytelet token and tyxt of her werkkez"—she also invalidates the truth of such experience because she is saying that it is only a thing of language, simply the "title" or "book" rather than adventure itself: knightly "werkkez" may be no more than what is told about them in the writings of the poets. And Gawain, the "word" of chivalry who "walkez" everywhere yet speaks "no wordez" at all, is empty language. He is "cortays and coynt" enough with his "hetes" ("oaths") to show "a ȝonke þynk" much about the subject—"and teche sum tokenez of trweluf craftes" (1521–27). But, she protests, "ar ȝe lewed," you who wield so much renown? Do you think me "to dille" ("too stupid") to understand your "dalyaunce" (1528–29)?

The politics of Morgan's plot is behind this metalanguage, as the innuendoes target the stability of the public word about Arthur's court and the viability of that word in one of his knights. Gawain has just been reduced quite literally to the vacancy of an echo, and he must scramble to evade the accusation by refusing to be fictionalized into the role of teacher she has assigned to him, insisting instead that he is required to be "seruaunt to yourseluen" (1548). And yet his affected modesty remains rhetorically subordinate to her discourse: he becomes her echo, repeating the essential diction of her rebuke.

> "Bot to take þe toruayle to myself to trwluf expoun,
> And towche þe temez of tyxt and talez of armez
> To yow þat, I wot wel, weldez more slyȝt
> Of þat art, bi þe half, or a hundreth of seche
> As I am, oþer euer schal. . . ." (1540–44)

You, he says, wield more *slyȝt* of the art of exposition by one-half than one hundred of me could ever muster; by the truth of my word ("trawþe"), such talk would be "folé" many times over (1544–45).

But he is already caught in the folly he would control. Attempting to protect his "trawþe" by giving her own words back to her in copy-speech, he reiterates the language of seduction and thus moves closer to the second kiss of this visit (1555), even as he would fend off her approach as merely idle talk about the "tyxt" of chivalry. He invites what he repudiates, but invites it through the *expounyng* he refuses to speak. As he will not "towche" the "temes" of love's book, her "text," "tale," and "armes" were never more desirable in the ambiguity of their *circumlocutio*.

FALSSYNG þe SYNGNE

The importance of the kisses, three so far, in the plot of Gawain's fall from the purity of the pentangle is obvious in the symmetry of their repetition on day three, when three kisses are given (1868). It has been customary to note that his weakness of will is signified further by the shift in the symbolic imagery of the poem, the displacement of the pentangle by the green girdle.[39] Yet I have been suggesting that it is more than the kiss that prefigures acceptance of the lace. It is plain that Gawain's wearing of her garment has specific bearing on the moral and political interests of the plot. But this act of cross-dressing participates as well in the cross-dressing of language set in motion the moment the "fader of nurture" began to imitate the rhetoric of Lady Bertilak (919). Appropriated by Gawain as a poetics of political and moral self-defense, her discourse is also his undoing, and the wearing of the girdle completes the semiology. "Who-so knew þe costes þat knit ar þerinne" (1849)—the observation delivered as Gawain is about to accept the lace—punctuates the connection; for the *costes* of this fabric are not simply the "qualities" by which Gawain may defer fate but also the "terms" magically "woven" within it.[40]

Saying and not saying what she means, Lady Bertilak demands engagement. She is a figure of diglossia, speaking in "two tongues" by virtue of enclosing within her speech a discourse already spoken by others—Lord Bertilak, Morgan, and probably Merlin too. Like other diglossic signs (the ax on the tapestry, the *forwarde*, the talking head), Lady Bertilak's voice is a figure of literary language in this poem. In contrast to pentagonal discourse, with its geometry, measure, and self-explication, her voice sanctions no control on the separation between rhetorical figure and syntactical sense, utterance and meaning. She is the *soverayn* who denies her own dominion. And thus, as the instrument of Morgan's revenge, her attack on the moral integrity of one of Arthur's knights is all the more subversive as a manipulation

[39] Emphasized by Ackerman in "Gawain's Shield."
[40] Cf. this sense of *cost* at 546–47.

of his language. Gawain, to be sure, succumbs of his own accord to the
seductions of Lady Bertilak, but his fall begins early in the mimesis of
her style: imitating her, Gawain refuses the role of "teacher" and
remains "seruaunt." He cannot speak in his own person. Gawain is not
Gawain. He is, as she says, a "worde" of "no wordes." Morgan's magic
has found its *folé*. And the dominion of Arthur's court has been taken
down in the principle which constituted it, the putative autonomy of
its sovereign word.

Linguistic trickery is no less at work upon Gawain's arrival at the
chapel for the final exchange of blows, when the Green Knight says to
him: "Of steuen mon may þe trowe" (2238). As every reader knows,
Gawain is and is not "a man of his word." At the first swing of the ax,
the ambiguity of his "word" surfaces as Gawain flinches and the Green
Knight repeats the charge of Lady Bertilak earlier: "Þou art not Gawayn"
(2270). The connection between this failure of courage and the equivocal name of Gawain is extended into a more general vacancy of language as the Green Knight quickly protests that he "ne kest no kauelacion
in kyngez hous Arthor" when he put his head on the block a year prior
(2275). But Gawain's rejoinder, the more notable because of its length
under the circumstances, is not a *cri de coeur* from a man facing his
executioner; it is not idiosyncratically his own, except insofar as idiosyncrasy now identifies Gawain's argot: in a string of colloquialisms,
he echoes the idiom of others: I flinched once, he insists:

> "Bot þaȝ my hede falle on þe stonez,
> Icon not hit restore." (2282–83)

"Bryng me to þe poynt," he says, with an ungainly pun on his own
fate; "do hit out of hond"; "haf here my trawþe" (2284–87). And the
last word was never more uncertain as it rings hollow among clichés.

In contrast, it might seem that Bertilak's discourse is more specific,
since he discloses the purpose of the beheading exchange to Gawain
after the final blow. Striking a note of similarity with the earlier commentary on the pentangle, Bertilak explicates the symmetry of the
three blows: the first feinting swing for keeping the original agreement
made at Camelot; the second feint for obeying the next agreement to
exchange the yield on each day of the sojourn at the castle; the third
and wounding blow for failing to disclose the gift of the green girdle
(2338–59). Although Bertilak moves even closer to unveiling the apparent grounds of the plot against Gawain when he finally names himself
(2445), the geometry and legality of his disclosure are not absolute.
Beyond them, says Bertilak, is yet another plot—the "myȝt" of Morgan
la Faye:

> ". . . þat in my hous lenges
> And koyntyse of clergye, bi craftes wel lerned,
> Þe maystrés of Merlyn." (2446–48)

This lengthy explanation (running to 2456) is crucial to the role of
Morgan and Merlin in the story; but like the circuitous discourse of
Lady Bertilak's earlier inquiry into Gawain's "lettrure of armes," this
passage, too, is anacoluthic. And the breach in syntax occurs in the
context of another "breach," the disclosure that within the story of
Gawain's testing is yet another story, the obscure liaison between
Morgan and Merlin. Specifically, the "kontyse of clerge" has been the
means by which Morgan was able to stage the "wonder" at Camelot
in the hope of scaring Guenevere to death by the man who "gostlych
speked / With his hede in his honde bifore þe hyȝe table" (2461–62).

Morgan failed, needless to say, since Guenevere is very much alive
at Camelot. But the reference to "gostly speech" is most relevant to the
success of Morgan's revenge, since it characterizes not simply the
Green Knight's challenge; it also carries forward the suggestions of
split language associated with the decapitation and with the "magic"
of linguistic evasion in so many parts of the poem. In this case, "gostly
speech" introduces still more trickery in the plot: it aligns the seductive
colloquy in Lady Bertilak's bedroom with an earlier trick in Arthurian
legend, Lady Guenevere's revelation of Morgan's secret sexual liaison
with Guiomar. Behind one story of seduction is the ghost of another,
and behind them all is an "explanation" that leaves more unsolved
than it answers. The *koyntese* of Merlin, we are told, provided Morgan
with her means of revenge: the word signifies "curious," "clever,"
"quaint," "near at hand," "handy," "uncanny," and "sexual." They all
seem to apply vaguely to the obscure figure of Merlin.

Koyntese

But *koyntese* in the sense of "near at hand" also applies to the real figure
of Morgan in the poem, the "þe auncian lady" of Bertilak's castle who
turns out to be Gawain's aunt (2463). She has been on the margin of
this story from the outset, a woman excluded from recognition by King
Arthur, as feminist readings of the poem have noted. But the revenge
for her exclusion is carried out not only through the configuration of
women. Morgan's "magic," though related to incestuous memories
that Arthur would repress, returns much more pervasively in what I
have been calling the "writing" in this story. If Morgan is "displaced"
from recognition, the exposure of that displacement is the return of the
"gostly speech" written into the circuitous and evasive conversation

that undermines Arthur's knight at every crucial turn. Since Morgan set out to subvert the *surquidré* of Arthur, the pride of his dominion, then the exposure of writing within oral discourse, the figuration of textuality by the text itself, focuses on displacement in language as the principal strategy by which power establishes itself to begin with. And here in the end, the ghost of the letter surfaces to subvert Arthurian dominion one last time.

Surmising that he has been given the final explanation of the plot against him, Gawain stands "in study" pondering the disclaimer of the motives behind the three blows (2369). He repudiates first "coward-dyse and couetyse boþe," but the morality of this self-indictment is also qualified by his obvious indignation. He could have stood head to head with his opponent and come away unscathed (surely not be-headed), girdle or no girdle (2375). Red-faced in shame (2371), he grabs at the green belt around his waist, unties the knot, and flings it fiercely at its owner, saying: "Lo! þer þe falssyng, foule mot hit falle!" (2378). Bertilak shortly characterizes Gawain's response with full approval: "þou art confessed so clene," he says (2391), obviously accepting the girdle as a "token of vntrawþe," which Gawain later calls it (2509).

Many critics would accept Bertilak's characterization of Gawain's confession as "clene."[41] But we would do well to recognize that his blaming the sign is of a piece with his subsequent blaming the women of history for the woes that have befallen their "bigyled" men (2413). While his confession begins with self-recrimination, it leads to a defi-nite ambiguity about the cause of it; for the reference of "in *yow* is vylany and vyse" equivocates between the belt of the next line and the speaker himself (2375). We note he does not say, *mea culpa*, in me is villainy and vice. Rather he deflects the specific object of blame, just as he digresses into indicting Eve, Delilah, and Bathsheba a few moments later.

In short, if we follow Bertilak's sense of Gawain's "cleanness"—that he is like a "perle bi þe quite pese" (2364)—we are led to conclude that his blaming the sign of the girdle is a mark of his courtesy and truth, and the antifeminist passage thus becomes an instance of his unwill-ingness to name Lady Bertilak explicitly as the agent of his beguiling.[42] Or, we may see his "courtesy" in these matters exemplified later by the Arthurian court: as Gawain appropriates the stories of Biblical women to excuse his own failure, so do Arthur's knights appropriate Gawain's story of his adventures at Bertilak's court.[43] They finally justify the

[41] E.g., Howard and Zacher, *Critical Studies*, p. 172; Burrow, *A Reading of "Sir Gawain,"* pp. 127–33; Benson, *Art and Tradition*, pp. 236–38; Shoaf, *The Poem as Green Girdle*, p. 70.

[42] E.g., Waldron, ed., *Sir Gawain and the Green Knight*, l. 2425 and note.

[43] Arthur, *Medieval Sign Theory*, pp. 134–41, 152 ff.

transformation of the lace as "token of vntrawþe" into a sign of "þe renoun of þe Rounde Table" (2519). And Gawain himself ends up, with the sign of the wound, as a figure of "wanhope."[44]

However, the shift in the valorization of the girdle has a purpose larger than identifying the character of the hero. First of all, the reading of the girdle assigned by the Round Table does not simply supersede Gawain's. The two readings remain in conflict; they are misprisions of the sign, referring back neither to betrayal and "falssyng" (Gawain's designation) nor to honor and "renoun" (Camelot's reading). A medieval logician would say that the girdle does not signify *de re* and thus does not "signify" in the strict sense at all; rather, it "supposits" for itself directly as a sign, and that kind of linguistic reflexivity—the capacity of language to be "material" by referring back to itself as inscription or speech—constitutes a large part of what the language of this poem accomplishes.

This interest, as I have said, is theoretical, but it is much more immediately moral and political, insofar as the "material" reflection on language in the poem exposes the displacement by which dominion asserts itself. It is not surprising, therefore, to find in Gawain's parting remarks to Bertilak on the "wyles of wymmen" a considerable amount of double-play in his talk. He opens by declining his host's invitation to return to the castle for more "reuel" and "ryche fest" (2401). Begging the indulgence of Lady Bertilak, "boþe þat on and þat oþer, myn honoured ladyez," he concedes defeat by their "kest," their deceiving or veiling words, which have "koyntly bigyled" him throughout the sojourn (2412–13). As if he already guesses what Bertilak is about to tell him, "that other" is none other than Morgan la Faye herself, who is privy to the *koyntyse* of Merlin. But Gawain knows not what he says, for he cannot realize the subtext of his undoing; and yet it splits his utterance as he becomes involved in separating his own behavior from its motivations by lamenting the fate of Adam, Samson, and David, all of them "wrathed wyth [the] wyles" of women (2420).

> "And alle þay were biwyled
> With wymmen þat þay vsed.
> Þag I be now bigyled,
> Me þink me burde be excused." (2425–28)

The last line is especially pointed in light of his opening deference to Lady Bertilak and his subsequent veneration of her girdle. He says that he "ought to be excused" because he was beguiled. And so he will wear the sash not for its "wynne golde," nor as a "saynt" ("belt"); not

[44] Ibid., pp. 115–16, 128, 158.

for its "sylk," its "syde pendaundes," or its "wele" ("wealth"); and he will not wear it for its "worchyp" ("honor") nor for its "wlonk werk-kez" ("beautiful workmanship"). Instead, he will wear it only as a "syngne of my surfet" (2430–33). Having exceeded the bounds of propriety, he says that he will be forever mindful of "excess." But is there no "surfet" too in the style of this oration? Are we not to sense hyperbole in the argument that the deeds on which the fate of famous leaders and nations, if not the human race itself, was determined are here somehow comparable to the impropriety of accepting a woman's lace? The exaggeration becomes even more obvious in the assignment of the fault. *Mea culpa, mea maxima culpa*—the lace will signify, says Gawain, the "fayntyse of þe flesche crabbed": "How tender hit is to entyse teches of fylþe" (2435–36). But what deeds or thoughts merit the particular terms of this apology? What is the direction of this inflation?

If it authenticates Gawain's mistake in the bedroom, as many would argue, so also does the hyperbole void moral responsibility in this sign of fault. It has been falsified by the very act of veneration. And as it refers back to itself merely as exaggeration, bypassing the *significatio* of a moral category, the "flesh" of the lace begins to point unavoidably toward the lady who wore it. It is her metonymy at the same time as it is a metaphor of his sin, and it is precisely this equivocality that plays itself out as Gawain addresses Lord Bertilak about his regret and transgression with Lady Bertilak's lace. How "tender" it is, he says, to "entyse" its beholder; he will look to this "luf-lace" always when "pryde schal me pryk for prowes of armes"; then will it "leþe" ("sof-ten") his heart (2437–38). Is this an apology for sin or a subtle seduction from afar? And who is doing the seducing—Gawain in an adulterous *circumlocutio* to the husband he would cuckold? Or is Lady Bertilak seducing Gawain with the magic of her split language imitated one last time in the mouth of the lover who would repent? At the very least, the lace is still the sign of her body which softened his heart once and now will do so ever after, not only because he wears it but also because the "costes þat knit ar þerinne" are clearly echoing as the "terms" by which he again cross-dresses her language (1849). No won-der he apologizes with the words "me *burde* be excused": the verb of his defense was never so irresistibly confused with the noun of his desire—used throughout this poem for Lord Bertilak's "wife."

Though Bertilak, who will go on to explain the *koyntyse* of the plot, does not acknowledge the ambiguity of this apology, neither does Gawain. We are left with the silence of the split between the speaking of Gawain in high veneration of the girdle by which he signifies himself, and the writing within his voice seeking the desire and lust for the woman he has, until now, denied all along. The text will not resolve the question of this silence—whether he controls or is controlled by the metalanguage of his apology. And that aporia is to the point of the *assay* written into the testing of *surquidré* in the Arthurian court. For it is not just the discourse of Gawain, but the narrative, too, which has participated in "falssyng" the sign from the beginning.

ARTHUR'S COURT AND ENGLAND'S

If *Gawain* ends by exonerating the politics it sets out to criticize, the elusive language of this text does not give the last word to the lords and ladies of the aristocracy. Nor does Morgan have a final say about Arthur and Guenevere. For her "magic" is no more autonomous as the subtext of criticism than the split discourse of the Green Knight, Lady Bertilak, or Sir Gawain. Originating from the expressed intention of undermining the fame of Arthur, the language of critique turns back upon itself to venerate the same seduction it seeks to fault, not only because the retinue of Arthur puts on the green sash to celebrate the story of Gawain but also because the hero himself has remained true to his reputation as celebrated lover and "fader of nurture" when he immortalizes the sign of desire in the rhetoric of repudiation.

That kind of reflexivity is not the result of the power of *significatio* in the signs of fourteenth-century philosophy or politics. It is an effect of the fall of the ax, the "spelle" or errancy of language which cuts into everyone's utterance in this poem with a reflexivity they rarely hear. It establishes itself notwithstanding the competing interest of spoken forms to assert their own signification and their own dominion. It creates the possibility for the representation of language to take precedence over its object and even to occlude it. And thus it testifies to the diglossia between speaking and writing which was playing itself out in so many other aspects of culture during the fourteenth century. The philosophical and historiographical traditions were certainly engaged by this division, but not nearly as forthrightly as *Gawain*, which spells out the consequences of diglossia as they never could. As poetry, it is entitled to take more risks.

And one of those risks is to present the dominion and autonomy of orality in medieval tradition as an imperative that exceeds the realm of a specific monarchy or academic discipline or, for that matter, a given time and place; the persistence of the oral is much more broadly based in the infrastructure and mythology of culture before the advent of print. Like other medieval myths, it is motivated by a searching determination to mediate contradiction and reconcile opposition, in this case to forestall the inevitable divisions introduced by the assimilation of written and textual skills. But by contrast, *Gawain* is a diglossic extravaganza cutting into the logic and propriety of myth just as the "spelle" of the ax cuts into the propriety of Arthurian dominion. What the voices of court "spelle" thereafter is possessed by a spell that no one controls. Myth, to be sure, has a voice in this poem, but it is articulated by a talking head, a figure of archaic feudal orality suspended alone as a prerogative without context or author.

The chronicles of England make it abundantly clear that the rule of the kingdom is synonymous with the presence of the monarch in his spoken word when they assimilate Edward III's voice to his viability in holding on to political power at home and ensuring his patrimony in France. They assume the same dominion of oral forms when they tell the story of the suppression of written authority by the lords appellant seeking to purge Richard II's royal chamber in 1388, and when they explain, *mutatis mutandis*, the king's deposition as a direct result of arrogating the law *in ore suo*, into his own spoken word. It is no accident that this charge (from the articles of deposition in 1399) occurs at the end of a reign in which Richard saw his own voice fail miserably to find efficacy in the signs and badges distributed to spread his dominion.

The representation of sovereign rule in *Gawain* is not very far from this political context (especially when we consider the possibility that the poem may have been written by a Cheshire poet in and for Richard's affinity).[45] When the royal court of Camelot laughs off the sign of fault and reinscribes it as a badge of renown, it is as if the reincorporation of the knight into society after alienation can take place only with the effacement of any signs of difference within the community. Exposing the power play of this displacement, *Gawain* casts an ominous shadow on the appropriation of dominion in the royal court of England. The poem darkens the mythology of this politics by engaging the old and venerated relation between the behavior of the sign in language and the manipulation of power in the social order. It draws a telling connection between the arrogation of dominion in the political arena and the presumption of autonomous control in the order of language. By separating speaker from context, personal from material supposition, discourse from meaning, it spells out the unavoidably random connection between the voices of political rule and the sanction of dominion they would claim. Fulfilling itself and simultaneously voiding itself of the contextual conditions of its own production, the language of this poem is like its several tests: its *assay* is a writing and

---

[45] Bennett, "*Sir Gawain and the Green Knight* and the Literary Achievement of the North-West Midlands," p. 83, and *Community, Class and Careerism*, pp. 131–35. Cp. Pearsall, "Origins of the Alliterative Revival," pp. 7–17.

a cutting, an act of dividing the oral prerogative in order to qualify its compromising hold on the politics of state.

As that politics in the courts of Arthur and Richard nourished the *surquidré* of an autonomous and sovereign discourse, a voice that recognizes only itself, the metalanguage of high literacy in this poem presents a disturbing alternative, no less ghostly than the "auncian lady" shadowing the halls of Bertilak's castle and pulling all the strings behind the scene. Although *Gawain* is indebted to the oral tradition of poetry and the genealogy of English dominion in the "Brutus bokez," it is not appropriated by history, oral or written, and it does not reiterate the political order of King Arthur for its own time. The exploration of linguistic and cultural diglossia which the poem confronts is made in spite of its past, not because of it; the text engages that past sharply and critically from within the very bounds of the context which produced it. It discloses the arbitrary acquisition of power in the exercise of sovereign voice. It interrupts the theory of the descent of power from on high in the Christian order of perfect forms and from history in the genealogy of royal lines. It reveals the compromise at stake in the exercise of sovereign discourse over the potential errancy of people and their signs.

As a romance that appears so otherwise parochial in its dialect and anachronistic in its political statement, *Gawain* does not romanticize the past, no more so than *Don Quixote* romanticizes the middle ages a few centuries later. The feudalism of its setting in the time of Arthur and the orality of its formulaic phrases and motifs from an equally misty origin bespeak loudly the historical nostalgia of the fourteenth century. But the poem does not embrace nostalgia. It holds that echo from the past at arm's length, like the dialect of a distant region no longer conversant with the needs of the moment. And in that conclusion it most certainly embraces its time, with a newer historical consciousness than any of the chronicle histories were able to achieve.

Chapter Seven

"WITHOUTEN ANY REPPLICACIOUN": DISCOURSE AND DOMINION IN THE *KNIGHT'S TALE*

> ". . . This is a short conclusiuon.
> Youre owene mouth, by youre confessioun,
> Hath dampned yow, and I wol it recorde."
> —Theseus, *Knight's Tale*

INTRODUCTION

In the previous chapter, I suggested that by exploring how written and oral conventions "displace" each other, *Sir Gawain* focuses on a critique of language which is only implied or ignored in philosophical and historiographical projects of the fourteenth century. The capacity of language to reflect on itself (metalanguage) becomes all-important as a property of poetry because it responds specifically to the nature of rule in the court of King Arthur. The poem shows how metalanguage creates an environment that prevents displacement from succeeding as a structure of dominion, and thus it exposes the heart of Arthurian politics as a nostalgic ideal.

Chaucer's *Knight's Tale* is relevant to this discussion because it, too, is concerned with metalanguage and political dominion. Like *Gawain*, Chaucer's romance is utterly scrupulous about the conflict of oral and written conventions; it delights in reflecting on its own modes of utterance; and it foregrounds reflexivity as the means of exposing the displacement of both linguistic and political control. Like its alliterative counterpart, the *Knight's Tale* studies the problem of sovereignty through a variety of oppositional structures, such as the conflict between Theseus and Saturn. But, unlike the alliterative poem, based as it is on books and oral stories about the legendary foundations of England, Chaucer proceeds from a specific text of Boccaccio and reaches into the distant past of pagan Athens and Thebes. Morcover, we know the provenance of his poem, and so we can say a little more about its possible historical context than we can about *Gawain*.

Because the tale of Arcite and Palamoun is cited in the Prologue to the *Legend of Good Women* (written sometime between 1386 and 1388), the *Knight's Tale* predates the Canterbury period. By exactly how many years we do not know. Nor do we know precisely what status Chaucer imagined it to have before he included the poem in the collection. But we do know, on the basis of many stylistic details, that both the narrator and the audience do not always square perfectly with the pilgrim-knight and the company of twenty-nine listeners on their way to Becket's shrine. Once included in the collection, the address of the Knight is manifestly to the pilgrims, a fictional group; but this move also redacts the wider audience to whom Chaucer may have originally read the poem, a real group of listeners—perhaps the king's court, perhaps his group of friends and *litterati*.[1] This well-known crux in the tale, signified prominently at the end of each of the four parts when the narrator changes directions to address the audience, is not often appreciated for the way in which it involves a shift from an experience of the narrative as something *heard* to something *read*, maybe even read silently and privately.[2]

Certainly the poem as a whole must be considered as Chaucer has given it to us, as the first tale in the Canterbury "Book" and thus a contribution to the structure and theme of pilgrimage chronicle. But acknowledging that it may very well predate the collection and its pilgrim-teller allows us to see in sharper relief what Chaucer needed to overcome in order to include it within the larger fiction. Therefore, I consider the *Knight's Tale* without going on to the remaining tales of its manuscript (fragment I) or the total collection for two reasons: in order to see how Chaucer, like the *Gawain*-poet, found in romance a genre with an acknowledged tradition of interest in the relation of poetry to history; but also to see how the editorial adjustments of voice and audience in the tale may be tied to the historical adjustment between oral and written traditions at the time.[3]

Managing this division in language, as we have seen, was of no little consequence to those people concerned with dominion in the last quarter of the fourteenth century. In the political arena, England during the 1380s was ruled intermittently by a regency commission; Richard did not assume complete control of the realm until his twenty-second birthday, in 1389. Between these years, the royal prerogative was

---

[1] See Strohm, *Social Chaucer*, for an audience of merchants, clergy, and writers.

[2] NB Chaucer opens *Troilus* with the "double sorrow of Troilus to *tellen*," acknowledging that his verses "wepen as I *write*" (1 and 7). The *Treatise on the Astrolabe* starts with "every discret persone that *redith* or *herith* this litel tretys" (41–42). Benson, ed., *Riverside Chaucer*, used throughout.

[3] For similar approaches to the relation of textual properties and sociopolitical context, cf. Patterson, *Chaucer and the Subject of History*, pp. 165–230, and Ganim, *Chaucerian Theatricality*, pp. 115 ff. Neuse, *Chaucer's Dante*, pp. 105–39, corroborates the staging of "oral performance" and audience involvement.

a highly contested issue, and it arose often as a question about the king's right to speak. For instance, as a member of Richard's party, Chaucer would have been aware of the controversial situation of Michael de la Pole, appointed to the chancery in 1383 and impeached by parliament in 1386. Chaucer was King Richard's appointee in that parliament. During his tenure as chancellor, de la Pole was a willing participant in the execution of Richard's orders via the *signet* letter, the first significant expression of his personal voice in the affairs of government.

But the king was defeated, and in 1387 he called upon the justices to look into the question of whether the lords in 1386 had the right to impeach his royal appointments and set the agenda of parliament. When the justices verified in law that the prerogative of the king had been derogated, the lords proceeded against him anyway a year later by extending the purge to his entire chamber. Once again, another panel of justices advised parliament that cases involving the prosecution of the king's own appointments had no precedent for trial in parliament. But still the lords set aside for a second time the legal history documented by the judges and went forward with what they called the "ley du parlement" to prosecute and condemn to death Robert de Vere, Nicholas Bembre, Simon Burley, and many other members of the royal party, while the king was forced, quite literally, to sit by and watch without any voice to intervene.

As a member of the king's party, Chaucer could not have been ignorant of the nature of the proceedings, even though he was outside of London at the time. Since he had served in government, he would have been aware that each of the events between 1383 and 1388 questioned seriously the status of the text as an instrument of validating action. As we have seen, both the philosophical and historiographical projects of the time study the relation of sovereignty to language, but neither of them focuses on its own discourse as a qualifying condition of how such inquiry may proceed. *Gawain* centers precisely on this problem in the Arthurian court, and the *Knight's Tale* opens the historical focus even wider. The ongoing rivalries over the right to the voice of power during the years of King Richard's minority illustrate graphically the problems of displacement in discourse which metalanguage would exploit.[4] Chaucer's poem engages this problem through a study of the conflict between spoken and written modes: self-reflexive language in a story about ancient Athens constitutes a specific reaction to the political problem of dominion in the England of the 1380s.

---

[4] Patterson, *Chaucer and the Subject of History*, pp. 180 ff., notes the "logic of displacement" in the Knight's representation of chivalry.

Spoken or Written?

Whether Chaucer's narrative was read aloud or in silence, his audience still *overheard* the fiction of a narrator-Knight speaking orally to a group of listeners on their way to Canterbury. Listening for the text may occasion audiences to think that they are presented with the choice of having either a silent or audible experience of the word. On the oral side, we have the argument that a text composed in a largely illiterate or semiliterate culture, such as fourteenth-century England, "must therefore create within itself much that in an oral situation is obvious."[5] A text like the *Knight's Tale* must compensate for what is presumably "lost" with inscription by figuring the listening audience, signifying transitions between episodes, delineating images sharply, and above all restoring the principal loss—the author. From the point of view of the oral apology for medieval poetry, writing necessitates the self-conscious creation of the poet in the text, the "double agent" familiar in Machaut, Dante, and Chaucer.

This argument makes some sense out of the oral qualities of medieval texts, but it does not confront adequately why the fiction of the speaker necessarily exists to re-create an oral circumstance, and why the author more broadly would feel the need to occlude the writtenness of the text. There is extensive medieval evidence to confirm the resistance to writing in the belief that inscription is simply speech written down. But it would be oversimplified to assume that an oral apologetics was the essential project of fourteenth-century authors.[6]

What could the fiction of the poet in a written text have meant to the audience Chaucer read to during the 1380s and 1390s? He was probably associating during those years with people of learning and letters, some of whom were professional writers, like Gower. They would surely have recognized the paralinguistic signals of speech in a poem; but they would have heard and read them as *conventions*, like the epic elements in a romance or domesticity in a fabliau. In other words, to a literate person like Gower or Chaucer, the very effort to compensate for oral circumstances would itself be recognized as an acknowledgment made from the remove of the manuscript page.[7] The

[5] Brewer, "Orality and Literacy in Chaucer," p. 109. Cf. Lindahl, *Earnest Games*, p. 161: "Fourteenth-century England was a predominantly oral culture, particularly insofar as poetry was concerned." On similar assumptions in the Ellesmere MS, see Parkes, "The Influence of Concepts," p. 134, followed by Coleman, *Medieval Readers and Writers*, pp. 198–201. Cf. scholarship on the "dramatic principle" in Kittredge, *Chaucer and His Poetry*; Lumiansky, *Of Sundry Folk*; Bronson, *In Search of Chaucer*; Bowden, *Chaucer Aloud*; Koff, *Chaucer and the Art of Storytelling*.

[6] Cf. J. H. Fisher, "Chaucer and the Written Language," in Heffernan, ed., *The Popular Literature of Medieval England*, pp. 237–51.

[7] Cf. Neuse, *Chaucer's Dante*, p. 120.

gap between spoken and written properties would be obvious, and any attempt to close it would suggest that the difference between the two channels of language was being foregrounded for a purpose. To begin this exploration, Chaucer appeals to the well-known syntax of oral telling, parataxis.

The verb "tellen" in the first line of the poem would not in particular call attention to itself as a signal of speech, except for the fact that it is followed by about twenty lines composed almost entirely of paratactic clauses, strung together by coordinating conjunctions and emphasized by clusters of anaphora. The effect of this style is the figuration of a narrator speaking directly to his audience by repeating and interrupting himself before he arrives at the narrative present of the wailing women. No one misses these properties of a colloquial style, the leisurely movement from scene to scene assuring the listener of being included in the moment of the telling, the feeling of participation with the narrator in shared experiences and values, and the anticipation of sympathetic response to what will follow.[8] Through such effects of style, speaking is figured in the text to the extent that we must wonder about the "objectivity" of the narrator over his "olde stories," as well as the one he is telling; and that factor is all the more before us, lest we forget it, because of the Knight's own fictional status. With yet another echo of interruption before proceeding ("This duc, of whom I make mencioun"; 893), the distance between the voice of telling and the text of record continues to widen.

Some readers have been inclined to describe this kind of separation as an editorializing "break" in the "dramatic illusion." The Knight is thus "outside" of the scene looking in and taking a firm hold on the reins of his story, maintaining an omniscient perspective not unlike the author's. Scholarship on this point, with some exceptions, tends to agree that he succeeds; but I follow the lead of those readers who find a number of moments when perspectival authority is forfeited because of the way the narrator reads his material.[9] His principal trope of control is the rhetorical "color" of *occultatio*, the feigned exclusion of material from the narrative.[10] It has struck readers as a device by which the narrator establishes distance and reserve, what some think of as his "dignity." But it merits further consideration.

---

[8] See Neuse, *Chaucer's Dante*, pp. 104, 120–24, 131.

[9] E.g., see Jordan, *Chaucer and the Shape of Creation*, pp. 152 ff.; Muscatine, *Chaucer and the French Tradition*, pp. 175 ff.; Howard, *The Idea of the "Canterbury Tales,"* pp. 230 ff.; Kolve, *Chaucer and the Imagery of Narrative*, pp. 134 ff.; in contrast with Neuse, "The Knight"; Thurston, *Artistic Ambivalence in Chaucer's "Knight's Tale"*; Aers, *Chaucer, Langland and the Creative Imagination*, p. 174; and Wetherbee, "Romance and Epic in Chaucer's *Knight's Tale*," pp. 319 ff.

[10] See Kelly, "*Occupatio* as Negative Narration."

OCCULTATIO

In the first instance of this trope at the opening of the tale, the narrator apologizes with "I wolde have toold yow fully the manere / How wonnen was the regne of Femenye," but then he turns around to adumbrate the high points of the history "bitwixen Atthenes and Amazones" (880). Although familiar enough in medieval and classical rhetoric, *occultatio* as the Knight uses it is not, strictly understood, a rhetorically neutral device for "passing over" decorously certain details in order to get on with the story. As a *feigned* exclusion, it invites consideration of what is "left out," and thus it raises the question of how well the Knight realizes the implications of what he is saying. In this first instance, *occultatio* is clearly a figure "of speech," since it feigns the exclusion of text, which the narrator will leave unread. But its putative bearing on the speaker and the story cannot and will not be occluded, especially since it carries rather provocative undertones. Accordingly, the narrator concludes, "al that thyng I moot as now forbere."

> I have, God woot, a large feeld to ere,
> And wayke been the oxen in my plough. (874, 886–87)

Deferring to tell us how Theseus subdued the fiercely independent Queen Hypolita, the narrator is simultaneously saying, via a well-worn periphrasis, that his text is long and intricate like the Book of Nature; but he is also saying, whether he knows it or not, that carnal desire (the oxen in his plow) has diminished, presumably following the untold tale of the "grete bataille" between the sexes (879). The conflation of textual and sexual semiologies (borrowed here from *Le roman de la Rose* and quoted later by the Miller in his Prologue) cannot be occluded by the speaker, though from what we can tell, he would not acknowledge their bearing on what he is telling his listeners. Perhaps that is why he is so mindful of his procedure, which he continues to defend in the next few lines. But we have gotten the point, and we will hear *occultatio* function as a figure for the feigned exclusion of writing at many points in narrative yet to come.

For instance, as soon as the narrator sums up the account from his source about how the two knights were discovered, brought to Athens, and condemned to prison, he changes directions abruptly through *occultatio*: "what nedeth wordes mo?" (1029). Although the deferral calls up short the emphasis on time—the knights will dwell in prison "perpetually" (1024); Theseus will rule for the "terme of his lyf" (1029)—it is also a hinge into the central locus of desire in the poem, the prison garden in which Emelye is promptly introduced. After the lovers argue over her, the narrator again uses *occultatio* to defer explaining why Perotheus loved Arcite enough to seek his release from prison. And in this case, the Knight unequivocally identifies his rhetorical figure with oral language and the excluded material with inscription: "of that storie list me nat to write" (1201). By *write* he can only mean "speak," but the valence is obvious, and to punctuate it he repeats the metaphor of speaking as writing a few lines later: "This was the forward, pleynly for t'endite" (1209). One could dismiss these lines as editorial "inconsistencies" that Chaucer should have altered after he assigned the poem to a fictional speaker in the Canterbury collection.[11] But left as we find them, as metaphors of speaking, they focus attention precisely on the broader interests of the poem, how voice would preempt writing and even exclude it. *Occultatio* is the spoken side, as it were, of the verso page of inscription: if it "feigns" the exclusion of other texts, it also fails to acknowledge a crucial aspect about its own feigning, that it configures writing as a species of voice, not something other than speech, but speech itself. As a result *occultatio* is both a feigned and a real occlusion in the *Knight's Tale*, and what it obscures from the outset is writtenness per se.

The length and detail of the poem justify, in some respects, the narrator's reliance on rhetorical figures to control the progress of his story. But, in consequence of what he does not realize about his style, his editorializing is linked specifically to the theme of control in the poem, the "governaunce" of Theseus over Athens and Thebes. Theseus is a figure of political dominion. The narrator-Knight is a figure of controlling language. The political theme and the narrative style are thus conjoined. And before the end of Part I, we are given vivid evidence of that conjunction when the two knights begin to lament their situation as political prisoners.

As a result of the rivalry for Emelye, their confinement heats up over the issue of betrayal: they accuse each other of violating the spoken bond by which they were "ysworn ful depe" always to "forthren" each other: "This was thyn ooth," says Arcite to Palamoun, "and myn also, certeyn" (1132–39). Nor was their agreement limited to personal behavior; as "my brother sworn," Arcite continues, "thou art ybounded as a knyght / To helpen me" (1147, 1149–50). The stability of the spoken bond of the word has a public reference, and its falsification is a matter of public shame. But violating the chivalric ethos is not sanctioned by appeal to any public response, not in this context. Its only sanction is the violation of language itself, which in this passage figures the spoken oath as "bound" in two very different respects. Palamoun is

---

[11] Muscatine, *"The Canterbury Tales,"* p. 90.

first of all "ybounden" to his spoken word of fealty; but he is also quite literally "bound" in prison by the "pure fettres on his shynes grete" (1279). The bond of the word which would enfranchise him is thus split into signifying that it also imprisons him from claiming his beloved beyond the prison wall. The exposure of this ambiguous "other side" of the spoken word is probed further in Arcite's charge that his friend has been "fals."

He would prove his own right to Emelye on the grounds that Palamoun's claim to her is divided in its utterance.

> "For paramour I loved here first er thow.
> What wiltow seyen? Thou woost nat yet now
> Wheither she be womman or goddesse." (1155–57)

He refers to his friend's address to Emelye through the window as if she were "Venus" who had chosen "thus to transfigure" herself in front of him (1104–1105). But Arcite is not just playing sarcastically with Palamoun's vocabulary. Beyond his reach is a sophisticated argument from fourteenth-century logic about the conditions of priority in language. In naming the woman in the garden as a deity, Palamoun has spoken in "simple supposition," which has no claim on the evident individuals of perception or cognition. But Arcite, in contrast, has spoken of "love as to a creature," and such "personal supposition" is the only kind of language that identifies evidently what it bespeaks. Lest we think this distinction in medieval *suppositio* too rarefied for the context, the language of logic enters the text specifically when Arcite says, "I *pose* that thow lovedest hire biforn" (1162). In other words, "for the sake of argument" or, more precisely, "in supposition only do you have a claim to Emelye." But in truth Palamoun's spoken word has no priority; it is divided against itself.

And yet Arcite's claim to her is no less divided; for he would count on the proverb, "who shal yeve a lovere any lawe?" (1164) to sanction his own right, when in fact it was used just as often to impugn the license of lovers. Chaucer so translated the line specifically with that signification in his source, which is *Boece* (3.m.12.52–55). Like the focus earlier in this scene on the oath and then the spoken words of Palamoun to "Venus," here once again the attention is on oral functions of language and specifically on their division, which is signified in these instances by what they tend to occlude.

But before the scene ends, the division of language emerges in still another way. Faced with perpetual damnation in prison, Arcite characterizes the futility of arguing over Emelye with a sharp alteration in style.

"We stryve as dide the houndes for the boon;
They foughte al day, and yet hir part was noon.
Ther cam a kyte, whil that they were so wrothe,
And baar awey the boon bitwixe hem bothe." (1177–80)

This kind of lapse in style from "high" to "middle" or "low" has been well noted in critical response to the tale.[12] But the change is not only among the "levels" of literary style: it marks a shift to the diction, imagery, and syntax of a distinctly oral way of using language. Elsewhere in the *Knight's Tale*, as I will note in due course, such stylistic adjustments also signify a shift from literate to spoken discourse. In this case, like hounds wrangling over a bone, the knights have been wrangling over language, which calls attention to itself as divided in its loyalties to both speech and inscription.

In this respect, the style of the passage points in the same direction as the narrator's *occultatio*, toward the split in language and the conflict of resolving what is said with what is signified. That is explicitly the problem of the knights' argument in the prison scene. But it is also the problem of the poem's style writ large, and in this respect the *Knight's Tale* cites more broadly the conflict between spoken and written language which was so much at issue in the political world of England during the 1380s. Scholarship has never been certain about political "allusions" in the *Knight's Tale*. But in view of the problem of occlusion in the style of this work, the lines ending the prison argument deserve a closer look. Unable to resolve "the bone bitwixe hem bothe," Arcite comments ruefully:

"And therfore, at the knyges court, my brother,
Ech man for hymself, ther is noon oother." (1181–82)

He is speaking colloquially, so much so that his expression became proverbial after Chaucer. But we do not miss the anticlimax of the expression. From the "boon" of contention, which can only be Emelye, to the king's court, we anticipate something—anything—more than the banality of "each man for himself." The anticlimax is all the more divisive because it aligns the law of love, which binds no lover, with the law of prison, which binds everyone. And "here in this prisoun" is explicitly the image on which the scene terminates (1185). If there is only remote correspondence at the level of imagery between "prison" and "court" in these lines, they conjoin in a most unlikely way by the devastating resonance of *here*: the word inevitably coordinates the

---

[12] E.g., Muscatine, *Chaucer and the French Tradition*, pp. 185 ff. Cp. Brewer, "Orality and Literacy in Chaucer," pp. 112 ff., on the "mix" of orality and literacy in such passages.

place of oral combat in prison with the space defined within the hearing or reading of the text in Chaucer's time, which could very well have been the court of King Richard II. The language of the prison is "here" within the audience of this text, by virtue of the specific ways in which speaking would take precedence over its own written mode. That is the force of an occlusive discourse. But it is also a political fact of life at court in the 1380s.[13]

If *occultatio* sharpens the focus on what is left out, other "colors" of rhetoric in the poem also urge a similar attention. Before the end of Part I, the most powerful stylistic feature is the rhetorical question. We hear it with particular force from Arcite who complains, once he has been freed from prison, that he is worse off separated from Emelye than he was when he could see her from behind prison bars. The hyperbole of his lament—prison was once "paradys" (1230, 1237)—prepares for the resounding negative import of his question:

> "Allas, why pleynen folk so in commune
> On purveiaunce of God, or of Fortune,
> That yeveth hem ful ofte in many a gyse
> Wel bettre than they kan hemself devyse?" (1251–54)

He should have known better. But more than an inkling of pragmatic inquiry is carried by this question, although Arcite is not in any way prepared to pursue its philosophical reach. The rhetorical equation of divine "purveiaunce" with "Fortune" is so provocative that for the next several lines Arcite's comments draw freely from descriptions of life under *fortuna* included in Boethius' *Consolation of Philosophy*; and yet not once do we get the sense that Arcite is reading the subtext to his own benefit. The question asked rhetorically continues the figuration of voice as somewhat deaf to its own implications of a very well-read text.

Arcite's question prefigures the subsequent inquiries posed by Palamoun. While he asks about different matters, his style is the same. And thus the poem cites itself, in the same way as the speaker's question doubles back upon itself. Palamoun, still in prison, asks a version of Job's question about why the innocent suffer. His voice is rich with echoes of a Christian tradition he could not know; and for that reason the figuration of writing in his remarks is all the more mysterious and obscure. But most striking is the clear alignment between writing and the political terminology of his complaint:

[13] Cf. Patterson, *Chaucer and the Subject of History*, p. 202: the Knight "displaces" his own anxieties about chivalry on to Palamoun and Arcite.

> Thanne seyde he, "O crueel goddes that governe
> This world with byndyng of youre word eterne,
> And writen in the table of atthamaunt
> Youre parlement and youre eterne graunt,
> What is mankynde moore unto you holde
> Than is the sheep that rouketh in the folde?" (1303–1308)

The force of Palamoun's question, as he understands it, is heavily rhetorical, "for slayn is man right as another beest" (1309). But the text provides another way of considering the question, and it is exposed by the suggestions in Palamoun's diction. The "sheep" cowering in the "folde" is a pagan way of misunderstanding the "eterne graunt" of the divine word written in the tables of stone. Palamoun, like Arcite before him, could not acknowledge the Christian echoes of his language, but the point is that the Knight does not either; and the uncertainty of his purpose becomes increasingly obvious as he proceeds.

What are we to make, for example, of the unreadable text governing this world and the invocation of its administration by "parlement"? Palamoun claims that Arcite is a "lord" who, like himself, is at the mercy of those who "governe" without any care of the governed. He asks with ringing despair:

> "What governace is in this prescience,
> That giltelees tormenteth innocence?" (1313–14)

His reach is momentarily philosophical: "what is the nature of a fore-knowledge that would torment the innocent"? But the force of his rhetoric returns him to the prison house and the real world where the "theef" roams freely while the "trewe man" suffers (1325–26). A text, he says, may contain the answer, but he cannot read it: "The answer of this lete I to dyvynes" (1323). The theological invitation, however, is not truncated here in sarcasm. As a pagan, Palamoun is limited to a specifically mundane view of things; and that is why the "governance" and "parlement" he speaks about have immediate and local illustration in those who live "in prison and arreest" (1310). So also is the text of his reference local: although obscure, it is not austere and mysterious, like the visionary book of St. John in the Apocalypse. Palamoun's text is written in a "table of atthamaunt"; he says it is the obdurate word of rule in this world—unreadable because arbitrary and inexplicable.

Rhetorical and real questions in this passage compete with each other, and although they are unresolved, they are hardly without purpose. Like the stylistic adjustments earlier in Part I, the split in the question participates in the juxtaposition of voice and writing. In this case, writing is figured as obscure and occluded to the speaker, and moreover, the disposition of that concealment is given a specifically political valence. At the same time as Palamoun would question dominion, his voice is denied access to an adamant written word and returns tautologically to where he began: his language is prison-bound. He cannot realize the occlusion in his own speaking, and that is why his prison is the world, as he implies. But the occlusion of his voice is also a political statement about the real circumstances of sovereign voice in the affairs of state during the 1380s. The court of King Richard, to be sure, is not yet the prison of despotism. But the power struggles fought during his minority over the sovereignty of voice and the willful appropriation of writing finds a definite echo in the uncertain disposition of talk and text in the prison scene of the *Knight's Tale*.

The narrator takes no side in the disputes launched by Arcite or Palamoun. But he does speak about their situation directly to the audience at the end of Part I, and his address has an unequivocal connection with the style of the questions asked earlier by the characters:

> Yow loveres axe I now this questioun:
> Who hath the worse, Arcite or Palamoun?
> That oon may seen his lady day by day,
> But in prison he moot dwelle alway;
> That oother where hym list may ride or go,
> But seen his lady shal he nevere mo.
> Now demeth as yow liste, ye that kan,
> For I wol telle forth as I bigan. (1347–54)

No one familiar with the convention of the *demande d'amour* takes this question at face value, as a request for a considered reply, since, to begin with, it is out of place. Conventionally the *demande* occurs at the end of a narrative, as in the *Franklin's Tale*. Here it is relevant to the narrator's qualification of the philosophical reach of the questions posed by both Arcite and Palamoun about the nature of mankind in an indifferent world. In contrast to those inquiries, the narrator's question brings us down to earth; and in the process, it also trivializes what the knights want to know. The narrator's question introduces a point which for the moment can only be moot, and the narrator knows it. In the end we will discover whose situation is "the worse"—but not in any way as a specific answer to this question. The inquiry remains real in the narrative, though it is rhetorical as far as the narrator is concerned.

Moreover, the uncertainty of the Knight's question to us explains, in part, why Chaucer did not redact the fiction of the audience which the question creates. Prior to inclusion in the collection of tales, the narrator's address to "yow loveres" might accommodate any number of people, an audience not unlike the one assumed in *Troilus and Criseyde*. However, since the Knight is addressing the twenty-nine travelers, we might expect him to say, as other pilgrims address each other, "Lordynges." But he does not, and accordingly we have to wonder about who he is talking to. The expression, in short, addresses a wide audience, either listening or reading silently; but once in the collection, it addresses listeners particularly, and very few of them at that. The noun of address is deliberately strained in the same way as the Knight's question pulls in different directions for both rhetorical and pragmatic answers. At the end of Part I, we do not have a text that is "compensating" for itself by trying to create what is obvious in an oral circumstance. To the contrary, Chaucer has focused specifically on *not* compensating for his writing by leaving both voice and audience undecided. He will not compromise text to speech, and that is a political statement of some significance in the debate about sovereign voice in England during the 1380s.

MIRRORING LANGUAGE

Although *occultatio* organizes narrative progress in the *Knight's Tale*, Chaucer has expanded the trope well beyond its customary function in medieval and classical rhetoric. Rather than a figure of simple narrative dignity and neutrality, *occultatio* "colors" much of the style of this poem: the gesture of feigning exclusion continues to suggest that something is being really concealed in the progress of the narrative; and this split signifies a variety of other oppositions—from the verbal battles between the knights over Emelye to the separation between utterance and significance in what they say.[14] The narrator's voice is qualified by the very trope with which he would otherwise claim control. Because this division in the text involves the disposition of political authority in pagan Athens, I have suggested that it is aligned with the larger problem of qualifying the voice of sovereign rule in England, and I will have more to say promptly about this matter. For now, however, it is appropriate to note that as Part I of the *Knight's Tale* probes the question of speaking and writing, Part II commences with consideration of Arcite's voice.

An echo of *occultatio* modifies the neutrality of the narrator from the outset. It is conventional, perhaps, for him to introduce the subject of Arcite's suffering in love by saying, "shortly to concluden al his wo"

---

[14] Cf. Wetherbee, "Romance and Epic in Chaucer's *Knight's Tale*," p. 324, on the Knight's rhetoric.

(1358); but the peremptory note of beginning with a "conclusion" is
evident in the swift movement from the single word exemplifying the
lover's anguish ('ful ofte a day he swelte and seyde "Allas'!"; 1356) to
the subsequent passage detailing his physical condition in "the loveris
maladye / Of Hereos" (1373–74). Whether or not Arcite is being ide-
alized or satirized has not passed unnoticed in readings of the poem,
but it deserves another look. It is apparent that next to Arcite's physical
distortion (with "eyen holwe" and "hewe falow and pale as asshen
colde," 1364–65) his voice is also distorted: he is a figure of *discordia*
"waillynge al the nyght, makynge his mone" (1366), in contrast to the
concordia of "song or instrument" (1367). Music drives his "spirtz"
downward, "so lowe" that "no man koude knowe / His speche nor
his voys, though men it herde" (1369–71). Like Boethius at the opening
of the *Consolation*, Arcite is "up so doun" (1377).

But this figure of philosophical inversion is also a trope of the
double-sided voice of Arcite in this passage, the split between wailing
and song, voice and hearing, listening and misunderstanding. The
narrator is describing the lover's condition with some adaptation from
his source, and yet his own voice is being mirrored in what he describes. As the passage opens with the *occultatio* of "concluden," so it
terminates with more pressing citation of the trope: "What sholde I al
day of his wo endite?" asks the Knight (1380). He has already told
some of Arcite's woe, and he has yet to tell a great deal more; so what
is he "passing over" with this figure? It is clear that the convention
involves a good deal more than editing Boccaccio's *Teseida*. Changing
narrative directions takes on the significance it has established earlier
in Part I: at the same time as the narrator would give voice to his
subject, his own voice becomes implicated in the account, and that
involvement is spelled out pointedly in the verb of his narration. Is the
narrator's "endite" a metaphor for a tedious account (a "writing") of
what might be more swiftly told orally? Or, is the speaker unwittingly
"indicting" the experience of Arcite at the same time as he is sympa-
thizing with him? The division of these questions in the verb confronts
the neutrality of speech with its own divided interests, suggesting that
the "voys" the narrator describes is not unlike his own: we hear it, to
be sure, but there is something about it "that no man koude knowe."
And yet this denial of knowing exposes simultaneously that the other
voice of the narrator in the scene is Arcite's. Between the two of them
is a gap in the text which anyone can know: the poem cites itself as
inscription in the very gesture of signifying the import of unrecogniz-
able voice for the scenes to follow.

Arcite's "maladye" at the opening of Part II has ordinarily been
regarded as the prefiguration of his "double identity" after he returns

to Athens incognito, changes his name (to Philostrate), and secures himself as a page in the chamber of Emelye. However, these developments in the story also mirror the doubling of Arcite's voice as we have read it in the account of his sickness, and this division finds its most explicit image in the "mirour."

> And with that word he caught a great mirour
> And saugh that chaunged was al his colour. (1399–1400)

The emphasis is apparently on the change in Arcite's "visage"; it is of "another kynde"; and he thus takes it in mind to dissimulate himself at the court of Theseus. But the dissimulation of his identity also fulfills the foreboding note that no one could know his voice. As the mirror becomes the dark conceit in which Arcite's face is "disfigured" (1403), so also does it distort the "figure" and "colour" of his voice. The mirror is explicitly linked to language when the narratorial convention, "with that word," doubles as an echo of Arcite's own voice—specifically the vacancy he feels in desiring the "presence" of his lady (1398). The verb "caughte," therefore, participates in the signification of Arcite's disfiguring: he not only grabs hold of the mirror to see himself; his "word" is also taken or seized by its representation—"dis-figured." As his word is thus caught in its figuration, so too is the narrator's, since his convention of telling is in this instance on loan to his character.

The double identity of Arcite is the formation of much more than the convention of the lover's malady. It articulates the larger concerns of the poem with the doubling of language. As *occultatio* modulates this effect in the scene with Arcite in Part II, so also is it responsible for the shift to Palamoun, and once again it figures a split between spoken and written discourse. The orality of the narrator's procedure is noted first: "And speke I wole of Palamon a lite" (1450). Then abruptly the narrator delves into the pit of Palamoun's "derkness" in prison "thise seven yeer," all the more "perpetual" because of his "double soor" as prisoner and unrequited lover (1451–58). Although extremes of characterization and "aventure" typify the genre, the next move in the narrative stretches the convention almost out of whack:

> Who koude ryme in Englyssh properly
> His martirdom? For sothe it am nat I;
> Therfore I passe as lightly as I may. (1459–61)

What is the tone here? Presumably this is the kind of material for a serious writer, a Chaucer perhaps, not for a humble horseback teller. But the irony of textualizing oral performance in this way is of a piece with the suddenness of the shift away from the agony of prison and the hyperbole of Palamoun's "martirdom": are we simply redacting

Boccaccio and altering narrative directions or oscillating between an appreciation and a dismissal of Palamoun's "soor"? It is manifestly "double": he is in prison and in love; and yet his pain is at once spoken "perpetually" and written "as lightly as I may." To surmise that Chaucer should have edited the passage more suitably for the collection is to miss how deliberately the narrator is made to stumble over two very different experiences of language, and one more relative clause extenuates the problem before Palamoun gets out of jail: "as olde bookes seyn, / That al this storie tellen moore pleyn," Palamoun escaped "by aventure or destynee (1463–65)." The "aventure" is as much of the telling as of the plot.

AVENTURE

The arbitrariness of romance is repeatedly directed by the narrator to the storyline. But Chaucer has attended as well to the "aventure" of telling, the uncertainty of separating saying from hearing, listening form reading, uttering from understanding. He figures this split most obviously in editorializing "asides" to the audience, such as those under discussion thus far. But the split language of the text finds other expressions, and the next one in Part II is Arcite's springtime song of love overheard "by aventure" as Palamoun is hidden nearby in a bush. Overhearing has already figured so prominently as a condition of reading that the scene becomes a metadrama of the narrative performance and reception of the *Knight's Tale* itself.

As Arcite sings a conventional poem of the season, a "roundel," loud enough to be heard by his silent auditor, the passage anticipates his eventual discovery by Palamoun through various metaphors of "hearing" unexpected "voices."

> But sooth is seyd, go sithen many yeres,
> That "feeld hath eyen and wode hath eres."
> It is ful fair a man to bere him evene,
> For al day meeteth men at unset stevene.
> Ful litel woot Arcite of his felawe,
> That was so ny to harknen al his sawe. (1521–26)

The proverb that the woods have ears carries out the preoccupation of romance with unanticipated meetings, but in this passage the contingency is of the listening process per se. For the second proverb, about meeting unexpectedly, extends rather ironically the metaphor of saying "sooth," since it is first concealed in the verb "bere" ("to sing" as well as "to bear") and then echoed in "unset stevene." That phrase may signify that people meet sometimes at an "unanticipated time," but only in metaphor, since the literal translation of "stevene" is "voice" or "sound." Palamoun is about to decipher the identity of the singer by, first of all, hearing his "unassigned voice": that is the "sawe" to which he will "harken."

The play on the identity and origin of voice as the "aventure" of discovery is taken in still another direction when the narrator shifts his style markedly from a literary and poetic idiom to a conversational one. "Sodeynly," he says, Arcite's roundel leaves him in a "studie,"

> As doon thise loveres in hir queynte geres,
> Now in the crope, now doun in the breres,
> Now up, now doun, as boket in a welle. (1530–33)

The narrator is concerned with hearing accurately in order to identify the disguised speaker. But the shift in style of this passage from courtly poetry to the colloquial argot and syntax of the barnyard redirects attention back upon the very medium of the description. Like the lovers described, the style of the passage—now up, now down—comments on itself; and thus overhearing is no longer limited strictly to what Palamoun is listening to. The passage is rich with an oral style that configures response as an aural event. Although that kind of effect may be perfectly in line with the Knight's public address to the pilgrims, the text of the tale has qualified pointedly its own oral reception. Palamoun, after all, is concealed as listener of Arcite's courtly poetry. In the most extended illustration of dramatic irony in the poem, he overhears a song and conversation whose significance is totally lost on him and, what is more, lost on its speaker—until Arcite names himself. The metadrama of the situation inevitably suggests that response to the narrator's tale exceeds the oral channel of language, and the imbrication of literary and colloquial styles reiterates the point: listening alone puts one in the unavoidable situation of a Palamoun—"no man koude know" what he hears. But "overhearing" what neither speaker nor listener can comprehend proceeds from very different properties than those available to the ear—from a response to *writing*, which has time to pause over the telling difference between "roundel" and "boket in a welle."

I have been arguing that the anticipation of romance with the "aventure" of events in the plot has been subtly reworked by Chaucer back into the happenstance of the telling. But the errancy of the genre is not pointless; it has a use.[15] And in this poem it is used to suggest that although speakers control language, they are also in turn controlled by it. It may seem arbitrary that the narrator's *occultatio* should reflect

---

[15] Cf. Parker, *Inescapable Romance*, on postmedieval romance.

back upon him as well as forward on the development of the storyline, or that the ironic situation of Palamoun listening should mirror the listening experience of the tale. But the "aventure" of such situations is a factor of reflexivity in the language of the poem, over which the narrator exerts only partial control. He is "read," as we have seen, by his own virtuosity with the coincidence of idiom or event.

One coincidence of this sort in Part II is the unlikely alignment between the scene of the knights' accidental meeting and the subsequent scene in which Theseus discovers them fighting in the grove over Emelye. It has been observed by several commentators that the Knight does not quite understand the full range and significance of what he says preliminary to the discovery of this "aventure" when he discourses on the "purveiaunce" of the "ministre general."[16] He does not realize, for instance, that he has forgotten momentarily about free will as he proceeds with heady ideas on the destiny which foresees things that may happen in a day even if they have not happened in a thousand years. He is not quite certain about whether he means that Theseus is this divine foreknowledge or whether the duke simply foresaw that one day he would decide to go hunting. And he certainly does not foresee that his sober notion of determinism is suddenly interrupted by the path of the hart which leads, by chance, to the discovery of Palamoun and Arcite. The entire action of the poem turns on this totally accidental distraction, and, for all we can tell, the narrator is more fascinated by the coincidence than he is in directing the significance of it.

The "aventure" of romance could hardly be illustrated more lucidly than by the mirror reflection of the knights' unexpected meeting and Theseus' coincidental discovery. But my point is that happenstance is not only an event of plot; it is also a property of voice, and for that reason the second scene extends the implications of the first. As the narrator sets out to reflect on the unexpected in a world governed by the "ministre general," he paradoxically loses sight of the fact that he has stumbled upon the path of the hart and then the principal actors of the drama. The telling is inhabited by an "aventure" no less significant than the unanticipated discovery of the action. Moreover, since the first scene is about the inability of both speaker and listener to realize the significance of what is spoken, the "aventure" of the scene with Theseus is anticipated specifically as a disjunction in narrative voice: not only is the narrator-Knight an unlikely spokesperson of such complicated ideas as divine providence, he is incongruously aligned

[16] E.g., Leicester's critique of Howard, *The Idea of the "Canterbury Tales"* (*The Disenchanted Self*, pp. 230–31).

with his own knight, Arcite, speaking a poetry whose significance remains, for the moment at least, out of his reach. Consequently, accidental discovery in this scene continues the larger concern of the poem with the "two sides" of language, what it attempts to describe and what it says about itself. No matter how firmly "the world had sworn / The contrarie of a thyng by ye or nay" (1666–67), the narrator, who makes this observation at the opening of his speech, will not be able to hear the contrary side of his own voice. Division is unpredictable in language, and that is why the "aventure" of romance is so well-suited to reflecting on the historical forces "of werre, or pees, or hate, or love" (1671) in the fourteenth century.

That narrator and character are momentarily aligned is not unusual in this poem, since we have already seen that certain styles of speaking, like the rhetorical question, are used interchangeably by them. Because *occultatio* is so common to the narrator, we find it as well in the discourse of his characters. Upon being discovered by Theseus fighting with Arcite in the grove, Palamoun's first words in self-defense echo the rhetoric of his narrator, but in this instance the trope has become a means of qualifying the voice of the speaker. "Sire, what nedeth wordes mo?" says Palamoun to Theseus (1715). He is then constrained to narrate everything thus far concealed by the plot, that he has escaped from the prison tower, that Arcite is working incognito for Theseus himself, and that both of them love Emelye, who until now does not even know that they exist. If it is an agonizing moment for the speaker, his failure in love and friendship has been colored by the rhetorical style of his narrator: the feigned exclusion of what he is saying tends to obscure the real loss he obviously feels. And what *occultatio* does not occlude in this regard, overstatement does, when Palamoun requests repeatedly in his apologia that both he and Arcite "deserved to be slayn" (1741).

WITHOUTEN ANY REPPLICACIOUN

As Theseus is ready to take him at his word and condemn both fighters to death, his response pays no particular attention to the speaker's rhetoric. With single-minded judgment, Theseus answers:

> ". . . This is a short conclusion.
> Youre ownene mouth, by youre confessioun,
> Hath dampned yow, and I wol it recorde." (1743–45)

The echo of the narrator's style of opening with a conclusion is a cue to the participation of this passage in the division of language elsewhere. Yet neither he nor Theseus responds to that possibility in the language of confession. Palamoun has been condemned by his "mouth." But the women of the hunting party, including Emelye, have been listening, too, and they have heard something in Palamoun's voice which has been overlooked. Their response may be construed as a reading of the lover's lament. "Have mercy, Lord, upon us wommen alle!" (1757). That is all they say. But in the dramatization of their anguish, they exemplify the other side of Palamoun's confession, the wounding and pain concealed within the various tropes of his rhetoric.

The response of Theseus—to rescind the death sentence of both knights—is explained specifically as a revision of his own previous "word": he will not be, he says, "a leon . . . in word" (1775). The metaphor of the word as lion is defined as the utterance of a ruler who refuses to acknowledge "division" ("That lord hath litel of discrecioun, / That in swich cas kan no divisioun"; 1779–80). The women's complaint has confronted him with a division which he cannot ignore. It is the dramatization of the pain occluded by the rhetoric of public confession, and Theseus must yield to it.

But he does so only momentarily because he goes on to treat very casually, if not to mock, those unfortunate lovers who live under the aegis of the God of Love. Stopping to note that he himself was once a servant of love, he forgives the knights their "trespas" on his previous edicts. Yet he still moves directly to protect the integrity of his "word" by returning to its previous division. Now, he says, the decision to settle the dispute about Emelye in a joust is a word of "plat conclusioun, / Withouten any repplicacioun" (1845–46). To his earlier sentence of death the women had reply. This time rebuttal is excluded; his word will have no reply. But it will also have no replication: he means what he says, or rather, the only possible meaning is contained exclusively within his utterance, which cannot be divided. Recognizing no reply and no other meaning but its own, his voice is sovereign—and there is no outside of sovereign discourse.

Such a configuration of voice constitutes the political rule of Athens. There is no outside of power. But it becomes increasingly clear that the narrator emulates the "sighte" of Theseus, specifically his dominion over what may be included and excluded from his "conclusion." Although their voices converge explicitly toward the end of the poem, the signals of it are already in place early on, as in Theseus' remark on the finality of his word in this scene: "upon my trouthe, and as I am a knyght" (1855). Middle English "trouthe," of course, is synonymous with spoken oath, and with it Theseus seals his judgment. But speaking "as a knight" is the narrator's eager reading of Theseus' political status as "Duc," whose certainty of voice he himself would emulate.

And to enforce his own finality, the narrator-Knight ends this section of his performance with a return to his familiar tropes of control:

> Who looketh lightly now but Palamoun?
> Who spryngeth up for joye but Arcite?
> Who kouthe telle, or who kouthe it endite,
> The joye that is maked in the place
> Whan Theseus hath doon so fair a grace? (1870–74)

Rhetorical questions tend once again to deflect pragmatic inquiry away from the extremity of the situation. The knights are "up for joye" as everyone else is "doun on knees" (1875) in respect of the new dispensation. Caught up too in the joy of the moment, the narrator unwittingly includes himself as teller among all those who wonder in his tale, when the "who" of his *occultatio* is aligned by anaphora with the same fictional reference of his two previous pronouns. And the fourth occurrence, the "who" of "endite," stretches the alignment still further, as the Knight who speaks can be "enditing" only in metaphor. The metaphor of writing (as speaking) closes this section with the same enunciation it has been given from the opening of the poem. It cannot be taken, therefore, as a figuration of voice offered in compensation for the silent inscription of text, not when it has such obviously ulterior motives. For the moment, the narrator speaks like Theseus, "withouten any repplicacioun." But the putative innocence of this prerogative is not to last for long.

Telling or Looking?

In Part III the narrator's editorial procedure for including material from his sources opens with paradoxical reference to *forgetting*. He says that we would think him negligent "if I foryete to tellen" the details about how the royal lists for the joust were constructed (1882). But, the "forgetting" of such an elaborately itemized construction manifestly echoes the narrator's well-exercised rhetoric of *occultatio*. Feigning to exclude and feigning to forget are the same trope; and in this case, it is deployed in the service of yet another crucial aspect of oral delivery, the art of memory. Remembering by means of the "commonplaces"— associating details with physical places in the mind's eye—appeals to the oral art of recalling in the absence of the artificial memory of the written record. Chaucer's poetry, as scholarship has demonstrated in many ways, represents this very old medieval practice of recollecting.[17]

---

[17] As Howard, *The Idea of the "Canterbury Tales,"* has demonstrated.

For instance, the combination of mnemonic representation and graphically visualized images in the "picture" of the lists in Part III illustrates how Chaucer's lettered art "is shaped by, and continually responsive to, an oral-audial environment"; the listener's need to "see" is supplied by a speaker's ability to paint or illuminate with words—*ut pictura poesis*, in Horace's phrase, or in Gregory the Great's "pictures are the books of the illiterate."[18] This approach to the imagery of narrative in Chaucer's poetry offers valuable insight into the question of why orality persisted in the literate traditions of the fourteenth century, particularly through the suggestion that even in silent reading the oral expectation for a "picture" of the word is still expected.

However, the oral properties of the *Knight's Tale* are qualified in so many ways that we need to consider further how Chaucer was responding to the "oral-audial environment." Indeed, he seems to be interested, with the *Gawain*-poet, in taking to task the customary assumption from many sources of the middle ages that a writer must compensate for the "mere" writtenness of his medium. Chaucer's inquiry continues in Part III as the narrator's familiar trope of control compromises the distance and oversight he would otherwise presume as his point of view. How he sees things is as much a part of the picture as the visual elements of his description. His voice is once again figured in his text by the repetition of oral conventions, and the *occultatio* of "forgetting" dominates his attempt to organize:

> But yet hadde I foryeten to devyse
> The noble kervyng and the portreitures,
> The shap, the contenaunce, and the figures
> That weren in thise oratories thre. (1914–17)

Here strong physical imagery constitutes a mnemonic device for recalling that the three temples to be described (those of Venus, Mars, and Diana) will serve as common "places" for mentioning three aspects about each deity (shape, appearance, and iconography.) But the continued listing of details within an extenuated *occultatio* divides attention between the pictures in the text and the figuration of narrative voice, which is set in relief by still other oral devices, notably anaphora and parataxis.

> Nat was foryeten the porter, Ydelnesse,
> Ne Narcisus the faire of yore agon,
> Ne yet the folye of kyng Salomon,
> Ne yet the grete strenghte of Ercules. (1940–43)

[18] Kolve, *Chaucer and the Imagery of Narrative*, p. 15. On Gregory, see L. G. Duggan, "Was Art Really the 'Book of the Illiterate'?"

As the list goes on, the random association of images betokens the narrator's own confusion about how to stop and change directions: "Why sholde I noght as well eek telle yow al . . ." (1967). The tone of his rhetoric is uncertain, but it is not comic or disdainful, as some would argue; the context for such derogation is simply too vague in the tale.[19] Rather, the narrator once again feigns to continue speaking, and that posture has a very definite context in the tale, since it is related specifically in this passage to how he looks at the visual art of his description.

First of all, he plays to the oral circumstance of a shared familiarity with his subject matter, the painting on the walls of Venus's temple: there "maystow se" and "thus may ye seen" (1918, 1947), that is, now in the mind's eye of the narrator's retelling or in books we have read or heard read to us. He could recall, he says, "a thousand mo" images of life under the sign of Venus (1954). But, as soon as the narrator turns in the next verse to the statue of the goddess Venus herself, who is "naked, fletynge in the large see, / And fro the navele doun al covered," he is no longer narrating from the detached remove of recalling an old text. He is now standing as eyewitness in the arena like one of his characters, looking up at the naked goddess in front of him and observing her "glorious to se" and "ful semely for to se" (1955–57, 1960).

He brings himself up short, as usual, saying he will now tell us about the portraiture on the walls of the next temple, that of Mars. But here, too, his looking at the details of iconography gets the better of his telling, and all of a sudden he steps once more as eyewitness into the space of his book:

> Ther saugh I first the derke ymaginyng
> Of Felonye. . . . (1995–96)
> Yet saugh I Woodnesse. . . . (2011)
> Yet saugh I brent the shippes. . . . (2017)
> Saugh I Conquest. . . . (2028)
> Ther saugh I how woful Calistopee. . . . (2056)
> Ther saugh I Dane. . . . (2062)

Although Chaucer had read this narrative shift in Boccaccio's *Teseida* and had used it extensively in the *Hous of Fame*, the convention is developed for unique purposes in the *Knight's Tale*. The discourse corrects itself on occasion when the narrator changes from the indicative mood of these verses back to the subjunctive mood, for example,

[19] Contrast D. W. Robertson, Jr., *A Preface to Chaucer*, pp. 260–66, 370–73, with Neuse, "The Knight."

of "ther maistow seen" Lygurge coming into the arena with Palamoun (2128). But the tear has occurred, and once it does, it repeats itself without apparent supervision.

The medieval convention of the narrator as eyewitness is made specific to this poem in the same way as the formality of *occultatio*: an entirely familiar convention of oral delivery is set in a context that resists its putative objectivity and control.[20] For although we might say that the narrator's verb "saugh" is simply metaphorical of an act of seeing which never occurred, we cannot ignore the parallel between the metaphor of sight in this instance and the metaphor of writing elsewhere in the poem. In this case, however, the opposition of voice and sight is much more difficult to reconcile within the hierarchical order assumed by metaphor. It makes every bit of difference to realize that the order of metaphor would impose itself in the very moment when voice is being displaced into the event of gazing up at Venus naked.[21] Seeing, in other words, plays the same part as writtenness in the *Knight's Tale*: it asserts the differentiation that voice would occlude. The verb "saugh," therefore, remains *literal* in the basic sense of the word: its writtenness resists the narrator's metaphor as he compromises the margin of his tale and prefigures by his own gaze the vision of Arcite and Palamoun yet to come.

The confusion between telling and looking thickens when the narrator stops on his mention of "Dane" (cited above) to give a short clarification: he did not mean to say "Diana" but "Daphne"—the one who was changed into a tree; whereas "Diana" calls to mind another transfiguration:

> Ther saugh I Attheon an hert ymaked,
> For vengeaunce that he saugh Diane al naked;
> I saugh how that his houndes have hym caught
> And freeten hym, for that they knewe hym naught. (2065–68)

What starts out as a recapitulation, made with all respect for listeners unable to turn back the page for clarification, is transfigured into a visual scene before his eyes; and, as if to emphasize this elision in discourse, he closes with one more displacement, this time concerning literary imagery per se: "Ther saugh I many another wonder storie" (2073). As with the description of Venus which caused the narrator to

---

[20] Cp. Spitzer's assessment of this convention in "A Note on the Poetic and Empirical 'I' in Medieval Authors."

[21] That his vision also displaces his "repressed knowledge" of the dark side of chivalry in the iconography of Mars, see Patterson, *Chaucer and the Subject of History*, p. 226.

lose his balance earlier, the temple of Diana proves to be far more complicated than he knows.

For having finished with the grisly account of what Acteon failed to see as he watched Diana bathing, the narrator turns his attention to Emelye during the early hours of the morning at the shrine of her goddess, when no one else but the maids is looking on.

> This Emelye, with herte debonaire,
> Hir body wessh with water of a welle.
> But how she dide hir ryte I dar nat telle,
> But it be any thing in general;
> And yet it were a game to heeren al.
> To hym that meneth wel it were no charge;
> But it is good a man been at his large. (2282–88)

As *occultatio* feigns concealment once again, it does not disguise the fact that what the narrator dares not tell is still being told through the power of insinuating what Emelye did when she washed her body "in general." And yet, he says, it would be fun to hear it all, shifting responsibility to the third person: "to hym that meneth wel" there would be no blame in providing the details of what he saw. For after all it is good "for a man" (not this one, of course) to be "at large"—to have free rein in looking around when no one else is and to speak freely about what he sees. If the narrator was in and out of the arena earlier, he now foregrounds that displacement of perspective as a man's game of taking prerogatives with language. We cannot say that he plays unwittingly, as he obviously enjoys winking to a familiar audience. But we can definitely say that he does not see himself as we read him, identifying himself with Acteon and recognizing it not, even as the syllables of that name are on his lips one last time in the opening verses of Emelye's prayer to her deity. "Keepe me," she says, from "thy vengeaunce and thyn ire, / That Attheon aboughte" (2302–2303). There is not a danger in the world that Emelye is a likely target for the dogs of desire, since it is Acteon who "bought" it. But her narrator does not see it that way, and we know why.[22]

Such a manipulation of prerogative is no more nor less than the custom of any teller in the medieval context, where the hierarchy of gender would hardly shudder when a male narrator projects a woman, instead of himself, as Acteon. But in this passage the sovereignty of perspective is mediated specifically around gender, since women— usually naked or bathing—become the site of narrative displacement,

---

[22] Cp. Crane, "Medieval Romance and Feminine Difference in *The Knight's Tale*," p. 54: the "narrator avoids making Acteon's error."

the occasion of a split in the discourse between telling and looking, saying and meaning, suppositing and signifying. As much as the voice of narration would take its cue from the speech of Theseus and proceed "withouten any repplicacioun," seeing and writing are telling a very different story about dominion. The "sighte above" which the narrator would emulate has become a figure in the text, produced by the language it would otherwise oversee.

Such a reversal does not square very well with the oral presumption that writing is a form of speech visualized in a picture for those unable to read. The visual image is no longer in tertiary position, following for the sake of illustration what is first spoken and then written. Now the picture is "like a poem" in a most radical sense: both are a kind of *writing* no longer dictated by voice. It is everywhere apparent that the art of medieval illumination and painting has found its way into the *Knight's Tale* in the depiction of extended images like the prison garden in Part I and the royal lists in Part III. Their representation by the narrator in the text suggests that Chaucer had meditated long and hard over medieval illuminations of the act of reading, in which the reader is painted, book in hand, with the "image" of his story visualized before him.

But the *Knight's Tale* demonstrates that Chaucer did much more than imitate the customary structure of this relation between teller and text. He suggests, *pace* Gregory the Great, that the picture does not simply compensate for the written word, making up for what is obvious in oral circumstances. Chaucer has divided writing from the control of voice, and he has been assisted by the very tradition that had relied upon the painted image as mirror of speech. In Part III of the poem, voice is just as much a part of the picture as the iconography of oaths or the gods, and although that reversal is also to be found in medieval illumination, Chaucer has played out the consequences of its irony. The seeing inscribed in telling unravels what narrative voice would want to assume about its own neutrality and innocence. That we may observe a coordination between the "orality" of the poem—its recitation and its conversational properties—and certain "dominant" images, such as the prison garden and the jousting arena, is a conclusion that is not completely congruent with the subtle and consistent qualification of voice in the poem. We hear it throughout in the manifest ambiguity of *occultatio*, which strains to the breaking point when the Knight would "feign" excluding himself from the scene of Emelye's bath. He has failed to account for his own figuration in the story: he becomes Acteon. And that is an occlusion he has not counted on.

To assume, therefore, that *occultatio* is a figure of feigned exclusion in the *Knight's Tale* is justifiable only in part. It is also a figure of real exclusion. In Part III the doubling of the figure occurs specifically within a narrative apology of sight, which remains blind to itself, to its own self-defense; the voice of seeing fails to read itself, and by extension something about the narrative is left unread. *Occultatio* is the occasion of this unreadability. In view of the double-sided quality of the figure, it is appropriate now to recall that early in the poem, the image of unreadable inscription is cited explicitly as a *text* when Palamoun laments his fate in prison. The world, says Palamoun, is ruled by a blind fate "writen in the table of atthamaunt" whose inscription cannot be read or interpreted. The image of the unreadable text occurs expressly twice more in the poem.

When Emelye prays to Diana at her temple, she is given the provocative sign of the burning brands dropping blood and spitting out sounds. But Emelye cannot interpret the sign, "she ne wist what it signyfied" (2343). The deity herself, as if in answer to this failure of interpretation, speaks *in viva voce*, and yet only part of her oracular statement is understood: Emelye will be married to one of the knights. The other part of the oracle, the most important part (which man), is deferred to an unreadable text.

> "And by eterne word writen and confermed,
> Thou shalt ben wedded unto oon of tho
> That han for thee so muchel care and woe,
> But unto which of them I may nat telle." (2350–53)

Whether Diana is prohibited from reciting a text she has already read or is herself unable to decipher its inscription is a moot point, except for the fact that it highlights the function of unread writing as a critical element of the poem. Emelye is in the same unfortunate situation as Palamoun earlier, and that conjunction around the sign of the closed book in the poem is no less oracular than the fire in the first dish on Diana's altar, dying and then igniting again. Unreadable signs for both Palamoun and Emelye augur that they will be married in the end. The narrator, to be sure, knows this outcome at this moment of the telling, but not because he has read the pagan text obscured to Palamoun or Emelye. What he does not know, and cannot know, is that his own tale is being brought into unusual juxtaposition with an unreadable book.

This conjunction appears once again in the third occurrence of the image in the poem, and this time most strikingly within the trope of apologizing for exclusion. In response to Arcite's dying words—"Mercy, Emelye!"—the narrator ponders the whereabouts of his soul.

> His spirit chaunged hous and wente ther,
> As I cam nevere, I kan nat tellen wher.
> Therefore I stynte; I nam no divinistre;
> Of soules fynde I nat in this registre,
> Ne me ne list thilke opinions to telle
> Of hem, though that they writen where they dwelle.
> Arcite is coold, ther Mars his soule gye! (2808–14)

As the effort of lofty pathos falls to the grave in this anticlimax, the narrator defers the destiny of Arcite to a writing he does not know how to "telle." He cannot read or recite from its "registre"; the "hous" of the dead is the "text" in which the destiny of pagan souls is recorded; but only a "divinistre" can interpret its mysterious inscription—because, presumably, it is oracular. Nor will the narrator recite from a book of learned opinions on pagan myth; whether or not he can read the writing of commentary, that text, too, is closed for now— like the "hous" where dead pagans "dwelle" and the grave where Arcite is "coold" (2815).

It is difficult to interpret the implications of the narrator's somewhat dismissive tone in this passage. But one thing is clear: the image of the unread text reflects the unique response of medieval Christianity to pagan books and the pagan world in general. The notion of a text that is obscure or indecipherable has a well-documented history in the middle ages, the so-called *liber occultorum* or "book of things hidden," the "book of secrets."[23] Among its many exemplifications, one of the most common is the last book of the Bible, Apocalypse, because its oracular signs remain shrouded in mystery. More specifically, in Apocalypse 20.12, the image of the book that is to be opened was commonly interpreted in exegesis as the "closed book" (*liber occultus*) recording the souls of the dead; it was a "secret" text insofar as its contents were to be read at the end of time by God. This convention of the *liber occultorum* has a certain bearing on the "registre" that records the whereabouts of Arcite's dead soul.

But the narrator's attitude toward this text is colored more generally by a typical view of paganism in the Christian middle ages. When he says, "ne me list thilke opinions to telle," he is hardly speaking in affected modesty about a subject he has mastered. Rather, he is echoing the presumption that neither the authors nor the audiences of pagan books knew enough to provide the kind of interpretation now available in the medieval Christian world. And thus the Knight's shifting

---

[23] E.g., see the *Allegoria in sacram scripturam* (PL 112, 987); Hugh of St. Cher, 7:422 (verso); Bersuire, 2:462D; and my discussion in *The Idea of the Book*, pp. 162–63.

tone in this passage is of a piece with the three images of the occluded text in his tale. Yet as the narrator defers further interest in the unread text of the pagan world, it never crosses his mind that his own discourse may displace a similar unreadability.

That it crosses Chaucer's mind is more than evident because the narrator puns unwittingly on his own poem when he says that he cannot locate the destiny of souls "in *this* registre." He is not ruminating around the hidden places of the *liber occultorum* in Apocalypse. But he is looking for the dead, and if the record will not signify their location, it is *occultus* because it resists plain and simple self-disclosure. Narrative voice in the *Knight's Tale* would strain toward that plainness and simplicity in the continuing negotiation of *occultatio* between what to include and what to leave out.[24] In the most basic sense, the "voice" of that figure is *oral* to the extent that it would deny any other than the feigned sense of this negotiation. And yet it is clear that *occultatio* also initiates a real occlusion in the speaker's voice, something he does not hear. With one more echo of the figure, "I kan nat tellen wher," the narrator is confessing his inability to read the pagan book; but he has no idea that he has also just feigned the exclusion of a text he really does not see, the fusion of the unread book of paganism with his own poem. It is that occlusion which constitutes what I have been calling the *writtenness* of the tale. Chaucer is interested in it precisely because it is so obvious and yet so habitually subsumed within the oral form of voice.

Pagan Metaphor

The focus on unreadable signs which I have been pointing to in the *Knight's Tale*, whether they are explicit as texts or buried within the rhetorical style of narrative voice, asserts a clear alignment with the life and attitudes that medieval Christians regarded as pagan. In the *Man of Law's Tale*, Chaucer draws this parallel between the unreadable book and paganism directly when he refers to "thilke large book / Which that men clepe the hevene ywriten was" (190–91). In this Book of the Heavens, the "sterres" are words and sentences recording the life and death of every individual—including Hector, Achilles, Pompey, Julius Caesar, and "the strif of Thebes" (200). But, says the narrator of the tale, although that Text is open to everyone and "clerer than is glas, / Is writen, God woot . . . mennes wittes ben so dulle / That no

---

[24] I have not yet seen a discussion of *liber occultorum* in connection with rhetorical *occultatio* in a medieval text.

wight kan wel rede it atte fulle" (194–203). Chaucer may well have read this description of the cosmos in Bernard Silvestris' *Cosmographia*, but he obviously changed the source to stress the unreadability of the Heavenly Book. Unlike Bernard, who would qualify as the kind of "divinistre" capable of reading pagan myth in the *Knight's Tale*, pagans themselves have "wittes . . . so dulle" that they cannot make out its inscription. That this description is applicable to the unread texts of the *Knight's Tale* is established when the Man of Law includes "the strif of Thebes" as one of the undecipherable sentences written on the sky. But the point is that the pagan perspective is one the narrator-Knight comes to share when he too shrugs his shoulders at unreadable signs or turns a deaf ear to his own voice. And because he does not know the implications of such writing in his own figures of speech, his discourse too is closed, like the pagan images of the text he mentions. Speaking without replication, therefore, is not only a pagan phenomenon identifiable with the government of a bygone age in Athens and Thebes; it is also a way of talking about the past in fourteenth-century England.

We have heard it, for instance, at the end of *Sir Gawain* when the hero returns wearing the green girdle as a sign of his failure, and King Arthur and his retinue transform it into a declaration of their "renoun." The heroic ideal acknowledges no signs of difference, let alone fault, in the expression of its sovereignty. Like Theseus, Arthur speaks "withouten repplicacioun"—and his knights follow suit. So potent is the single-mindedness of this voice of no reply that the scribe who added the closing French line to the poem transposed it into a verbal challenge to all future readers and listeners: "you, too, shall have nothing more to say—*you who think evil: shame on you.*"

No one takes the rhetoric of this claim at face value, not without forgetting most of the poem. But the split here between what I have been calling the "oral" value of writing and the subversion of it in the text spells out a difference that was repeatedly compromised in various sociopolitical contexts of the 1380s. However history may judge the events of this decade, the facts are that pivotal points were decided by the successful suppression of differences between the spoken and written claim to political power. Michael de la Pole, as noted, was the ready participant in authorizing the requests of Richard's orders written under the Privy Seal. He was impeached by the lords in 1386 (perhaps before Chaucer's eyes), and in the subsequent year when the justices verified that parliament had derogated the royal prerogative by their actions, the lords suppressed their decision. In 1388 parliament once again suppressed all opposition to its procedures as the lords went about purging the king's chamber, ending their deliberations with the oath forbidding all replies in times to come. It is tempting to think that this oath of no reply and the ending line of *Gawain* have something to do with each other.

Be that as it may. I have been suggesting that the Knight's representation of dominion in ancient Athens responds to the discourse of sovereign rule in medieval England. The pagan scene in the *Knight's Tale* is a moral metaphor, as readers often remark, but it is also a political one for the times. And although Theseus' rule and word may seem benign, they remain pagan. The narrator is not saying that England is Athens, but he tends to lose sight of his own appreciation as he gets caught up in the stateliness and governance, the "voice," of his hero. Chaucer, we can be sure, is not caught up in the coordination of voices, however benign they may sound. Indeed, it is the presumption of neutrality in the speaker's voice that has caught Chaucer's poetic and political ear. Feigning to exclude, as the narrator utters throughout, pays only lip service to the gesture of all-inclusiveness. There is something about it that "no man koude knowe"—that passes over or excludes what it would seek to recognize. *Occultatio* is thus not only a rhetorical strategy of tale telling but a political response to the stormy struggle of claiming sovereignty in the England of the 1380s.

In Part IV this figure of speech is more prominent than anywhere else. Though critics have often noted that the teller's management of his material becomes comic as the poem comes to a close, I do not see humor or repudiation in the editorializing. Chaucer allows his narrator all the rhetorical lead he wants, in the interests of fair play to a speaker who presumes his own neutrality or benevolence. We hear it most clearly in the "orality" of discourse, when a speaker extenuates his assumption that we as listeners are in there with him, sharing his sympathies and values. I recall, once more, that those are sympathies for a pagan world, and therein is the rub of Chaucer's paradoxical rhetoric.

ORALIZING SCRIPT

He emphasizes this tension in the battle scene of Part IV when he begins with *occultatio* and proceeds with a lengthy adaptation from the style of the alliterative revival.

> Ther is namoore to seyn, but west and est
> In goon the speres ful sadly in arrest;
> In gooth the sharpe spore into the syde.

> Ther seen men who kan juste and who kan ryde;
> Ther shyveren shaftes upon sheeldes thikke;
> He feeleth thurgh the herte-spoon the prikke.
> Up spryngen speres twenty foot on highte;
> Out goon the swerdes as the silver brighte;
> The helmes they tohewen and toshrede;
> Out brest the blood with stierne stremes rede;
> With myghty maces the bones they tobreste.
> He thurgh the thikkeste of the throng gan threste;
> Ther stomblen steedes stronge, and doun gooth al,
> He rolleth under foot as dooth a bal;
> He foyneth on his feet with his tronchoun,
> And he hym hurtleth with his hors adoun. (2601–16)

It seems odd that Chaucer would imitate alliterative convention since he wrote nothing else in that style and even derogated it in the Parson's repudiation of verse in "rum, ram, ruf."[25] But in this case, the shift to a manifestly different meter compares with the many other occasions of stylistic alteration in the poem. Alliteration accents the balance and parallelism of syntax, the anaphora of organizing items in series, the synecdoche of a battle instrument signifying an army; the repetition of the generic article ("*the* swerdes as *the* silver brighte; *the* helmes"); the repetition of formulary phrases ("in goon the speres"), and so forth.

Medieval historians of military events, as we have seen, would strain at length with such stock-in-trade devices: their purpose was oratorical, to vitalize the bare writtenness of a textual account and bring it to life with the breath of rhetoric. The narrator-Knight is striving for a similar effect, and he reaches for the familiar style of chivalric contesting in the alliterative line. However, if the sudden shift to this style breathes life into the text, it also reflects back on the convention itself. The narrator would be there on the scene of battle, as he once was at Tramyssene, Palatye, and elsewhere. And yet the teller as eyewitness is also a narrative commonplace, which inevitably mediates the experience of violent combat. "They tohewen and toshrede" at once delivers the clash of weapons and also dissolves it into countless formulary battle phrases from the pages of medieval romance and chronicle history. The same is true of the definite article or the synecdoche: the whole army of Arcite or Palamoun gathers under the *the* of sword and helmet. But still the generality of the article or the noun abstracts any one individual out of the grit of conflict.

---

[25] *Pars. Prol.* (43). See Everett, *Essays on Middle English Literature*, pp. 140–42, on Chaucer's "ear" for alliterative effects.

Although the narrator would want us there with him, encouraged by the style of fine oral delivery, Chaucer has framed his performance in the undisputed imitation of a lettered art. And that frame puts stress on the prerogative which voice would claim for itself in this poem. We cannot miss the importance of this tension when the two orders of language—the narrator's voice and the voices of characters in the fiction—become mixed up with each other to bring the battle scene to a conclusion. Describing the din of the crowds celebrating Arcite's momentary victory, the narrator forgets himself once again and enters into dialogue with the fictional heralds and musicians, ordering them to quiet down because he cannot hear himself think:

> The trompours, with the loude mynstralcie,
> The heraudes, that ful loude yelle and crie,
> Been in hire wele for joye of daun Arcite.
> But harkneth me, and stynteth noyse a lite,
> Which a myracle ther bifel anon. (2671–75)

The oral appeal to an audience of present listeners is clearly the intent of a number of stylistic devices at this point in the poem, beginning with the odd choice of words in the narrator's description of the violence done to the knight's body.[26] After many lines of anatomical details, "Nature" we are told, no longer has "dominacioun':

> And certeinly, ther Nature wol nat wirche,
> Fare wel physik! Go ber the man to chirche! (2759–60)

From the malfunctions of Arcite's internal organs to the high reach of a philosophical "Nature" is a long stretch of style, but the next, bidding good-bye to medicine and saying hello to church, assumes a colloquial familiarity with a moment that is anything but familiar. Arcite is breathing his last. Why the lapse into a conversational argot?

And why also begin his death speech with the rhetorical flourish of affected modesty? That trope is *occlutatio* in yet another key, feigning to be modest about an elegance of style or knowledge recognizable to everybody.

> "Naught may the woful spirit in myn herte
> Declare o point of all my sorwes smerte
> To yow, my lady, that I love moost." (2765–67)

One form of rhetoric leads to another, and shortly Arcite is given the anaphora of an accomplished orator ("Allas, the wo! Allas, the peynes

---

[26] See Neuse, *Chaucer's Dante*, p. 124, on the "theatrical" response to Arcite's death.

stronge"; 2771 ff.), which is followed by even more pointed rhetorical flourishes.

> "What is this world? What asketh men to have?
> Now with his love, now in his colde grave
> Allone, withouten any compaignye." (2777–79)

This time the shift from the higher reaches of philosophical causality is less jarring—but only momentarily; for the real inquiry of the question, like those asked earlier in passionate search for the reason and order in this world, threatens to descend into a mere rhetorical question, a nonquestion, at the moment when answers are needed most. And the irony of this anticlimax is assisted by the devastating understatement of realizing that the grave is a fine and private place where none embrace. Philosophy has its moment here, as the most important inquiry of the entire tale is put forth, but only fleetingly as the rhetoric that we have heard all too frequently from the narrator tends to evacuate Arcite's speech of the pain his language would otherwise summon forth.

A similar compromise colors the urgency of response heard from the women of Athens who fall into inconsolable wailing upon the death of Arcite.

> "Why woldestow be deed," thise wommen crye,
> "And haddest gold ynough and Emelye?" (2835–36)

From the distant vantage of the narrator, the women know not what they ask; theirs is an "incomplete perception," as one reader concludes.[27] But such a response fails to hear the narrator's voice controlling the style of the women's question. Their voice is subsumed within the rhetoric of an overstated question; it inevitably finesses real inquiry into the justice and fairness of an order that would presume categorically to include all loss, no matter how inexplicable. Women once again provide a "reading" of the spoken word, and as in the case with Palamoun's confession earlier, their speech is preempted by a voice that would claim to speak for all. Rhetorical figurality compromises a "voice" that is not there, but that is indelibly written all the same.

From nearly the first lines of the poem, Chaucer has been exploring the split interests of rhetorical figures, and as *occultatio* has been the most salient device for justifying a putatively innocent inclusion, it is fitting that now in the last moments of the narrative we see that figure anatomized beyond anything we have observed before. I refer to the famously delivered description of the funeral pyre, an *occultatio* with-

---

[27] Muscatine, *Chaucer and the French Tradition*, p. 190.

out restraint running longer than any other sentence in the poem and, for that matter, in the whole corpus of Chaucer's poetry. It is manifestly innocent of satire, dismissal, and humor—all of which have been heard in the passage by critics of the tale. But it is also prefigured by countless other instances of the figure which do not proceed from a neutral voice. Chaucer has previously split *occultatio* into its two divided interests, what it recognizes and fails to recognize about itself. In the description of the pyre, the figure becomes a sort of rhetorical net cast wide across the entire world of pagan ceremony for the dead. But between the opening of the figure ("how the fyr was maked. . . ."; 2919), and continuing to the predicate of the sentence some fifty-six lines later ("I wol nat tellen how"; 2963), *occultatio* has lost all rhetorical point. It is that loss of emphasis, and of order, which spells out the division of the figure we have noted so often in the poem.[28] The speaker has become exceedingly digressive in his syntax: between subject and verb almost anything can be included, and everything is—from the sticks and branches collected for the funeral fire, to the response of Emelye in attendance, to games Greeks were wont to play at wakes, and even to the oiled bodies of the wrestlers in those games.

One could, as I said, think this style humorous and distancing, which are attitudes of stoic detachment not unfitting to the occasion for pagans or Christians. But I do not find comedy or detachment in this passage. The assumption created by the digressive style is the oral expectation of shared sympathy and even participation in each detail of the moment. And thus digression becomes self-generating: "I will not tell you," says the narrator, "how the fire first caught the straw":

> Ne how Arcite lay among al this,
> Ne what richesse about his body is;
> Ne how that Emelye, as was the gyse,
> Putte in the fyr of funeral servyse;
> Ne how she swowned whan men made the fyr,
> Ne what she spak, ne what was hir desir;
> Ne what jeweles men in the fyre caste,
> Whan that the fyr was greet and brente faste;
> Ne how somme caste hir sheeld, and somme hir spere. (2939–47)

The oral presumption of control was never more self-assertive. Who, after all, would deny the speaker his digression as he would summon with staccato-like anaphora and parataxis a certain respect for the dead.

---

[28] Cp. Kolve's reading of the figure in this scene (*Chaucer and the Imagery of Narrative*, pp, 130–31).

But what are we to make of all those negatives? Not telling us what he is telling feigns a permission for speaking continuously and representing everyone, even within the breath of one sentence. And yet we must take account of the real effect of a syntax that negates so insistently everything it is trying to include. Do we not have here yet another version of including a sympathy which is simultaneously being denied? Is this not a consequence of split interests which have inhabited the narrator's voice from the very beginning?

If the voice of this long passage is thus split in its utterance, we can be sure that the narrator-Knight would be the last to admit it. He would clearly want to maintain that he is speaking in the spirit of fair and just representation to all details. And on that note he ends his account of the burial scene: the games of the wake are over—"the pley is doon"—and it is time to "make of my longe tale an ende" (2964, 2966). Still, deferring the play of the pagan wake to the play of telling the tale is not a narrative transition plain and simple. Although he is not disingenuous or dismissive, neither does he hear in his own voice the appeal to a benign connectedness between two orders of "play" which have very little in common. Voice, even in this innocuous transition, does not sustain the disparity it would encompass, and in the conclusion of the poem the rhetoric of innocent inclusion takes on yet another form, the grand philosophical argument delivered by Theseus on the "faire cheyne" binding all things (2987 ff.). This passage has been cited tirelessly in the pages of Chaucerian criticism as an illustration of the real innocence of an inclusive order for understanding the death of Arcite and the purpose of suffering in this world. But I suggest following the lead of those who find in it the limitation of a pagan understanding of suffering and death.[29] Such a limitation, as I will argue in closing, has been already structured in the poem by the characterization of voice as presuming more than it can possibly sustain. Theseus' voice, like his narrator's, is also strained.

TEXTUALITY

Few passages in the tale are as bookish as Theseus' closing disquisition, and every reader is duly advised to recognize beneath the surface the learned bibliography in the *Teseida*, the *Consolation of Philosophy*, the *Commentary on the Dream of Scipio*, the *Timaeus*, and—closer to home— Wyclif's *De universalibus*.[30] But before reaching, on the best of advice,

[29] E.g., Aers, *Chaucer, Langland and the Creative Imagination*, pp. 188ff., and Kolve, *Chaucer and the Imagery of Narrative*, pp. 137ff., though I reach different conclusions from them.

[30] See Kean's summary in *Chaucer and the Making of English Poetry* 2:41–49. Wyclif's treatise remains to be related to the speech.

for the old books in Chaucer's library, we would do well to recall the obvious, that references to them are culled from here and there to be woven into a spoken discourse. And it is in the spokenness of textual references that the passage makes its point about the inclusiveness of order in the universe. It is easy to overlook, for example, the diction of textuality in what Theseus is saying. The great "effect" and high "entente" (2989) of the First Mover are terms from Chaucer's lexicon of signifying the functions of language and the reading of books. In an epistle to Troilus after all is lost, Criseyde uses both terms to deflect her former lover from thinking the worst: "gret effect men write in place lite; / Th'*entente* is al, and nat the lettres space" (*Troilus* 5.1629–30). In the *Knight's Tale*, the word "effect" has been used at several critical moments to signify the transition from one section to another, as at the end of Part III, when the narrator says that he will stop discussing the gods, "And telle yow as pleynly as I kan / The grete *effect*, for which that I bygan" (2481–82). And to make the point that this is a textual, not just a spoken, maneuver, the poem quotes itself in the first word of the succeeding line: "*Greet* was the feeste in Atthenes that day" (2483).

So Theseus begins by quoting the narrator's "grete effect," and since he could not possibly know his source, citation in his discourse will pay respect to two different orders of language—what it points out in other books and what it points to in itself. Theseus speaks as if he were a writer, quoting learned commentary and using the vocabulary of the writer's trade as he oralizes the inscribed word. Such moves are nothing new in this tale, and accordingly they should caution against the opinion of many of Chaucer's critics that Theseus' discourse embraces purely and simply the rational freedom of the Timaean meter in the *Consolation of Philosophy*.[31] It is plain to everybody that Theseus quotes Boethius when he notes the binding of the elements, "the fyr, the eyr, the water, and the lond" (2992); but, unlike Boethius, Theseus treats the First Mover like an author well in control of the "cause" in what he writes: he knows fully the "why" and the "what thereof he mente" (2990). As if to participate in the same self-conscious reflection on the meaning of language as the First Mover, Theseus imitates the Divine Self-Knowledge when he insists:

> 'Ther nedeth noght noon auctoritee t'allegge,
> For it is preeved by experience,
> But that me list declaren my sentence." (3000–3002)

---

[31] It is the "solution to the problems" of the poem, according to Robertson, *A Preface to Chaucer*, p. 270.

Insisting on the self-evidence of what is said cannot be called a habit learned from toiling over the give-and-take of interpreting written documents and books. It appeals to an oral aptitude for "auctoritee," one that is based not in looking things up and checking them out but in the "proof" of "experience." The "sentence" is all, and not the letter's space. So far so good, until we take account of the double jeopardy of "sentence": the word refers to the *sententia* from the many old books on universal order ringing in the background of this famous passage; yet Theseus is also bearing witness to his own sentence, his words. They are self-validating of the order he would have us see in the world. Quoting himself in this way must inevitably compete with the authority he would say exists primarily in "the cause above" (2987). And with that phrase, his first in the speech, he has unwittingly cited the discourse of another authority, the narrator-Knight, who has been giving us all kinds of "causes above" in the lines of his tale for the way things have fallen out.[32]

Self-citation, once established, is not a factor of Theseus' "entente," no more so than he is responsible for citing the narrator. He continues that it is logical to assume the stability of the First Mover once we have established the stability of its order:

> "Thanne may men by this order wel discerne
> That thilke Moevere stable is and eterne." (3003–3004)

For every "part" derives from its "hool" only if its order "parfit is and stable." Any reader of Plato, Boethius, Augustine, or Wyclif will be satisfied with the reference, since those authors also treated the order of the world like a Text in which to trace the idea of order. But the logic of Theseus' "thanne" follows his ambiguous "sentence" and thus sets up a chain reaction in "discerning" how the "part" of this sentence does in fact validate the "whole" of the argument for order. The speaker vouches for stability "outside" in the world of books and experience, at the same time as the self-reference of his language returns him to his own utterance.

The split "reference" of the passage—at once to authority and to itself—locates an instability within the grand claim for stability which can only darken the stoic indifference wherein we are supposed to find consolation for the disorder of Arcite's death. "Descendynge" is indeed the right word to follow the "stable" order of Theseus' appeal (3010). All things are "corrumpable"; they are "speces" which merely "en-

---

[32] The *MED* editors define *above* as "higher up on the written page, at a point closer to the beginning of a book or document" (1b:a), and "earlier in a discussion, a speech, or a story" (1b:b). Chaucer is cited for *Melibee* (2660, 2975).

duren by successioun, / And nat eterne" (3015). The descent could not be more obvious; look at the "ook," the "hard stoon," or the "brode ryver" (3017, 3021, 3024). All things must come to their "ende":

> "Of man and womman seen we wel also
> That nedes, in oon of thise termes two
> This is to seyn, in youthe or elles age—
> He moot be deed, the kynge as shal the page." (3026–30)

Such are the examples of his argument, and in the moment of listening we are not inclined to refer back and question the symmetry of the descending order ending in man and woman. The narrator stops to double back and be sure that we understand his reference to the "termes two": they refer to either end of life, birth and death. But there is no provision in the grand sweep of speaking to pause over the fact that people in this world all come under the same category of necessary happenings as oaks and stones and rivers. The ends are the same. We are all "termes" in an argument, nothing more. In the gesture of signifying what the logicians would call the *res* of experience, Theseus remains bound within the "end" and "term" of language. He speaks for a stoic appreciation, "To maken vertu of necessitee" (3042). And yet the necessary causality he would document in the world is compromised by the self-referential necessity of his argument. He says there is an outside order where nature is but art and all discord is harmony not understood. But how do we get to the *res* and *haecceitas* of it if language cannot get outside of itself?

PRISON

Nobler minds of the fourteenth century than Chaucer's fictional Knight contemplated that question, and no one more compellingly than William of Ockham. We will recall that for him speech was a sign of *res* in the physical universe or the mind of God, and that writing was a sign of speech. Inscription remained speech written down, no matter how "nominalistic" we may construe Ockham's logic. Moreover, even though Ockham went farther than any other philosopher of the century in dividing "words" from essences, the individual *res* had to be identifiable with a mental sign, which he called the *vox* of the mind and which was simultaneous with the intuitive knowledge of the individual. Accordingly, Ockham never thought that reality evaporated into language. And yet even though he believed he had found a way out of the abyss of self-reference in language, access to the individual thing, in its own essence, remains mediated in his epistemology, and the source of the problem is the "voice" of the mental concept.

But something else is afoot in the logic of writing and speaking in Theseus' speech on order. To repeat, he would locate the reality of order in the physical universe, but his spoken representation of that order is fundamentally qualified by the metalanguage of his argument. Self-citation unveils the "text" of his argument (which is the tale itself), but he proceeds to appropriate it within the sound of his own voice. He oralizes the text, or, what amounts to the same thing, turns the text of his reference into an oral object. That too is a most conventional development. And we may recall, with John Wyclif, perhaps the most flourishing illustration of it in the fourteenth century. According to Wyclif, the text of Scripture, specifically its *forma verborum*, is the manifestation of the speech act that created the universe, the *Vox Dei*, and appropriately known in the exegetical commonplace of the *liber praesentiae Dei* ("the book of the presence of God").[33] The fundamentalism of Wyclif consists in his radical notion that the words of the Bible actually express the *Vox Dei*, and it is for this reason that he saw no problem, as his contemporaries certainly did, in advising that it be rendered in the language spoken by people in his time, the dialects of Middle English.

But the orality of the text in the argument of Theseus has a different direction. After Theseus delivers his axiom on the wisdom of necessity, he proceeds to silence those who "gruccheth"; they do no more than "rebel" against the memory of Arcite (3045–46). Silence is the word here in every sense, as Theseus gathers his whole argument into a statement about the kind of immortality Arcite now enjoys.

> "And certeinly a man hath moost honour
> To dyen in his excellence and flour,
> Whan he is siker of his goode name." (3047–49)

He recalls a venerable pagan ideal. People live on in what others say about them. Arcite has given up "his breeth," but the breath of others will make "a worthy fame"—as the narrator's breath is itself attempting through the heavy cadences of anaphora and parallelism in these lines (3052 ff). *Fama*, as Chaucer knew the term well (from the *Hous of Fame*), is the oral circulation of language about history, legend, and life. The orality of the book in Theseus' argument has been referred directly to a pagan ideal of immortality. He looks to an outside world of reference in old books for noble thoughts on order, but his own argument never identifies it with the sovereign good, which alone grants the freedom from the bondage of this world. He never ascends with

---

[33] Discussed above, in ch. 3.

Boethius on the wings of philosophy into the freedom of eternal sight or into the "book of the presence of God." Rather, the reference he would seek remains subordinated by the self-citation in his discourse which keeps returning language to the confines of its own utterance. His voice, therefore, is like the narrator's, occluding a writtenness it would seek to transform into speech.

It will be apparent by now in my own references to the occlusion and confinement of the oralized form of the book in Theseus' argument that another semiology is at work in this poem, and it qualifies further the alignment with paganism. Theseus himself gives it to us when he says, astonishingly in the context of encouraging his listeners, that we must all stop grumbling if we would escape "out of this foule prisoun of this lyf" (3061). As at least one other reader has noted, we do not have to look far for shadows of the prison house in what Theseus says.[34] His speech on order is full of "chains" and "bonds," even when we least expect them, as in the "progressiouns" and "successiouns" keeping all things in order (3013–14). Trying to lead us out of prison, Theseus keeps implying, as the knights said earlier, that the world is a version of it. But so also is his own language linked to the image of the chain when he asks: "What may I conclude of this longe *serye*?" (3067). The argument for order, though he knows it not, is itself imprisoning; and thus this devastating image takes up residence also with the writing hidden within. The argument for pagan fame in a person's good name is an oral ideal that locks up freedom as an unreadable text locks up its *sentence*. Paganism is an indecipherable book in the *Knight's Tale*, and nowhere more bindingly than in Theseus' argument for a way out of jail.

When he turns to speaking about how everyone listening may "departen from this place," the prison of the unread text confines him still. He says:

> "I rede that we make of sorwes two
> O parfit joye, lastynge everemo." (3070–71)

No one misses the incongruity of these sentiments after so much talk about how no joy lasts forever, nothing does. Yet the periphrasis and chiasmus are very odd here. Theseus does not name the two sorrows (Emelye's loss of Arcite and Palamoun's loss of Emelye) or the one joy (marriage) because he reaches for the eloquence of balance in chiasmus

---

[34] Kolve, *Chaucer and the Imagery of Narrative*, pp. 142 ff., sees this imagery as an extension of the metaphor of the prison garden earlier in the poem, not as a reflection on the language of argument in the speech itself.

(sorrow / two—one / joy); but he is still numbering and counting and squaring off items in series as he did before. Chaining is a factor of the occluded writing in the passage, and occlusion is precisely the final note of his decision. "And looketh now, wher moost sorwe is herinne" (3073). The most sorrow in this place (the parliamentary congress) rests in the bosoms of Palamoun and Emelye. But the other sorrow "her-inne," the one Theseus would encompass within the order of pagan fame, goes completely unnoticed—as hidden finally as the soul of its hero is lost somewhere in an unreadable register, unexplained by the philosophy of its consolation.

No Word Bitwene

That the narrator-Knight finds in Theseus a model of speaking which he himself would emulate is particularly pressing in the epilogue of the poem; for here the narrator would read a Christian gloss into the pagan ceremony of marriage. He has been listening well to his hero, but as hearing has been his principal experience of the word earlier, so it is again. He is particularly taken by the image of *binding* in Theseus' speech, just concluded. And when he cites it for his audience, it carries the limitation from its previous context in the prison of unread inscription. The narrator refers the joining of Palamoun and Emelye "by hond" to the "bond" that Christian pilgrims "highte matrimoigne or mariage" (3093–95). He is reading and interpreting the scene and his own language in a manner reminiscent of the medieval mythographer trained to read the events of the pagan world as "words" capable of forecasting Christian values. The narrator's response seems wonderfully symmetrical, as it appears to reverse the unreadability of the pagan tablets and registers cited earlier in the poem. Here the pagan story *is* read by a Christian teller—and read with the profoundest of Christian lessons.

But in truth his reading is strained, as any audience must feel when the narrator calls upon the God of Jesus Christ:

> . . . that al this wyde world hath wroght,
> Sende hym his love that hath it deere abooght. (3099–3100)

Theseus had just identified the creator of the universe with the "Firste Moevere" whom he called "Juppiter" (3035). By no stretch of the imagination can that planet-deity be synonymous with the God who sent his love into the world by purchasing it dearly in self-sacrifice. The connection from pagan to Christian is an afterthought, and we

hear the simplicity of it in the formulaic diction, phrasing, and sentiment of the last lines of the poem. Palamoun is now "in alle wele":

> Lyvynge in blisse, in richesse, and in heele,
> And Emelye hym loveth so tendrely,
> And he hire serveth so gentilly,
> That nevere was ther no worde hem bitwene,
> Of jalousie or any oother teene. (3101–3106)

Large abstract nouns may be appropriate to a conclusion, but the effect
of them here is to abstract feeling from the event of marriage in which
feeling should be everything. The narrator is pressing to close, but the
strain of his "*so* tendrely" and "*so* gentily" divide word from experience
at the moment when he would join them. Love exists in name only in
this epilogue, as distant from the heart of the bridal couple as Emelye's
"wommanly pitee" is distant from the Love of God in the narrator's
prayer (3082).

In short, there is precious little demonstrable love between the partners, at least not the kind the narrator would want to sacramentalize.
And he almost says as much when he comments that jealousy and
sorrow completely disappeared from their lives—not a "worde" of
such feelings was left "bitwene" them. Many medieval romances end
this way; we should not expect heady metaphysical reflection in conclusion. But the absence of the word of "pain between" is awfully
reminiscent of the lost "sorrow herein." Where *is* the word of love in
this marriage, and why has it so swiftly forgotten the sorrow in which
it originated? The "no word" between the marital partners is not unlike
the unreadable word of pagan inscription written in the texts that
shadow this narrative throughout. Thus the narrator closes his tale as he
began it, in a voice that passes over its own citation of an all-important
writing. He is certainly not feigning exclusion this time. But he no less
obscures the loss *herein* when he concludes that his tale has explained
it with every breath of speech. As Theseus would talk "withouten any
repplicacioun" only to lose sight of the reply his discourse makes to
itself, so too does the narrator: his affirmation that no word of contention was to be heard between the partners conceals a most audible and
readable reply as the language of the epilogue circles back upon itself
with the haunting realization that no word here, in all the abstractions
and formulary phrases, replicates either the death of Arcite or that
other death which bought love so dearly for this world.[35]

[35] Cf. Aers, *Chaucer, Langland and the Creative Imagination*, pp. 194–95, on "order,"
"necessity," and "love" as empty abstractions in this speech.

Poetry and Society

I have been arguing that the *Knight's Tale* is not an ironic satire on the discourse of its narrator or the principal character, Theseus. Rather, it explores the silence or blindness of their voices, the gap between what voice says about another person, text, or world and what it says about itself. This separation is rendered explicitly in the poem as a split between oral and written discourse, and thus I have referred to the metalanguage of the text as a writing unread by its speaker. In the most fundamental sense, Chaucer has exposed the writtenness of writing as the poem in hand, a book of voices already written. Every reader comes into possession of the "recited" nature of Chaucer's poetry. But my argument has been that he begins the *Canterbury Tales* with a poem that probes the implications of the differentiation inherent in every reading, oral or silent. By singling out writing as something other than voice, Chaucer has reacted sharply to medieval literacy as well as to the relation of oral and written language in the sociopolitical context of his time.

In the *Knight's Tale*, the narrator quite specifically forecloses scrutiny of pagan texts, and that gesture is repeated, though far more subtly, in the apparently innocent functions of *occultatio*. The massive extension of this trope in the poem comes to signify the capacity of voice to compromise the self-discovery of its own utterance. Even in the powerful speech of Theseus at the end, the argument for metaphysical order turns around inevitably to become the order of syntax and diction in the *series* of points argued for consolation in the face of loss. And his sovereignty of sentence is no less political than grammatical.

Such a foreclosure is not unusual, when we recall its occurrences in medieval philosophy and politics. It is to be found particularly in advice from literates about the visual images of manuscripts. Literacy itself had a strong oral cast. Small wonder, then, that theologians should worry about giving away too much of the power in their own voice by allowing the translation of Latin, or that politicians should take such liberties with the written word. The border between the two channels of language was paper thin. Why not, therefore, dispense with the law when it suited the purposes of powerful voices in parliament? So what if it threw to the wind the inherited rights of kings? Voice was a kind of First Mover, especially *noble* voice, whether it issued from pulpit, lectern, or parliament. Writing was its obedient servant, a mere echo of its dominion. How could it possibly so extricate itself as to confront its own speaker with the audacity of self-discovery? The order of knowledge and the order of the state—as we hear from the mouth of Theseus—could never proceed in the face of such a reversal of the way things had always been. And that is why the oral habits and customs of a distant past still held on so subtly in a world making increasing use of documents and books. Literacy was a deeply political infrastructure of late medieval culture.

As a writer on the scene of government for years, Chaucer did not fail to respond to the political implications of language. We do not have his thoughts on the matter; but we do have his reflection on the sovereign voice of Theseus and the narrator-Knight's imitation of it. Both of them assume the neutrality of their own disposition, and that attitude is a perfect insight into the putative innocence of the relation between voice and letter in medieval literacy from at least the time of Augustine. By thus qualifying the neutrality of voice, by revealing that the benign gestures of the narrator leave an awful lot unsaid and unaccounted for, Chaucer has in effect delivered a statement about sovereign discourse in the politics of his time.

He suggests, with Palamoun, that the apparently benign order of "governance" executes an indecipherable text when its signs are at best arbitrary and at worst tyrannical. England is governed by an unread-able book. And it is not held in the hands of a monarch, not in the 1380s, but by a "parlement" whose vacillations are inscrutable. That body is a pagan interpreter of an adamant text to the extent that it has failed to realize its own blindness—not unlike all those cultures outside the Christian pale which have historically denied its precepts. But if governance is a matter of the blind leading the blind, it is so because dominion has resided in language in a way that has always been latent or suppressed. The capacity to foreclose or compromise the difference of writing—the *orality* of a text—bears witness to the paradox that dominion is a creation of language. It may be inherited by divine right, as Wyclif believed, or it may be synonymous with an originary intui-tion, as Ockham thought. But Chaucer puts before us a different propo-sition in the *Knight's Tale*.

His poem is a bold exploration of the cryptic allusion to contempo-rary politics early in Part I:

> ". . . at the kynges court, my brother
> Ech man for hymself, ther is noon oother." (1181–82)

No other what? No other rule but the squabble of self-interest? No other truth about rule than that pitiful anticlimax? No other rule but the king's? One thing is sure: Richard did not have full control of England at the time of this poem, and Chaucer's membership in the king's circle, among his other associations, put him in the know about how much the machinations outside the royal chamber counted for in governing the realm. Government, in other words, is the rule of what each man can claim for himself, at parliament no less than the court of the king. Its worst consequences are obvious, for example, in the tragic events of 1388. After that outrageous year, old feudal mythologies of venerating power in an unimpeachable origin have little meaning.

But as much as Chaucer's anticlimactic lines derogate the order of government in England, they also look shamelessly at what feudalism had always occluded, that dominion consists in displacement, and nowhere more obviously than in the displacement of a voice which knows nothing other than its own utterance. Writing, however compromised, was the irritant reply of that self-protecting dominion, and it was ventured in various ways, such as Wyclif's fundamentalism and Ockham's epistemology. But neither of them went as far as the *Gawain*-poet and Chaucer. The poets could take more risks with the sources of power in learning and government; they could even invent them; they could go so far as to say that the origin of language was something which language itself could invent. Ockham himself would never say that, and Wyclif would recoil at the thought.

Yet by embracing openly the seemingly endless self-reflexivity of language, neither Chaucer or the *Gawain*-poet closes off poetry into the prison of an abyss, unmoored from history. Both of them return language to the truth that history (particularly the chronicle history of Edward III and Richard II) had quite forgotten about itself—that constructions of a pagan past or Christian present must confront the language of their own composition. Only then will the dominion inherent within know more fully the range of its implications.

BIBLIOGRAPHY

Ackerman, Robert W. "Gawain's Shield: Penitential Doctrine in *Gawain and the Green Knight*." *Anglia* 76 (1958): 254–65.

Acta inter Bonifacium VIII, Benedictum XI, Clementem V et Philippum, Pulchrum regem Christianum. Troyes, 1614.

Adam of Usk. *Chronicon Adae de Usk, 1377–1421*. 2d ed. Edited and translated by Edward Maunde Thompson. London, 1904.

Adams, Marilyn M. "Intuitive Cognition, Certainty and Skepticism in William of Ockham." *Traditio* 26 (1970): 389–98.

———. "Ockham on Identity and Distinction." *Franciscan Studies* 36 (1976): 5–74.

———. *William Ockham*. 2 vols. Notre Dame, Ind., 1987.

Aers, David. *Chaucer, Langland and the Creative Imagination*. London, 1980.

———. *Community, Gender, and Individual Identity: English Writing 1360–1430*. London, 1988.

Alféri, Pierre. *Guillaume D'Ockham: Le Singulier*. Paris, 1989.

Alford, John A. "The Grammatical Metaphor: A Survey of Its Use in the Middle Ages." *Speculum* 57 (1982): 728–60.

———. "Literature and Law in Medieval England." *Publications of the Modern Language Association of America* 92 (1977): 941–51.

Alvarus Pelagius. *Collirium adversus Hereses Novas*. Edited by R. Scholz. In *Streitschriften* 2:491–514.

Amsler, Mark E. "Literary Theory and the Genres of Middle English Literature." *Genre* 13 (1980): 389–96.

Annales Ricardi Secundi. In *Johannis de Trokelowe, et Henrici de Blaneforde, monachorum S. Albani*. Edited by Henry T. Riley. Rolls Series. London, 1866.

Anonimalle Chronicle, 1333–1381. Edited by V. H. Galbraith. Manchester, 1927.

Anselm of Canterbury. *De grammatico*. Edited by D. P. Henry. Notre Dame, Ind., 1964.

———. *Monologion*. Edited by P. Franciscus S. Schmitt. Stuttgart, 1964.

———. *Proslogion*. Edited by P. Franciscus S. Schmitt. Stuttgart, 1961.

Aquinas, Thomas. *Summa Theologiae*. Vol.12. Edited and translated by Paul T. Durbin. London and New York, 1968 (Blackfriars ed.).

Aristotle. *Poetics*. Translated by S. H. Butcher as *Aristotle's Theory of Poetry and Fine Art*. 4th ed. New York, 1955.

Arthur, Ross G. *Medieval Sign Theory and "Sir Gawain and the Green Knight."* Toronto, 1987.

Aston, Margaret. "Devotional Literacy." In *Lollards and Reformers*, pp. 101–33.

———. "Lollards and Images." In *Lollards and Reformers*, pp. 135–92.

———. "Lollardy and Literacy." *History* 62 (1977): 347–71.

———. *Lollards and Reformers: Images and Literacy in Late Medieval Religion*. London, 1984.

————. "Wyclif and the Vernacular." In Hudson and Wilks, eds., pp. 281–330.

Asworth, E., ed. *Tradition of Medieval Logic and Speculative Grammar from Anselm to the End of the 17th Century: A Bibliography from 1836 Onwards*. Toronto, 1978.

Auerbach, Erich. *Literary Language and Its Public in Late Latin Antiquity and in the Middle Ages*. Translated by Ralph Manheim. New York, 1965. From *Literatursprache und Publikum in der lateinischen Spätantike und im Mittelalter* (Bern, 1958).

————. *Mimesis: The Representation of Reality in Western Literature*. Translated by Willard Trask. Garden City, N.Y., 1957. From *Mimesis: Dargestellte Wirklichkeit in der abendländischen Literatur* (Bern, 1946).

Augustine. *Confessionum libri XIII*. Edited by Martin Skutella. Rev. Lucas Verheijen. Corpus Christianorum Series Latina, 27. Brepols, 1981.

————. *De magistro*. Edited by K. D. Daur. Corpus Christianorum Series Latina, 29. Brepols, 1970.

Auksi, P. "Wyclif's Sermons and the Plain Style." *Archiv für Reformationgeschichte* 66 (1975): 5–23.

Baker, Geoffrey le (of Swinbrook). *Chronicon*. Edited by Edward M. Thompson. Oxford, 1889.

Barber, Richard, ed. and trans. *The Life and Campaigns of the Black Prince*. London, 1979.

Barg, M. A. "The Villeins of Ancient Demesne." In *Studi in Memoria di Federigo Melis* 1:213–37. 5 vols. Naples, 1978.

Barnes, Harry Elmer. *A History of Historical Writing*. 2d. ed. New York, 1962.

Barron, Caroline M. "The Tyranny of Richard II." *Bulletin of the Institute of Historical Research* 41 (1968): 1–18.

Barthes, Roland. *Mythologies*. Translated by Annette Lavers. New York, 1972. From *Mythologies* (Paris, 1957; rpt. 1970).

Bartlett, Robert. *Gerald of Wales, 1146–1223*. Oxford, 1982.

Baugh, Albert C. "Improvisation in the Middle English Romances." *Proceedings of the American Philosophical Society* 103 (1959): 418–54.

Bäuml, Franz H. "Medieval Texts and Two Theories of Oral-Formulaic Composition: A Proposal for a Third." *New Literary History* 16 (1984): 31–49.

————. "The Theory of Oral-Formulaic Composition and the Written Medieval Text." In Foley, ed., pp. 29–45.

————. "Varieties and Consequences of Medieval Literacy and Illiteracy." *Speculum* 55 (1980): 237–63.

Baxter, J. H. and C. Johnson, eds. *Medieval Latin Word-List*. London, 1950.

Bean, J. M. W. *From Lord to Patron: Lordship in Late Medieval England*. Philadelphia, 1989.

Bellamy, John G. *Law of Treason in England in the Later Middle Ages*. Cambridge, 1970.

Bennett, Michael J. *Community, Class and Careerism: Cheshire and Lancashire Society in the Age of "Sir Gawain and the Green Knight."* Cambridge Studies in Medieval Life and Thought, 18. Cambridge, 1983.

————. "*Sir Gawain and the Green Knight* and the Literary Achievement of the

North-West Midlands: The Historical Background." *Journal of Medieval History* 5 (1979): 63–88.

Benson, Larry D. *Art and Tradition in "Sir Gawain and the Green Knight."* New Brunswick, 1965.

———. "The Literary Character of Anglo-Saxon Formulaic Poetry." *Publications of the Modern Language Association of America* 81 (1966): 334–41.

Bernard of Clairvaux. *S. Bernardi opera.* Edited by J. Leclercq and H. M. Rochais. 8 vols. Rome, 1957–77.

Bersuire, Pierre (Petrus Berchorius). *Opera omnia.* 6 vols. Cologne, 1730–31.

Bird, Ruth. *The Turbulent London of Richard II.* London, 1949.

Blanch, Robert J. "Imagery of Binding in Fits One and Two of *Sir Gawain and the Green Knight.*" *Studia Neuphilologica* 54 (1982): 53–60.

———. *Sir Gawain and the Green Knight: A Reference Guide.* Troy, N.Y., 1985.

Bloch, Marc. *Feudal Society.* Translated by L. A. Manyon. 2 vols. London, 1961.

Bloch, R. Howard. *Etymologies and Genealogies: A Literary Anthropology of the French Middle Ages.* Chicago, 1983.

Bloom, Allan D. *The Closing of the American Mind.* New York, 1987.

Blum, Jerome. *The End of the Old Order in Rural Europe.* Princeton, 1978.

Boehner, Philotheus. *Collected Articles on Ockham.* Edited by E. M. Buytaert. Franciscan Institute Publications 12. St. Bonaventure, N.Y., 1958. Includes Boehner's previously published essays: "The Metaphysics of William Ockham," pp. 373–99 (1947–48); "The Notitia Intuitiva of Non-Existents According to William Ockham," pp. 268–300 (1943); "Ockham's Political Ideas," pp. 442–68 (1943); "Ockham's Theory of Signification," pp. 201–32 (1946); "Ockham's Theory of Supposition and the Notion of Truth," pp. 232–67 (1946).

———. "The Realistic Conceptualism of William of Ockham." *Traditio* 4 (1946): 307–35.

Bois, Guy. *The Crisis of Feudalism: Economy and Society in Eastern Normandy c. 1300–1500.* Cambridge, 1984.

Borroff, Marie. *Sir Gawain and the Green Knight: A Stylistic and Metrical Study.* New Haven, 1962.

Bowden, Betsy. *Chaucer Aloud: The Varieties of Textual Interpretation.* Philadelphia, 1987.

Brandt, William J. *The Shape of Medieval History: Studies in Modes of Perception.* New Haven, 1966.

Breisach, Ernst, ed. *Classical Rhetoric and Medieval Historiography.* Studies in Medieval Culture, 19. Kalamazoo, Mich., 1985.

Bresslau, Harry. *Handbuch der Urkundenlehre.* 2d ed. 2 vols. Leipzig, 1912–1931.

Brewer, Derek. "Orality and Literacy in Chaucer." In *Mündlichkeit und Schriftlichkeit im englischen Mittelalter,* pp. 85–119. Tübingen, 1988.

———. *Tradition and Innovation in Chaucer.* London, 1982.

Bridbury, A. R. *Economic Growth: England in the Later Middle Ages.* London, 1962.

Bronson, Bertrand H. *In Search of Chaucer.* Toronto, 1960.

The Brut, or the Chronicles of England. Edited by F. W. D. Brie. 2 vols. Early English Text Society, 131 and 136. London, 1906–1908.

Burgess, Glyn S. and A. D. Deyermond et al., eds. *Court and Poet: Selected Proceedings of the Third Congress of the International Courtly Literature Society.* Liverpool, 1981.

Burrow, John A. "Bards, Minstrels, and Men of Letters." In Daiches and Thorlby, eds., pp. 347–70.

——. *A Reading of "Sir Gawain and the Green Knight."* London, 1965.

——. *Ricardian Poetry: Chaucer, Gower, Langland and the "Gawain"-Poet.* Yale, 1971.

Cable, Thomas. *The English Alliterative Tradition.* Philadelphia, 1991.

Caenegem, R. C. *Royal Writs in England from the Conquest to Glanvill: Studies in the Early History of the Common Law.* Publications of the Seldon Society, vol. 77. London, 1959.

Calderwood, James L. *Shakespearean Metadrama: The Argument of the Play in "Titus Andronicus," "Love's Labor's Lost," "Romeo and Juliet," "A Midsummer Night's Dream," and "Richard II."* Minneapolis, 1971.

Callus, D. A. "The Oxford Career of Robert Grosseteste." *Oxoniensia* 10 (1945): 42–72.

Camargo, Martin. "Oral Traditional Structure in *Sir Gawain and the Green Knight.*" In Foley, ed., 121–37.

Camille, Michael. "The Book of Signs: Writing and Visual Difference in Gothic Manuscript Illumination." *Word and Image* 1–2 (1985): 133–48.

——. *The Gothic Idol: Ideology and Image-Making in Medieval Art.* New York and Cambridge, 1990.

——. "The Language of Images." In *The Age of Chivalry: Art in Plantagenet England, 1200–1400,* ed. Jonathan Alexander and Paul Binski, pp. 33–40. London, 1987.

——. "Visual Signs of the Sacred Page: Books in the *Biblia moralisée.*" *Word and Image* 5 (1989): 111–30.

Carruthers, Mary J. *The Book of Memory: A Study of Memory in Medieval Culture.* Cambridge, 1990.

Catto, Jeremy. "Andrew Horn: Law and History in Fourteenth-Century England." In Davis and Wallace-Hadrill, eds., pp. 367–92. Oxford, 1981.

Chambers, R. W. "The Continuity of English Prose." In *Harpsfield's Life of More,* ed. E. V. Hitchcock. Early English Text Society, 186. London, 1932.

Chambers, R. W. and Marjorie Daunt. *A Book of London English, 1384–1425.* London, 1931.

Chandos, John, the herald of. *The Life of the Black Prince.* Translated by M. K. Pope and E. C. Lodge. Oxford, 1910 (rpt., New York, 1974).

——. *La vie du Prince Noir.* Edited by Diana B. Tyson. Beihefte zur Zeitschrift für Romanische Philologie, 147. Tübingen, 1975.

Chaucer, Geoffrey. *The Riverside Chaucer.* 3d ed. Edited by Larry D. Benson. Boston, 1987.

Chaytor, H. J. *From Script to Print: An Introduction to Medieval Literature.* Cambridge, 1945.

Chenu, Marie-Dominique. *Nature, Man, and Society in the Twelfth Century:*

Essays on New Theological Perspectives in the Latin West. Translated by Jerome Taylor and Lester K. Little. Chicago, 1968.

Chrimes, S. B. "Richard II's Questions to the Judges, 1387." *Law Quarterly Review* 72 (1956): 365–90.

Christianson, Paul. "Chaucer's Literacy." *Chaucer Review* 11 (1976): 112–27.

———. "Evidence for the Study of London's Late Medieval Manuscript-Book Trade." In Griffiths and Pearsall, eds., pp. 87–108.

Chronique de la traïson et mort de Richart Deux, roy Dengleterre. Edited and translated by Benjamin Williams. London, 1846.

Cicero. *De oratore libri tres.* Edited by Augustus S. Wilkins. 1892 (rpt., Amsterdam, 1962).

Cipolla, Carlo M. *Literacy and Development in the West.* Baltimore, 1969.

Clanchy, Michael T. "England in the Thirteenth Century: Power and Knowledge." In *England in the Thirteenth Century: Proceedings of the 1984 Harlaxton Symposium,* ed. W. M. Ormrod. Suffolk, 1985.

———. *From Memory to Written Record: England, 1066–1307.* Cambridge, 1979.

———. "Looking Back from the Invention of Printing." In *Literacy in Historical Perspective,* ed. Daniel P. Resnick. Washington, D.C., 1983.

Coleman, Janet. *Ancient and Medieval Memories: Studies in the Reconstruction of the Past.* Cambridge, 1992.

———. "*Dominium* in Thirteenth- and Fourteenth-Century Political Thought and Its Seventeenth-Century Heirs." *Political Studies* 33 (1985): 73–100.

———. *Medieval Readers and Writers: 1350–1400.* New York, 1982.

Cook, Robert G. "The Play-Element in *Sir Gawain and the Green Knight.*" *Tulane Studies in English* 13 (1963): 5–31.

Courtenay, William J. Review of *William Ockham,* by M. Adams. *Speculum* 64 (1989): 641–43.

———. "The Reception of Ockham's Thought in Fourteenth-Century England." In Hudson and Wilks, eds., pp. 89–107.

———. *Schools and Scholars in Fourteenth-Century England.* Princeton, 1987.

Covington, Michael A. *Syntactic Theory in the High Middle Ages: Modistic Models of Sentence Structure.* Cambridge Studies in Linguistics, 39. Cambridge, 1984.

Crane, Susan. *Insular Romance: Politics, Faith, and Culture in Anglo-Norman and Middle English Literature.* Los Angeles, 1986.

———. "Medieval Romance and Feminine Difference in *The Knight's Tale.*" *Studies in the Age of Chaucer* 12 (1990): 47–63.

Créton, Jean. *Histoire du Roy d'Angleterre Richard.* Edited and translated by John Webb. *Archaeologia* 20 (1824): 1–423.

Crosby, Ruth. "Chaucer and the Custom of Oral Delivery." *Speculum* 13 (1938): 413–32.

———. "Oral Delivery in the Middle Ages." *Speculum* 11 (1936): 88–110.

Curschmann, Michael. "Oral Poetry in Mediaeval English, French, and German Literature: Some Notes on Recent Research." *Speculum* 42 (1967): 36–52.

Curtius, Ernst Robert. *European Literature and the Latin Middle Ages.* Translated by Willard R. Trask. New York, 1963.

278 BIBLIOGRAPHY

Cuttino, G. P. *English Medieval Diplomacy*. Bloomington, Ind., 1985.

Daiches, David and Anthony Thorlby, eds. *Literature and Western Civilization: The Medieval World*. London, 1973.

Damascene, John. *Institutiones Grammaticae*. Edited by A. L. G. Krehl. Leipzig, 1820.

Damiati, Marino. "Gugliemo d'Ockham: Povertà e potere. I. Il problema della povertà evangelica e francescana ne se. XIII e XIV. Origine del pensiero politico d. G. d'Ockham." *Studi Francescani* 75 (1978): 1–516.

Davenport, W. A. *The Art of the "Gawain"-Poet*. London, 1978.

Davis, R. H. C. and J. M. Wallace-Hadrill, eds. *The Writing of History in the Middle Ages: Essays Presented to Richard William Southern*. Oxford, 1981.

Day, S. J. *Intuitive Cognition: A Key to the Significance of the Later Scholastics*. Franciscan Institute Publications. St. Bonaventure, N.Y., 1947.

De Man, Paul. *The Resistance to Theory*. Minneapolis, 1986.

De Rijk, Lambertus M. *Logica Modernorum: A Contribution to the History of Early Terminist Logic*. 2 vols. Assen, 1962–1967.

Derrida, Jacques. *Of Grammatology*. Translated by Gayatri C. Spivak. Baltimore, 1976. Originally published as *De la grammatologie* (Paris, 1967).

Dialogus de Scaccario. Edited by Charles Johnson. London, 1950.

Dobson, Richard Barrie. *The Peasants' Revolt of 1381*. London, 1970.

Dronke, Peter. *Poetic Individuality in the Middle Ages: New Departures in Poetry, 1000–1150*. Oxford, 1970.

Du Boulay, F. R. H. *An Age of Ambition: English Society in the Later Middle Ages*. London, 1970.

Duby, Georges. *The Early Growth of the European Economy: Warriors and Peasants from the Seventh to the Twelfth Century*. Translated by Howard B. Clarke. Ithaca, N.Y., 1974.

———. *The Three Orders: Feudal Society Imagined*. Translated by Arthur Goldhammer. Chicago, 1980.

Du Cange, Carlo. *Glossarium mediae et infimae latinitatis*. 10 vols. Paris, 1883–1887.

Duggan, Hoyt N. "The Role of Formulas in the Dissemination of a Middle English Alliterative Romance." *Studies in Bibliography* 29 (1976): 265–88.

Duggan, Lawrence G. "Was Art Really the 'Book of the Illiterate'?" *Word and Image* 5 (1989): 227–51.

Duls, Louisa D. *Richard II in the Early Chronicles*. Studies in English Literature, 79. The Hague, 1975.

Dumézil, Georges. *The Destiny of the Warrior*. Translated by Alf Hiltebeitel. Chicago, 1970.

Dyer, Christopher. "The Social and Economic Background to the Rural Revolt of 1381." In Hilton and Aston, eds., pp. 9–42.

Edwards, A. G. S. "The Influence and Audience of the *Polychronicon*." *Proceedings of the Leeds Philosophical and Literary Society* 17, no. 6 (1980): 113–19.

Edwards, A. S. G. and Derek Pearsall. "The Manuscripts of the Major English Poetic Texts." In Griffiths and Pearsall, eds., pp. 257–78.

Egidius Romanus. *De Ecclesiastica Potestate*. Edited by R. Scholz. Weimar, 1929.

Eisenstein, Elizabeth. *The Printing Press as an Agent of Change: Communications and Cultural Transformations in Early Modern Europe*. 2 vols. Cambridge, 1979.

Elliott, John R., Jr. "Richard II and the Medieval." *Renaissance Papers 1965* (1966): 25–34.

Erzgraber, Willi. "Problems of Oral and Written Transmission as Reflected in Chaucer's *House of Fame*." In *Historical and Editorial Studies*, ed. Mary-Jo Arn and Hanneke Wirtjes, pp. 113–28. Groningen, 1985.

Eulogium Historiarum sive temporis. Edited by F. S. Haydon. 3 vols. Rolls Series. London, 1858–65.

Evans, G. R. "Wyclif on Literal and Metaphorical." In Hudson and Wilks, eds., pp. 259–66.

Everett, Dorothy. *Essays on Middle English Liteature*. Oxford, 1955.

Faith, Rosamond. "The 'Great Rumour' of 1377 and Peasant Ideology." In Hilton and Aston, eds., pp. 43–73.

Febure, L. and H.-J. Martin. *The Coming of the Book*. Translated by D. Gerard. London, 1976.

Ferguson, C. A. "Diglossia." *Word* 15 (1959): 325–40.

Ferguson, Margaret W. "Saint Augustine's Region of Unlikeness: The Crossing of Exile and Language." *Georgia Review* 29 (1975): 842–64.

Figgis, John Neville. *The Theory of the Divine Right of Kings* (Cambridge, 1896). 2d ed.: *The Divine Right of Kings*. Cambridge, 1922 (rpt., New York, 1965).

Finlayson, John. "Definitions of Middle English Romance." *Chaucer Review* 15 (1980): 44–62, 168–81.

———. "The Expectations of Romance in *Sir Gawain and the Green Knight*." *Genre* 12 (1979): 1–24.

Finnegan, Ruth. *Literacy and Orality: Studies in the Technology of Communication*. Oxford, 1988.

———. *Oral Poetry: Its Nature, Significance, and Social Context*. Cambridge, 1977.

Fisher, John H. "Chaucer and the Written Language." In Heffernan, ed., pp. 237–51. Knoxville, 1985.

Fisher, Sheila. "Leaving Morgan Aside: Women, History, and Revisionism in *Sir Gawain and the Green Knight*." In *The Passing of Arthur: New Essays in Arthurian Tradition*, ed. Christopher Baswell and William Sharpe, pp. 129–51. New York, 1988.

———. "Taken Men and Token Women in *Sir Gawain and the Green Knight*." In *Seeking the Woman in Late Medieval and Renaissance Writings*, ed. Sheila Fisher and Janet E. Halley, pp. 71–105. Knoxville, 1989.

Fitzgerald, M. J. "Supposition and Signification: An Examination of Ockham's Theory of Reference." *Dissertation Abstracts International* 43, no. 4 (1982): 1172A.

Fleishman, Suzanne. "Philology, Linguistics, and the Discourse of the Medieval Text." *Speculum* 65 (1990): 19–37.

Foley, John Miles, ed. *Comparative Research on Oral Traditions: A Memorial for Milman Parry*. Columbus, Ohio, 1987.

Foucault, Michel. *The Order of Things: An Archeology of the Human Sciences*. New York, 1971.

Fradenberg, Louise. "Spectacular Fictions: The Body Politic in Chaucer and Dunbar." *Poetics Today* 5 (1984): 493–517.

Froissart, Jean. *The Chronicle of Froissart, translated out of French by Sir John Bourchier Lord Berners.* 7 vols. London, 1903 (rpt., New York, 1967).

———. *Oeuvres complètes de Froissart: Chroniques.* Edited by Dervyn de Lettenhove. 25 vols. Brussels, 1868–1877.

Funkenstein, Amos. "Periodization and Self-Understanding in the Middle Ages and Early Modern Times." *Medievalia et Humanistica*, n.s., 5 (1974): 3–23.

Gabel, L. C. *Benefit of Clergy in England in the Later Middle Ages.* Smith College Studies in History, 14. Northampton, Mass., 1929.

Gál, Gedeon. "William of Ockham Died 'Impenitent' in April 1347." *Franciscan Studies* 42, no. 20 (1986): 90–95.

Galbraith, V. H. *Anonimale Chronicle.* Manchester, 1927.

———. "The Literacy of the Medieval English Kings." *Proceedings of the British Academy* 21 (1935): 201–38.

———. *The Making of Domesday Book.* Oxford, 1961.

———. "Nationality and Language in Medieval England." *Transactions of the Royal Historical Society*, 4th ser., 23 (1941): 113–28.

———. "A New Life of Richard II." *History* 26 (1942): 223–39.

———. "Richard II in Fact and Fiction." *Listener* 51 (1954): 691–92.

Ganim, John M. *Chaucerian Theatricality.* Princeton, 1990.

———. "Disorientation, Style and Consciousness in *Sir Gawain and the Green Knight*." *Publications of the Modern Language Association of America* 91 (1976): 376–84.

———. *Style and Consciousness in Middle English Narrative.* Princeton, 1983.

Gashé, Rodolphe. *The Tain of the Mirror: Derrida and the Philosophy of Reflection.* Cambridge, 1986.

Gellrich, Jesse M. "Deconstructing Allegory." *Genre* 18 (1985): 197–213.

———. *The Idea of the Book in the Middle Ages: Language Theory, Mythology, and Fiction.* Ithaca, N.Y., 1985.

———. "Orality, Literacy, and Crisis in the Later Middle Ages." *Philological Quarterly* 67 (1988): 461–73, 480.

Geoffrey of Monmouth. *The Historia Regnum Britannie of Geoffrey of Monmouth: The First Variant Version.* Edited by Neil Wright. Vol. 2. Cambridge, 1988.

Gilson, Étienne. *History of Christian Philosophy in the Middle Ages.* New York, 1955.

Given-Wilson, Chris. *The Royal Household and the King's Affinity: Service, Politics, and Finance in England, 1360–1413.* New Haven, 1986.

Gless, Darryl J. and Barbara H. Smith, eds. "The Politics of Liberal Education." *South Atlantic Quarterly* 89 (1990).

Goldast, M. *Monarchia Sancti Romani Imperii.* 3 vols., Hanover, 1611; Frankfurt, 1614, 1613 (rpt., Graz, 1960).

Göller, Karl H., ed. *The Alliterative "Morte Arthure": A Reassessment of the Poem.* Cambridge, 1981.

Goody, Jack. *The Domestication of the Savage Mind.* Cambridge, 1977.

———. *The Interface Between the Written and the Oral.* Cambridge, 1987.

————. *The Logic of Writing and the Organization of Society*. Cambridge, 1986.

————, ed. *Literacy in Traditional Societies*. New York, l968.

Goody, Jack and Ian Watt. "The Consequences of Literacy." *Comparative Studies in Society and History* (1962–63): 304–45.

Gottfried, Robert S. *The Black Death: Natural and Human Disaster in Medieval Europe*. New York, 1983.

Gower, John. *Vox Clamantis*. In *The Complete Works of John Gower*, ed. G. C. Macaulay. 4 vols. Oxford, 1899–1902.

Graff, Harvey J. *The Labyrinths of Literacy: Reflection on Literacy Past and Present*. Philadelphia, 1987.

————. *The Legacies of Literacy: Continuities and Contradictions in Western Culture and Society*. Bloomington, Ind., 1987.

————. *Literacy in History: An Interdisciplinary Research Bibliography*. New York, 1981.

————. *The Literacy Myth: Literacy and Social Structurre in the Nineteenth-Century City*. New York, 1979.

Gransden, Antonia. *Historical Writing in England*. Vol. 2, *Ca. 1307 to the Early Sixteenth Century*. London, 1982.

Graus, F. "Social Utopias in the Middle Ages." *Past and Present* 38 (1967): 3–19.

Green, D. H. "Irony and Medieval Romance." *Forum for Modern Language Studies* 6 (1970): 49–64.

————. "Orality and Reading: The State of Research in Medieval Studies." *Speculum* 65 (1990): 267–80.

Green, Donald C. "The Semantics of Power: *Maistree* and *Soverayntee* in the Canterbury Tales." *Modern Philology* 84 (1986): 18–23.

Green, Richard F. "King Richard's Books Revisited." *Library* 31 (1976): 235–39.

————. *Poets and Princepleasers: Literature and the English Court in the Late Middle Ages*. Toronto, 1980.

Green, Richard H. "Gawain's Shield and the Quest for Perfection." *English Literary History* 29 (1962): 121–39.

Griffith, Richard R. "Bertilak's Lady: The French Background of *Sir Gawain and the Green Knight*." In *Machaut's World: Science and Art in the Fourteenth Century*, ed. Madelaine P. Cosman and Bruce Chandler, pp. 249–66. New York, 1978.

Griffiths, Jeremy and Derek Pearsall, eds. *Book Production and Publishing in Britain, 1375–1475*. Cambridge, 1989.

Guido Terreni. *Quaestio de Magisterio Infallibilis Romani Pontificis*. Edited by B. F. M. Xiberta. In *Opuscula et Textus* 2. Munster, l926.

Haines, Francis D., Jr. "The Tragedy of John of Gaunt." In *Ashland Studies for Shakespeare 1961*, ed. Margery Bailey, pp. 59–73. Ashland, Ore., 1961.

Hanna, Ralph. "Unlocking What's Locked: Gawain's Green Girdle." *Viator* 14 (1983): 289–302.

Hanning, Robert W. "*Beowulf* as Heroic History." *Medievalia et Humanistica*, n.s., 5 (1974): 77–102.

————. "Sir Gawain and the Red Herring: The Perils of Interpretation." In *Acts of Interpretation: The Text in Its Contexts, 700–1600: Essays on Medieval and*

Renaissance Literature in Honor of E. Talbot Donaldson, ed. Mary J. Carruthers and Elizabeth D. Kirk, pp. 5–23. Norman, Okla., 1982.

———. *The Vision of History in Early Britain*. New York, 1966.

Hansen, H. M. "The Peasants' Revolt of 1381 and the Chronicles." *Journal of Medieval History* 6 (1980): 393–415.

Harding, Alan. "The Revolt against the Justices." In Hilton and Aston, eds., pp. 165–93.

Hargreaves, Henry. "Wyclif's Prose." *Essays and Studies*, n.s., 19 (1966): 1–17.

Harwood, Britton J. "*Gawain* and the Gift." *Publications of the Modern Language Association of America* 106 (1991): 483–99.

Havelock, Eric A. *The Literate Revolution in Greece and Its Cultural Consequences*. Princeton, 1982.

———. *A Preface to Plato*. Cambridge, 1963.

———. *When the Muse Learns to Write: Reflections on Orality and Literacy from Antiquity to the Present*. New Haven, 1986.

Heffernan, Thomas J., ed. *The Popular Literature of Medieval England*. Tennessee Studies in Literature, 28. Knoxville, 1985.

Henry, D. P. "The Early History of the *Suppositio*." *Franciscan Studies* (1963): 205–12.

Higden, Ralph. *Polychronicon Ranulphi Higden; together with the English translations of John Trevisa and of an Unknown Writer of the Fifteenth Century*. Vols. 1–2 edited by Churchill Babington. Vols. 3–9 edited by Joseph R. Lumby. Rolls Series. London, 1865–66.

Hill, John M. "Middle English Poets and the World: Notes Toward and Appraisal of Linguistic Consciousness." *Criticism* 16 (1974): 153–69.

Hilton, Rodney H. *Bond Men Made Free: Medieval Peasant Movements and the English Rising of 1381*. New York, 1973.

———. *Class Conflict and the Crisis of Feudalism: Essays in Medieval Social History*. London, 1985.

———. *The English Peasantry in the Later Middle Ages*. London, 1975.

Hilton, Rodney H. and T. H. Aston, eds. *The English Rising of 1381*. Cambridge, 1984.

Hirsch, E. D. *Cultural Literacy: What Every American Needs to Know*. Boston, 1987.

Historia Vitae et Regni Ricardi Secundi, Angliae Regis. Edited by George B. Stow, Jr. Philadelphia, 1977.

Hobbs, J. E. "An Early Press in Canterbury." *Library* 33 (1978): 172.

Hornsby, Joseph Allen. *Chaucer and the Law*. Norman, Okla., 1988.

Howard, Donald R. *The Idea of the "Canterbury Tales."* Berkeley, 1976.

Howard, Donald R. and Christian K. Zacher, eds. *Critical Studies of "Sir Gawain and the Green Knight."* Notre Dame, Ind., 1968.

Hudson, Anne. *Lollards and Their Books*. London, 1985.

———. *The Premature Reformation: Wycliffite Texts and Lollard History*. Oxford, 1988.

———. "Wyclif and the English Language." In Kenny, ed., pp. 85–103.

———, ed. *Selections from English Wycliffite Writings*. Cambridge, 1978.

Hudson, Anne and Michael Wilks, eds. *From Ockham to Wyclif.* Studies in Church History, Subsidia 5. Oxford, 1987.

Hugh of St. Cher. *Opera omnia.* 8 vols. Venice, 1732.

Hugh of St. Victor. *The Didascalion of Hugh of St. Victor: A Medieval Guide to the Arts.* Translated by Jerome Taylor. New York, 1961.

Hult, David F. *Self-Fulfilling Prophecies: Readership and Authority in the First "Roman de la Rose."* New York, 1986.

Hunt, R. W. "Oxford Grammar Masters in the Middle Ages." *Oxford Studies Presented to Daniel Callus,* Oxford Historical Society, n.s., 16 (1964): 163–193.

———. *The Schools and the Cloister: The Life and Writings of Alexander Nequam (1157–1217).* Edited by Margaret Gibson. Oxford, 1984.

Huot, Sylvia. *From Song to Book: The Poetics of Writing in Old French Lyric and Lyrical Narrative Poetry.* Ithaca, N.Y., 1987.

Hutchison, Harold F. *The Hollow Crown: A Life of Richard II.* London, 1961.

———. "Shakespeare and Richard II." *History Today* 11 (1961): 236–44.

James of Viterbo. *De Regimine Christiano.* Edited by H.-X. Arquilliere. In *Le plus ancien traité de l'église: Jacques de Viterbe, De Regimine Christiano (1301–02).* Paris, 1926.

Jankofsky, Klaus P. "Public Executions in England in the Late Middle Ages: The Indignity and Dignity of Death." *Omega* 10 (1979): 43–57.

Jeffrey, David L., ed. *Chaucer and Scriptural Tradition.* Ottowa, 1984.

Joachim of Fiore. *Liber de Concordia Noui ac Veteris Testamenti.* Edited by E. Randolph Daniel. Philadelphia, 1983.

John of Salisbury. *Metalogicon.* Translated by Daniel D. McGarry. Berkeley, 1962.

———. *Metalogicon Libri IIII.* Edited by Clemens C. I. Webb. Oxford, 1929.

———. *Polycraticus.* Edited by Murray F. Markland. New York, 1979.

Jones, James H. "Commonplace and Memorization in the Oral Tradition of the English and Scottish Popular Ballads." *Journal of American Folklore* 74 (1961): 97–112.

Jones, Richard H. *The Royal Policy of Richard II: Absolutism in the Later Middle Ages.* New York, 1968.

Jordan, Robert M. *Chaucer and the Shape of Creation: The Aesthetic Possibilities of Inorganic Structure.* Cambridge, 1967.

Jousse, Marcel. *La Manducation de la parole.* Paris, 1975.

Kaeuper, Richard W. *War, Justice, and Public Order: England and France in the Later Middle Ages.* Oxford, 1988.

Kamps, Ivo. "Magic, Women, and Incest: The Real Challenges in *Sir Gawain and the Green Knight.*" *Exemplaria* 1 (1989): 311–36.

Kantorowicz, E. H. *The King's Two Bodies: A Study in Medieval Political Theology.* Princeton, 1957.

Kaske, R. E. "Holy Church's Speech and the Structure of *Piers Plowman.*" In *Chaucer and Middle English Studies in Honor of Rossell Hope Robbins,* ed. Beryl Rowland, pp. 320–27. London, 1974.

———. "Sir Gawain and the Green Knight." *Proceedings of the Southeastern Institute of Medieval and Renaissaince Studies* 10, ed. G. Mallary Masters (Special Issue, 1979): 24–44. Chapel Hill, 1984.

———. "The Speech of 'Book' in *Piers Plowman*." *Anglia* 77 (1959): 117–44.

Kean, Patricia M. *Chaucer and the Making of English Poetry*. 2 vols. London, 1972.

Keen, Maurice. "Chivalry, Heralds, and History." In Davis and Wallace-Hadrill, eds., pp. 393–414. Oxford, 1981.

———. "Wyclif, the Bible, and Transubstantiation." In Kenny, ed., pp. 1–16. Oxford, 1986.

Keil, Henry, ed. *Grammatici Latini*. 8 vols. Leipzig, 1855–1923.

Kelber, Werner. *The Oral and the Written Gospel: The Hermeneutics of Speaking and Writing in the Synoptic Tradition, Mark, Paul, and Q*. Philadelphia, 1983.

Kellogg, Robert. "Oral Narrative, Written Books." *Genre* 10 (1977): 655–65.

Kelley, Francis E. "Ockham: Avignon, Before and After." In Hudson and Wilks, eds., pp. 1–18.

Kelly, Henry A. "*Occupatio* as Negative Narration: A Mistake for *Occultatio / Praeteritio*." *Modern Philology* 74 (1977): 311–15.

Kempe, Margery. *The Book of Margery Kempe*. Edited by S. B. Meech and H. E. Allen. Early English Text Society, o.s., 212. Oxford, 1961.

Kenny, Anthony. "Realism and Determinism in the Early Wyclif." In Hudson and Wilks, eds., pp. 165–77.

———. "The Realism of the *De Universalibus*." In Kenny, ed., pp. 17–29.

———. *Wyclif*. Oxford, 1985.

———, ed. *Wyclif in His Times*. Oxford, 1986.

Ker, W. P. *Medieval English Literature*. Oxford, 1969 (originally published in 1912).

Kilworldly, Robert. *De ortu scientiarum*. Edited by A. G. Judy. Oxford, 1976.

Kittay, Jeffrey. "Utterance Unmoored: The Changing Interpretations of the Act of Writing in the European Middle Ages." *Language in Society* 17 (1986): 209–30.

Kittredge, George L. *Chaucer and His Poetry*. Cambridge, 1972 (originally published in 1915).

Knighten, Merrell Audy, Jr. "Chaucer's *Troilus and Criseyde*: Some Implications of the Oral Mode." *Dissertation Abstracts International* 36 (1986): 8076A.

Knighton, Henry. *Chronicon*. Edited by Joseph R. Lumby. 2 vols. Rolls Series. London, 1889–95.

Koff, Leonard. *Chaucer and the Art of Storytelling*. Los Angeles, 1988.

Kolve, V. A. *Chaucer and the Imagery of Narrative: The First Five Canterbury Tales*. Stanford, 1984.

Kretzmann, Norman, Anthony Kenny, and Jan Pinborg, eds. *The Cambridge History of Later Medieval Philosophy: From the Rediscovery of Aristotle to the Disintegration of Scholasticism, 1100–1600*. Cambridge, 1982.

Lagarde, G. de. *La naissance de l'esprit laïque au déclin du moyen-âge*. Vol. 4, *Guillaume d'Ockham: Défense de l'empire* (Paris, 1962); vol. 5, *Guillaume d'Ockham: Critique des structures ecclésiales* (Paris, 1963).

Langland, William. *The Vision of William Concerning Piers the Plowman, together with Richard the Redeless*. Edited by Walter W. Skeat. 2 vols. Oxford, 1886.

Lapsley, Gaillard. "Richard II's 'Last Parliament.'" *English Historical Review* 53 (1938): 53–78.

Laun, J. F. "Recherches sur Thomas de Bradwardin, précurseur de Wyclif," *Revue d'histoire et de philosophie religieuses* 9 (1929): 217–33.

Lawton, David. *Chaucer's Narrators*. Chaucer Studies, 13. Cambridge, 1985.

———. "The Diversity of Middle English Alliterative Poetry." *Leeds Studies in English* 20 (1989): 143–72.

———. "The Unity of Middle English Alliterative Poetry." *Speculum* 58 (1983): 72–95.

———, ed. *Middle English Alliterative Poetry and Its Literary Background*. Cambridge, 1982.

Leclercq, Jean. *The Love of Learning and the Desire for God: A Study of Monastic Culture*. Translated by Catharine Misrahi. New York, 1961. From *L'Amour des lettres et le désir de Dieu* (Paris, 1957).

Leff, Gordon. "The Bible and Rights in the Franciscan Disputes over Poverty." In *The Bible in the Medieval World: Essays in Memory of Beryl Smalley*, ed. Katherine Walsh and Diana Wood, pp. 225–35. Oxford, 1985.

———. *Bradwardine and the Pelagians*. Cambridge, 1957.

———. *Heresy in the Later Middle Ages*. 2 vols. Manchester, 1967.

———. "The Place of Metaphysics in Wyclif's Theology." In Hudson and Wilks, eds., pp. 217–32.

———. *William of Ockham: The Metamorphosis of Scholastic Discourse*. Manchester, 1975.

LeGoff, Jacques. *Time, Work, and Culture in the Middle Ages*. Translated by Arthur Goldhammer. Chicago, 1980.

Leicester, H. Marshall, Jr. *The Disenchanted Self: Representing the Subject in the "Canterbury Tales."* Los Angeles, 1990.

Lerer, Seth. *Literacy and Power in Anglo-Saxon Literature*. Lincoln, 1991.

Lévi-Strauss, Claude. *The Savage Mind*. Translated by George Weidenfield. Chicago, 1969. From *La Pensée Sauvage* (Paris, 1962).

———. *Structural Anthropology*. Translated by Claire Jacobson and Brooke Schoeph. New York, 1963. From *Anthropologie structurale* (Paris, 1958).

———. *Tristes Tropiques*. Translated by John and Doreen Weightman. New York, 1974. From *Tristes Tropiques* (Paris, 1955).

Lewis, Charlton T. and Charles Short. *A Latin Dictionary*. Oxford, 1966.

Lindahl, Carl. *Earnest Games: Folkloric Patterns in "The Canterbury Tales."* Bloomington, Ind., 1987.

Lonergan, Bernard J. *Verbum: Word and Idea in Aquinas*. Edited by David B. Burrell. Notre Dame, Ind., 1967.

Loomis, Roger S. "Morgan Le Fee in Oral Tradition." In *Studies in Medieval Literature: A Memorial Collection of Essays*. New York, 1970.

Lord, Albert Bates. *The Singer of Tales*. Cambridge, 1960.

Loux, Michael J. "The Ontology of William of Ockham." In *Ockham's Theory of Terms: Part I of the "Summa Logicae,"* ed. and trans. Loux, pp. 1–21. Notre Dame, Ind., 1974.

———. "*Significatio* and *Suppositio*." *New Scholasticism* 53 (1979): 407–27.

Lumiansky, R. M. *Of Sundry Folk: The Dramatic Principle in the "Canterbury Tales."* Austin, 1955.

Luria, Aleksander R. *Cognitive Development: Its Cultural and Social Foundations.* Edited by Michael Cole. Translated by Martin Lopez-Morillas and Lynn Solotaroff. Cambridge, 1976.

Luscombe, David. "Wyclif and Hierarchy." In Hudson and Wilks, eds., pp. 233–44.

Lyall, R. J. "Materials: The Paper Revolution." In Griffiths and Pearsall, eds., pp. 11–29.

Lydgate, John. *The Minor Poems of John Lydgate.* Part 2. Edited by H. N. MacCracken. Early English Text Society, o.s., 192. London, 1934.

Macfarlane, Alan. *The Origins of English Individualism.* Oxford, 1978.

Magoun, Francis P., Jr. "Oral-Formulaic Character of Anglo-Saxon Narrative Poetry." *Speculum* 28 (1953): 446–67.

Malony, Thomas S. "The Semiotics of Roger Bacon." *Mediaeval Studies* 45 (1983): 120–54.

Mann, Michael. *The Sources of Social Power.* Vol 1, *A History of Power from the Beginning to A.D. 1760.* Cambridge, 1986.

Manning, Bernard L. "John Wyclif." In *Cambridge Medieval History.* General editors: H. M. Gwatkin and J. P. Whitney. Vol. 7, pp. 486–507, 900–907. Cambridge, 1911–36.

———. *The People's Faith in the Time of Wyclif.* Cambridge, 1919.

Manning, Stephen. "Rhetoric, Game, Morality, and Geoffrey Chaucer." *Studies in the Age of Chaucer* 1 (1979): 105–18.

Marrou, H. I. *A History of Education in Antiquity.* Translated by George Lamb. New York, 1956.

Marsilius of Padua. *Defensor Minor.* Edited by C. K. Brampton. Birmingham, 1922.

Martin, John E. *Feudalism to Capitalism: Peasant and Landlord in English Development.* Atlantic Highlands, 1984.

Mathew, Gervase. *The Court of Richard II.* London, 1968.

Matonis, A. T. E. "Middle English Alliterative Poetry." In *So Meny People, Longages and Tonges,* ed. Michael Benskin and M. L. Samuels. Edinburgh, 1981.

Maurer, A. "Method in Ockham's Nominalism." *The Monist* 61 (1978): 426–43.

McFarlane, Kenneth B. "Bastard Feudalism." *Bulletin of the Institute of Historical Research* 20 (1947): 173–75.

———. *John Wycliffe and the Beginnings of English Nonconformity.* London, 1952.

———. "Parliament and 'Bastard Feudalism.'" *Transactions of the Royal Historical Society,* 4th ser., 26 (1944): 53–79.

McGrade, Arthur Stephan. "Ockham and the Birth of Individual Rights." In *Authority and Power: Studies on Medieval Law and Government Presented to Walter Ullmann on his Seventieth Birthday,* ed. Brian Tierney and Peter Linehan, pp. 149–65. Cambridge, 1980.

———. *The Political Thought of William of Ockham: Personal and Institutional Principles.* Cambridge, 1974.

McKisack, May. *The Fourteenth Century, 1307–1399.* Oxford History of England, 5. Oxford, 1959.

McKitterick, Rosamond. *The Carolinginans and the Written Word*. Cambridge, 1989.

———, ed. *The Uses of Literacy in Early Mediaeval Europe*. Cambridge, 1990.

McLuhan, Marshall. *The Gutenberg Galaxy: The Making of Typographic Man*. Toronto, 1962.

McNamara, Grace Helen. "*Regio Dissimilitudinis* and *Homo Claudus*: Conceptual Indebtedness of the *Pearl* Poet to St. Augustine of Hippo." *Dissertation Abstracts International* 40 (1979): 242A.

McNamara, John Francis. "Responses to Ockhamist Theory in the Poetry of the *Pearl* Poet, Langland, and Chaucer." *Dissertation Abstracts International* 29 (1968): 3148A-49A.

Medcalf, Stephen, ed. *The Later Middle Ages*. New York, 1981.

———. "*Piers Plowman* and the Ricardian Age in Literature." In Daiches and Thorlby, eds., pp. 643–96.

Meech, Sanford. B. "An Early Treatise in English Concerning Latin Grammar." In *Essays and Studies in English and Comparative Literature*, pp. 81–126. University of Michigan Publications in Language and Literature, 13. Ann Arbor, 1935.

Middleton, Anne. "The Idea of Public Poetry in the Reign of Richard II." *Speculum* 53 (1978): 94–114.

———. "William Langland's 'Kynde Name': Authorial Signature and Social Identity in Late Fourteenth-Century England." In *Literary Practice and Social Change in Britain, 1380–1530*, ed. Lee Patterson, pp. 15–82. Los Angeles, 1990.

Miller, J. Hillis. "The Triumph of Theory, the Resistance to Reading, and the Question of the Material Base." *Publications of the Modern Language Association of America* 102 (1987): 281–91.

Minnis, Alistair J. *Medieval Theory of Authorship: Scholastic Literary Attitudes in the Later Middle Ages*. London, 1984.

Momigliano, Arnoldo. *Essays in Ancient and Modern Historiography*. Oxford and Middletown, Conn., 1977 (originally published in 1947).

Moody, Ernest A. *The Logic of William of Ockham*. London, 1935 (rpt., New York, 1965).

Moorman, Charles. "The Origins of the Alliterative Revival." *Southern Quarterly* 7 (1969): 345–71.

Moran, Jo Ann Hoeppner. *The Growth of English Schooling, 1340–1548: Learning, Literacy, and Laicization in Pre-Reformation York Diocese*. Princeton, 1985.

Mueller, Janel M. *The Native Tongue and the Word: Developments in English Prose Style, 1350–1580*. Chicago, 1984.

Muralt, André de. "Ockham's Nominalism and Unreal Entities." *Philosophical Review* 86 (1977): 144–76.

———. "Ockham's Theory of Natural Signification." *The Monist* 61 (1978): 444–59.

———. "La toute-puissance divine, le possible et la non-contradition: Le principe de l'intelligibilité chez Occam." *Revue Philosophique de Louvain*, 4th ser., 84, no. 63 (1986): 345–61.

Murdoch, J. E. and E. D. Sylla, eds. *The Cultural Context of Medieval Learning*. Dordrecht, 1975.

Murphy, James J., ed. *Medieval Eloquence: Studies in the Theory and Practice of Medieval Rhetoric*. Berkeley, 1978.

Muscatine, Charles. "*The Canterbury Tales*: Style of the Man and Style of the Work." In *Chaucer and Chaucerians: Critical Studies in Middle English Literature*, ed. D. S. Brewer. University, Ala., 1966.

———. *Chaucer and the French Tradition*. Berkeley, 1957.

———. *Poetry and Crisis in the Age of Chaucer*. Notre Dame, Ind., 1972.

Near, Michael R. "Anticipating Alienation: *Beowulf* and the Intrusion of Literacy." *Publications of the Modern Language Association* 108 (1993): 320–32.

Nederman, Cary J. "Royal Taxation and the English Church: The Origins of William of Ockham's *Ars Princeps*." *Journal of Ecclesiastical History* 37, no. 3 (1986): 377–88.

Neuse, Richard. *Chaucer's Dante: Allegory and Epic Theater in "The Canterbury Tales."* Berkeley, 1991.

———. "The Knight: The First Mover in Chaucer's Human Comedy." *University of Toronto Quarterly* 31 (1962): 299–315.

Neuss, Paula. "Images of Writing and the Book in Chaucer's Poetry." *Review of English Studies* 32 (1981): 385–97.

Nichols, Stephen G. "Discourse in Froissart's *Chroniques*." *Speculum* 39 (1964): 279–87.

———. "Introduction: Philology in a Manuscript Culture." *Speculum* 65 (1990): 1–10.

———. "Remodeling Models: Modernism and the Middle Ages." *Recherches et Rencontres* 1 (1990): 45–72.

———. Review of *Implications of Literacy*, by Brian Stock. *Speculum* 61 (1986): 208–209.

Oakden, J. P. *Alliterative Poetry in Middle English*. 2 vols. Manchester, 1930–35 (rpt., Hamden, 1968).

Oman, Charles W. *The Great Revolt of 1381*. Oxford, 1906.

———. *The History of England from the Accession of Richard II to the Death of Richard III (1377–1485)*. Political History of England, 4. London, 1906.

Ong, Walter J. "Agonistic Structures in Academia: Past to Present." *Interchange* 5 (1974): 1–12.

———. *Interfaces of the Word: Studies in the Evolution of Consciousness and Culture*. Ithaca, N.Y., 1977.

———. *Orality and Literacy: The Technologizing of the Word*. London, 1982.

———. "Oral Residue in Tudor Prose Style." *Publications of the Modern Language Association of America* 80 (1965): 145–54.

———. *The Presence of the Word: Some Prolegomena for Cultural and Religious History*. New York, 1970.

———. *Rhetoric, Romance, and Technology: Studies in the Interaction of Expression and Culture*. Ithaca, N.Y., 1971.

———. "Tudor Writings on Rhetoric, Poetic, and Literary Theory." *Studies in the Renaissance* 15 (1968): 36–69.

Opie, Iona and Peter. *The Lore and Language of Schoolchildren*. Oxford, 1959.

Oresme, Nichole. *Le Livre politiques d'Aristote*. Edited by Albert D. Menut. Transactions of the American Philosophical Society, n.s., 60, pt. 6. New York, 1970.

Orme, Nicholas. *English Schools in the Middle Ages*. London, 1973.

Park, John K. *William Ockham's Life and Thought*. Seoul, 1983.

Parker, Patricia. *Inescapable Romance: Studies in the Poetics of a Mode*. Princeton, 1979.

Parkes, Malcolm B. "The Influence of the Concepts of *Ordinatio* and *Compilatio* on the Development of the Book." In *Medieval Learning and Literature: Essays Presented to R. W. Hunt*, ed. J. J. G. Alexander and M. T. Gibson. pp. 115–41. Oxford, 1976.

————. "The Literacy of the Laity." In Daiches and Thorlby, eds., pp. 555–77.

Parks, W. Ward. "The Oral-Formulaic Theory in Middle English Scholarship." *Oral Tradition* 1 (l986): 639–94.

————. *Verbal Duelling in Heroic Narrative: The Homeric and Old English Traditions*. Princeton, 1990.

Parry, Milman. *The Making of Homeric Verse: The Collected Papers of Milman Parry*. Edited by Adam Parry. Oxford, 1971.

Partner, Nancy. *Serious Entertainments: The Writing of History in Twelfth-Century England*. Chicago, 1977.

Patrologia Latina (*PL* in notes). Edited by Jacques-Paul Migne. 221 vols. Paris, 1841–1905.

Patterson, Lee. *Chaucer and the Subject of History*. Madison, 1991.

————. "'What Man Artwo'?: Authorial Self-Definition in *The Tale of Sir Thopas* and *The Tale of Melibee*." *Studies in the Age of Chaucer* 11 (1989): 117–75.

————, ed. *Literary Practice and Social Change in Britain, 1380–1530*. Los Angeles, 1990.

Pattison, Robert. *On Literacy: The Politics of the Word from Homer to the Age of Rock*. New York, 1982.

Pearsall, Derek. "The Alliterative Revival: Origins and Social Backgrounds." In *Middle English Alliterative Poetry and Its Literary Background: Seven Essays*. Cambridge, 1982.

————. "Chaucer's Poetry and Its Modern Commentators: The Necessity of History." In *Medieval Literature: Criticism, Ideology, and History*, ed. David Aers, pp. 123–47. Brighton, 1986.

————. *Old English and Middle English Poetry*. London, 1977.

————. "The Origins of the Alliterative Revival." In *The Alliterative Tradition in the Fourteenth Century*, ed. Bernard S. Levy and Paul E. Szarmach, pp. 1–24. Kent, Ohio, 1981.

Peck, Russell A. "Chaucer and the Nominalist Questions." *Speculum* 53 (1978): 745–60.

Pernoud, M. A. "Innovation in William of Ockham's References to the *Potentia Dei*." *Antonianum* 45 (1970): 65–97.

————. "The Theory of the *Potentia Dei* According to Aquinas, Scotus and Ockham." *Antonianum* 47 (1972): 69–75.

Petronella, Vincent F. "Regal Duality and Everyman: Dante to Shakespeare." *Humanities Association Review* (Canada) 30 (1979): 131–46.

Poole, R. L. *Chronicles and Annals: A Brief Outline of Their Origin and Growth*. Oxford, 1926.

Porter, Joseph A. *The Drama of Speech Acts: Shakespeare's Lancastrian Tetralogy.* Berkeley, 1979.

Priscian. *Institutiones Grammaticae.* Edited by Martin Hertz. Vols. 2 and 3. In *Grammatici Latini,* ed. Henry Keil. 8 vols. Leipzig, 1855–1923.

Putnam, Bertha H. *The Enforcement of the Statutes of Labourers.* New York, 1908.

Quinn, William A. and Audley S. Hall. *Jongleur: A Modified Theory of Oral Improvisation and Its Effects on the Performance and Transmission of Middle English Romance.* Washington, D.C., 1982.

Quintilian. *Institutionis oratoriae libri duodecim.* Edited by M. Winterbottom. 2 vols. Oxford, 1970.

———. *The Institutio oratoria of Quintilian.* Translated by H. E. Butler. Cambridge, 1966–69 (originally published in 1920–1922).

Ramsey, Lee C. *Chivalric Romances: Popular Literature in Medieval England.* Bloomington, Ind., 1983.

Ranald, Margaret Loftus. "The Degradation of Richard II: An Inquiry into the Ritual Backgrounds." *English Literary Renaissance* 7 (1977): 170–96.

Ray, Roger D. "Medieval Historiography Through the Twelfth Century: Problems and Progress of Research." *Viator* 5 (1974): 33–59.

———. "Rhetorical Scepticism and Verisimilar Narrative in John of Salisbury's *Historia Pontificalis.*" In Breisach, ed., pp. 61–102.

Read, S. "The Objective of Ockham's *ficta.*" *Philosophical Quarterly* 27 (1977): 14–31.

Reed, Robert Rentoul, Jr. *Richard II: From Mask to Prophet.* Pennsylvania State University Studies, 25. University Park, Pa., 1968.

Reeves, Marjorie E. "History and Prophecy in Medieval Thought." *Medievalia et Humanistica,* n.s., 5 (1974): 51–75.

———. *The Influence of Prophecy in the Later Middle Ages: A Study in Joachism.* Oxford, 1969.

Renoir, Alain. "Descriptive Techniques in *Sir Gawain and the Green Knight.*" *Orbis Litterarum* 13 (1958): 126–32.

Richard Redeless (anon.). *See* Langland, William.

Richter, Michael. "A Socio-Linguistic Approach to the Latin Middle Ages." *Studies in Church History* 11 (1975): 69–82.

———. "Urbanitas-Rusticitas: Linguistic Aspects of a Medieval Dichotomy." *Studies in Church History* 16 (1979): 149–57.

Rickert, Edith. "King Richard II's Books." *Library* 13 (1933): 144–47.

Rishanger, William. *Chronica.* In *Chronica monasterii S. Albani (1259–1307),* ed. Henry T. Riley. London, 1865.

Ritzke-Rutherford, Jean. "Formulaic Microstructure: The Cluster." In Göller, ed., 70–82.

Roberts, C. H. "The Christian Book and the Greek Papyri." *Journal of Theological Studies* 50 (1949): 155–68.

Roberts, Josephine A. *Richard II: An Annotated Bibliography.* 2 vols. Garland Shakespeare Bibliographies, 14. New York, 1988.

Robertson, D. W., Jr. *A Preface to Chaucer: Studies in Medieval Perspectives.* Princeton, 1962.

Robertson, Elizabeth. *Early English Devotional Prose and the Female Audience.* Knoxville, 1990.

Robertson, J. C. and J. B. Sheppard, eds. *Materials for the History of Thomas Becket.* Rolls Series. London, 1875–85.

Robson, J. A. *Wyclif and the Oxford Schools: The Relation of the "Summa de Ente" to Scholastic Debates at Oxford in the Later Fourteenth Century.* Cambridge, 1961.

Rosenberg, Bruce A. "The Oral Performance of Chaucer's Poetry." *Folklore Forum* 13 (1980): 224–37.

Rosier, Irene. *La grammaire spéculative de modistes.* Lille, 1983.

Rotuli Parliamentorum: The Rolls of Parliament. 6 vols. London, 1783.

Rowland, Beryl. "*Pronuntiatio* and Its Effect on Chaucer's Audience." *Studies in the Age of Chaucer* 4 (1982): 33–51.

———. "Speech, the Principle of Contraries, and Chaucer's Tales of the Manciple and Parson." *Mediaevalia* 6 (1980): 209–22.

Ryan, John J. *The Nature, Structure, and Function of the Church in William of Ockham.* Missoula, Mont., 1978.

Ryan, Michael. *Marxism and Deconstruction: A Critical Articulation.* Baltimore, 1982.

Saenger, Paul. "Silent Reading: Its Impact on Late Medieval Script and Society." *Viator* 13 (1982): 367–414.

Salmon, Vivian. "The Representation of Colloquial Speech in *The Canterbury Tales*." In *Style and Text: Studies Presented to Nils Erik Enkvist,* ed. H. G. Ringbom, pp. 263–77. Stockholm, 1975.

Salter, Elizabeth. "The Alliterative Revival." *Modern Philology* 64 (1966–67): 146–50, 233–37.

Salter, Elizabeth and Derek Pearsall. "Pictorial Illustration of the Late Medieval Poetic Texts: The Role of the Frontispiece or Prefatory Picture." In *Medieval Iconography and Narrative: A Symposium,* ed. Flemming G. Anderson, Esther Nyholm et al., pp. 100–23. Odense, 1980.

Sandquist, T. A. "The Holy Oil of St. Thomas of Canterbury." In *Essays to Wilkinson,* pp. 330–44. Toronto, 1969.

Sapora, Robert William, Jr. *A Theory of Middle English Alliterative Meter, with Critical Applications.* Cambridge, 1977.

Saussure, Ferdinand de. *Course in General Linguistics.* Translated by Wade Baskin. New York, 1959. Originally published as *Cours de linquistique générale,* ed. Charles Bally et al. (Geneva, 1916).

Sayles, G. O. "Richard II in 1381 and 1399." *English Historical Review* 94 (1979): 820–29.

Scattergood, V. J. "Literary Culture and the Court of Richard II." In *English Court Culture in the Later Middle Ages,* ed. V. J. Scattergood and J. W. Sherborne, pp. 29–43. London, 1983.

Scheller, R. W. *A Survey of Medieval Model Books.* Haarlem, 1963.

Scholz, R. *Unbekannte kirchenpolitische Streitschriften aus der Zeit Ludwigs des Bayern (1327–1354).* 2 vols. Rome, 1911–14.

———. *Wilhelm von Ockham als politischer Denker und sein Breviloquium de Principatu Tyrannico.* Leipzig, 1944 (rpt., Stuttgart, 1952).

Schotter, Anne Howland. "Vernacular Style and the Word of God: The Incarnational Art of *Pearl*." In *Ineffability: Naming the Unnameable from Dante to Beckett*, ed. Peter S. Hawkins and Anne Howland Schotter, pp. 23–34. New York, 1984.

Scott, Kathleen L. "Design, Decoration and Illustration." In Griffiths and Pearsall, eds., pp. 31–64.

Scott, T. K. "Ockham on Evidence, Necessity and Intuition." *Journal of the History of Philosophy* 7 (1969): 27–49.

Scott-Giles, Charles W. "King Richard II." In *Shakespeare's Heraldry*. London, 1950.

Shoaf, R. A. *The Poem as Green Girdle: Commercium in "Sir Gawain and the Green Knight."* Humanities Monograph, 55. Gainesville, 1984.

Siegel, Paul N. *Shakespeare in His Time and Ours*. Notre Dame, Ind., 1968.

Smalley, Beryl. "The Bible and Eternity: John Wyclif's Dilemma." *Journal of the Warburg and Courtauld Institutes* 27 (1965): 73–89.

———. *Historians in the Middle Ages*. New York, 1974.

———. "John Wyclif's *Postilla super totam bibliam*." *Bodleian Library Record* 4 (1953): 186–205.

Southern, Richard W. "Aspects of the European Tradition of Historical Writing." Three parts in *Transactions of the Royal Historical Society* 20 (1970): 173–96; 21 (1971): 159–79; 22 (1972): 159–80.

———. *The Making of the Middle Ages*. New Haven, 1953.

Spade, Paul V. "Ockham's Rule of Supposition: Two Conflicts in His Theory." *Vivarium* 12 (1974): 63–73.

———. "Synonymy and Equivocation in Ockham's Mental Language." *Journal of the History of Philosophy* 18 (1980): 9–22.

Spearing, A. C. "Central and Displaced Sovereignty in Three Medieval Poems." *Review of English Studies* 33 (1982): 247–61.

———. *Criticism and Medieval Poetry*. London, 1964.

———. *The "Gawain"-Poet: A Critical Study*. Cambridge, 1970.

———. *Readings in Medieval Poetry*. Cambridge, 1987.

Spiers, John. *Medieval English Poetry*. London, 1957.

Spitzer, Leo. "A Note on the Poetic and Empirical 'I' in Medieval Authors." *Traditio* 4 (1946): 414–22.

Stanbury, Sarah. *Seeing the "Gawain"-Poet: Description and the Act of Perception*. Philadelphia, 1991.

Starkey, David. "The Age of the Household: Politics, Society, and the Arts c. 1350–c. 1550." In *The Later Middle Ages*, ed. Stephen Medcalf, pp. 225–90. London, 1981.

Steel, Anthony B. *Richard II*. Cambridge, 1941.

Steinmetz, David C. "Late Medieval Nominalism and the *Clerk's Tale*." *Chaucer Review* 12 (1977): 38–54.

Stock, Brian. *The Implications of Literacy: Written Language and Models of Interpretation in the Eleventh and Twelfth Centuries*. Princeton, 1983.

———. *Listening for the Text: On the Uses of the Past*. Baltimore, 1990.

———. "Medieval Literacy, Linguistic Theory, and Social Organization." *New Literary History* 16 (1984): 13–29.

Stow, George B. "Richard II in Thomas Walsingham's Chronicles." *Speculum* 59 (1984): 68–102.

Strauss, Leo. *Persecution and the Art of Writing*. Glencoe, Ill., 1952.

Street, Brian V. *Literacy in Theory and Practice*. Cambridge, 1984.

Strohm, Paul. *Social Chaucer*. Cambridge, 1989.

Szittya, Penn R. *The Antifraternal Tradition in Medieval Literature*. Princeton, 1986.

Tachau, Katherine H. *Vision and Certitude in the Age of Ockham: Optics, Epistemology and the Foundations of Semantics, 1250–1345*. Leiden, 1988.

Taylor, John. *English Historical Literature in the Fourteenth Century*. Oxford, 1987.

———. "Richard II's Views on Kingship." *Proceedings of the Leeds Philosophical and Literary Society, Literature and History Section* 14, no. 5 (1971): 189–205.

———. *The "Universal Chronicle" of Ranulph Higden*. Oxford, 1966.

Tedlock, Dennis. "Toward an Oral Poetics." *New Literary History* 8 (1977): 507–19.

Thomas à Kempis. *Of the Imitation of Christ*. London, 1961.

Thompson, Faith. *Magna Carta: Its Role in the Making of the English Constitution, 1300–1629*. Minneapolis, 1948.

Thompson, James W. *The Literacy of the Laity in the Middle Ages*. Berkeley, 1939.

Thompson, Sir Edward Maunde. "A Contemporary Account of the Fall of Richard the Second." *Burlington Magazine* 5 (1904): 160–72, 267–78.

Thomson, David. *A Descriptive Catalogue of Middle English Grammatical Texts*. New York, 1979.

———. "The Oxford Grammar Masters Revisited." *Mediaeval Studies* 45 (1983): 298–310.

Thomson, Williel R. *The Latin Writings of John Wyclyf*. Toronto, 1983.

Thurston, Paul T. *Artistic Ambivalence in Chaucer's "Knight's Tale."* Coral Gables, Fla., 1968.

Tierney, Brian. *Foundations of the Conciliar Theory*. Cambridge, 1955 (rpt., Cambridge, 1969).

———. "Ockham: The Conciliar Theory and the Canonists." *Journal of the History of Ideas* 15 (1954): 40–70.

———. *Origins of Papal Infallibility, 1150–1350*. Leiden, 1972.

Tolkien, J. R. R., E. V. Gordon, and N. Davis, eds. *Sir Gawain and the Green Knight*. 2d ed. Oxford, 1967.

Tout, T. F. *The History of England from the Accession of Henry III to the Death of Edward III (1216–1377)*. Political History of England, 3. London, 1905.

Trimpi, Wesley. *Muses of One Mind: The Literary Analysis of Experience and Its Continuity*. Princeton, 1983.

Troll, Denise A. "The Illiterate Mode of Written Communication: The Work of the Medieval Scribe." In *Oral and Written Communication: Historical Approaches*, ed. Richard L. Enos. Newbury Park, Calif., 1990.

Troyan, Scott D. "Rhetoric Without Genre: Orality, Textuality and the Shifting

Scene of the Rhetorical Situation in the Middle Ages." *Romanic Review* 81 (1990): 377–95.

Tuck, Anthony. *Richard II and the English Nobility*. London, 1974.

Turville-Petre, Thorlac. *The Alliterative Revival*. Cambridge, 1977.

Tyler, Stephen A. *The Said and the Unsaid: Mind, Meaning, and Culture*. New York, 1978.

Ullmann, Walter. *The Carolingian Renaissance and the Idea of Kingship*. Birbeck Lectures 1968–69. London, 1969.

―――. *The Individual and Society in the Middle Ages*. Baltimore, 1967.

―――. *Principles of Government and Politics in the Middle Ages*. London, 1961.

Vance, Eugene. *Mervelous Signals: Poetics and Sign Theory in the Middle Ages*. Lincoln, Neb., 1986.

―――. "Medievalisms and Models of Textuality." *Diacritics* 15 (1985): 55–63.

Vignaux, P. *Nominalisme au XIVe siècle*. Paris, 1948.

Vincent of Beauvais. *Speculum maius*. Dijon, n.d.

Vising, Johan. *Anglo-Norman Language and Literature*. London, 1923.

Waldron, Ronald A. "Oral-Formulaic Technique and Middle English Alliterative Poetry." *Speculum* 32 (1957): 792–804.

―――, ed. *Sir Gawain and the Green Knight*. Evanston, 1970.

Walsingham, Thomas. *Chronicon Angliae (1322–1388)*. Edited by E. M. Thompson. Rolls Series. London, 1874.

―――. *Gesta abbatum monasterii Sancti Albani*. Edited by Henry T. Riley. 3 vols. Rolls Series. London, 1867–69.

―――. *Historia Anglicana*. Edited by Henry T. Riley. 2 vols. Rolls Series. London, 1863–64.

Ward, John O. "Some Principles of Rhetorical Historiography in the Twelfth Century." In Breisach, ed., pp. 103–65.

Watts, Willaim H. and Richard J. Utz. "Nominalist Perspectives on Chaucer's Poetry: A Bibliographical Essay." *Medievalia et Humanistica*, n.s. 20 (1993): 147–72.

Weisheipl, J. A. "The Curriculum of the Faculty of Arts at Oxford in the Early Fourteenth Century." *Mediaeval Studies* 26 (1964): 143–85.

Wengert, R. G. "The Sources of Intuitive Cognition in William of Ockham." *Franciscan Studies* 41, no. 19 for 1981 (1984): 415–47.

Wenzel, Sigfried. "Chaucer and the Language of Contemporary Preaching." *Studies in Philology* 73 (1976): 138–61.

Wesling, Donald. "The Difficulties of the Bardic: Literature and the Human Voice." *New Literary History* 8 (1981): 69–81.

Westminster Chronicle, 1381–1393. Edited by L. C. Hector and Barbara F. Harvey. Oxford, 1982.

Wetherbee, Winthrop. "Romance and Epic in Chaucer's *Knight's Tale*." *Exemplaria* 2 (1990): 303–28.

White, Hayden. *The Content of Form: Narrative Discourse and Historical Representation*. Baltimore, 1987.

―――. "The Value of Narrativity and the Representation of Reality." *Critical Inquiry* 7 (1980): 5–27.

Wickson, Roger. *The Community of the Realm in Thirteenth Century England*. London, 1970.

Wilkinson, B. *Constitutional History of Medieval England*. Vol. 2. New York, 1952.

———. "The Deposition of Richard II and Accession of Henry IV." *English Historical Review* 54 (1939): 215–39.

Wilks, Michael J. "Predestination, Property and Power: Wyclif's Theory of Dominion and Grace." *Studies in Church History* 2 (1965): 220–36.

———. *The Problem of Sovereignty in the Later Middle Ages*. Cambridge, 1964.

William of Ockham. *Breviloquium de Principatu Tyrannico super Divina et Humana, Specialiter autem super Imperium et Subiectos Imperio, a quibusdam Vocatis Summis Pontificibus Usurpato*. Edited by R. Scholz: *Wilhelm von Ockham als politischer Denker und sein Breviloquium de principatu tyrannico*. Leipzig, 1944 (rpt., Stuttgart, 1952).

———. *Contra Benedictum*. Edited by J. G. Sikes and R. F. Bennett. In *Opera Politica*, vol. 1. Manchester, 1940.

———. *De Imperatorum et Pontificum Potestate*. Edited by R. Scholz. In *Streitschriften* 2:453–80. Rome, 1914.

———. *Dialogus*. Edited by Melchior Goldast. In *Monarchia Sancti Romani Imperii* 2:392–957. Frankfurt, 1614 (rpt. Graz, 1960).

———. *Octo Quaestiones de Potestate Papae*. Edited by J. G. Sikes and R. F. Bennett. In *Opera Politica*, vol. 1. Manchester, 1940.

———. *Opus Nonaginta Dierum*. Chapters 1–6: Edited by J. G. Sikes and R. F. Bennett. In *Opera Politica* 1:289–374 (Manchester, 1940). Chapters 7–124: Edited by R. F. Bennett and H. S. Offler. In *Opera Politica* 2:375–858 (Manchester, 1963).

———. *Quodlibeta Septem*. Strasbourg, 1491 (rpt., Louvain, 1962).

———. *Scriptum in librum primum sententiarum: Ordinatio* (Prologus et Distinctio prima). Edited by Gedeon Gál and Stephen Brown. Vol. 1 of *Opera Theologica*. St. Bonaventure, N.Y., 1967.

———. *Scriptum in librum primum sententiarum: Ordinatio* (Distinctiones 2 and 3). Edited by Stephen Brown and Gedeon Gál. Vol. 2 of *Opera Theologica*. St. Bonaventure, N.Y., 1970.

———. *Scriptum in librum primum sententiarum: Ordinatio* (Distinctiones 4–18). Edited by Gerald I. Etzkorn. Vol. 3 of *Opera Theologica*. St. Bonaventure, N.Y., 1977.

———. *Scriptum in librum primum sententiarum: Ordinatio* (Distinctiones 19–48). Edited by Gerald I. Etzkorn and Francis Kelley. Vol. 4 of *Opera Theologica*. St. Bonaventure, N.Y., 1979.

———. *Summa Logicae, Pars Prima, Pars Secunda et Tertiae Prima*. Edited by P. Boehner. St. Bonaventure, N.Y., 1957–1962.

———. *Tractatus Logicae Minor*. Edited by E. M. Buytaert. *Franciscan Studies* 24 (1964): 55–100.

Williams, Benjamin, ed. *Cronique de la Traïson et Mort de Richart Deux Roy Dengleterre*. English Historical Society Publications, 12. London, 1848.

Williams, Raymond. *The Long Revolution*. London, 1961.

Wilson, R. M. *The Lost Literature of Medieval England*. London, 1952.

Wittgenstein, Ludwig. *Philosophical Investigations*. Translated by G. E. M. Anscombe. Oxford, 1953 (rpt., Oxford, 1968).

Wittig, Susan. *Stylistic and Narrative Structures in the Middle English Romances*. Austin, 1978.

Wolter, Allan B. *The Philosophical Theology of John Duns Scotus*. Edited by Marilyn McCord Adams. Ithaca, N.Y., 1990.

Wood, Rega. "Intuitive Cognition and Divine Omnipotence: Ockham in Fourteenth-Century Perspective." In Hudson and Wilks, eds., pp. 51–61.

Workman, Herbert B. *John Wyclif: A Study of the Early English Church*. 2 vols. Oxford, 1926.

Wright, Thomas, ed. *Alliterative Poem on the Deposition of King Richard II. Ricardi Maydiston De concordia inter Ric. II et civitatem London*. Camden Society, 1838 (rpt., New York, n.d.).

Wyclif, John. *English Wycliffite Sermons*, vol. 1. Edited by Anne Hudson. Oxford, 1983.

———. *Fasciculi Zizaniorum*. Edited by W. W. Shirley. Rolls Series. London, 1858.

———. *Johannis Wyclif: Tractatus de civili dominio*. Vol. 1 edited by J. Loserth. Wyclif Society, 1885–1904 (rpt., New York, 1966).

———. *Johannis Wyclif: De dominio divino* (and Richard FitzRalph, *De pauperie Salvatoris*). Edited by R. L. Poole. Wyclif Society, 1883–1922 (rpt., New York, 1966).

———. *Johannis Wyclif: De ente (libri primi tractatus primus et secundus)*. Edited by S. H. Thompson. Oxford, 1930.

———. *Johannis Wyclif: De ente (librorum duorum excerpta)*. Edited by M. H. Dziewicki. Wyclif Society, 1883–1892 (rpt., New York, 1966).

———. *Johannis Wyclif: De eucharistia, tractatus maior*. Edited by J. Loserth. Wyclif Society, 1892 (rpt. New York, 1966).

———. *Johannis Wyclif: De veritate sacrae scripturae*. Edited by R. Buddensieg. 3 vols. Wyclif Society, 1883–1922 (rpt., New York, 1966).

———. *Johannis Wyclif: Tractatus de apostasia*. Edited by M. H. Dziewicki. Wyclif Society, 1889 (rpt. New York, 1966).

———. *Johannis Wyclif: Tractatus de ecclesia*. Edited by J. Loserth. Wyclif Society, 1886 (rpt., New York, 1966).

———. *Johannis Wyclif: Tractatus de logica*. Edited by M. H. Dziewicki. 3 vols. Wyclif Society, 1883–1922 (rpt., New York, 1966).

———. *Johannis Wyclif: Tractatus de officio regis*. Edited by A. W. Pollard and C. Sayle. Wyclif Society, 1887 (rpt., New York, 1966).

———. *Johannis Wyclif: Tractatus de potestate papae*. Edited by J. Loserth. Wyclif Society, 1907 (rpt., New York, 1966).

———. *Tractatus de universalibus*. Edited by Ivan J. Mueller. Oxford, 1985.

———. *Trialogus*. Edited by G. V. Lechler. Oxford, 1869.

Yates, Francis. *The Art of Memory*. Chicago, 1966.

Zumthor, Paul. *Introduction à la poésie orale*. Paris, 1983.

———. *La lettre et la voix de la "littérature" médiévale*. Paris, 1987.

———. *Speaking of the Middle Ages*. Translated by Sarah White. Lincoln, Neb., 1986. From *Parler du moyen âge*. Paris, 1980.

INDEX

Abelard, Peter, 21, 40, 58
Ackerman, Robert W., 218n
Adam of Usk, 171–72, 187n
Adams, Marilyn M., 40n, 43n, 45n, 47n, 48n, 50n, 51n, 54n, 55n, 56n, 75n
Aers, David, 231n, 262n, 269n
allegory, 11, 94
alliterative revival, 195–98, 257
Alvarus Pelagius, 71
Ambrose, 11, 39, 40, 59
amplificatio, 131–32, 135–36, 141, 147, 149, 163
Annunciation, 80, 110
Anonimalle Chronicle, 153–54, 162, 169
Anselm of Canterbury, 19–21, 30, 34, 83, 191
Anti-Christ, 99–101, 106
antiqui, 15, 82
Aquinas, Thomas, 41, 108
archaism, 156, 171
Archbishop of York, 188
Aristotle, 25, 41, 45, 49, 51, 56, 69, 82, 119; *Poetics* 13n; *Politics*, 69
Arthgallo (king), 172
Arthur, Ross G., 212n, 221n
Arundel, Thomas, 176
Aston, Margaret, 17n, 80n, 92n, 96n, 108n 111n, 112n, 150n
Aubrey de Vere, 173
Auerbach, Erich, 4, 4n, 113n, 114n
Augustine, Saint, 13, 83; and autonomous language, 14; and Ockham, 77; and phonocentrism, 8; on speaking, 7; *Confessiones*, 7, 14; *De magistro*, 8; *De trinitate*, 49. *See also* William of Ockham; Wittgenstein, Ludwig; Wyclif, John
Auksi, P., 108n
authority, 90, 94

Bagot, William, 172
Ball, John, 155–58, 163–66, 168; letter of, 164
Barg, M. A., 158n
Barthes, Roland, 23

Bartlett, Robert, 124n
Baugh, Albert C., 195n
Bäuml, Franz, 4n, 197n
Bean, J. M. W., 134n, 150n, 173n
Bembre, Nicholas, 181–83, 229
"benefit of clergy," 26
Bennett, Michael J., 225n
Benson, Larry D., 196n, 197n, 200n, 207n
Beowulf, 196, 205
Berengarius, 109
Bernard of Chartres, 12
Bernard of Clairvaux, 21
Bernard Silvestris, 256
Black Prince, Edward of Woodstock, Prince of Wales, 105; epitaph of, 146; fame of, 129, 140, 141; as Hector, 129; as orator, 139, 141; and rule, 148
blank charter, 185
Bloch, R. Howard, 17n
Bloom, Allan D., 16n
Blum, Jerome, 155n
Boccaccio, Giovanni, 14, 227; *Teseida*, 240–41, 249, 262
Boehner, Philotheus, 47n, 53n, 61n, 70n
Boethius, 49, 234, 236, 240, 262–64, 267
Bonaventura, 124n
book: burning of, 161, 162; and dominion, 101, 116, 190; and *liber occultorum*, 254–55; and *liber praesentiae*, 117, 266; as *liber vitae*, 95, 115; and nature, 24, 91, 93, 232; and orality, 102, 266; and Sacred Scripture, 24; and voice, 76. *See also* Scripture; textuality
Brandt, William J., 123n, 133n
Brewer, Derek, 230n, 235n
Brut, 134, 185
Buridan, John, 55n
Burley, Simon, 175–76, 183, 187, 229
Burrow, John A., 202n, 212n, 213n, 215n

Cable, Thomas, 196n
Caedmon, 4
Calais, 134, 136
Calderwood, James L., 185n
Camargo, Martin, 198n

Camelot, 200–202, 211, 219–22, 225
Campsall, Richard, 46
capital punishment, 152, 179
Caradoc, 199
Carolingians, 3, 4, 6, 114–15
categorematic terms, 53–54, 74, 83
Catto, Jeremy, 150n
Chandos, John, 142–43, 147, 175
Chaucer, Geoffrey, 14; *Franklin's Tale*, 238; *Hous of Fame*, 249, 266; *Knight's Tale*, 191, 227–72; *Legend of Good Women*, 227; *Man of Law's Tale*, 255; *Parson's Tale*, 258; *Treatise on the Astrolabe*, 228n; *Troilus and Criseyde*, 90n, 228n, 239, 263
Cheshire, 186, 225
chivalry, 134
Chrimes, S. B., 178n
Christianson, Paul, 33n
chronicles: and history, 133, 201, 272; as history, 133, 199; genre of, 124, 134, 137, 191; and *Knight's Tale*, 258. *See also* historicism
church: particular, 63; primitive, 97; universal, 61, 103, 116
Cicero, 11, 153
Cistercians, 18
Clanchy, Michael, 3n, 25n, 27n, 28n, 29n, 30n, 31n, 149n
Clement VII (pope), 105
Clermont, John de, 142–43
Clopton, Walter, 179
cognition, 40–41, 45; habitual, 48, 50; of individuals, 41–42, 75, 83; intuitive, 41, 44–45, 48; and mediation, 56, 71–75; and power, 75–78. See also *haecceitas*; sign; William of Ockham: on *fictum*
Coleman, Janet, 9n, 13n, 20n, 36n, 45n, 48n, 51n, 61n, 62n, 64n, 70n, 125n, 190n
commons, 154–57
consignification, 53, 132, 133, 150; and dominion, 75. *See also* supposition theory
Constantine (emperor), 99
Courtenay, William, 176
Courtenay, William J., 41n, 80n, 81n
Court of Chivalry, 179, 186n
Crane, Susan, 251n
Crécy, 129, 131
Curschmann, Michael, 197n

Curtius, Ernst R., 113n

Dante Alighieri, 14, 70, 143, 230
deconstruction, 75
de la Pole, Michael, 172, 174–78, 181, 229, 256
demythologizing, 107, 112
Derrida, Jacques, 8, 17, 17n, 57n
Dialogus de Scaccario, 159
dictio scripta, 55, 76. *See also* writing
diglossia: in Anglo-Saxon England, 34; defined, 6; in *Gawain*, 200, 216–18, 224; in *Knight's Tale*, 235, 241; and literacy, 115–19, 152–53; in Richard II's reign, 184, 186–88; and social class, 157–71. *See also* literacy; writing
discourse: defined, 14; and displacement, 34–35, 119, 189, 214, 229, 255; and literacy, 167, 190; and voice, 15, 36, 77, 151, 191, 213, 226, 246, 271. *See also* dominion; displacement; voice
displacement: defined, 17, 19; and dominion, 35, 36, 114, 272; in *Gawain* 199–201; in *Knight's Tale*, 227, 229, 250–51, 272; and literacy, 22, 97, 169; and orality, 113, 191; and property, 133, 148; and voice, 148; and women, 220, 204, 251. *See also* metalanguage
Domesday Book, 158, 178, 184, 188
dominion, 23, 35, 61, 97; and Bible, 102; defined, 14–15, 64; and Genesis, 65; from God, 67, 98; and government, 229, 257; lay, 98; mediated, 75; papal, 62, 99; and romance, 200, 227. *See also* displacement; literacy; orality; textuality
Donatus, 10, 59, 14
Don Quixote, 226
Duby, Georges, 23
"due process," 181–82
Duggan, Hoyt N., 197n
Duke of Lancaster. *See* John of Gaunt
Dumézil, Georges, 23
Duns Scotus, John, 41, 47
Durham, 34
Dyer, Christopher, 155n

Eadmer, 31
ecclesia. *See* church
ecclesiology. *See* church
Edmund of Langley, 173

Edward II, 174, 176–77
Edward III, 105, 130, 133, 136; and feu-
    dalism, 151; and history writing, 134;
    and oral history, 146; and patrimony,
    138, 225; and rule, 148
Egidius Romanus, 62
empire: from God, 72; from pope, 71
empiricism, 40–41, 82
essence, 81, 84, 87, 108, 110, 115. *See also*
    universal (species)
Evans, G. R., 94n, 110n
Everett, Dorothy, 258n
Exton, Nicholas, 183

Faith, Rosamond, 156n, 157n, 158n, 159n
feudalism, 23, 119, 138, 148, 150, 190,
    226, 272
Figgis, John N., 187n
Fisher, Sheila, 204n
FitzRalph, Richard, 98
flyting, 31, 135, 142, 198, 205, 209
forgery, 31
formalism: in Ockham, 67; in Wyclif, 116
formulas, oral, 27, 145, 196–98
Froissart, Jean, 130–31, 135, 138, 141–43,
    146
Funkenstein, Amos, 124n, 126n

Gabel, L. C., 26n
Gál, Gedeon, 78n
Galbraith, V. H., 171n
Ganim, John M., 228n
Gellrich, Jesse M., 92n, 159n
Geoffrey le Baker, 130–31, 141, 144
Geoffrey of Monmouth, 124, 172, 201
Gerald of Wales, 124n, 171
gesta Dei, 131
Giles of Rome, 187
Gilson, Étienne, 75n
Given-Wilson, Chris, 173n, 186n
Gloucester, Duke of. *See* Thomas of
    Woodstock
Godefroid of Fontaines, 64
Goody, Jack, 5n, 6n, 19n, 23n, 24n, 33n,
    34n, 119n
government: ecclesiastical, 67, 69; secu-
    lar, 70–71, 119. *See also* dominion; em-
    pire
Graff, Harvey, 5n
grammatica, 12, 83, 90, 118
Gransden, Antonia, 124n, 127n, 133n

Graus, F., 156n
Great Schism, 105
Green, D. H., 4n
Green, Richard F., 188n
Gregory IX (pope), 31
Gregory XI (pope), 105
Gregory of Tours, 10
Gregory the Great, 10, 14, 129, 248, 252
Grindcobbe, William, 160
Grosseteste, Robert, 26, 82–83
Guillaume de Lorris, 14

haecceitas (haecceity), 42–43, 47, 265
Harding, Alan, 161n
Hargreaves, Henry, 108n
Havelock, Eric, 10n
Henry I, 31
Henry II, 26
Henry IV, 171, 173
Henry, D. P., 53n
herald of John Chandos, 131–32, 141,
    144–46, 201
Higden, Ranulf, 124, 128–29, 137
Hilton, Rodney H., 138n, 155n, 156n,
    157n, 164n
historicism, 36, 51, 58, 123, 150–51, 170,
    189, 201, 226
Horace, 129, 248
Howard, Donald R., 212n, 231n, 244n, 247n
Hudson, Anne, 80n, 96n
Hugh of St. Victor, 3, 12, 24–25
Huot, Sylvia, 4n, 12n, 15n, 143n
Hutchison, Harold F., 175n

ideology, 6, 35, 138, 150. *See also* literacy
illiteracy, 157, 161, 166, 171, 212, 248
illuminated manuscripts, 12, 32, 160, 252.
    See also visual art
imitation, 17, 22, 112. *See also* mimesis;
    representation
inscription. *See* scribe; writing
interpretation: of Scripture, 100, 105; and
    sola scriptura, 93–95
intuition. *See* cognition
Isidore of Seville, 11, 126, 131

Jean de Meung, 14
Jerome, Saint, 11, 129
Joachim de Fiore, 16
Joan of Kent, 106
John XXII (pope), 61, 64, 66

John Duns Scotus, 107, 125
John Gower, 230
John of Gaunt, Duke of Lancaster, 105–6,
    132, 154, 172–73, 176
John of Paris, 64
John of Salisbury, 127n
Jones, Richard H., 171n, 175n, 177n,
    179n, 184n, 187n

Kaeuper, Richard W., 155n, 157n, 158n,
    190n
Kamps, Ivo, 200n, 204n
Keen, Maurice, 124n
Kelber, Werner, 10n
Kelley, Francis E., 60n, 61n, 65n
Kempe, Margery, 4
Kenningham, John, 87
Kenny, Anthony, 95n
Kittay, Jeffrey, 11n
Knighton, Henry, 132, 166–67
knowledge. *See* cognition
Kolve, V. A., 248n, 262n, 267n

Lagarde, G. de, 68n, 70n
Lancastria *coup*, 178. *See also* Richard II:
    and deposition
Langland, William, 165
Langton, Simon, 31
language: as artificial, 83–84, 92; and do-
    minion, 74–78, 89–92; and *lingua angel-
    ica*, 166; mental, 20, 39, 44, 46–47, 50,
    76, 85, 126; and politics, 59, 75, 118;
    vernacular, 156. *See also* discourse;
    sign; teaching
law, 28–29; of judges (1387), 178; *lex liber-
    tatis*, 65–67; *lex tua*, 183; and "ley du
    parlement," 179–83; and sovereign
    voice, 184; and textual tradition, 163,
    170, 177–78, 180, 183–84, 190, 229. See
    also *Magna Carta*
Lawton, David, 195n, 196n
Leclercq, Jean, 12n, 126n
Leff, Gordon, 41n, 53n, 55n, 56n, 61n,
    62n, 68n, 70n, 71n, 93n, 94n, 95n, 101n,
    102n, 116n
Leicester, H. Marshall, 244n
Lerer, Seth, 4n, 15n, 22n, 32n, 34n
Lévi-Strauss, Claude, 17, 23
liber vitae. *See* book
Lindahl, Carl, 230n
literacy: and autonomy, 4, 14, 34, 128; de-

fined, 4, 14, 19, 25, 34, 149; develop-
    ment of, 26, 189; and dominion, 18, 59,
    77, 115, 119, 146, 152, 165, 167, 169,
    180, 189, 226, 270–71; and gender, 166–
    67, 251; and ideology, 4, 16, 35; and la-
    ity, 26, 162–63; Latin, 4, 15, 59, 112,
    168; vernacular, 4, 96, 111, 113, 165–66.
    See also orality; textuality; writing
Locke, John, 40
logocentrism, 9, 58, 88, 105. *See also*
    book; voice; writing: as speech
Lollards, 17, 157; and Wyclif, 80
Lombard, Peter, 87
Lord, Albert B., 197n
Loux, Michael J., 51n, 53n, 56n
Lucan, 140n
Ludwig of Bavaria, 61, 68, 71, 73
Luscombe, David, 92n
Lutterell, John, 60
Lyall, R. J., 33n
Lydgate, John, 32

Machaut, Guillaume de, 230
Macrobius, 153, 262
magic, 200
Magna Carta, 28, 174, 181, 182
Mann, Michael, 156n, 175n
Manning, Bernard L., 81n
Map, Walter, 153n
Marsilius of Padua, 63, 70
Mathew, Gervase, 173n, 175n
McFarlane, Kenneth B., 80n, 175n
McGrade, Arthur S., 60n, 65n, 68n, 70n,
    72n
McKisack, May, 173n, 175n, 187n
McKitterick, Rosamond, 3n, 6n, 114n,
    115n, 119n
McLuhan, Marshall, 6n, 18n, 25n
Medcalf, Stephen, 165n
mediation, 22, 24, 64, 42, 69; in Ockham,
    44; and rule, 71, 74
memory: and history, 9, 13, 128, 146; in
    Knight's Tale, 247, 266; and orality, 3–4,
    12, 126–27, 160. *See also* reading: oral;
    ruminatio
metalanguage: and displacement, 35;
    and *Gawain*, 200, 215, 222–24; and his-
    torical representation, 152; and
    Knight's Tale, 227, 266, 270; and Ock-
    ham's logic, 40, 51, 76. *See also* dis-
    course; displacement

meter. *See* alliterative revival
Michael of Cesena, 61, 78
Middleton, Anne, 165n
Mile End, 155, 160, 169. *See also* Richard II
mimesis, 20, 97; in *Gawain*, 219. *See also* imitation; representation
moderni, 15, 82, 149
monarchy, 101, 104, 116, 155, 127
Monk of Evesham, 189
Mortimer, Roger, 180
mouth: in *Knight's Tale*, 246; of prophet, 188; of Richard II, 152, 187, 188; of Wat Tyler, 163; as witness, 27; of Wyclif, 168
Mueller, Janel M., 36n, 80n, 110n, 111n
Muscatine, Charles, 233n, 235n, 260n
mythology: and autochthony, 159; and mediation, 149; and orality, 22–25, 224; and sacred space, 91. *See also* book; magic; voice: and oaths

Nambikwara, 17, 23
narrative: and history, 124, 131; and law, 28; and politics, 233
Neolithic period, 23
Neoplatonism, 39, 63, 77, 89, 91n
Neuse, Richard, 228n, 249n, 259n
New Law, 65
Nichols, Stephen G., 130n
nominalism: and Ockham, 40, 57–58, 125, 199
non-contradiction: logic of, 56, 76
Norman Conquest, 25, 127
nostalgia, 190, 191, 226

oaths. *See* voice
occultatio, 205, 232–39, 247–55, 261, 270. *See also* Chaucer: *Knight's Tale*
Offa (king), 160, 161
Old Law, 65
Oman, Charles W., 155n, 158n, 165n, 171n
Ong, Walter, 3n, 6n, 25n, 39n, 149n
oral chronicle, 142, 171, 146. *See also* narrative
orality: defined, 34, 149, 271; and dominion, 185, 224; and mythology, 22, 24; secondary, 3, 9–13; transmission of, 4, 6, 39–41, 113, 117, 128, 195–98, 225–26, 248. *See also* literacy; voice

oral performance, 143–47, 195–97, 228n, 252, 257–59
oral tradition, 10, 18, 31, 79, 97, 170, 210

paganism: in the church, 100; and dominion, 73; as metaphor, 254–57; and reading, 255; and textuality, 267
parataxis, 140–41, 199, 231, 248, 261
Paris, Matthew, 129
Parkes, Malcolm, 5n, 153n
Parks, W. Ward, 142n, 199n
parliament: in *Knight's Tale*, 237; law of, 179; of 1386, 178, 179, 229; of 1388, 174, 180, 229
Partner, Nancy, 124n
Paschal II (pope), 31
paternity: and rule, 69–71
Patterson, Lee, 228n, 229n, 236n
Pattison, Robert, 113n, 114n
Paul, Saint, 10, 63, 73
Pearsall, Derek, 195n, 198n
Peasants' Revolt. *See* rising of 1381
Peter of Blois, 26
Peter the Venerable, 12
phonocentrism. *See* voice; writing
plain style, 108, 113–14
Plato, 10, 56, 51, 82, 264; *Timaeus*, 24, 262
Platonism, 39, 87–88
plenitude of power, 61, 64, 66, 71
"Pleasaunce" of Richard II, 186
Poitiers, 139–45
positivism. *See* William of Ockham
Priscian, 13
propaganda, 127, 170–80
property: and dominion, 65, 67, 138, 142; and language, 22, 35, 42, 51; and ownership, 27, 31, 64, 102–3
propositions. *See* language
pseudo-Dionysius, 92

Quintilian, 153

rationality: and textuality, 19–22
reading: oral, 8, 10, 30, 101, 230, 239, 248; silent, 11, 198, 212, 228, 230, 239
realism: in *Gawain*, 210; metaphysical, 87, 89, 109; and nominalism, 40; and spoken language, 79–80; and Wyclif, 115–16, 199
real language: defined, 86. *See also* cognition; language

reception: theory of, 95
recitation. *See* oral performance
reform: religious, 80, 96–97, 104, 113–15
Reformation, 93, 96, 116
regio dissimilitudinis, 9
representation, 47, 58; and mediation, 77
res gestae, 131, 171
retinue: of King Arthur, 202, 224, 256; of Black Prince, 175; of Edward III, 135; of Richard II, 177, 185
rhetoric, 114, 199; and chronicle history, 127–28, 137–39, 150–51; and orality, 25, 138, 233; and persuasion, 171, 218; and writing, 143, 259
Richard II, 151, 271; and deposition, 152, 171, 187–88, 225; at Mile End, 168–69, 175; as *persona mixta*, 188; and regency commission, 177, 179, 182, 228; and royal affinity, 172–75, 178, 185–86, 225; and royal signet, 175–77; and symbolic oil, 188
Richard (Fitzalan), Earl of Arundel, 176, 185
Richard the Redeless, 186
Rickert, Edith, 188n
ring structure, 198, 199
rising of 1381, 112, 152, 153–66
Ritzke-Rutherford, Jean, 198n
Robert de Vere, 173–74, 181, 229
Robertson, D. W., 249n, 263n
Robson, J. A., 82n
Roland, 23, 205
romance: conventions of, 242, 244; as genre, 171, 228; and history, 195
Roman de la Rose, 232
Roscelin, 58
royal prerogative, 170, 174, 176, 178–81, 188, 228, 256. *See also* dominion; voice
ruminatio, 12, 126. *See also* reading
rusticus, 153–54, 169. *See also* commons

Saenger, Paul, 11n, 15n
Salisbury, John of, 4
Salter, Elizabeth, 195n
Sandquist, T. A., 188n
Saussure, Ferdinand de, 57, 57n, 59
scholasticism, 44, 55, 58; and Ockham, 40, 59, 125; and Wyclif, 107, 111, 113
Scott, Kathleen L., 32n

scribe, 12, 32
Scripture, 24, 91; Apocalypse, 91, 237, 254, 255; Corinthians, 10, 24, 63; Exodus, 63; Ezekiel, 187; Genesis, 191; Isaiah, 188; Matthew, 72, 99, 100, 104, 109; Romans, 62. *See also* interpretation
seals: 29, 30; Franciscan, 77; papal, 31; precious, 29; privy, 175, 176; royal, 162, 175, 188; and voice, 176
seeing: in *Knight's Tale*, 247–52
Seneca, 129
sermo humilis. *See* plain style
Shakespeare, William, 185, 187, 188, 189; *Richard II*, 188
sign, 7, 20, 25–29, 48, 56; artificial, 83; in *Gawain*, 221, 222; in *Knight's Tale*, 253; and mental concept, 49; and presence, 88–89; used by Richard II, 185; and universal, 82; and voice, 58–59. *See also* cognition; language; universal (species)
signet. *See* seals; sign
signification: defined, 52, 58. *See also* cognition
Sir Gawain and the Green Knight, 191, 195–229, 248, 256, 272
Skirlaw, Walter, 176
Smalley, Beryl, 91n
sokmen: and oral custom, 158
sola scriptura, 93–95, 116. *See also* interpretation
Southern, Richard W., 124n
Spade, Paul V., 56n
Spearing, A. C., 200n
species. *See* universal (species)
speech. *See* voice; vox; writing
Stafford, Edmund, Bishop of Exeter, 187
Stanbury, Sarah, 211n
Steel, Anthony B., 171n, 175n, 180n
Stock, Brian, 3n, 6n, 18n, 19n, 20n, 21n, 22n, 29n, 41n, 119n
Stow, George B., 170n, 173n
Stow, John, 139
Street, Brian, 5n, 6n, 119n
Strohm, Paul, 228n
sub specie aeternitatis, 7
Sudbury, Simon, Archbishop of Canterbury, 154, 163
supposition theory (*suppositio*), 45, 57–58; in *Gawain*, 222; in *Knight's Tale*, 234;

material, 54, 76; personal, 52, 53; simple, 54. *See also* consignification; syncategorematic terms

surquidré, 203, 207, 221–26. *See also* retinue: of King Arthur; *Sir Gawain and the Green Knight*

syncategorematic terms, 53

Szittya, Penn R., 80n

Tachau, Katherine H., 46n, 51n

Taylor, John, 128n, 134n, 150n, 164n, 173n, 185n, 188n

teaching: in Latin, 96, 114; in vernacular, 102, 107, 112

textuality, 18–20, 22, 95, 146; and community, 4, 18; in *Gawain*, 201, 215–18; in *Knight's Tale*, 237, 241, 253, 263; and orality, 25, 133. *See also* metalanguage; voice: and text

Thomas à Kempis, 76

Thomas Aquinas, Saint, 41, 108

Thomas (Beauchamp), Earl of Warwick, 176, 185

Thomas of Woodstock, 173, 176, 179–80, 185

Thompson, Faith, 181n

Thompson, James W., 5n

translation, 157, 270; and *lingua anglica*, 166; and sedition, 166

treason, 164, 179–80, 182

Tresilian, Robert, 181

Trevisa, John, 126–27

Trinity, 21, 85

Trivet, Nicholas, 123

Troll, Denise A., 12n

Troyan, Scott D., 199n

Tuck, Anthony, 171n, 173n, 174n, 175n, 176n, 180n, 186n

Turville-Petre, Thorlac, 195n, 196n

Tyler, Wat, 155–58, 163, 165, 168–69

universal (species), 41–51, 57–58, 81–88, 91–103. *See also* church; essence

universal history. *See* chronicles

Urban VI (pope), 105

verbum, 21, 53, 89, 109–10. *See also* voice; *vox Dei*

Vincent of Beauvais, 124

Virgil, 129

visual art, 149; in *Knight's Tale*, 250–52. *See also* illuminated manuscripts

voice, 11, 47–48; and dominion, 128, 148, 187; and oaths, 27, 160, 177, 181–91, 208–9, 217, 246; and origin, 9–15, 138; and patrimony, 133–36, 147, 225; and sight, 250–53; and sign, 8, 49, 74, 77; sovereign, 151, 168, 188, 238–39, 256, 262, 269–71; and text, 8–12, 133, 191, 231, 236–39, 247, 266. *See also* orality; sign; vox; *vox Dei*

vox, 40, 46, 50–51, 125; as *vox literata*, 13; as *vox mentalis*, 76

vox Dei, 9, 13, 101, 126, 266

Waldron, Ronald A., 195n, 221n

Walsingham, Thomas, 124, 129–32, 153, 163, 167–69, 173

Ward, John O., 127n, 150n

Wars of Alexander, 197

Watt, Ian, 5n

Wetherbee, Winthrop, 239n

white hart: badge of, 185–86

Wilks, Michael J., 101n, 102n, 105n

William of Ockham, 39–78, 83, 107, 125, 149, 191, 265, 271–72; at Avignon, 60; and expediency, 68; on *fictum* and *intellectio*, 45–49, 56; and functionalism, 66, 68; and Ockhamism, 82; and Ockham's razor, 46; and positivism, 70. *See also* nominalism; sign; universal (species)

William of Sherwood, 53n

Wilson, R. M., 196n

Wilton dyptich, 185

Winchester, Law of, 155

Wittgenstein, Ludwig, 8n, 14n; on Augustine, 8, 14

Wittig, Susan, 198n

women: and displacement, 220, 251; and literacy, 26, 166, 167, 168; and reading, 246, 260. *See also* literacy: and gender; translation

Wordsworth, William, 115

writing, 83; as autonomous, 4, 34–35, 115, 199, 202; as *dictio scripta*, 55, 76; as inscription, 15, 92, 111, 161, 230–33, 255, 269–70; and magic, 25–27, 30–31, 204–5, 218–20; as proof, 3, 30, 183–84,

writing *(continued)*
　199–200; resistance to, 30, 33, 149, 163,
　230; as speech, 8–9, 13, 49, 59, 76–77,
　90, 95, 101, 105, 115, 126–28, 199, 230,
　247, 265; and technology, 4, 10. *See also*
　language; literacy; orality
Wyclif, John, 61–62, 79–120, 148, 155,
　157, 187, 266, 271–72; and Augustine,
　87, 89, 114; death of, 167; and English

language, 80; on eucharist, 106–11;
and fundamentalism, 97, 100–102, 114,
272; and *Knight's Tale*, 262; and nominalism, 81, 115. *See also* Lollards; realism; reform

Yates, Francis, 126n

Zumthor, Paul, 3n